P9-DMU-539

www.wadsworth.com

wadsworth.com is the World Wide Web site for Wadsworth and is your direct source to dozens of online resources.

At *wadsworth.com* you can find out about supplements, demonstration software, and student resources. You can also send email to many of our authors and preview new publications and exciting new technologies.

wadsworth.com
Changing the way the world learns®

cash4book.com
instant quote, free shipping, fast payment

Governing America's Urban Areas

ALAN L. SALTZSTEIN
California State University at Fullerton

THOMSON

WADSWORTH

Australia • Canada • Mexico • Singapore • Spain
United Kingdom • United States

THOMSON

WADSWORTH

Publisher: Clark Baxter
Executive Editor: David Tatom
Development Editor: Susan Alkana
Assistant Editor: Julie Iannacchino
Editorial Assistant: Dianna Long
Technology Project Manager: Melinda
  Newfarmer
Marketing Manager: Janise Fry
Marketing Assistant: Mary Ho
Advertising Project Manager: Stacey Purviance
Project Manager, Editorial Production:
  Ray A. K. Crawford
Print/Media Buyer: Karen Hunt
Permissions Editor: Stephanie Keough-Hedges

Production: Carlisle Publishers Services
Photo Researcher: Sandra Lord
Copy Editor: Lora Kalb
Cover Designer: Brian Salisbury
Cover Image: Pigeons & Skyscrapers,
  San Francisco © Bryan Peterson
Cover Printer: Transcontinental/Louiseville
Compositor: Carlisle Publishers Services
Printer: Transcontinental/Louiseville

COPYRIGHT © 2003 Wadsworth, a division of
Thomson Learning, Inc. Thomson Learning™ is
a trademark used herein under license.
ALL RIGHTS RESERVED. No part of this work
covered by the copyright hereon may be
reproduced or used in any form or by any
means—graphic, electronic, or mechanical,
including but not limited to photocopying,
recording, taping, Web distribution,
information networks, or informatin storage
and retrieval systems—without the written
permission of the publisher.

Printed in Canada
1 2 3 4 5 6 7 06 05 04 03 02

For more information about our products,
contact us at:
Thomson Learning Academic Resource Center
1-800-423-0563

For permission to use material from this text,
contact us by
Phone: 1-800-730-2214   **Fax:** 1-800-730-2215
Web: http://www.thomsonrights.com

**Library of Congress Control
Number: 2002105129**

ISBN: 0-15-507379-6

Wadsworth/Thomson Learning
10 Davis Drive
Belmont, CA 94002-3098
USA

Asia
Thomson Learning
60 Albert Street, #15-01
Albert Complex
Singapore 189969

Australia
Nelson Thomson Learning
102 Dodds Street
South Melbourne, Victoria 3205
Australia

Canada
Nelson Thomson Learning
1120 Birthmount Road
Toronto, Ontario M1K5G4
Canada

Europe/Middle East/Africa
Thomson Learning
Berkshire House
168-173 High Holborn
London WC1 V7AA
United Kingdom

Latin America
Thomson Learning
Seneca, 53
Colonia Polanco
11560 Mexico D.F.
Mexico

Spain
Paraninfo Thomson Learning
Calle/Magallanes, 25
28015, Spain

Contents

Preface

Our cities are the richest in the world, centers of the vibrant American economy, and home to some of the world's finest commercial centers, museums, parks, and public attractions. But near the finer parts of our cities are neighborhoods of poverty, which include homelessness, high rates of unemployment, and significant crime. These neighborhoods remind many of depressing third-world cities. Parts of our cities occasionally explode in violence and mayhem. Why is there such poverty and depravation amid plenty? Why can't a successful society manage to govern its cities more successfully? Part of the reason is related to choices we make about how to govern our metropolitan areas.

Our concern here is those large concentrations of population that make up our largest cities and the surrounding suburbs and smaller cities that are economically, technologically, and socially related to them. Urban areas, by definition, require larger governments. Many services that can be produced informally in smaller areas must be managed by government in large cities. Water systems, waste disposal, transportation, and air pollution abatement are examples; in smaller cities, these needs can be produced privately or informally. In addition, migrants come to our cities without the support systems and community attachments that normally would aid their integration into society and assist them in moving up the economic ladder. Often government services replace matters that were once handled by extended families, churches, and informal social organizations.

One would assume that strong governments would follow from the need for increased public services. Yet, in the United States, the opposite happens. Rather than strong, large governments capable of making regional decisions, our urban areas are governed by many small, frequently parochial governments with little overall direction. Further, we divide power within our governments. Hence a paradox exists; *urban areas demand greater governmental services and powers, but metropolitan governance is usually divided between numerous small governments with limited jurisdictions and little visibility among the public.* Lacking strong governments, we often fail to meet the needs of the citizens. The paradox—how it comes about, the problems it brings to cities, and how it might be resolved—is the thesis of the book. All chapters are related to this topic.

To understand the paradox, we need to know much about the city—its historical roots and the changes in its society and economy. Chapter 1 spells out the paradox in more detail. Chapter 2 looks at the historical, social, and economic growth of American cities and evaluates their contemporary settings.

Traditions of American governance, going back to the founding of the Republic, frame any discussion of how urban governments are structured. We rely on conflicting principles of democratic governance, one associated with James Madison and the other attributed to Thomas Jefferson, to frame our discussion of the best way to run a city. These are discussed in Chapter 3. Chapter 4 looks closely at the variety of governmental structures and practices in the contemporary city. The field of public administration and the reform movement within urban management developed from the same roots in the progressive movement in the early years of the twentieth century. The council-manager plan, discussed in depth in Chapter 4, is the most elaborate application of progressive principles. Its widespread use in cities gives social scientists a laboratory in which to test the costs and benefits of many of the important principles of public administration.

In Chapter 5, the role of the federal government in cities is discussed. Chapter 6 looks at power and leadership in the city, drawing both on the experience of those who have studied power theoretically and the practical experiences of noted power wielders in our major cities. Chapter 7 examines urban riots and civil disturbances, the opposite of a civil society.

The final three chapters turn to questions of reform and change, looking for ways of resolving the paradox of urban governance. Chapter 8 focuses on ways of improving the connection between citizens and the governing process; many analysts are concerned about declining "social capital." Chapter 9 evaluates urban areas that form regional governments or combine and coordinate the separate jurisdictions within an urban area. In Chapter 10, the argument is summarized and ways of resolving the paradox are examined.

A CONCERN FOR TEACHING

The goal is a clear brief text for use in undergraduate and graduate classes in urban politics, urban management, and urban studies. I have taught these courses for decades in urban universities to a primarily working-class clientele. Much of what I have wanted in a metropolitan politics text is incorporated here. The aim is to interest the reader in the setting and dynamics of cities and hopefully to encourage them to explore their own communities and urban settings.

- Cases focusing on the dynamic interaction of participants are included in all chapters. Many of these highlight recent urban problems and concerns; the Orange County bankruptcy, community-based policing, and life in the contemporary inner city. Others highlight historical events and activities; the urban machine, the making of Levittown, and the urban career of Theodore Roosevelt.

- The common theme, the paradox of urban governance, focuses student interest throughout the text and offers the instructor a point of view to contrast with other approaches.

- Numerous charts and tables incorporate new data, particularly from the 2000 census. Analysis of the quantitative material provides the students with rudimentary skills in drawing inferences.

- The size and style of the text, brief and simply written, permits the instructor to incorporate supplementary texts, important articles, and studies of their local setting. Unlike other areas of the discipline, urban politics can be experienced by the student. Thus, local studies, interviews with local officials, and the use of guest lecturers can easily enrich the course.

- The text provides a broad treatment of urban concerns, city and suburb, in all parts of the country. It is designed to be useful in all parts of the country; it is free of the eastern big city bias common in some of the urban texts.

- For students of *public administration,* the study of urban areas has always been an important area of concern. Local governments employ the largest number of public servants in the country, and they are the portion of the public sector that has grown most significantly. City officials today expect their employees to have an elementary knowledge of urban governance.

A Few Words of Thanks

The text is the culmination of years of teaching and practical experience in metropolitan governance. Thus, the influences on my efforts are many, and some may go unnoticed. I want to particularly thank my editor at Wadsworth, David Tatom, for encouraging me initially and extending his support when others might have questioned the project. Susan G. Alkana, freelance development editor for Wadsworth, has worked tirelessly to improve the manuscript. Her many suggestions and her ability to interpret comments from reviewers have made this book a much better one. Most importantly, her sunny disposition and repeated encouragement have been a real inspiration to me.

I would like to thank the reviewers who have been exceedingly helpful in improving the manuscript. These include the following: Hugh Inton of the University of Toledo; James G. Hogan of Seattle University; Brian Janiskee of

California State University at San Bernadino; Ed Miller of the University of Wisconsin at Stevens Point; and Carol Ann Traut of the University of South Dakota. Particularly important were the suggestions of two old friends, Roger Durand of the University of Houston, Clear Lake, and Richard Young of Seattle University. Both of these gentlemen are long-time practitioners of the teaching trade. Their advice was invaluable. Richard deserves special praise for his detailed scrutiny of the manuscript and his ability to bring forth relevant ideas from his encyclopedic knowledge of politics, teaching practice, and social theory. His support of this effort has meant a great deal to me.

My many students from my years of teaching at California State University, Fullerton deserve special praise. I have been fortunate to teach undergraduates and graduates within an urban setting. My students come with a variety of experiences; some as practicing administrators, and others come from the mosaic of cultures that now comprise the population of greater Los Angeles. Our many students who have recently immigrated to the United States as well as those with longer roots in the country provided me with an everyday laboratory. Many of them are recognized in the cases and discussions. They include innovative, hard working city managers, county officials facing indictment, police officers on the beat, and social workers who help the poor. From all of them, I have had the opportunity to learn.

The faculty deserve special mention for their willingness to support and work with an urban oriented and political science based Masters of Public Administration program. My colleague, Raphe Sonenshein, has been a multi-faceted source of ideas, insights, and knowledge of politics, generally and particularly the Los Angeles setting.

Most important are the seven women in my life; my wife, Grace, daughters Sylvia, Anneke, Jennifer, and Rachel, and granddaughters Julia and Emily. I love all of you very much.

About the Author

Alan Saltzstein is Professor of Political Science and Chair of the Division of Political Science and Criminal Justice at California State University, Fullerton. Much of his career has involved instruction and coordination within the Masters of Public Administration program at CSUF. He also regularly teaches undergraduate courses focusing on urban-related concerns.

His research emphasizes two areas. He has written on urban-related matters, including studies of Los Angeles politics, city managers, and the politics of city finance. He is the editor and major contributor to *California Government in National Perspective*. His concern for human resources management and personnel administration includes studies of family friendly benefits in the federal sector, and his edited book *Public Employees and Policymaking*. He holds a Masters in Public Administration from the University of Minnesota, and Ph.D. in Political Science from UCLA.

Chapter One

The Paradox of Urban
Governance

D enny Levy, 36 a videographer witnessed the impact from the ground.

"I saw this plane flying low over the buildings down the center of
Manhattan" said Levy. "It went toward the World Trade Center. It sounded
like its engine was broken. Your brain tricks you. I thought it went past the
building then it went a little to the left and took a plunge at the building.

"Then there was this burst of stuff coming out of the building. There was
no fire and no explosion. I wondered why the plane was making so much
noise and was so low.

"You could tell it was a passenger plane, that it was in trouble or trying to
get close for a view. You'd never think a plane would go dead center into a
building. It was like a missile.

"I thought it was an accident, except he took a sudden left. He went right
for it. It was so creepy. I thought 'Oh my God I just saw 300 people die.' "
(Matea and Farley, 2001)

*Matea Gold and Maggie Farley "America Attacked: Strike Against the Nation; Terrorist Attack," Los Angeles
Times, 12 September 2001. Reprinted by permission of Los Angeles Times Syndicate International.*

The tragedy of September 11, 2001, began a worldwide chain of events that altered all aspects of political life. An assault on world terrorism commenced, including a major war in Afghanistan. New international alliances formed,

radically changing the world political system, and consensus politics within the United States, at least temporarily, replaced the bitter partisanship of the early months of the Bush administration. But nowhere did the tragedy have greater effect than in the governing process in New York City.

When the planes hit the World Trade Center, most of the things that hold that great city together were suspended. Thousands died and tens of thousands lost their jobs; many of those were the struggling poor. The immediate loss of more than 300 firefighters and three dozen police officers, the needs of injured citizens, the presence of numerous unsafe buildings, and the continuing fires strained the capacity of New York's public safety officers. No city in America is as highly dependent on public transportation as is New York, but that, too, ground to a halt. The stock market closed as members of the financial community scrambled to find new office space and restore coordination with international financial markets.

The resilience of the citizens of New York, and the national commitment to restore the city to its former greatness has helped to heal a grieving city and nation. Mayor Guiliani's energy, selfless actions, and his reassuring voice comforted many and energized those dealing with the aftermath of the tragedy. One of the most memorable World Series in recent memory helped restore people's confidence in the city's future.

The attempt to restore the city, however, is dogged by a series of problems.

- The towers contained 13 million square feet of office space; more than the total in downtown Chicago. The loss began a downward spiral in the city's economy. While the nation struggled with the beginnings of a recession, the economy of New York severely declined. An estimated 40,000 people were immediately out of work. Declines in air traffic and tourism into New York have led to further declines in city revenue precisely at the time when more public resources are needed. The current budget deficit is conservatively estimated at $40 billion; by far the largest in the city's history. Tax relief is needed to keep industries and taxpayers from leaving the city.

- Massive public investment in transportation systems, street repair, the clean up of the Towers site, and new safety measures are needed to return city services to their previous level. However, the decline in public resources will make this difficult to accomplish, and increasing taxes may further the decline of the economy.

- Federal and state officials promised massive aid to assist the city government. However, as the national economy declines and costs mount for the war effort, it is uncertain how significant the contribution from other governments will be.

- Interests in New York City are anxious to restore the financial community and the Manhattan economy to its pre–September 11 greatness. However, the city faces competition from surrounding cities as firms decide whether to remain in the city center. Many of the firms that were housed in the Trade Center towers now are located temporarily in outlying cities in New Jersey and Connecticut or in the New York suburbs. The city then loses the jobs and taxable resources of these firms. Will they return to the city if the Towers are rebuilt?

- Replacing the Towers requires intense cooperation between the public and private sectors. The land must be cleared, new utilities and public improvements put in place, and private developers must be able to invest. A common way of redeveloping the downtown of cities is to forgo taxes to developers willing to make the investment. But as tax money is lost, the strain on the public treasury increases.

Since at least the 1830s, New York has been the preeminent financial center of the nation. Though the center of population moved westward and new, powerful cities were created, New York has remained the center of economic life for the nation. In spite of competition from other cities, many of the nation's powerful financial firms and the stock market were located close together in lower Manhattan. The region's governments, in good as well as bad economic times, have responded to the needs of the financial community. The World Trade Towers, in fact, were public buildings owned by the New York Port Authority.

The city will resume hegemony in the financial world only if the many governments within the New York political system can cooperate. The New York region is divided into numerous municipalities, school districts, authorities, and special districts that span three states. Thus, cooperation requires meeting the needs and interests of several independent governments. Federal and state officials must be influenced to find resources and make policy changes needed to promote recovery. State government action is required for most major changes in city government including increased taxes.

American urban government, however, is a divided government. Numerous governments exist within all urban areas and their powers are limited by state and local laws and customs. Concerted action then requires unusual coordination, cooperation, and the ability to overcome the resistance in American character and political philosophy to strong city governments. The rebuilding of New York must contend with what I term the "Paradox of American Urban Government": urbanization creates the need for strong governments, but the American political system resists powerful city governments. The return of New York to greatness and improving the governance of all large American cities involves the resolution of this paradox.

Many who have looked are our cities from abroad are critical of what they see. Here are two such views:

The growth of great cities has been among the most significant and least fortunate changes in the character of the population of the United States during the century that has passed since 1787. There is no denying that the government of cities is one of the conspicuous failures of the United States. . . . What Dante said of his own city may be said of American cities:

they are, like the sick man who finds no rest upon his bed, but seeks to ease the pain by turning from side to side. (Bryce, 1907: 628)

My only impression was of a huge, noisy city with an enormous number of neon signs and automobiles; hence vast quantities of exhaust fumes that were choking people. Basically, New York was like any other capitalist city; it had terrible poverty and slums. On the whole New York has a humid, unpleasant climate and the air is filthy. (Krushchev, 1974: 382)

The governing of urban areas in the United States baffles most citizens and has troubled foreign visitors as diverse as Lord James Bryce in the 1880s and Nikita Khruschev in the 1960s. These critics wondered why, in such a rich and dynamic land, urban problems are handled so poorly. Why are there so many governments, yet few with clear authority over important concerns? Why so many elected officials, most with limited control over important sources of power? Why such large divisions in wealth and living conditions between the rich and the poor? Why such pronounced conflict between races, classes, and ethnic groups?

The field of American urban politics is defined by these questions. In this book, we will examine the many components that comprise the paradox of American Urban Government, which I describe in the following way:

1. Urbanization creates a need for increased governmental services. The need for governmental services should result in strong urban governments that are capable of making representative decisions, extracting necessary resources and efficiently administering public policies.

2. In the United States, the opposite occurs. Numerous governments with weak political structures are the norm in urban areas.

OUR URBAN AREAS: LANDSCAPE OF CONTRAST

Urban areas are regions of significant population in high concentration, including both central city and suburb. Dynamic contrasts define our urban areas: expensive buildings etch the skyline of most downtowns; visitors see new multi-story glass towers, athletic stadiums, music centers, and urban shopping malls. International investment firms, professional office centers, and innovative businesses locate in the hubs of many of our large urban areas. In suburban areas, and in "edge cities," those new urban centers on the periphery of our metropolitan complexes (for example, Tysons Corner, Virginia; Newport Beach, California; and Cobb County, Georgia) one sees shiny new high rises, carefully planned residential areas, glamorous shopping malls, and well-developed park systems. Innovative school systems, high-tech police departments, and efficient management describe many suburban and "edge city" governments.

However, there is another environment in most urban areas defined by decaying streets, run down schools, and poverty, and this scene is adjacent to every shiny downtown and near to every suburb and edge city. Its presence creates fear in the affluent because the streets are lined with the homeless, urban gangs, and substance abusers. Thus, wealthier residents come to these parts of the city as little as possible. They move to outlining areas and endure long commutes to work.

Periodically the frustrations of the poor break out in destructive rampages and violence. Former San Antonio mayor, urban scholar, and federal Secretary of the Department of Housing and Urban Development Henry G. Cisneros surveyed Los Angeles following the riots of 1992.

> What I saw was a city in which the smoke was everywhere. . . . Sirens screamed every few seconds, as teams of fire engines escorted by the California Highway Patrol-literally convoys of twenty vehicles, the patrol cars to protect the firefighters—raced from one fire to the next. Men drove pickup trucks to electronics stores, bashed in the glass storefronts and then hurriedly loaded VCRs and television sets on the trucks and sped away to the next store. This same scene could be reenacted in another American city some other night. . . . Like piles of dry wood with red-hot coals underneath, other American cities can also ignite. . . . In the slow burn of hundreds of communities, we're reaping a harvest in inattention, of withdrawal, of an unwillingness or incapacity to invest in all of our people. (1993: 18–21)

The problems we think of as those in the inner cities are also a part of the outlining areas. In some suburban area, schools deteriorate, the streets are un-kept, and crime increases. Wealthier residents leave these areas and move to the far reaches of the urban fringe.

Poverty amid plenty is a problem for the rich and the poor. The wealthy leave the poorer neighborhoods, taking their taxable resources with them. Public investment then declines as cities must either increase taxes or invest less in public improvements. Residents endure a long journey to work and have less time for family and friends. The deprived areas then decline further as new jobs move farther away and the poor have limited access to them.

We legally separate cities from suburbs, and in most urban areas tax receipts from the residents are the primary source of city income. Central cities then are left with the problems associated with poverty but lack the resources to deal with them. One wonders, wouldn't all of us be better off if we invested more in the city? With better roads, freeways, and mass transit, could we make the at-tractions of the city more accessible to all and make our businesses more effi-cient? With better schools, parks, and social centers, could we create more useful citizens, provide a broader range of opportunities for the residents, and prevent urban violence? Would the well-off residents live closer to the central city if city governments and public facilities were organized more efficiently and had in-creased resources? If all lived nearer the inner city, open spaces could be pre-served, and some public facilities could be built at lower cost. Perhaps the costs of an urban society could be more equitable, paid for, and the benefits more widely distributed?

"But we're not homeless. We're on a camping trip."

© The New Yorker Collection 1999 David Sipress from cartoonbank.com. All Rights Reserved.

Attacking these problems is related to many basic concerns; the socialization of people, the managing of the economy, and the place of our cities in an international economy. Fitting the pieces of an urban society together involves many concerns beyond the scope of a single volume. Therefore, **we will focus on the governance of our major metropolitan areas and their political and governmental organization.** Our inquiry asks; Can we govern urban areas more effectively? With better governance, Can we improve the city for both rich and poor? The goal is a more efficient metropolis where more wealth is created and distributed more evenly. My hope is that there is a better way of governing the urban area that can lead to the improvement of all residents.

A VIEW OF THE INNER CITY

Anthropologist Elijah Anderson observed life in the inner cities of Chicago and Philadelphia. Below is a composite of his insights:

Small groups of seven and eight year old street kids hang out on the corners and in the local alleys. They watch the traffic go by, observing the recurring drug sales, though many pretend not to see. Streetlore is that local drug dealers employ some of them as lookouts for crack houses or to signal dealers when a new shipment of drugs has arrived at a pickup point.

On a summer day residents hang out of their windows to catch a breeze or sit on stoops to watch the traffic go by. There is much street life here; young men, young women, old people, middle-aged people. To walk the streets is to observe many pregnant young women, walking or standing around with one or two children. Their youthful faces belie extended bellies, but they carry on.

The streets are noisy and very much alive with sociability—yells. Screams loud laughter and talk, car screeches, rap music, and honking horns. A car pulls up and honks its horn for a passenger; another honks to urge the stopped car in the middle of the street to move on. But people are basically courteous, not wanting to provoke others. There are smiles and a certain level of camaraderie. Everybody knows everybody here as best they can, some try to watch out for others.

But many have their hands full watching out for themselves. Like aluminum siding at an earlier time, decorative iron bars have become a status symbol in the neighborhood, and residents acquire them for downstairs windows and doors as serious protection against thieves and "zombies" (crack addicts). And they show real concern about strangers who seem questionable.

In the underclass neighborhood, the drug trade is everywhere; and it becomes ever more difficult to separate the drug culture from the experience of poverty. The neighborhood is sprinkled with crack dens located in abandoned buildings or in someone's home. On corner after corner, young men peddle drugs the way a newsboy peddles papers. To those who pass their brief inspection they say "psst, psst I got the news. I got the news. Caine blow. Beam me up Scotty," code words easily understood by those who know. . . Almost as any denizen of these streets has come to accept the area as a tough place, a neighborhood where the strongest survive and where, if people are not careful and streetwise, they become ensnarled in the games of those who could hurt them.

SOURCE: From Elijah Anderson, "Neighborhood Effects on Teenage Pregnancy," in *The Urban Underclass* (Washington D.C.: The Brookings Institution).

WHY DO OUR CITIES FAIL?

We live in a very rich land, and most of us dwell in large urban areas near a central city. By urban areas, I refer to the central city, the smaller cities surrounding it (usually referred to as suburbs), and those edge cities near to the central city. If you live near an edge city, you may rarely travel to the central city, but your livelihood and your life style are dependent on it. Tyson Corners, Virginia, Newport Beach, California; or Arlington, Texas would not thrive without the attachment to the larger central city that is near. Economists and city planners argue that the economic and social vitality of our communities depends on the health of our central cities. Why, then, can't the United States create cities worthy of our heritage?

Two reasons are often cited for America's failure to create more effective cities:

1. *A cultural bias favoring rural areas and small towns.* This thinking goes at least as far back as Jefferson, who feared the development of cities and hoped

that the country could remain one of small towns and independent farms. He purchased Louisiana, in part, to realize this dream. Commenting on a yellow fever epidemic that led to the deaths of many in 1800, he stated:

When great evil happens I am in the habit of looking out for what good may arise from them as consolations to us and Providence has in fact established the order of things, as most evils are the means of producing some good. The yellow fever will discourage the growth of great cities in our nation, and I view great cities as pestilential to the morals, the health and the liberties of man. True, they nourish some of the elegant arts, but the useful ones can thrive elsewhere, and less perfection in the others, with more health, virtue and freedom would be my choice. (Glaab 1963: 52)

According to Morton and Lucia White, authors of a classic study of the role of the city in American literature;

For a variety of reasons our most celebrated thinkers have expressed different degrees of ambivalence and animosity toward the city, attitudes which may be partly responsible for a feeling on the part of today's city planner that he has no mythological or mystique on which he can rest or depend while he launches his campaigns on behalf of urban improvement. We have no persistent or pervasive tradition of romantic attachment to the city in our literature or in our philosophy, nothing like the Greek attachment to the *polis* or the French writers affection for Paris. (White and White 1962: 12–13)

Could it be that Americans pay less attention to cities than they do to small towns and rural areas because philosophically we find virtue in the country and have never been comfortable with city life?

2. *Economic and technological processes that have led to the decline of many central cities and some metropolitan areas.* The central city of 1900 was the locus of economic life because production was dependent on major waterways and railroad lines and workers needed to live close to their place of employment or be transported by mass transit. With the development of the internal combustion engine, air transport, and modern means of communication, the central city lost much of its economic importance. Economic and social changes in recent times accelerated the deterioration of the central city. Ladd and Yinger summarize recent changes quite clearly:

Over the last twenty years, powerful economic, social and fiscal trends have buffeted the major central cities of the United States. The shift in employment from manufacturing to services, the suburbanization of middle income households, migration from the northeast to the southwest, the urbanization of poverty, the tax revolt, and recent cuts in federal aid all have made it more difficult for many cities to finance out of their own resources such basic public services as police and fire protection, sanitation and the building and maintenance of streets. (Ladd and Yinger 1989: 2)

Some cities rise and others fall as the economic and technological factors change. Thus, economic and social change that benefits the nation as a whole may result in obsolete cities and decaying city centers. Some urban areas can adapt to these changes by taking advantage of their strengths, while others may decline because economic and technological factors no longer favor them. Government can have some effect on a city's ability to take advantage of the changes, but technological and economic factors are more important. Therefore, central city decline, is an inevitable consequence of larger changes in society.

The argument of this book accepts the logic of both of these approaches, but emphasizes the importance of a third explanation. We will look closely at how American urban areas are governed and ask if our political traditions and practices are, in part, responsible for the difficulty of governing and managing large urban areas. *Perhaps the way we organize cities, how we select leaders, and how we divide authority among governments makes it difficult for us to plan city resources properly and build public facilities to respond to public problems.*

I propose that the problems of our central cities are related to the way urban areas are governed. A look at urban areas from this perspective focuses on several questions:

- Do citizens who are good representatives of the public govern cities?
- Are city officials given sufficient authority to make good decisions?
- Are urban areas structured politically to make sound decisions for the benefit of all citizens?
- Does the public have sufficient confidence in their local leaders to allow them to govern?
- Does the relationship between the federal, state, and local government permit city officials to govern properly?

Most analysts answer these questions similarly:

- City officials' background and values are not representative of the citizens
- The legal traditions and Supreme Court rulings give cities limited authority to govern
- Most urban areas contain many city governments, counties, special districts, and school districts, so decisions for the entire area are difficult to make numerous governments baffle the citizens because they don't know who is responsible for government policy
- This diversity of governments acts to constrain cities rather than giving them freedom to make good decisions.

These traits are similar to those of the political system in general. U.S. Congressmen, Senators and state legislators complain of the difficulties of divided government, and the public expresses limited confidence in their leadership as well. Urban officials, however, face a fundamentally different setting than do politicians at other levels because urban areas need more government than do other levels of government. Thus, decentralized, divided, and less visible local governments create greater problems for those who want to govern cities.

WHY URBAN AREAS NEED MORE GOVERNMENT

If urban areas differ from other parts of our country politically, it is important to carefully define what we mean by urban. The meaning of the term has been the subject of debate in both academic and governmental circles. We talk about urban and rural representatives, and the federal government awards differing amounts of aid depending on the definition of terms like *urban* and *rural*. Behind these political designations is an important distinction. Life in a large urban area (city, edge city or suburb) is very different from living in a small town or rural area. Compare what you know of life in downtown Manhattan, or suburban Highland Park, Illinois, with that of a small rural town. What should strike you immediately is the great difference in the need for governmental action to meet basic needs and provide the important matters of life for the New Yorker or the midwestern suburbanite. Urban life depends, to a much greater extent, on numerous kinds of collective actions usually supplied through government.

The great sociologist Louis Wirth was among the first to think systematically about why urban areas are different from other parts of the country, and his essay "Urbanism as a Way of Life" remains the best statement of the distinguishing features of urban areas. He defined urban areas as "relatively large, dense and permanent settlements of socially heterogeneous individuals" (Wirth 1964: 64). Thus, size, density, and heterogeneity, to Wirth are the primary traits of an urban area. When these conditions occur, Wirth argues, society is fundamentally different than in rural settings.

Why are urban societies different than rural ones? Wirth argues that size, density and heterogeneity act together to produce much more complex relations among people. Population concentration is a consequence of a large–scale technology where goods are produced for the society as a whole by large organizations. People must be able to get to and from these organizations easily. They must live close together and be able to get back and forth from work, commercial areas, and home easily. Urban society requires that its citizens be housed near their work and that they can readily get from home to work and shopping areas. Thus, housing and transportation must be efficiently obtained.

People in an urban society, who are by definition heterogeneous, have different values, customs, and traditions. Each group desires to preserve its religions practices, its forms of social life, food, and recreation. Therefore, each groups needs different organizations and institutions to assist them in meeting their personal needs. However, people with different values must share schools, stores, and recreation areas. Friction, irritation, and often conflict among people and groups are more common as people from different backgrounds must share a smaller space. Lacking personal understanding of one's neighbors, neutral parties are needed to keep peace among conflicting groups. Government officials are needed to mediate among differing peoples. People live in one neighborhood, work in another, and shop in a third. They depend on transportation networks and commonly accepted rules of trade. The increased scale of life removes man from nature, requiring a dependence on others for daily tasks that in simpler environments one could maintain themselves.

Wirth also argues that social life in urban areas is fundamentally different from life in small towns and rural communities. Individuals interact as *roles* they play rather than as people they know. Police officers are not people you went to school with; they are people you don't know personally. To you they are enforcers of abstract rules and laws; they perform tasks defined by the organizations they work for. Disputes are settled by judges and social workers rather than ministers and family friends. In rural societies or small towns, teachers and police officers are people that most citizens have seen in the neighborhood, in church, or at social events. Their roles as citizens and friends merge with their role as a government official. In the city and suburb, however, most people interact with police officers, schoolteachers, and even the after-school soccer coach in their professional roles only. They may live miles away from their place of work and rarely interact personally with citizens beyond their official duties. Thus, specialists trained for particular tasks replace personal relationships.

VANDALIA, ILLINOIS, THE POLITICS OF A SMALL TOWN

In the early 1960s, Joseph Lyford wanted to find out what was going on in a typical American small town. He selected Vandalia, Illinois, a farming community of 5,500 people and spent several days talking to residents and observing town life. The interviews and his insights were published in a moving book entitled *The Talk in Vandalia*.

Residents of the town knew one another well and interacted with other town's people frequently. . . . What is clear is that it is impossible to be in Vandalia very long without being noticed. Vandalia's social and moral regularity depends greatly on several thousand pairs of eyes. There is nothing malicious or prying about this sort of surveillance. In a small town, one does not peer, one sees, whether one wishes to or not. When a housewife goes to market, she learns where she has been soon afterwards from an interested friend. Ministers have come to rely heavily on kind-hearted parishioners for information on what members of their flock lie ill at home or in the hospital. In a town where the lives of their neighbors are the yarn of everyone's knitting, it is possible to be immoral, but utterly past imagination for one to remain undetected" (Lyford 1962: 42) One can assume that this closeness serves to control potential deviant behavior. Speeding cars, fights on the playground, or missing items in the general store are topics of conversation and result in informal, but potent sanctions.

Politics in Vandalia are remarkably calm and lacking in conflict. "Candidates do not run for office, they file for it, on ballots that do not mention party affiliation. The

(continued)

(continued)

campaign for mayor is not usually one of Vandalia's most exciting events. Last year's canvas was enlivened somewhat when one candidate promised that, if elected, he would fire the police chief. The reformer was elected, but the police chief is still the police chief, and there have been no outraged cries from the electorate about broken campaign promises. It is understood that it is pretty hard for the mayor of Vandalia to fire anybody. The mayor claims he ran for mayor because 'they couldn't get anybody else.' Nominations for political leadership are bestowed somewhat as they are in certain primitive societies, on persons who are the least skillful at evading the designation." (Lyford 1962: 39) One would expect few changes in policies in such a system.

Vandalia is not without problems. The economy has been declining for some time, and many of its industries threaten to leave. With few job possibilities for its young people, the more energetic youth leave for the big city. City leaders are concerned about economic growth and have developed plans to improve the job base. These plans, however, rarely involve government actions. Banks, the Chamber of Commerce, and contributions of civic groups and individuals were used to entice new industries to locate in Vandalia. Significantly, government played no part in these efforts.

SMALL TOWNS AND URBAN GOVERNMENTS

Compare the job of government in a small town like Vandalia to that in an urban area. Government must do more in the urban area—it must assume new tasks. Political scientist Richard Rose points out that urbanization is always related to increases in the size of government. He states:

> Historically urbanization has had a major impact on the size of government for people living in cities require services not needed in the countryside and are far better placed to make their demands effective politically. In contemporary Western societies, population movements within metropolitan regions . . . create pressures for the expansion of government. The relative burden of maintaining central city services increases as the number and average income of city residents drops, while the cost of maintaining roads, bridges, libraries and other central place services remains constant or increases. New suburbs have no backlog of social investment; they require many public facilities to be built at present day inflated capital costs. (Rose 1984: 40)

The increase in the need for government takes on several forms. To begin with, **government or government-related organizations must run many basic services that could be purchased or created individually in less dense environments.** In small towns and rural areas, water can be obtained through individual wells and waste is disposed in septic tanks. Trash can be burned or buried in a communal dump, and roads can be individually maintained.

In cities and suburbs, however, water systems are needed to secure enough water for the area, insure quality, and prevent damage to the environment. Central sewer systems are required to ensure quality public health. Roads and streets must be systematically designed and efficiently constructed to get goods from producers to consumers and transport people to and from their jobs. City growth limits the amount of open spaces that, in smaller environments, become places for people to play and exercise. Government must provide parks and recreation facilities in cities, often requiring the purchase of expensive land or the setting aside of properties that would otherwise generate income for the taxpayers. Government must oversee the design and often the operation of these facilities.

Changes in social life also lead to increased demand for government. In the small town, social deviations are controlled by common values, informal contacts among residents, and private organizations like churches and social groups. When someone misbehaves, ministers, friends, and neighbors inform other family members. Consequently, social life may be controlled, limited, and stifling, as novels of small towns frequently demonstrate. Government influence, however, is minimized.

In urban areas, these informal controls on behavior weaken. People do not know their neighbor, and they must rely on government agencies to settle disputes. My then-teenaged daughters once invited friends for an afternoon party that included a small rock band complete with drum set and electric guitar. Shortly after the group warmed up, a police officer came to our door saying that neighbors had complained. Why had the police come rather than the neighbor? Because the neighbors did not know us and in today's suburb, the police replace connections among neighbors. Colleague from a small North Dakota town skipped school one day in his youth. His parents received three calls from friends within an hour of the start of school, and soon he was in the classroom. In cities, we have truant officers who look for children out of school. In these examples, neutral agents of government rather than acquaintances must control deviant behavior. Thus, government costs must increase as police officers, jails, and court systems replace informal contacts between tavern owners, clergy, and household members. Divorce, illegitimacy, and crime increase in urban areas in part because people are placed in an anonymous setting that places fewer informal constraints on behavior.

Thirdly, many argue that **urban areas create a metropolitan culture** that demands certain kinds of facilities that often are produced by government. Concert halls, stadiums, and museums are expected in large cities. Urban residents demand such facilities and city leaders fear that the lack of these will lead to the city's decline. For that reason, government is the frequent provider or facilitator of cultural and athletic facilities.

Lastly, as urban areas grow, problems are created that require government intervention to ameliorate; **urbanization creates its own demand for government.** Air quality declines, often reaching unhealthy levels unless government officials regulate emissions. Our once pristine beaches become polluted from the runoff of water as it travels down dirty streets and through overloaded sewer systems. Increases in traffic lead to great inconvenience and economic decline

The satellite view of Earth demonstrates the scope of urbanization in the United States. Clusters of lights outline our metropolitan areas.

AP/Wide World Photos

if freeways and mass transit are not built. Lead from passing cars poisons those who live too close to the freeway. "Brown outs" occur because the demand for electricity exceeds the capacity. Generally, it is government that builds or regulates the facilities that deal with those problems.

Thus in all cities, as they grow from small towns to large urban centers, more government is needed.

- The public sector replaces private means of providing services and settling disputes.
- As a city increases in size needs arise that can only be handled by government. Public costs are an inevitable consequence of urbanization. Regardless of one's political philosophy or one's concern for the tax burden, large cities require more sewers, roads, police officers, social workers, teachers, health inspectors, and baseball fields. While some may argue the need for specific services and the costs of providing particular elements, most would agree that large cities require increases in most of these services.

Evidence of growth in government costs is apparent in Figure 1.1. Displayed are total expenditures for all cities larger than 100,000 in population since 1955. Two measures are compared, the total expenditures and those ex-

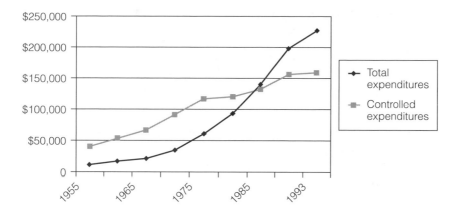

FIGURE 1.1 Growth in City Expenditures, 1955 to 1993.

United States Census of Governments.

penditures controlled for changes in the consumer price index (CPI). The CPI takes into consideration changes in the value of money—it controls for inflation that may have occurred. The figure demonstrates that costs have increased. The increase in total expenditures, particularly from 1970 forward, is most dramatic. Controlled expenditures reveal that costs have steadily increased; though there was little increase from 1975 to 1985. Problems in the economy, and the tax revolt discussed in Chapter 7, most likely had an effect on city spending.

HOW OUR URBAN AREAS RESPOND
TO THE NEED FOR GOVERNMENT

Governing institutions are organizations that have the authority to make decisions for the residents and raise the money necessary to carry out those decisions. A logical response to the need for more government is the creation of strong, governing institutions that represent people well and provide the means to respond to the need for new services. One might expect that political leaders would create effective representative governments in our cities that could oversee this growth in government fairly and efficiently. Urban areas would then be governed by these principles:

- A limited number of governments so that the concerns of all members of the effected population would be heard.

- Governments that enable central authority to clearly define and implement solutions to public problems. Political systems that organize public opinion to effectively provide important electoral choices.

- A public that is interested in the affairs of the city and maintains effective control over elected leaders.

  However, in our major urban areas, the opposite is the case.

Many Governments

For the purposes of this book, *governments are defined as publicly created organizations with clearly defined duties run by elected or appointed officials who can make authoritative decisions and impose costs on the public.* Our urban areas include several different kinds of governments that rule over us. Officials of governments determine how services will be administered and may raise taxes and fees to pay for the services. Most governments can also borrow money.

Control of all local governments ultimately resides with the state. Legally, states are independent governments; their sovereignity is protected by the United States Constitution. All local governments are wards of the state. States can redefine the jurisdiction of all local governments, and state laws directly impact what local governments can do.

Governments in urban areas are divided into four major categories.

Counties

All states divide their territory into local governments to aid in the distribution of state services and to provide minimal local government functions. Commonly we call these governments *counties,* though they are referred to as Boroughs in Alaska, Judicial Districts in Rhode Island, and Parishes in Louisiana. Counties are normally governed by several elected officials, including commissioners and judges. Frequently sheriffs, treasurers, and county attorneys are also elected to oversee specific functions. Counties perform functions delegated to them by state law and at the instigation of the commissioners. They act as agents of local government in unincorporated areas; those areas that are not contained in cities. Thus, in unincorporated areas, counties and *special districts* (discussed later) perform the normal duties of cities; police, fire, public works, etc. (see Figure 1.2).

As administrative arms of the state, counties frequently provide services that are local in nature but mandated by state law. Counties are the common supplier of welfare, public health, the court system, and jails, and usually maintain regional parks, much of the road system, and disposal facilities. The duties of counties, however, vary significantly in different states.

Counties vary greatly in size and population. San Bernardino County in California is larger in area than many states; while others are only a few square miles in area. Los Angeles County and Cook County, Illinois, include several million people each; while many counties have fewer than 1,000 residents. Some states, like Texas, divide the state into hundreds of counties; in Alaska, there are but five.

In some urban areas, counties provide most of the urban services. San Francisco, St. Louis, Baltimore, Jacksonville, and Nashville are usually referred to as city-counties. In these cases, one government performs the functions normally given to cities and counties. New York City is actually the combination of five separate counties, or boroughs, that were consolidated to form the present city. Thus, the city of New York performs both city and county functions for what used to be a five-county area.

The organization of the County of Orange is typical of many urban counties. The electorate chooses the five members of the Board of Supervisors in large districts, and voters choose those positions outlined in black. Consequently power is divided among the elected officials. The multiple lines of authority make it difficult to determine who is actually in charge. In 1994, Orange County declared bankruptcy because the county treasurer and the Board of Supervisors divided responsibility on investment policies. The power of the treasurer to invest money was not supervised by the primary decision-makers, the Board of Supervisors. Supervisors claimed they had little authority over the treasurer's decisions.

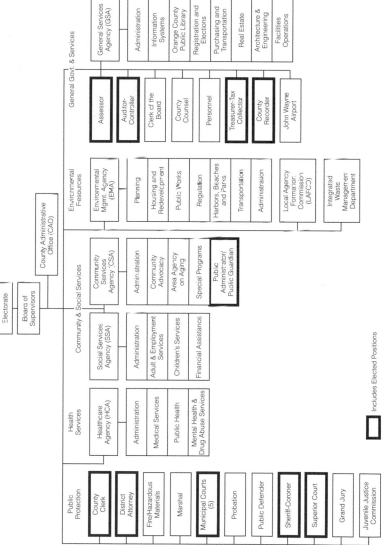

□ Includes Elected Positions

FIGURE 1.2 Organization Chart, County of Orange, California.

Cities

Cities, or municipalities, are created to provide more specific public services to a territory within a county. Areas incorporate as cities for the purpose of providing services specifically tailored to those within the city boundary. State laws generally set standards by which residents can create cities and expand them through the addition of land, commonly called *annexation*. Potential city residents are expected to petition state or county agents for the purpose of incorporating as a city. Once incorporated, elections are held for city offices, and the elected officials can determine the governmental tasks that are carried out within the new city. This makes city duties those determined primarily by the residents and their delegates, within the boundaries of state and federal law.

Cities perform a wide range of governmental functions. Public safety, fire protection, parks and recreation, public works, city planning, and building inspection are the common responsibilities of cities. The breadth of functions performed varies depending on the practices of the state. In New York City and Chicago, for example, schools are a city responsibility. In most other cities, schools are governed by special districts. In combined city-counties, welfare, health, and the court system become city responsibilities. New York City's responsibilities include a university system, while some Minnesota cities provide liquor stores.

Cities are run by elected officials; city council members, mayors, and occasionally other separately elected officials. City councils vary is size and responsibility, and mayors differ in authority and responsibility. Professionally trained executives, usually called city managers, are delegated primary administrative responsibility in some cities, while others vest the day to day running of the city to city council members or mayors.

Special Districts

Special districts are governments established for a single or limited number of governmental functions. They are run by elected or appointed officials who have the authority to administer that particular service and tax the residents for it. They differ from cities and counties because they are limited to a small number of prescribed services. Special districts vary significantly in size—some span several counties in more than one state, while others are restricted to small neighborhoods.

Large districts with major responsibilities for transportation are usually referred to as *authorities*. The larger authorities span several counties and are responsible for major public improvements. The Port Authority of New York and New Jersey, for instance, administers the Port of New York and many transportation facilities in a 17-county region. It is governed by commissioners appointed by the governors of the two states and derives most of its revenue from the facilities it operates. Thus, it is able to act independently of other governments in the region. Transportation authorities that have responsibility for transportation planning, bus systems, and mass transit are common in larger urban areas.

Schools are governed by special districts in most states. Historically, Americans have separated school government from other governmental functions, but in recent years, state control of schools has increased in most states. As a special district, school districts may span the boundaries of several city governments. Separate districts can also be created for lower- and upper-level education systems. School districts are generally guided by elected school board members who appoint a school superintendent.

Cities often create special districts to guide and plan the redevelopment of portions of the city. Commonly, *redevelopment districts* are defined as the portion of the city where upgrades will be made to the use of the land. The district has the power to condemn property and borrow money to clear the land and build new streets, roads, and sewers. The debt is to be paid by the increase in property value as the properties are sold and new structures built. The city council members often serve as directors of the redevelopment district.

Most urban areas contain numerous special districts for other functions of government. Water is often distributed through water districts governed by elected boards. Portions of urban areas may contain special districts for public services as varied as street lighting, libraries, recreation, and sanitation. The size of special districts can be tailored to conform to the interests of particular neighborhoods or communities, or they can span several cities to supply a service to a broader area.

Townships

Some states in New England and the Middle West divide the state into small units referred to as *townships.* Townships are expected to provide minimal public services for largely rural areas. Where townships are present, the county has very limited functions.

The Impact of Many Governments Figure 1.3 compares the number of local governments in 1952, 1992, and 1997. Note that the numbers of governments declined markedly between 1952 and 1992, and they increased slightly

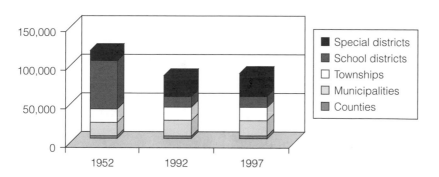

FIGURE 1.3 Changes in the Number of Local Governments.

Source: Statistical Abstract of the United States.

between 1992 and 1997. Over 80,000 local governments were present in 1997. Since 1952, significant declines have occurred in school districts as a consequence of a national movement to consolidate small districts. Non-school special districts, on the other hand, have nearly tripled during this time period. Analysts attribute this increase to the increase in population in unincorporated areas, the ability of special districts to avoid spending, and debt limitations imposed on cities.

Figure 1.4 looks at the number of local governments in the five largest urban areas. All urban areas contain large numbers of local governments, but the New York Region contains the most, with over 6,700. Los Angeles with less than 1,000, has the smallest numbers. The different frequencies reflect the ease with which state law permits the creation of governments and districts and the historical practice of government in the regions.

The benefits and costs of numerous governments are disputed by scholars and will form one of the major debates of this book (see Chapter 9). Some argue that the presence of numerous governments promotes competition among them, resulting in more efficient operations and greater consumer choice of services (Ostrom 1971: 22–35). However, David Rusk maintains that urban areas with fewer separate cities handle urban problems more effectively; they are more integrated racially, attract new businesses more readily, and are in better shape financially (Rusk 1995). Houston, for instance, maintains a great deal of open land within the city, and the City of Houston contains most of the population of urban area. Consequently, as the city expanded, wealth remained within the city boundaries. When integration of the school system was required, white residents could not escape to the suburbs; thus creating a more integrated school system. The opposite occurred in Detroit where suburbs surrounded the central city. White residents fled to the suburbs and new industry was placed in suburban communities rather than the city. Because the suburbs had their own school systems, it was difficult to integrate the schools. Hence, the Detroit region today is extremely segregated by both race and class. Racial

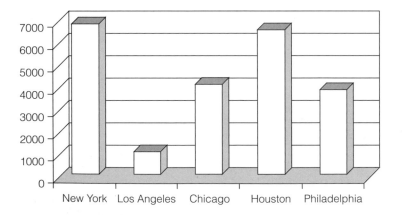

FIGURE 1.4 Local Governments in the Five Largest Urban Areas, 1997.

Source: U.S. Government Census of Governments: Government Organization 1997.

and class divisions may have had an effect on economic development. Potential businesses in Houston dealt with a united city that offered new jobs and a good school system for all workers regardless of race or class. In Detroit, the industrialist was faced with a divided city and uncertainty about the quality of schools for their workers.

Governments with Divided Powers

Local governments are created by states and ultimately serve at the whim of state officials. However, states commonly grant cities, and often counties, *charters* that define the structure of government for a city and permit autonomy of action within the confines of the charter. A charter is best viewed as a small constitution for the city. It defines the duties of elected and appointed officials and prescribes the manner of election. Charter changes have become a major way in which residents can alter the operation of their local governments. Reform of local government has frequently taken the form of a change in the city charter.

History of Divided Power

Charters reflect the values that proponents wish to see in their government. Tyranny of elected officials was foremost in the minds of the Founding Fathers when they created the American Constitution (see Chapter 4). They desired a government that would control the potential evil of factions— small groups of people acting in their own self-interest. Factions, assumed to reflect the nature of man, could be controlled only by creating structural roadblocks within the operation of government. The authors proposed a system of separation of powers and checks and balances designed to make it very difficult for any small group to dominate the governmental process. They hoped good government would emerge from a competition among contending powers with no one group gaining primacy. The smooth running of government and the efficient production of public services were secondary concerns.

Early city charters mirror these concerns. The common form of city government in the early years of the republic was the *mayor-council form of government,* which divides power between a city council, mayor, and other elected officials and appointed commissions. In keeping with the Constitutional principles, city council members were elected in districts, and mayors by the city as a whole. Both the mayor and city council shared responsibility for legislation, appointing of officials, and oversight of the administration. The mayor heads the executive branch; the city council members are the chief legislators. Through policy proposals and the veto power, the mayor is an important influence on legislation. The mayor's power, however, is relatively weak.

Early local governments delegated significant power to city councils, partly in reaction to the appointed mayors who had dominated colonial local governments. Early mayors were commonly selected from among council members until approximately 1820 (Kweit and Kweit 1990: 92). The division of the city into districts that represented different sectors of the city followed from the need to provide checks on the power of local mayors (Jones 1983: 244).

Toward the end of the nineteenth century reformers desired more central authority. Commonly, changes were put in place that limited the number of separately elected officials, gave mayors the power of appointment and budgetary authority, and provided for separately elected mayors with four-year terms. We commonly refer to this kind of government as the *strong mayor form* and the earlier structure as the *weak mayor government*. The difference between strong and weak mayors, however, has always been one of extent rather than kind. It is more accurate to think of mayor–council government as a range of powers divided between mayor and council.

Mayor-council forms of government were in place during the era of the political machine, roughly from 1880 to 1920, and are frequently blamed for its excesses. Powerful, centrally run governments, usually called machines or the boss system, thrived on ethnically based districts or wards that were coterminous with city council districts, partisan elections, and mayors with strong control over the administration. Urban machines were a product of a time of immense industrial and commercial change and significant immigration. With urban problems mounting and little response from the federal government, local governments were forced to act quickly to provide a minimal infrastructure; new roads, sewers, schools, welfare, and health facilities. The party system coordinated by a mayor, or boss, became a vehicle for uniting diverse ethnically based wards and providing the resources for a rapidly expanding public sector. (This period is discussed in more depth in Chapter 4.)

Divided Power in Early Twentieth Century

The problems of city government became the focus of a reform movement during the early years of the twentieth century. Advocates felt the problems of city government were caused by an electoral system that encouraged narrow, personal concerns rather than the interests of the city as a whole and an administrative system that prevented the application of techniques of modern management. Wards, partisan elections, and the incentives for career politicians, they argued, created a government where the concerns of particular groups and interests were satisfied at the expense of those of the city as a whole. A system was needed that encouraged those who were not aligned to particular groups, so they proposed several different kinds of governmental structures. The most common legacy of this movement within today's cities is called the *council-manager plan*. The plan consists of a small council, generally five to seven members, elected at large rather than in wards, with the members serving for little or no pay. This body would set general policy only, similar to the board of directors of a corporation.

Administering city policy is a city manager who headed an organization of civil servants. The city manager was trained in techniques of modern management and hired for his professional skill. Other employees were to be selected through an examination process determined by the skills of the positions. The manager's presence would permit the city council to meet less often because many of the concerns that were formally matters of politics—hiring new employees, awarding contracts, and determining construction priorities—could now be handled as administrative matters. The emerging science of management, could take many matters out of the hands of politicians (see Chapter 4). Another reform structure, the *commission plan,* elects a small number of officials citywide who also served as the heads of major departments. Thus, voters selected a police chief, a public works director, and a parks and recreation director, for instance, and these officials also composed the city council.

Government Structures Today

All of these concerns and values are reflected in the wide array of governmental structures in American cities today. Figure 1.5 displays the frequency of the kinds of local government in 2000. Strong mayor, weak mayor, and council-manager structures occur with great frequency. Nearly half of all cities use the council-manager structures. The mayor-council form is most common in the largest and smallest cities and constitutes 43 percent of the total. The commission plan has few adherents today, as most city charters reflect the founders' skepticism of centralized control. Townships are found in small cities predominantly in New England.

Division of Authority

Among major cities, the City of New York represents the most centralized structure of government. New York mayors enjoy significant powers—they appoint most members of their administration and commission members without confirmation by the city council, and they have authority to propose the city budget.

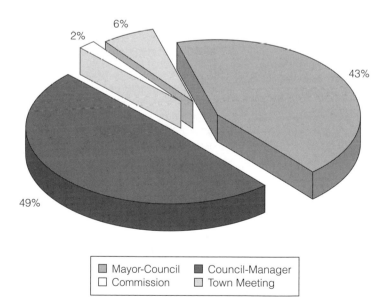

FIGURE 1.5 Forms of Municipal Government.

Source: International City Management Association Municipal Yearbook 2001.

In other mayor–council cities, it is common for power to be more divided between mayor and council. Councils normally must confirm mayoral appointments and have the power to propose nominations in some cities. In several cities, the chief administrative officer reports to both the council and the mayor. Independent commissions have direct operating responsibility in some cities. In Los Angeles, for example, the Public Works Commission is directly responsible for the city's public works department. The director of that department reports to the commission, not the mayor or the city council.

In council–manager cities, legislative authority is centralized in the city council. In practice, the city manager exerts significant influence on the making of policy in addition to her/his responsibilities for administration of policy. Studies of the practice of government in council–manager cities conclude that authority is not neatly divided between council and manager (see Chapter 4).

Other features of local government divide authority. Most cities and counties elect officials beyond the mayor and city council. Treasurers, chief legal officers, and sheriffs are examples. Cities are created by state government and states exert significant influence on city policy. Frequently, cities must appeal to the state legislature to raise taxes and alter planning and zoning practices. City decisions can also be questioned by the residents through the machinery of direct democracy. In most cities, an elected official can be recalled by a petition of residents and a new election. Many cities permit public issues to be decided by initiative and referendum (that is, direct votes of the public on policy issues). State initiatives and referenda also can affect city and county policies.

GOVERNMENTAL COMPLEXITY IN GREATER LOS ANGELES

Mayor Tom Bradley established the Los Angeles 2000 Committee in December of 1985, to prepare a strategic plan for the city as it faced the new millennium. More than 150 business and civic leaders representing many constituencies and perspectives met for months with the assistance of numerous social scientists and city staff members. Following is an excerpt from their final report that deals with problems associated with government. Note their concern for the complexity of governmental institutions.

Our forms of local government do not reflect the region's growth during the century nor are they designed to meet regional problems like traffic, solid waste disposal and air pollution. The basic form for the County of Los Angeles, for example, was established in 1913, when the population was 600,000 or approximately eight percent of today's numbers.

During the last decades there has been a growing tendency to respond to a perceived diminution of quality of life usually due to failure of infrastructure and particularly our road and highway system to keep up with growth by creating ever increasing numbers of jurisdictions and agencies. There are now 86 separate municipalities in Los Angeles County alone, each of which exercise local police power over public safety, land use, and growth policies, building codes and so on. Since each city is essentially free to set its own policies regardless of area needs, one begins to see how difficult it is to adopt and implement county-wide policies.

While local residents often decry traffic congestion and apply maximum pressure on local elected officials to make these problems go away, the difficulty is that clear responsibility is not defined. This fact contributes to bureaucratic gridlock in the transportation area. For example, any rail system in the Los Angeles metropolitan area would involve the following governing bodies and agencies: the City of Los Angeles (Mayor, City Council, Planning and Transportation Departments, and Commissions), the Los Angeles County Transportation Commission (11 commissioners); the Southern California Rapid Transit District (11 commissioners); Southern California Association of Governments; California Transportation Commission (9 Commissioners); the Federal

Department of Transportation; and the Urban Mass Transit Administration.

Any municipality along any proposed route would also be involved. The state legislature meanwhile hovers in the background ready to propose new legislation altering routes and dictating the composition of various decision making bodies while the national administration uses its influence to favor or oppose projects through federal transportation agencies. Add local pubic participation to this mix and it is possible to see why other nations can build hundreds of miles of new rail systems while we slog through multiple layers of bureaucracy.

SOURCE: From Los Angeles 2000 Committee, *Los Angeles 2000* (Los Angeles: Los Angeles 2000 Committee, 1985), 68–69.

Little Political Coordination   The difficulties of creating central policy in a dispersed and fragmented system could be overcome were it possible to organize interests that cross jurisdictional boundaries. The national government, for example, is governed by numerous overlapping jurisdictions and contains independent commissions and significant divided rule. The organization of political parties and the work of interest groups coordinate policy across the branches of government.

In urban areas, such coordination rarely happens. Most local elections are nonpartisan, and it is unusual for local leaders to coalesce with state and national leaders around distinct policy goals. Interest groups are less active and rarely influence policy among several local governments. It is unusual, for instance, for candidates for school boards and city councils to run a coordinated campaign.

The federal government, with its significant resources and influence over the political system, might also be able to exert a coordinating influence on urban areas. Through federal grants and the power of the central government to mandate practices, coordination of the diverse governments in urban areas might be accomplished. At times in our history, the federal government has exerted significant influence in urban areas, but it is more common for the influence of the federal government on cities to be quite limited. Constitutionally, states and the federal government share authority. States are provided legal rights, and the federal government has limited ability to directly affect city affairs. Historically, Congress has provided limited interest in the problems of urban areas. Politically, interest in the concerns of cities has varied with the values of the dominant party. Thus, as we will see in Chapter 6, the influence of the federal government in urban areas has been sporadic and limited.

Low Public Awareness With strong interest on the part of the public, it might be possible for general concerns of the population to directly affect public policy and overcome some of the effects of divided government. Local governments, after all, are designed to be closer to the people and should represent their interests with greater clarity than that of other levels of government.

The reality of local electorates, however, suggests that is not the case. Local elections frequently take place during off years when no state or national elections are held. Voting turnout in such elections is generally much lower than that of national elections. Karnig reports average turnouts nationwide of fewer than 30 percent of the registered voters, compared to roughly 50 percent for national elections. In fact, the percentage of the local government electorate voting has been declining since 1962 (Karnig and Walter 1986: 118). Turnouts under 10 percent are not uncommon in some local elections. In May of 1999, Ron Kirk was re-elected mayor of Dallas in an election where only 5 percent of the registered voters took part! Voter knowledge and information about their local officials is also lower than that of state and national officials. Peterson states the situation well:

> Lower levels of citizen involvement in local politics can be understood as rational responses to the structural context in which the public finds itself. The cues facilitating political involvement in national politics are in many cases noticeably absent. Much of the time, political parties do not structure conflict, issues do not have as burning an importance and candidates do not ambitiously compete for office. Information on local politics is hard to obtain from newspapers and the decisions taken by local officials are made in obscure settings. Interest groups do not mobilize mass involvement. (Peterson 1972: 128)

Those involved in local government are often unrepresentative groups. Their ability to represent the population as a whole is limited by the bulk of the population's lack of interest in politics.

Results of Authority Divisions

Consequently, we are left with what I call the **Paradox of American Urban Government,** which I introduced at the beginning of the chapter but restate here:

1. Urbanization creates a need for increased governmental services. The need for governmental services should result in strong urban governments that are capable of making representative decisions, extracting necessary resources and efficiently administering public policies.
2. In the United States, the opposite occurs. Numerous governments with weak political structures are the norm in urban areas.

The paradox limits the ability of leaders within an urban area to respond to the problems of urbanization. **This book focuses on this paradox; where it comes from, how our governments cope with its effects, and how it could be resolved.** Each chapter deals with a part of the paradox; therefore the reader should keep its components in mind.

Part I focuses on the effects of urbanization on government and the governing structures. The aim here is to understand the nature of urbanization as it affects governments and the kind of governmental systems Americans have developed. Chapter 2 examines the social and economic structure of our cities. The first part of the chapter focuses on city development from 1790 until 1940, especially the period of industrialization during the first part of the twentieth century when the structure and organization of our older cities was formed. The later part brings this discussion to the present day, looking particularly at the emergence of the suburban society following World War II and the more recent changes in our cities.

Chapters 3 and 4 examine the political organization of cities. American cities are famous for having very different kinds of political structures; different ways of electing officials and dividing powers between various elected and appointed officials. The structures reflect different ideas about how best to connect citizens and governing officials. Chapter 3 examines the origins of American thinking about local government as reflected in the views of James Madison and Thomas Jefferson and describes and evaluates the urban machine—the initial response of city government to the age of industrialization.

Chapter 4 looks at contemporary approaches to city government. The elements of the reform movement, the council-manager plan, and contemporary uses of the mayor-council structure are examined. Federal and state urban policies and local government finance are also examined in Chapter 5. The influence of the federal government has varied significantly over time and has taken different forms. As financial policy has changed at the state and federal level, so has the ability of cities to cope with the problems of urbanization.

The problems of dispersed power can be overcome through the development of strong leadership. Chapter 6 looks at the nature of power and leadership in American cities. It examines what is known about the distribution of power in urban areas and looks at leaders' ability to work with sources of power and influence.

Violence has always been a part of urban life. Civil disorders and riots occur frequently in urban areas. To many, they highlight the failure of governments to connect the citizen to the political system. The causes and impact of urban violence are discussed in Chapter 7.

Part II examines changes in government that attempt to overcome the paradox. Two major ways of dealing with the consequences of urbanization are neighborhood governance, discussed in Chapter 8, and regional governance, discussed in Chapter 9. The interest in neighborhood governance tries to improve the ties between neighborhoods and central governments by creating smaller governing units that are closer to the residents. The regional governance solutions propose larger units of government that more fully encompass the urbanized area.

In the final chapter, Chapter 10, we return to our paradox and examine how it can be resolved. We look at some longer-range reform proposals that emphasize action from the courts and federal and state governments, and assess the prospects for change in American urban governance.

SUMMARY

As New York begins the long process of recovery from the Trade Towers disaster, it faces a set of problems common to all American cities. The downtowns of most American cities are centers of both wealth and poverty; despair and potential destruction coexist next to the offices of multi-millionaires and the gleaming products of the twenty-first century economy. This book argues that the cause of some of these problems is related to a political system that fails to provide resources and the political will sufficient to deal with these problems.

Political and organizational problems are magnified in cities because of the consequences of urbanization. Using Louis Wirth's definition, urbanization is a "relatively large, dense and permanent settlements of socially heterogeneous individuals" (Wirth 1964: 64). The governmental effect of urbanization is the need for increased spending. When more people live in close proximity to one another, more must be spent on streets, sewers, and public protection. Citizens need more recreation areas and demand cultural centers; social problems between people and groups increase, requiring government officials to be mediators and resource providers. As more cars create pollution and clog the streets, more must be spent to improve transportation patterns and crack down on polluters.

Politically, the consequence of urbanization should be strong representative governments that can provide more services efficiently. If good services are produced, all would benefit, the urban area would operate more efficiently, and citizens would be proud of the accomplishments of their governments.

However, American cities have not responded to this need by creating strong governments. Instead, they have created many divided governments with limited powers. Few governing bodies represent the entire urban area. Decisions are made in the interests of small groups of residents, and the concerns of the region are neglected. Often, we separate the rich and poor politically, and wealthier residents enjoy better public services than do the poor.

Thus the paradox of American Urban government occurs; *there is a need for governmental power, yet political institutions disperse power.* The purpose of this book is to look closely at the components of this paradox and investigate how it can be resolved.

REFERENCES

Anderson, Ellijah. 1991. "Neighborhood Effects on Teenage Pregnancy." In *The Urban Underclass,* eds. Christopher

Jencks and Paul E. Peterson Washington, D.C.: The Brookings Institution.

Bryce, James. 1907. *The American Commonwealth*. London: MacMillan and Company.

Cisneros. Henry G. 1993. *Interwoven Destinies: Cities and the Nation*. London: W. W. Norton and Company.

Glaab, Charles N. 1963. *The American City: A Documentary History*. Homewood, Ill: The Dorsey Press.

Gold, Matea and Maggie Farley. 2001. "America Attacked: Strike Against the Nation; Terrorist Attack." *Los Angeles Times,* September 12.

Jones, Bryan D. 1983. *Governing Urban América: A Policy Focus*. Boston. Little, Brown and Company.

Karnig, Albert, and B. Oliver Walter. 1986. "Municipal Voter Turnout: A Longitudinal Analysis." Paper presented at the American Political Science Association.

Kweit, Robert W., and Mary Grisez Kweit. 1990. *People and Politics in Urban America*. Pacific Grove, CA: Brooks/Cole.

Krushchev, Nikita. 1974. *Krushchev Remembers: The Last Testament,* translated and edited by Strobe Talbott. Boston: Little Brown and Company.

Ladd, Helen F., and John Yinger. 1989. *America's Ailing Cities: Fiscal Health and the Design of Urban Policy*. Baltimore: Johns Hopkins University Press.

Los Angeles 2000 Committee. 1985. *Los Angeles 2000*. Los Angeles: Los Angeles 2000 Committee.

Lyford, Joseph P. 1962. *The Talk in Vandalia*. Charlotte, NC: McNally and Loftin Press.

Ostron, Elinor. 1971. "Metropolitan Reform: Propositions Derived from Two Traditions." In *Readings in Urban Politics,* eds. Harlan Hahn and Charles H. Levine. New York: Longman, 1984.

Peterson, Paul E. 1981. *City Limits*. Chicago: University of Chicago Press.

Rose, Richard. 1984. *Understanding Big Government: The Programme Approach*. Beverly Hills, CA: Sage Publications.

Rusk, David. 1995. *Cities Without Suburbs: Second Edition*. Washington, D.C.: The Woodrow Wilson Center Press.

White, Morton, and Lucia White. 1962. *The Intellectual Versus the City: From Thomas Jefferson to Frank Lloyd Wright*. Oxford, England: Oxford University Press.

Wirth, Louis. 1964. "Urbanism as a Way of Life." In *Louis E. Wirth on Cities and Social Life: Selected Papers,* ed. (with and Introduction by) Albert J. Weiss. Chicago: University of Chicago Press.

PART I

Contours of America's Urban Areas

Chapter Two

The Social
and Economic Structure
of American Cities

The concentration of the poor, less-skilled residents in our central cities, the high percentages of minority residents in the central cities and whites in suburban communities, and the flight of taxable resources to the suburbs contribute to the paradox of urban governance. Why did this pattern of settlement and government organization occur? The reasons are related to the historical development of American cities. In this chapter, we briefly survey the growth of American cities from the inception of the republic to the present day.

We examine several important questions in the chapter related to the paradox.

- Why are the poor living near the central city?
- Why are many of those poor racial and ethnic minorities?
- Why do we find jobs now more common in the suburbs than in the central cities?
- Why, over time, has the welfare of the central city become less important to those who live outside of the city center?

We begin our study by looking at the social and economic structure; who lives in cities, what kinds of activities are carried out, and how the mix of people and the means of production create wealth, social differences, and sources of tension and conflict. We assume politicians' actions respond to the demands placed on government by changing social and economic conditions. In the United States, social and economic conditions changed significantly in four periods of time.

- The era of the *walking city* existed from the founding of our country until about 1870. In this era cities were small in population and primarily centers of commerce and trade.

- The time from 1880 until 1940 is referred to as the era of *large-scale industrialization*. During this time the population of cities increased dramatically as large numbers of immigrants and rural folks moved, forming several large cities. Large industries emerged to hire the new residents, and numerous technological and organizational changes occurred to make large, complex cities possible.

- From 1945 to 1970, our cities changed radically again. This time period is best described as the era of *suburbanization*. Technological, social, and government changes acted in concert to encourage the movement of population and employment to the edge of the old city and beyond. Our urban areas became much larger in area, and our old central cities declined, but continued to be the refuge for new settlers.

- Finally, we come to the present time; the era of the *dispersed city*. Since 1980, a dizzying array of changes have taken place. International competition for wages and labor have placed our cities in competition with cities all over the globe. New forms of technology and communication are germinating wealth in some parts of the country but have left others with declining resources, and new immigrants are moving to our cities. This last period is hardest for us to comprehend because it continues to evolve. It has encouraged a further decentralization of city wealth and favored the expansion of smaller cities at the expense of larger areas. However, some cities have prospered.

We will look at the nature of city life in each of these time periods. As we discuss each period in time, think about the effects of the changes in life on the political system. What kind of decisions would political leaders face? What kinds of political problems would you anticipate were present in major cities? Why would the described conditions make it difficult to run the city effectively? Picture yourself as a political leader of the time; What do you think your main concerns would be?

THE WALKING CITY

From the founding of the country until after the Civil War, American cities were centers of commerce and trade. The vast majority of the population lived on small farms, and many raised all of their own food and provided for their own shelter. President Lincoln's upbringing was typical of much of the American population. Housing was provided simply from the environment—sod houses in Nebraska, and log cabins in Kentucky. Cities were small settlements where one could trade surplus crops and buy essential goods and services and small luxuries. Because the citizens had few surplus resources, the cities had little potential wealth. Larger cities connected the country to the outside world, initially, through ships and later railroads. These cities contained more extensive commercial goods and small industrial shops.

Cities as we know them today, however, did not exist; even our largest cities then would be considered small today. New York City was the only city with a population greater than 50,000 in 1800; the fifth largest city in that year, Charleston, South Carolina, contained a scant 18,000 people. New York City reached 100,000 people by 1820, but it was not until 1850 that as many as five cities had populations greater than 100,000.

David Donald's description of Springfield, Illinois, in his prize-winning biography of Abraham Lincoln, aptly describes many cities of this era:

> To the Eastern observers, Springfield in the 1830s was a frontier town. Though there were a few brick edifices, many of the residences were still log houses. If the roads were wide, they were unpaved; in the winter, wagons struggled through axle-deep mud, and in the summer the dust was suffocating. The town had no sidewalks, and at crossings, pedestrians had to leap from one chunk of wood to another. Hogs freely roamed the streets, and there was a powerful stench from manure piled outside the stables.
>
> But this was the most cosmopolitan and sophisticated place Lincoln had ever lived. Though Springfield had been in existence only since 1821, it was now a thriving community of 1,500 residents. The Sangamon County Courthouse occupied the center of town, which was laid out in a regular rectangular grid. The north-south streets were numbered. Those running east-west were named after American presidents. The courthouse—soon to be replaced by the new state capital—was surrounded by nineteen dry goods stores, several groceries, four drug stores, two clothing stores, and a bookstore. Four hotels cared for transients. In addition to schools and an "academy" the town boasted six churches. (Donald 1995: 67)

City populations began to grow in the middle of the eighteenth century as farmers sought outside markets for their products and the rail system and steamboats connected the hinterland to the centers of trade. Cities also followed the expansion of the frontier, providing access to the older Eastern seaboard, permitting commerce and trade, and acting to stabilize the life of the new residents by providing rudimentary pubic services, police and fire departments, churches, social clubs, and the various sources of leisure activities well described in Western movies.

As the population expanded, smaller cities took on added importance. After 1820, the increase in city populations outpaced rural areas, indicating that city life was replacing the farm as the centers of life. By 1860, the nation contained over 101 cities with a population of 10,000 or more. Lincoln's motives for leaving the farm and taking up the study of law were undoubtedly typical of many. His early life was dominated by the difficulties of farming. Lincoln sought a more interesting and less physically demanding life; and that could be found only in the town (Donald 1995: 38).

What were these cities like? Wade describes them well:

The "historic city" was characterized by compactness. It had to be small because it was a "walking city". People went to work, to shop, to visit and to play on foot. Some of the wealthy lived outside the municipal limits and commuted to their businesses by carriage, but most people, rich and poor, walked. Hence they lived closer together than they ever would again. To be sure the affluent appropriated the high land and the desirable locations and the poor huddled in shacks along the waterfront or tucked into allies and lanes. Yet no great spaces separated mansions from hovels. In addition commercial and manufacturing facilities were mixed with housing. In small retail shops owners or clerks lived above the store and tanneries, meatpacking plants, and breweries were often within sight and smell of the most elegant residences. Railroads and freight yards cut through the heart of the city, the tracks often moving along major streets. (Wade 1971: 94)

Thus, American cities began as densely populated centers, located along major commercial lines. Populations increased as the society became wealthier. Farms generated surplus goods, which could be bought and sold in cities. Merchants in smaller cities became intermediaries between locally produced goods and markets elsewhere where the goods desired by the citizens could be obtained. As cities expanded, production of goods also increased, but generally production was confined to small businesses, often taking place in homes.

Life in the early cities was chaotic, lively, and often unpredictable. The visitor approached them with care. Descriptions of the early cities by outsiders range from disgust to enchantment. Public services were limited and primitive because cities often grew quickly with little concern for orderly development or rational planning.

Little remains of the walking city today. Smaller commercial cities remain along our freeways but changes in technology and communications place these towns within the framework of the larger society, and in most cases, life is dominated by national concerns for those of nearby larger cities. The roots of two important characteristics of modern cities—utilitarian convenience and promotion—remain as legacies to this period of our history.

The location of our earliest cities was determined by natural conditions; waterways, ports, and flat, buildable land. With the development of railroads in the first part of the eighteenth century, however, the setting of rail lines influenced the location of cities, and the work of individual promoters became central to the future health of the city. Glaab and Brown point out that "Numerous cities in the West owe their importance to the fact that groups of energetic local promoters with substantial investments in local real estate were able through superior organization of their communities, superior advertising, or often simply through good luck to persuade railroads to build at their particular locations" (1967: 130). This tradition continues today; city officials frequently are promoters of their cities, and city governments and private organizations invest heavily in the promotion of their city. The surrounding social and economic forces then do not solely determine the characteristics of the city. Entrepreneurship, leadership skills, and community interests frequently influence the structure of the community.

Secondly, unlike European cities, the American city was formed as a utilitarian convenience. It was there to assist citizens carry out their own pursuits. In the words of one of our more thoughtful social critics, cities provide "a setting for individual pursuits rather than communal activities" (Rybczynski 1995: 109). Rybczynski adds, "People moved about from house to house, from neighborhood to neighborhood from town to town, from the East to the new frontier. The city—especially the new built city—was chiefly seen as an anonymous, practical convenience. Cities could be started from scratch, built up, and as quickly abandoned, or at least altered. Americans were attached to their homes, to their families, and to their political institutions, but . . . they carelessly left their cities to their own devices" (1995: 109). This temporary attachment limits the extent to which cities become connected to their residents. Limited citizen commitments may provide little incentive to attack the city's problems. One can easily move rather than work on the problems of the community. The weak commitment of residents to their communities continues to be a concern today, as we will see in Chapter 9, as some try to encourage citizens to become more attached to their communities.

THE INDUSTRIAL CITY, 1880–1920

Most facets of American life changed radically during the next period in city history. Many cities expanded from their commercial roots to become major producers of new products and exporters of mass-produced finished goods. Production was based on large quantities of raw materials (for example, iron ore, electricity, oil, and grain) and laborers, largely unskilled, to shovel raw materials, man assembly lines, and pack the finished products. Responding to the need for labor, millions of new immigrants came and settled in central cities, forming diverse ethnic communities.

These new cities had to provide public facilities on a very different scale than in the walking cities. Roads, sewers and water systems, and port facilities were needed for a much larger and more concentrated population. Changes in housing and transportation expanded the city and permitted the new concentration of people to get around. The change took place quickly; the number of people in Chicago, for instance, increased from less than 300,000 in 1870, to over 2 million by 1910. New York City was home to fewer than one million people in 1870, but 4.7 million lived there in 1910.

Figure 2.1 traces the emergence of large cities in this country over time. It tabulates the percent of the total population that is accounted for by the five largest cities. As you can see, from 1790 to 1860, this percentage changed only slightly and never was greater than 5 percent of the total population. Around 1870 this percentage began to rise. It dipped slightly in the late 1880s due to a

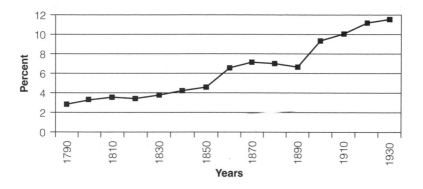

FIGURE 2.1 Percent of Total U.S. Population Living in Five Largest Cities, 1790–1930.

United States Government, Census of Population.

downturn in the economy, then it increased radically until 1930 when over 12 percent of the country's people were living in the five largest cities.

We can also see this change in the total population of the country. From 1860 to 1910, the total population expanded *seven times*. Most of that increase occurred in cities. In fact, as we will see, rural areas actually declined in population during these years. Another way of looking at this change is to compare the rural population with that living in cities. The United States Census Bureau defines *urban* as those cities larger than 2,500 in population. In 1790, only 5.1 percent of the population were classified as urban. By 1920, a majority of the country lived in cities with a population of 2,500 or more. From 1870 to 1920, the percentage of urban dwellers increased from 25 percent to over 50 percent (Judd and Swanstrom 1998: 17).

The new city bore little resemblance to the old. It was bigger and more complex in every way. How did such basic changes come about? Most argue that three factors explain the development of the industrial city; *technological changes* that permitted the mass production of goods and services, *transportation changes* that encouraged the flow of people and information in a concentrated area, and *the movement of people* needed to get the work done in the large cities. Again, clever entrepreneurs who could bring these new forces together led these changes.

Technological Changes

During the eighteenth century production changed from small cottage industries to large-scale industries employing thousands of people. Inventors and scientists devised ways of harnessing materials to produce goods that were cheaper and better than those produced by the small factories of the walking city. Many of these inventions could be used to create the means to bring together the large numbers of people and raw materials the new industries required. Changes in one form of production often led to other inventions that further increased the scale of the city. The mass production of steel, for instance, had a direct impact on housing and transportation needs. With steel rails, faster, stronger railroads were possible, and housing units of several stories could be built to house a greater concentration of people. Mass-produced energy ran the new factories. It permitted larger productive processes, and because energy could be transmitted efficiently, the location of industries could be coordinated with the need for workers and the delivery of raw materials. Advances in electricity also provided more street lighting and ran more efficient transit systems. One change thus affected several production processes. Together, these inventions and their adaptations provided the means for a larger, more concentrated city.

The contributions to these changes are too numerous to mention. We will highlight two, the production of steel and the generation of electricity, because they typify innovations of the time.

Steel The use of iron for making small implements had been known for centuries and was commonly produced in the United States in small furnaces widely scattered around the country. Local foundries produced hand-made iron products using very simple technologies in response to individual orders. Individually run furnaces were a common feature of the walking city, and very compatible with the structure of those cities. A family could run a furnace producing farm implements for nearby citizens (Bartlett 1988: 83–84). With production designed for small markets, there was little need for larger cities.

The value of iron products changed radically with the invention of the Bessemer process in the 1850s. High-grade steel, a much stronger and more malleable iron product, was now possible at a relatively low cost. The Bessemer process, however, required more complex production and greater concentration of materials than could be accomplished in small mills. To produce steel efficiently, large amounts of raw materials, expensive furnaces, and lots of manpower were needed. Steel could best be made where the raw materials could be cheaply obtained, sufficient capital to build the equipment was present, and a large labor force was available. Once produced, it was more efficient to ship the finished product rather than produce it in all cities.

Cities located on rail lines and waterways became the prime location for steel production, and technology required that it be produced in large quantities. That is how the city of Pittsburgh, became a center of steel production. Raw materials could be brought by boat from the northern Great Lakes region, and finished goods could be shipped out through the lakes and canals or by rail. Immigrants moved to the city as jobs in the industry became available.

Electricity Large factories needed radically increased amounts of power. In the mid-nineteenth century, electricity produced by waterpower was a major energy source for industry. Thus, the location of industries was extremely limited and very dependent on conditions of the waterways. The innovations of Thomas Edison and George Westinghouse in the late 1880s led to the development of power generators—the means to store electrical energy and the ability to transmit over long distances. The result was a significant increase in the availability of electricity and the ability to move energy to production sites. As Bartlett points out "The advantages of centrally generated electricity soon became clear. In 1900 perhaps electrical motors were providing 2 percent of the industrial horsepower in America. Twenty years later nearly one third was. In 1900 the nation's power companies generated 6-billion kilowatt-hours. Twenty years later they produced ten times that amount in power plants that were on average six times larger" (Bartlett 1988: 87).

The new industries offering good wages attracted new people to the cities. The money earned provided a market for stores and various kinds of entertainment. New inventions led to more industries. Abbott describes one of these emerging cities:

> Detroit was the grandest of all of these manufacturing capitals. It furnished roughly two-thirds of the world's cars and in the early 1920s with half its labor force employed by auto plants and their suppliers. Good wages attracted six hundred thousand new Detroiters in the 1910s and nine hundred thousand in the 1920s. Its symbol was the Ford motor company's giant new plant on 2,000 acres along the Rouge River. The plant was an autonomous industrial complex in which a network of low-slung buildings allowed Henry Ford to realize his ideal of a continuous flow of work that could be performed on one level. For industrialists and artists alike, it was one of the marvels of the age. (1987: 11–12)

As a consequence of these innovations and the presence of people with significant capital, large industries became the most efficient way to produce goods. Goods could then be exported, and as they were, the industries expanded requiring more resources and more employees. Cities became centers of production as well as commerce, and for the large cities, production was the more important function. The more efficient industrial city was one with a much larger population and a more complex social structure. It was vastly different than the walking city.

Transportation

In the walking city, the concentration of people and production in the central city could be handled with very simple means of transportation, primarily horses and horse-drawn carriages.

The horse-drawn omnibus holding at best 20 people was a major means of transportation in cities prior to the 1880s. The ride was less than pleasant according to an 1864 account in the *New York Herald:*

> Modern martyrdom may be succinctly defined as riding in a New York omnibus. The discomforts, inconveniences and annoyances are almost intolerable. From the beginning to the end of the journey a constant quarrel is progressing. The driver quarrels with the passengers and the passengers quarrel with the driver. There are quarrels about getting out and quarrels about getting in. . . . The driver swears at the passengers and the passengers harangue the driver. Ladies are disgusted, frightened and

insulted. Children are alarmed and lift up their voices and weep. . . . Thus the omnibus rolls along, a perfect bedlam on wheels. (Wade 1971: 69)

To survive in the industrial city, new means of transportation were needed and city members responded with the creation of cable cars, then electric trolleys, and finally subways and elevated railroads. With each of these changes, more people could be moved more quickly and further from the centers of employment and commerce. As transportation improved, the city could increase in size and spread out further from the city center.

Innovations permitted the city to grow *up* as well as out. Elevators, the use of steel skeletons, and the development of high-powered motors permitted the building of skyscrapers in the downtown area. Commerce and industry at this time required face-to-face interactions for most decisions. The business executive needed the coordination of suppliers, bankers, the insurance industry, and public officials to keep their factories running. Face-to-face interactions were necessary to coordinate such people; therefore, all of these parties needed to be located in the central city. Higher buildings made such interactions possible.

Transportation changes fueled significant changes in American cities. The city now could expand its territory because transportation lines could quickly connect outlining areas with the central city. Wealthier residents could move out of the central city, leaving the old area for the newly arriving immigrants. The separation of classes and races, still common today, was the result. American cities became mobile cities where people moved to new residences as they acquired wealth. Evidence of an improved lot in life was a move to a better location. Thus the trend, also still with us today, of neighborhoods without stable residents had its origin in the new transportation system.

The Movement of People

The emerging industries required large numbers of unskilled workers living near the new industries that were most likely to be located in the central city. Workers were needed to haul raw materials, perform routine tasks on primitive assembly lines, and prepare the finished product for shipment. Without large numbers of people mass-production could not occur. Without surplus labor, the cost of producing goods would limit the profits that could be made.

Two kinds of labor were attracted to the cities as industrialization advanced. Many migrated to the cities from American rural areas. Others were lured here by difficult economic, social, and political conditions in Europe and Asia. Most of these new groups moved to the city center, creating a crowded, vibrant, and chaotic concentration. Huge cities replaced the smaller walking cities in a very short period of time. Between 1860 and 1920, the number of people living in cities larger than 8,000 residents increased from 6.2 million to 54.3 million. In that span of 60 years, the country changed from a largely rural one to a dominantly urban society.

Migration The migration of rural Americans to the cities is an often-neglected contributor to the change in cities. Innovations and mechanization improved agricultural production in the late 1800s. The productivity of farm labor increased so strikingly that in 1890, far fewer workers on farms could produce much larger crops. Glaab and Brown point out that through the use of modern machines, the work of one man in a wheat field in 1896 could be more than 18 times as effective as it had been in 1830 (1967: 136). Though farm production increased significantly, fewer people were needed to run the farms, and farm families frequently produced several children. Settlers moved to the middle west to farm more productive land, and many of the small towns of the east declined. Farm life was difficult, and the city offered what seemed to be a more interesting life and less back-breaking work. It is estimated that 11 million people migrated to the city from American farms (1967: 136) from 1840 to 1900.

A second major group to move to the cities was African Americans from the rural south to the urban north and west. In 1880, over 90 percent of the African American population were residing in the rural south, most working as sharecroppers in the cotton fields, and living at a subsistence level. The development of railroads provided the first significant means of travel from the farms, as word spread of jobs and better treatment in the urban north. Most of this movement was concentrated in larger cities. The African American population of Chicago, for instance, steadily increased from 3,692 in 1870 to 50,000 in 1915 (Spear 1967: 11). In Detroit, the African American population had reached 40,000 by 1920, compared to 6,000 in 1910 (Sugrue 1996: 23).

Discrimination against African Americans was common in most cities during this time period. They were very limited in their job opportunities, schools were often formally segregated, and restrictive codes and practices limited housing opportunities. For these reasons, African Americans had different experiences than other ethnic groups in the cities. Segregation in most cities began when these communities were small, beginning a pattern that was to dominate city politics in the middle of the twentieth century. Because African Americans were so limited in their choice of housing, they were forced to pay higher rents, and most were restricted to inferior houses.

Employment opportunities for African Americans also differed from that of other ethnic groups. In Chicago, over 45 percent of African Americans were employed in four occupations: porters, servants, waiters, and janitors (Spear 1967: 30). Many other trades and occupations were closed to them. Because of the significant need for domestic workers and maids, the job opportunities for African American women were greater than for African American males. Unlike other ethnic groups, African American women outnumbered men in most cities and a far larger percentage of these women worked. In 1900, although one fourth of all women in the 11 largest cities of the north worked, nearly half of all African American women were classified as wage earners (Abbott 1987: 29).

In spite of these difficulties, African American migration to the cities increased significantly between 1910 and 1930. Spear refers to the movement following 1915 as "mass movement." As numbers increased, so did the segregation. In fact, Abbott (1987) argues that there was significantly greater integration prior to 1910. As the numbers increased, however, Whites restricted the movement of African Americans through their control of the real estate market and city hall.

Immigration Immigration to the United States from foreign countries produced a far larger number of new city residents during this time period than migration within the country. Economic, political, and social difficulties in Europe, and the image of America as a new society with the possibility of gaining personal wealth encouraged the exodus of waves of immigrants.

Social scientists tend to divide foreign immigrants into two groups. From 1840 to 1880, immigration averaged more than 2.5 million people per year. The first wave consisted primarily of Irish and German Catholics and English, German, and Scandinavian Protestants. While many of these immigrants remained in the entry ports of the large eastern cities, a significant number fanned out through the country, often into the growing cities of the middle west and west.

From 1880 to 1930, the number of immigrants increased radically, reaching a peak of 8.8 million in the decade 1901–1910 (Kweit and Kweit 1990: 49). This group was largely made up of people of peasant stock from the poorer countries of Eastern Europe, Italy, and Russia. A much larger proportion of these immigrants settled in large cities (Chudacoff 1975: 94). Rapidly, European immigrants became a major part of the population of the largest cities. In New York City, the number of foreign-born residents increased from 419,000 in 1870, to 2,300,000 in 1930. In Chicago, foreign-born residents totaled 145,000 in 1870, and 860,000 in 1930. In the largest cities, foreign-born residents and their children became the bulk of the population. By 1870, foreign-born residents and children with at least one foreign parent totaled 80 percent of the population in New York City and 87 percent of the population in Chicago.

Most immigrants arrived with little knowledge of English and a firm attachment to their own customs and traditions. Initially, at least, they hoped to find large numbers of their own kind and be able to live within an American city but retain their language and traditions. Frequently, ambitious members of the group had preceded them and served as intermediaries between the immigrants and the new society. These entrepreneurs then met the new settlers at the point of entry, found places for them to live in that portion of the city where others of their background were also living, and found jobs for them in the newly emerging industries. As more groups migrated, American cities became divided into sections dominated by different ethnic groups, each with its own religious institutions and customs. Thus, the new city was parceled out into many subcommunities, each with a different dominant language.

Politically, as we will discuss in Chapter 3, the new city presented a dazzling array of challenges. The new industrial structure and the increased number of residents required public services on a vastly greater scale. As mentioned in the first chapter, urban concentrations and large-scale industries generate radically increased need for centrally provided public services. The movement of goods required new roads and waterways, the crowded conditions produced health hazards unknown in the earlier cities, and socially, the new city was divided into numerous separate groups with little understanding or knowledge of American society.

The Diverse, Complex Metropolis

By 1910, the large American city was a complex mix of dynamic new industries, vibrant commercial areas, and diverse people with varying customs and traditions, as well as grinding poverty, interpersonal conflict, and unrest. It was an area of great diversity where fortunes were made and lost quickly and some were consigned to poverty and degradation. The city was one of extreme contrasts. Let us look at a few of these.

Theodore Dreiser describes Chicago in the 1890s through the eyes of a young girl leaving the Wisconsin farm, seeking a new life in the big city.

To the child, the genius with imagination, or the wholly untraveled, the approach to a great city for the first time is a wonderful thing. Particularly if it be even in that mystic period between the glare and gloom of the world when life is changing from one sphere or condition to another. Ah, the promise of night. What does it not hold for the weary? . . .

. . . In 1889 Chicago had the peculiar qualifications of growth which made such adventuresome pilgrimages even on the part of young girls possible. Its many growing and commercial opportunities gave it widespread fame, which made of it a giant magnet, drawing to itself, from all quarters, the hopeful and the hopeless—those whose fortunes and state of affairs had reached a disastrous climax elsewhere. It was a city of over 500,000 with the ambition, the daring, and the activity of a metropolis of

The lively bustle of the central city. Downtown Chicago in 1890; State Street, looking North from Madison.

© Bettmann/Corbis

By 1899, entrepreneurs designed modern buildings like the tall one on the left. Trolleys and some autos replaced horse-drawn carts and cabs.

© Corbis.

a million. . . . The sound of the hammer engaged upon the erection of new structures was everywhere heard. Great industries were moving in. The huge railroad corporations which had long before recognized the prospects of the place had seized upon vast tracts of land for transfer and shipping purposes. (Wade 1971: 145)

Dreiser's novel, *The Titan,* looks at the same Chicago through the eyes of one of its self-made business tycoons, Frank Algerton Cowpepper. A fictional account based on an actual Chicago corporate tycoon, the city is described as:

A very bard of a city, this singing of high deeds and high hopes. Its heavy brogans. Buried deep in the mire of circumstance. Take Athens, oh, Greece! Italy, do you keep Rome! This was Babylon, the Troy and Nineveh of a younger day. Here came the West and the hopeful East to see. Here hungry men, raw from the shops and fields, idyls and romances in their minds built them an empire, crying glory in the mud. Here were the Negro, the prostitute, the blackleg, the gambler, the romantic adventurer par excellence. A city with but a handful of native born; a city packed to the doors with all the riffraff of a thousand towns. Glaring were the lights of the bagnio; tinkling the banjos, zithers, mandolins of the so called gin mill; all the dreams and the brutality of the day seemed gathered to rejoice (and rejoice they did) in this newfound wonder of a metropolitan life in the west. (1945: 13)

© The New Yorker Collection 2001 Roz Chast from cartoonbank.com. All
Rights Reserved.

For many, however, the city was one of crowding, poverty, and disease. Irving Howe quotes the Yiddish writer David Ignatow's impressions of the Jewish ghetto of New York City:

> The new and alien people who came across the sea to this unimaginable city . . . felt themselves caught up in a terrible storm that would soon tear them limb from limb. Buses and trolleys rushed through the streets with devilish force. Waves of people pounded the streets, their faces like foam. The immigrants came to feel a sense of fright before the weight of these massed streets. It was all wild; all inconceivable. (1976: 72)

The large scale industrial city was a city of dynamic contrasts; variations in living patterns and land use, diverse living styles, vibrant downtowns, decrepit slums. In its positive features, it remains our image of what the city can be; in its baser acts, an agenda of reform. Important characteristics of the current metropolis can be traced to this period. Many of the qualities of these cities remain with us today.

- Racial and ethnic diversity began in this period and remains an important condition of central cities. Central cities continue to be the homes to newcomers and the poor.

- Industrialization and immigration created a vibrant, centralized downtown where most of the important matters of the society occurred. Michigan Avenue in Chicago, and Times Square in New York City, are examples of the excitement and dynamics of downtown. Our image of the good city as one with a glittering, crowded, and diverse downtown emerged during this period. Ever since, city officials have desired to recreate it.

- Changes in transportation permitted the city to spread out and create outlying living areas of lower density where those who could afford it could live with less conflict and congestion. Mass transit allowed the well-off to live in the best of both worlds; the bustling city by day and the quiet suburb at night and on weekends. Many still desire this kind of city.

- The beginnings of severe racial discrimination in northern and midwestern cities can be traced to this period. Prosperous members of white ethnic groups began to move to outlining parts of the city or suburbs. African Americans, however, were prevented from doing so as they were restricted legally and informally to the central city. Initially these restrictions encouraged vibrant communities within the African American ghettos. The so-called Harlem renaissance can, in part, be attributed to the inability of educated and professional African Americans to move as they gathered resources. Job discrimination and increases in the African American population concentrated more and more African Americans in small portions of the city. Thus, the inferior housing and living conditions many African Americans continue to endure in our central cities can be traced to this period.

THE SUBURBAN CITY, 1950–1970

Imagine the typical American city of 1960, and compare it with the city of the previous era. Industries operate differently; raw materials are now brought to the factory by trucks and airplane rather than by boat or rail; workers arrive in their own cars rather than walking or traveling by bus or mass transit; workers live in single family homes with spacious yards, usually outside the central city; and communications among corporate leaders are likely to be by telephone, often at great distance, rather than face-to-face. By 1960, large cities are found throughout the country, not primarily in the east and middle west; and the newer cities of the south and west are decidedly more prosperous than the older eastern and midwestern cities.

A look at the central cities and the outlying areas or suburbs of today reveals startling contrasts. Suburbs are often new, clean, family oriented. Central cities are often run down, with areas of high unemployment, higher crime rates, and they are largely minority. Single-parent homes and singles and couples without children are common in the central city; in the suburbs the two-parent family is the norm. Suburban communities often have good schools, elaborate park systems, and modern, clean streets. Central cities are more likely to have less accomplished school systems, run down parks, and a declining infrastructure.

How did these changes come about? Three important factors led to the change in city and suburb; the effect of these changes continues to define differences within our urban areas today.

- *Technological changes* took place that radically altered how goods were produced and distributed. Technology also affected how homes were produced, and with the perfection of the internal combustion engine, the means of transportation changed.

- *Historical conditions* brought on by the Great Depression and World War II initially put a lid on the impact of these changes. Thus, when the economy grew in the 1950s, the effect of innovations and government policies influenced the nature of the city more rapidly than would have been the case had political and economic conditions been more stable.

- *Government policies* and the use of public resources also were a significant cause of the changes that occurred. Government spending, price supports, restrictions, and major forms of public investment strongly influenced the changes in city structure.

Technological Change

Nothing has changed American cities more than the development of the internal combustion engine. The production of the Model T Ford in the early years of the twentieth century provided the means for cheap, reliable automobiles. Assembly line production and the standardization of parts lowered the cost of the finished product considerably. The price of the Model T actually decreased from $780 in 1910 to $360 in 1915 (Halberstam 1986: 81). Cars and trucks gradually became stronger and more reliable. Innovations in finance, permitting people to buy cars in time payments, spread the feasibility of car purchases to the middle class by 1930. Some indication of the spread of the automobile can be gained from statistics on automobile ownership. Car ownership in the United States increased from 1 in 13 inhabitants in 1920 to one in five by 1930 (Jackson 1985: 163).

As cars became reliable and affordable, workers could live miles from their work and choose where they wanted to live. They were no longer bound by the locations of their employers or mass transit. Shops and sources of entertainment likewise could locate wherever a market could be found.

Cities responded to the increase in automobiles by investing heavily in street building and using tax revenue rather than user fees and tolls to pay for it. Thus, travel on new roads did not appreciably add to the costs of driving. According to Jackson, special interest groups of road builders, service station owners, and developers and merchants lobbied cities and states to improve street quality. The development of smooth asphalt and concrete roadways also contributed to the expansion of road building (1985: 166–7).

The discovery of oil in the southwest and the expansion of the refining process provided a cheap source of energy for cars and trucks (Halberstam 1986: 84). Americans consistently keep the price of refined gasoline comparatively low, making cars affordable to operate as well as own.

By the middle of the twentieth century, cars dominated American life. They were a major production and consumption item for Americans with a stable income. "Cars are how Americans move around between and within their urban aggregations and they are now one of the fundamental things that cities produce and trade" states Bartlett. "They are industrial base and transportation system combined. The automobile has driven Americans to restructure their space" (1988: 105).

To Halberstam the combination of cars and cheap energy transformed the American landscape.

> Suddenly there were roads everywhere, paid for, naturally enough by a gas tax. Towns that had been too small for the railroads were reached now by roads and farmers could get to once-unattainable markets. Country stores that sat on old rural crossroads and sold every conceivable kind of merchandise were soon replaced by specialized stores, for people could now drive off and shop where they wanted. Families that had necessarily been close and inwardly focused, in part because there was nowhere else to go at night, became somewhat weaker as family members got in their cars and took off to do whatever they wanted to do. The car stimulated the expansiveness of the American psyche and the rootlessness of the American people; a generation of Americans felt freer than ever to forsake the region and the habits of their parents and strike out on their own. (1986: 86)

Technology affected the transportation of goods through the development of stronger, more efficient trucks. Raw materials could be delivered and finished products moved independently of waterways and fixed rails. Industrialists then had new options for the location of factories. If the logic of the assembly process required a larger area, they could look for cheaper land on the fringe of the city. In fact, trucks could get in and out of a factory located on the city's fringe more efficiently than in the crowded city center if roads and highways connected their location with other parts of the city.

As telephones, the mail system, and radios improved, face-to-face communication between components of the economy became less important. The business person could now contact suppliers and financiers efficiently by phone. Money could be transferred electronically rather than requiring direct bank transactions. Conference calls could clearly connect different sectors of the economy, making the trip to the central city less necessary. With the advent of air travel and cross-country highways, the east and the midwest lost some of the natural advantages for industrial location. If your business did not depend on heavy raw products, if it were more knowledge based, for instance, one could consider climate, physical features of the landscape, and the wishes of employees when deciding where to locate. Low cost, efficient air conditioning for homes, industries, and offices was developed by the middle of the twentieth century, making living and working in the south and southwest more attractive.

All of these changes moved the city in similar directions. The city could expand into the countryside. It could cover a much larger territory, and it was no longer bounded by physical conditions. If people wanted bigger houses and more open space, the city was now able to provide it for them. If industries could operate more efficiently in outlining parts of the city, they could now leave the crowded inner city. Other regions of the country could now compete with eastern and midwestern cities for the location of industries. Newer cities, in fact, had an advantage over some of the older cities because they were not burdened with a congested downtown, and they could more easily plan for the newer industrial economy. Together all of these trends encouraged the decline of the older central cities as places of work and living. Therefore, technological changes and the resulting impact of the economics of businesses encouraged growth in the suburbs at the expense of the older central cities of the east and midwest.

Historical Factors

The dispersed city of 1960 could have gradually emerged during the middle of the twentieth century as technological innovations took hold. Wise city officials, seeing that the logic of production and housing had changed, might have been able to alter city policies to incorporate the new city into their plans and remake the old central city to conform with the forces that now influenced city structure. However, historical events altered the pace at which most of these changes influenced the structure of the city. First, the Great Depression of 1929, and then the war effort during World War II, put a halt to the implementation of the changes.

In the prosperity of the 1920s, one can see the beginning of changes in city life that would lead to the present city form. As wealth increased, car sales expanded and wealthier residents established homes in suburban communities. The new suburbs were primarily for upper-class residents; while the prices of cars and housing kept the middle and working classes in the central cities. Cities did, however, invest significantly in road building and mass transit during the 1920s to accommodate location changes (Abbott 1987: 44). Traffic engineers were beginning plans for higher-speed highways that would connect city dwellers to locations further from the central city. One can see in these efforts, the beginnings of the mid-twentieth century urban form. These early efforts at urban planning provided means to encourage the middle class to move to the suburbs as public transportation improved and the wealth of the middle class increased.

The Depression, however, put most of these activities on hold. When the economy went into a steep decline, residents could no longer pay their mortgages or car payments. Bank failures produced defaults on loans that were building the infrastructure for new subdivisions. Cities' resources declined, so public improvements were halted. Some cities, burdened with debts and a significantly declined tax base, declared bankruptcy. As Abbott notes, "The physical deterioration of urban America matched the misery of millions of its residents. Between 1929 and 1933, the physical plant of the United States wore out faster than it could be replaced. Industrialists saw no reason to replace old machinery that was standing idle. Construction of new housing fell by 95 percent. Home owners put off repairs in hope of making their monthly payments" (1987: 48: see also Jackson 1985: 193).

During the Roosevelt years, significant efforts by the federal government repaired and replaced some of the declining infrastructure. As the economy began to rebound during the 1930s, much of the industrial capacity was rebuilt. World War II then altered the economy and production of public services in a different way. The economy was converted to war production, and consequently, consumer goods were severely limited. Automobile factories produced trucks and airplanes rather than private cars. Trucks were built for the military rather than industries or private haulers. Construction equipment was used to build military bases rather than new subdivisions and roads. Thus, the natural growth of cities was controlled by the needs of the war.

The war effort accelerated the changes in technology that had encouraged the new city form. The nation produced planes capable of hauling large amounts of cargo. The need for communication between troops led to advances in telephone and radio. Computers began as tools to handle the coordination of war related information. However, all of these new efforts were used primarily for the war effort, and much of it was focused in the so called Sun Belt areas of the west and south. The war effort controlled the application of technological change domestically, but also expanded the range of new technologies that were eventually transferred to the peacetime economy.

The means to significant change in society matured in the war years, so when the war was over, and the economy produced domestic goods again, all of these changes could be applied to the domestic economy. New production techniques were now available and the economy was ready to expand but the war and the depression had put a lid on these changes. When these constraints were gone, the city could spread to the suburbs and the Sun Belt. Cars were produced at prices the average family could afford. The skills that created Army bases rapidly could be used to build suburban homes. Trucks that hauled military equipment and troops could now be used to carry consumer goods to and from new factories. The change in urban life was much too rapid for city leaders and planners to comprehend, so changes occurred without careful planning.

THE MAKING OF INSTANT SUBURBIA:
BILL LEVITT AND LEVITTOWN

Nowhere were the effects of the changes in technology more dramatic than in the production of new homes. Large tracts of houses in outlying parts of the city literally sprang up over night; entire new communities for the middle class replaced open lands in a matter of months. Most of these were placed some distance from the central city and assumed that the owners had cars.

During the war, Bill Levitt served in the Navy building airfields in the Pacific as rapidly as was humanly possible while MacArthur led his rapid "island hopping campaign." His father

Levittown, New York, 1948.

AP/Wide World Photos

was a building contractor and he planned to work in his father's business when the war was over. At night, he brainstormed with his fellow officers, many of whom had also worked in the building industry. When he returned home, he pioneered the development of the suburban subdivision that became the backbone of the changing city. New homes were much in demand and the government was willing to aid the returning servicemen in acquiring a new home. The conditions were ripe for entrepreneurs who could apply new techniques to the building of houses.

Below, David Halberstam, in his stimulating book *The Fifties,* describes Levitt's successful efforts to create the new American suburb.

No industry suffered more than housing during the Depression and World War Two; housing starts fell from 1 million a year to fewer than 100,000. But during the same period the marriage rate, and surprisingly the birth rate increased sharply, the latter reaching 22 per 1,000 in 1943—the highest it had been in two decades. As everyone returned from the war, the housing situation was not merely tight—it was a crisis. Some 50,000 people were reportedly living in Army Quonset huts. In Chicago it was so bad that 250 used trolley cars were sold for use as homes. Estimates placed the number of new houses needed immediately at over 5 million. A federal housing bill was rushed through that contained very little in the way of controls, and a great deal in the way of federal insurance to protect builders by means of federal mortgage guarantees. The real estate boys read the bill, looked at one another in happy amazement, and the dry rasping noise they made rubbing their hands together could be heard as far away as Tawi Tawi, a writer named John Keats noted of the moment. The stored up energy of two decades was unleashed. In 1944 there had been only 114,000 new single houses started; by 1946 that

(continued)

(continued)

figure jumped to 937,000; to 1,118, 000 in 1948 and 1.7 million in 1950.

Bill Levitt was sure he was riding the wave of the future. 'We believe that the market for custom housing, like that for custom tailoring no longer exists. People who want to buy that kind of thing will be able to get it, but the real market is for the ordinary mass-produced suit of clothes. And you can build thirty thousand dollar houses by the six thousands,' he said even as he started his first development. In 1946 the Levitts pushed ahead with Bill Levitt's dream of creating his own community in Hempstead, by adding more and more acreage to what they already owned. There, some twenty miles from Manhattan, they set out to create the largest housing project in American history.

Levitttown was an astonishing success from the very beginning. The first Levittown house could not have been simpler. It had four and one half rooms and was designed with a young family in mind. The lots were 60 by 100 feet and Bill Levitt was proud of the fact that the house took up only 12 percent of the lot. The living room was 12 by 16 feet. There were two bedrooms and one bathroom. In his book *Crabgrass Frontier* Kenneth Jackson noted that in their simplicity, durability and value they were not unlike the Model T. The basic Levitt Cape sold for $7,990. In the beginning the Levitts threw in a free television and a Bendix washing machine as incentives.

SOURCE: From David Halberstam, *The Fifties* (New York: Villard Books, 1993), 134–37; and Kenneth T. Jackson, Crabgrass Frontier: The Suburbanization of the United States (New York: Oxford University, Press,1985)

The Changing Life of the African American

Occurring at the same point in time was another momentous change. In 1940, 77 percent of the African American population lived in the south; 49 percent in rural areas (Lemann 1991: 6). Most lived as sharecroppers in extremely seg- regated conditions, in severe poverty, and picked crops by hand. As Lemann describes:

Picking was hard work. The cotton balls were at waist high, so you had to work either stooped over or crawling on your knees. Every soft puff of cotton was attached to a thorny stem and the thorns pierced your hands as you picked—unless your entire hand was a callus, as most full time pickers' were. You put the cotton you picked into a long sack that was on a strap around your shoulder; the sack could hold seventy-five pounds so for much of the day you were dragging a considerable weight as you moved down the rows. The picking day was long, sunup to sundown with a half-hour off for lunch. There were no bathrooms. (1991: 8)

The system of legal segregation and intimidation enforced the sharecrop- per system. "The political institution that paralleled share-cropping was segre- gation; blacks in the South were denied social equality from Emancipation onward, and beginning in the 1890s they were denied the ordinary legal rights of American citizens as well. Segregation strengthened the grip of the sharecropper system by ensuring that most blacks would have no arena of opportunity in life except for the cotton fields" (Lemann 1991: 8).

For those in much of the south, this system of near slavery ended with the invention of the mechanical cotton picker in the 1940s. One picker could do the work of 50 people. Soon, most cotton pickers were replaced and the sharecropping system became obsolete. African Americans in the cotton fields faced an even bleaker life than they had experienced as sharecroppers. According to Lemann "(T)he advent of the cotton picker made the maintenance of slavery no longer a matter of necessity for the economic establishment of the South, and thus it helped set the stage for the great drama of segregation's end" (1991: 6).

The earlier migration of African Americans to the northern cities and the prosperity, real or perceived, of many there, served as a catalyst for another large movement in the mid-twentieth century. Through letters back home, occasional visits and the work of African American journalists, the north was viewed as the land of prosperity for the poor southern residents. African Americans who fought in World War II saw the conditions of their colleagues in the North and returned less willing to accept the near slavery conditions of the deep South.

From 1940 to 1970, over five million African Americans left the rural south; most going to northern cities. The African American population in several northern cities increased dramatically. In Detroit, the African American population increased from 150,000 in 1940, to nearly half a million by 1960. Chicago's African American population increased by 77 percent in the 1940s and another 65 percent from 1950 to 1960. Nearly one million African Americans lived in Chicago in 1960, compared with 278,000 in 1940. The mechanical cotton picker was now in use everywhere in the south, and the sharecropper system had been phased out on most plantations. In demography, there is an important distinction between migrations driven by *push* and *pull* factors; the latter go more smoothly. The attractions of Chicago still constituted a pull northward for any southern blacks, but now that plantation life had simply ceased to be an option back home, Chicago began to attract people who had been pushed there, too. "In black Chicago in the fifties, the slackening off of demand for unskilled labor had become obvious; blues songs of the era, like J. B. Lenoir's 'Eisenhower Blues' and John Brim's 'Tough Times' attest to the change. But the number of migrants kept rising—where else was there for the displaced sharecropper to go?" (Lemann 1991: 70)

Figure 2.2 compares the percentage of African Americans in the five largest cities for four time periods: 1940, 1950, 1960, and 1970. In each city the percentage significantly increased in each decade. The African American percentage exceeded 20 percent in all cities by 1970. In 1940, only Philadelphia contained an African American population greater than 5 percent. Detroit experienced the largest gain; from 8 percent in 1940 to 43 percent by 1970. Two trends explain these findings; African Americans moved to the central cities from the rural south while many Whites moved to the suburbs.

Jobs, of course, were also moving to outlining areas of the city and the new suburbs. Very few African Americans moved to the suburbs until the 1970s. Why not? Our third major change, government policies, helps us understand why African Americans remained in the central city.

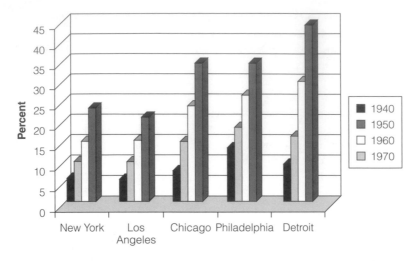

FIGURE 2.2 Percentage of African Americans in the Five Largest Central Cities.

U.S. Government Census of Population.

Government Policies

Governments spend, borrow, and tax. As they do, some people, regions, and locations will benefit and others will be hurt. Government actions affect the decisions of people and firms. They can promote the growth of some cities at the expense of others, or some kinds of industry or trade rather than another. Governmental actions are never neutral.

Actions of the federal government influenced the growth and development of cities at all times. The location of walking cities was strongly influenced by the placement of canals and railroads. The cities of the industrial era relied partially on federal government efforts to encourage commerce and trade, but these policies were, at best, quite limited.

During the suburban era, however, federal government policies were major contributors to the changes in city life. Federal efforts shaped the entry to the new middle-class suburbs, and helped restrict African Americans to the central city. *During this time, federal policies generally favored the suburbs rather than the central city and contributed to a general economic decline in the central city.* Some government policies discriminated against African Americans and acted to restrict their movement to the suburbs. Others made it easier for White, middle-class residents and business to move to the suburbs.

In this section, we will look at two policy areas where the influence of government was most pronounced—housing policies and transportation. Government policies had much to do with the kinds of housing that were encouraged, their cost, and the kind of people who were able to secure new housing. Government also became a major producer of highways during this time period, and the selection of roadways influenced the growth of the city.

Housing

Prior to the end of World War II, home ownership was limited to people of means. Mortgage insurers required large down payments, normally 40 percent, and often would extend loans of no longer than 10 or 15 years. However, owning a home has always been important to Americans. Jefferson thought the country could remain strong and democratic only if it remained a nation of farmers and small landowners. Scarlet O'Hara's father, in the movie *Gone With The Wind,* felt that "when you have land, you have everything." Many, though, had lost their homes in the depression, and with the victory in World War II, politicians wanted to respond to the needs of returning servicemen and provide the means for greater home ownership.

From 1934 through 1960, Congress approved several different housing programs. Loans for new housing by individuals was encouraged through the Federal Housing Administration (FHA) and the Veterans Administration (VA) loan programs. Those who qualified for loans paid a very low interest rate and could accrue the debt for as long as 30 years because the government insured the risk. Thus, a private lender could extend loans knowing that the government would pay much of the value of the loan in the event that the borrower had to default.

The building boom of the 1950s, dramatized in the discussion of Levittown, can be attributed to the success of these programs. More than 15 million homes were built in the 1950s, which was twice as many as produced from 1940 to 1949, and six times those built from 1930 to 1939. Most were financed by FHA and VA, and most, if not all, were purchased by members of the middle and lower-middle classes (Checkoway 1986: 121). Home ownership increased from 43.6 percent in 1940, to 62.9 percent in 1970 (Judd and Swanstrom 1998: 196). New construction techniques and government support made it cheaper to buy than rent in many cases (Judd and Swanstrom 1985: 205)

The apparent success of the FHA and VA programs, however, masks two important underlying problems. Racial and suburban biases dominated the implementation of these programs throughout the country. Until the courts intervened in the 1960s, the FHA pursued a policy of racial segregation in the awarding of loans (Citizens Commission on Civil Rights 1983, in Bratt, Hartman and Meyerson 1986: 299). The FHA Underwriting Manual, which was the guide for loan officials, stated that "If a neighborhood is to retain stability, it is necessary that properties shall continue to be occupied by the same social and racial classes. A change in social or racial occupancy generally contributes to instability and a decline in values" (Ibid). Though these policies were changed in the 1960s, they remained in effect during the time of greatest suburban expansion and they set a pattern of housing choice that continues today in many cities. Biases and prejudices of realtors and buyers were encouraged by overt government policies. Therefore, few new loans were given to African Americans. *Only 2 percent of the housing built in the 1950s under FHA mortgages went to minorities.* FHA employees encouraged developers to draw up restrictive covenants that prohibited the sale of homes to minorities in their new subdivisions (Ibid, 299). Sugrue notes that in Detroit the Federal Home Loan Bank

Board officials, in collaboration with local real estate brokers and lenders, sanctioned a series of maps that ranked all areas of the city based on the age of the structures, their condition, the infrastructure of the neighborhoods, and the level of racial and ethnic homogeneity. Every Detroit neighborhood with an African American population was ranked in the lowest category. Hence, few African Americans received loans while homes of Whites of similar economic status a few blocks away were underwritten (1996: 46).

FHA and VA policies also influenced the movement of residents to the suburbs. FHA-insured loan activities went to new residential developments on the edges of metropolitan areas, to the neglect of poor and minority neighborhoods (Checkoway 1986: 127). The FHA favored single-family construction and discouraged multifamily units. They rarely loaned funds to repair existing structures, which meant that it was easier to purchase a new home than repair an old one. Neighborhood evaluations were a factor in the securing of loans, biasing the process in favor of new neighborhoods rather than existing ones.

The federal government then encouraged home ownership for new homes in the suburbs purchased by White families. Minorities were restricted from most suburban homes and few mortgages were extended to old homes or apartment complexes in the central city. "The lasting damage done by the national government was that it put its seal of approval on ethnic and racial discrimination and developed policies which had the result of the practical abandonment of large sections of older, industrialized cities" (Jackson 1985: 217).

Federal legislation also provided public housing meant to house those at the bottom of the housing market in large rental housing projects owned and supervised by the government. In practice, public housing was concentrated in the inner city and in spite of early attempts to make it widely available, it became housing for the working poor (Bratt et al. 1986: 336–7).

Discrimination in tenant selection was wide spread. The case study, Public Housing in Post World War II Detroit, points out that public housing in the late 1940s was no more hospitable to African Americans than was the private market. Later, as the public housing units built in the 1940s and 1950s deteriorated, they became homes for the minority poor.

PUBLIC HOUSING IN POST WORLD WAR II DETROIT

In September 1945, veteran Charles Johnson returned to Detroit from service in the Pacific, hoping to make a life for himself and his family in the booming city. Johnson arrived at a particularly difficult time, especially for African Americans like himself. Tens of thousands of returning veterans put pressure on a housing market that could not even absorb the thousands of defense workers who had migrated to the city during the war. The small apartment buildings and houses in Detroit's black neighborhoods were bursting with tenants. Johnson found a temporary apartment on the West Side. He hoped that, like other veterans, he would be able to move into public housing. He spoke to another veteran, a white, who "had been given a list of places to investigate." Even if it was just one of the hundreds of Quonset huts that housed homeless veterans and their families, it would be better than a dreary, overcrowded, vermin-infested inner city apartment. On September 21, 1945, Johnson applied for public housing.

Johnson's hopes were quickly dashed. A Detroit Housing commission staff member informed him that "the Negro housing situation is extremely acute" and "we have more applications than dwelling units." He was put on a waiting list. But while waiting for his interview Johnson heard white veterans "receive assurances that they would be placed in housing developments in the very near future." He heard correctly. During World War II, Blacks flooded the city with applicants for public housing, but only 1,731 of 14,446 black applicants were placed.

Johnson was infuriated. He told the Housing Commission interviewer that he had not fought for his country to uphold racial discrimination. When she tried to explain the Commission's policy to him, he "was extremely angered and hardly appeared to be listening." Johnson left the office determined to get an answer. He moved up the chain of command. "Determined to make an issue of the matter," he headed straight for the office of the director of the Detroit Housing Commission, then to the mayor's office, and finally ended up meeting for an hour with George Schermer, the head of the Mayor's Interracial Committee. Schermer reported that "Johnson displayed very strong feelings." The veteran boldly stated that he "would refuse to accept placement in a segregated Negro project. He would insist on his right to be placed in any housing

development of his own choosing." Schermer was sympathetic to Johnson and suggested that he testify before the common Council about the situation. Johnson left frustrated; thoroughly convinced that the mayor, the Common Council, the Housing Commission and the Interracial Committee were unanimously committed to an anti-Negro policy. He followed up with a letter to the Detroit common Council. "We had won the War," he wrote "and are striving to win a complete peace. Each time Negroes are discriminated against, veterans or otherwise, a nail is driven in the coffin of peace."

Johnson's fate is unknown, but the situation for Blacks like him improved little in the post-war decade. From January 1947 through July 1952, 37,382 Black families and 56,758 White families applied for public housing. 41 percent of the white applicants and only 24 percent of the black applicants made the waiting list. Whites also moved off the waiting list more quickly than their black counterparts. The result was a striking discrepancy in the fortunes of black and white applicants: 9,908 whites but only 1,226 blacks obtained public housing in the city. Because of the city's discriminatory policy, most black demands for public housing went unmet through the mid 1950s. Blacks remained confined to a few inner-city projects, and despite tremendous efforts to alleviate the housing shortage by constructing subsidized low income developments on the city's periphery, virtually nothing was built.

SOURCE: From Thomas J. Sugrue, *The Origins of the Urban Crisis: Race and Inequality in Postwar Detroit.* 57–58. Copyright © 1996 by Princeton University Press.

Transportation

As truck and auto traffic increased, the quality of city roads and highways became an important concern in the post World War II years. Between 1945 and 1950, automobile registrations rose from 25 million to 40 million and they approached 60 million by 1955 (Chudacoff 1975: 239). Obviously, new highways were needed to efficiently handle this huge increase in cars. Determining how to properly design a system was difficult because several competing purposes were involved. Were highways needed to lessen traffic congestion in the central city, to enhance new businesses, or to protect the country from civil disasters? These competing concerns played a role in the extensive legislation that was passed beginning in the 1950s. The Interstate Highway system was initially meant to be a civil defense effort to move people and goods from one city to another and as a way of connecting diverse parts of the country. Little concern was voiced for the effect of road building on the structure of the city. However, urban interests were able to mandate that much of the funds would be spent in urban areas to relieve traffic congestion and encourage a more efficient economy.

The program was the largest of all federal programs at the time. Many argue that it also had the greatest impact on the shaping of urban society (Kantor 1986: 199). The interstate program and related transportation legislation in the 1950s had three important effects on urban society: 1) It encouraged suburban growth at the expense of the central city; 2) where urban freeways were built, poor neighborhoods were often torn apart with little concern for the livelihood of the residents; and 3) by failing to provide aid for mass transit, those systems deteriorated or were abandoned and left inner-city residents without the means to travel cheaply within the city or to the jobs that emerged in the suburbs.

The initial goal of the system was civil defense. To protect the country against enemy attack, it was hoped that people could be moved to other towns or to the countryside. Thus, early designs drew beltways around cities and connected one city to another. Land costs and problems of acquisition were minimized in the suburbs and the countryside. That led to loops around cities and connectors between urban areas being built first. New industries, wanting to efficiently transport goods from one city to another, also encouraged this pattern of construction.

Beltways and connecting links between cities encouraged the move to the suburbs at the expense of the central city. The new freeways meant that industries could move to the suburbs where they would be convenient for the residents (Tabb and Sowers 1984: 3). "By stimulating suburban growth" Kweit and Kweit note, "(T)hese highways did little to help cities and much to hurt them. Indeed the building of highways and the process of suburbanization became a vicious cycle with highways facilitating movement to suburbs and the growth of suburbs creating a need for highways" (1990: 268).

As the highway program moved to urban areas, however, many argue that the new roads were built with little concern for the quality of life of city residents. Neighborhoods were destroyed and few resources were allocated to relocate the residents. In many cities, poor neighborhoods were targeted for relocation while middle-class neighborhoods remained in tact. Often, freeways purposely avoided middle-class, White neighborhoods and disrupted homes of African Americans. According to Sugrue, "Detroit's highway planners were careful to ensure that construction of the new high-speed expressways would only minimally disrupt middle class residential areas, but they had little such concern for black neighborhoods, especially those closest to downtown. Instead they viewed inner-city highway construction in Detroit, as in other major American cities, North and South, as a 'handy device for razing slums' " (1996: 47). Throughout the 1950s little was done to assist those whose homes were razed by highway construction.

Finally, funding for mass transit was nearly non-existent until the 1970s. Many cities like New York, Los Angeles, and Chicago had developed efficient systems of mass transit, but without federal funding, these systems deteriorated and added further encouragement to the suburban exodus.

Together, all of these changes resulted in a very different kind of city in a rather short period of time. The White population spread to the burgeoning suburbs, replaced by the new urban African Americans. Several different Latino groups also migrated largely to the central cities during this time period. Urbanization along the Mexican border encouraged movement to the central cities of the southwest and west, Puerto Ricans moved to northern cities when economic conditions on the island declined, and significant numbers of Cubans moved to Florida following political unrest in their country. By 1970, a majority of the urban population was now living in suburban communities, and several central cities became predominantly minority. Figure 2.3 offers a graphic demonstration of this change in population from 1960 to 1970 in the five largest cities. The population is divided into central city and suburb. In all cities, the increase in population in the suburbs exceeds that of the central city. In three of the cities, Chicago, Philadelphia, and Detroit, the central cities actually lost population; in the case of Detroit, the population loss was over 10 percent. Only Los Angeles, a city with significant open areas within the central city, experienced population increase. Most of this increase occurred in the San Fernando Valley, an area with a suburban lifestyle and many new homes.

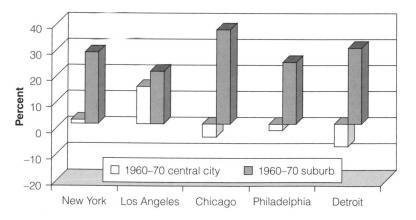

FIGURE 2.3 Percentage Change in Population from 1960–1970 in the Five Largest Cities.

U.S. Government Census of Population.

A CACOPHONY OF CHANGE:
THE AMERICAN CITY 1970–2000

American cities are in the midst of another array of changes. Cacophony, or jarring and discordant, may best describe the baffling period we are in. Cities are both wealthy and poor. Some are growing too much, some are declining. Regions of the country have different kinds of cities now and the world economy seems now to be a major player in shaping our cities.

Some of the changes in city life are extensions of trends in the previous period. Urban areas continue to grow at the expense of the rural hinterlands. By 1990, nearly 80 percent of the population was living in metropolitan areas, an increase from 63 percent in 1960. Suburbs continued to grow at a faster rate than did central cities, though one third of the metropolitan residents remain located in central cities. Central cities, however, continued to decline economically and remain the locations of poorer citizens. The minority percentage of the central city increased as new immigrants came and older residents moved to the suburbs.

Alongside these extensions of previous trends are several new conditions that together make the city of the twenty-first century a very different place. Six major changes will be briefly highlighted in this final look at the social and economic structure of cities.

1. Very pronounced regional changes have affected cities. The Sun Belt cities, those in the warm weather states, have grown while those in the east and midwest, the "Frost Belt," are declining.

2. Small cities and so-called edge cities, urban conglomerations in outlying parts of urban areas, have emerged as major sources of population and employment.

3. Immigration, particularly from Asia and Latin America, increased significantly since 1970 presenting new challenges to both central city and suburb.

4. Significant numbers of people have moved within our metropolitan areas. Some African Americans, Asians, and Latinos have moved to the suburbs as minority members have become part of the new professional class. Whites also moved from the central city in larger numbers than in earlier time periods.

5. Poverty, however, has become more heavily concentrated in central cities, and changes in the economic and social structures have added barriers to those who wish to escape poverty.

6. Cities today are a part of a world economy. Their economy is a part of global economic and social connections, rather than national trends. Those cities that are strongly connected to the world economy function differently than those who are not.

The "Frost Belt" and the Sun Belt

Since 1960, major increases in population and economic activity were concentrated in a band of newer cities stretching from North Carolina to southern California. Many different kinds of cities are included in this territory. What
they have in common is a warm climate and open land. While there are ex-
ceptions to this pattern, and problems defining which cities to include in the
Sun Belt (see Bernard and Rice 1983), the changes in population when one
compares cities above and below the 37th parallel are remarkable. Table 2.1
compares population in 1960 and 1990 for all cities that were within the top
10 in population in either year. The cities are divided into two categories; those
above the 37th parallel are referred to as Frost Belt cities, and those below it are
Sun Belt cities. All frostbelt cities lost population. Detroit, St Louis, and Cleveland lost more than 40 percent of their population in these years. All Sun Belt
cities have increased in population. Phoenix increased by over 120 percent and
Houston by 94 percent. All of these cities increased their population by at least
40 percent.

Why such different patterns of growth? Again, the explanations are economic, technological, and governmental. The American economy responded to
changes in the nature of production, transportation, and communications.
Cities became centers of information exchange, finance, and administration

Table 2.1 Frostbelt, Sunbelt Population Change, 1960–1990

	POPULATION CHANGE 1960–1990	PERCENT CHANGE
Frostbelt		
New York	569,393	−7
Chicago	−836,236	−23
Philadelphia	−416,935	−21
Detroit	−821,594	−44
Baltimore	−203,010	−2
Cleveland	−368,434	−42
Washington	−157,056	−21
St. Louis	−353,314	−47
TOTAL	**−3,726,999**	**28**
Sunbelt		
Los Angeles	1,003,942	4
Houston	692,453	74
San Diego	537,325	94
Dallas	327,146	48
Phoenix	544,233	124
San Antonio	347,885	59
TOTAL	**3,452,984**	**76**

rather than material production (Kasarda 1993: 82). Businesses and government could select their location based on preferences of employees and customers rather than the location of natural resources or physical facilities. As oil was discovered in the southwest and it replaced coal as a major source of energy, important resources were as plentiful in the Sun Belt. Given a choice of location, industries and government preferred the warm climates and open lands of the Sun Belt cities.

The development of low-cost air conditioning was an important catalyst in this process. Northerners could now move to warmer climates knowing that their personal climates could be controlled. Some have argued that Houston's rapid movement from a small southern town in 1950, to the fourth largest city in the country by 1980, was fueled largely by the discovery of oil and air conditioning.

Conterminously with these forces were a series of governmental actions that also encouraged growth of the Sun Belt and the decline of the Frost Belt. Federal defense spending during the Cold War became a major source of government spending, and a high proportion of it was spent in the Sun Belt. By 1975, for instance, the defense budget contributed only 3.8 percent of the personal income of the Frost Belt but 8.8 percent of the Sun Belt. Similar spending differentials were present in other aspects of government spending and in the tax code, which encouraged construction of new commercial and industrial structures rather than rehabilitation of old ones (Bernard and Rice 1983: 12). Others point out that Sun Belt cities more aggressively pursued new industries because they tended to be controlled by business interests. According to Mollenkopf "(M)ore than on any other dimension the southwestern metropolitan areas can be distinguished from those of the northeast by the small size of their governments, their private sector orientations, the lack of political conflict and by the relatively great social stratification which underlies their conservative political cultures" (1983: 42). Thus, Sun Belt cities could more readily meet the demands of new industries with less cost and fewer political conflicts.

The Rise of Small Cities

Changes in society also meant that the small city could compete with the metropolis for the location of industry and commerce. With advances in air transportation and new freeways, goods could get in and out of the small city quickly. Computers and advances in telephones and telecommunication improved the links between small and large cities. The advent of cable television and chain movie theaters brought many big city entertainments into the smaller town.

Therefore, from 1970 onward, smaller cities grew at the expense of the larger city and many small cities became metropolises. Figure 2.4 provides a vivid demonstration of the extent to which five cities emerged as major cities by 1990. These five cities were among the 50 largest cities in the nation in 1990 even though none were the top 50 in 1960. All five are located in the Sun Belt.

Smaller cities on the periphery of large cities have become prime locations for new growth. These *edge cities* (Garreau 1991) are located in suburban areas

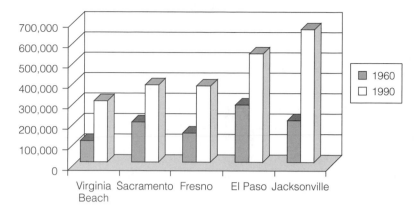

FIGURE 2.4 Smaller Cities: Population Change, 1960–1990.

U.S. Government Census of Population.

but contain commercial and business facilities similar to those in the central city. Headquarters of major firms and large high-tech industries are often found in these complexes. As these cities mature, they become competitors with the central city for the location of new housing and industry. Parts of Orange County, California, Clear Lake City near Houston, and portions of the Silicon Valley in Northern California, are examples of edge cities. In fact, the form of the modern metropolis can be viewed as a series of edge cities connected together by communication links. The downtown in this pattern becomes one of many central locations within the greater urban area. Greater Los Angeles can be viewed as an example of this new city structure. Downtown Los Angeles remains the most important of the urban centers, but the urban centers of Long Beach, Pasadena, Central Orange County, the Los Angeles Airport area, and the eastern San Fernando Valley all are viable central cities (Soja and Scott 1993: 13).

Immigration

Significant changes in immigration law in 1965 increased the number and home countries of immigrants coming to the United States. Quotas for particular countries were eliminated, and family unification and escape from political repression became the major determinants of the nation's willingness to accept new residents. Consequently, the number of immigrants increased from 2.5 million in 1960, to 5.8 million in 1990 (Ginsberg 1993: 36). The bulk of the new immigrants came from Mexico, Central America, and Asia.

New immigrants have profoundly reshaped the populations of our major cities. Figure 2.5 compares the percentage of residents who were foreign born in 1970 and 1990, for the five largest cities in 1990. Los Angeles has experienced the largest increase. Foreign-born residents total 38.4 percent of the population in 1990, compared with 14.6 in 1970. New York City and Houston have also experienced large increases in foreign-born residents. Generally,

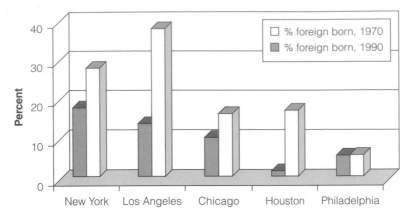

FIGURE 2.5 Percent Foreign Born in Five Largest Cities, 1970 and 1990.

U.S. Government Census of Population.

the immigrants have tended to come to the large cities; over half of the total foreign-born residents live in the five largest metropolitan areas (Waldinger and Bozorgmehr 1996: 13).

The 1990 minority percentage in the eight cities over 1 million in population ranged from 42.5 percent in San Diego to 79 percent in Detroit, a radical increase from previous decades. Figure 2.6 compares the components of the minority population in these cities. Important here are the differences in the population composition in these cities. African Americans are the most substantial component in Detroit, where they constitute over 70 percent of the population. They also make up a majority of the ethnic population in Chicago, New York, and Philadelphia. Latino's, however, are the largest ethnic group in Houston, San Diego, and Los Angeles. In short, the cities of the 1990s are more ethnically diverse and display different patterns of ethnic and racial composition.

The Dispersion of Minorities

Even with the concentration of minorities in central cities, a substantial number of African Americans, Latinos, and Asians moved to suburban communities and edge cities from 1970–1990. Increases in immigration and the movement of minority members within the metropolitan area have changed the complexion of suburban communities and edge cities. This is particularly true in the counties surrounding Los Angeles, where minority percentages increased markedly from 1980 to 1990. The outlying counties of Orange, Riverside, and San Bernardino experienced significant increases in the Asian and Latino populations from 1980–1990. The Latino population in all three counties was over 20 percent in 1990. The Asian population in Orange County increased from 4.5 percent to 10 percent in these years. Some of this change is attributed to movement of non-immigrant members of these groups, but foreign-born im-

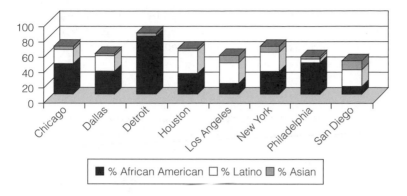

FIGURE 2.6 Percent Minority and Minority Composition in Cities Larger than One Million People, 1990.

U.S. Government Census of Population.

migrants are an important segment of the new suburban minority population. Thus, suburbs and edge cities today are no longer dominated by White Americans. Several, such as Santa Ana and Monterey Park, California, have become "majority-minority" cities.

Critics differ about the meaning of the outward movement of the minority population. Many of the suburbanized minorities live in racially isolated suburbs that are often older, declining areas not much different from the neighborhoods of the inner city (Clay 1979). Santa Ana, currently over 65 percent Latino, and East St. Louis, which is 96 percent African American, contain neighborhoods that are as highly minority concentrated neighborhoods as any in Los Angeles or St. Louis.

Yet, most agree that an emerging minority middle class has become integrated into suburban middle-class life and expanded significantly in the 1980s and 1990s. In a study of Chicago in the 1980s, Orfield located significant neighborhoods that were stably integrated. He estimates that one tenth of the white population in 1980 lived where there had been a significant African American or Hispanic population for more than a decade (1985: 185). Wilson points out that the African American migration to the suburbs in the 1970s was similar to that of Whites in that it was more common among the better educated and younger residents (1997: 38).

Ironically, the movement of successful minorities to the suburbs may contribute to the social problems of the inner city. As educated, upwardly mobile members leave, those who remain lack contact with those who have improved their position in society. William Julius Wilson's analysis of areas of high levels of poverty in Chicago in the 1970s concludes that the movement of the more educated and successful members of the African American community has actually contributed to the difficulties of those who remain. ". . . social isolation deprives the inner-city residents not only of conventional role models, whose strong presence once buffered the effects of neighborhood joblessness, but also social resources (including social contacts) provided by mainstream social networks that facilitate social and economic advancement in a modern industrial society. This form of social isolation also contributed to the formation and crystallization of ghetto related cultural traits and behaviors" (1996: 66).

Concentrated Poverty

Poverty in large cities has become increasingly concentrated in clearly defined neighborhoods. Wilson's detailed study of Chicago and Kasarda's examining national trends, reach similar conclusions. The number of areas with high levels of concentrated poverty increased significantly since 1970. As jobs left the inner city and as the economy required fewer unskilled and more knowledge-based jobs, residents of the inner cities became increasingly unemployed. Wilson refers to these high poverty areas as the new urban poverty. He describes them as, "(N)eighborhoods in which a substantial majority of individuals are either unemployed or have dropped out of the labor force altogether" (1996: 19). Wilson also identifies 12 Chicago-area communities where only one adult age 16 or over held a job in a typical week of the year (Ibid).

Kasarda argues that structural changes in employment, the decline of manufacturing, and the increase in service industries and knowledge-based employment have created the areas of high poverty. He concludes that concentrated poverty has affected some cities, like Chicago and Detroit, more severely than cities like Los Angeles, which was less dependent on heavy industry (1993: 109).

Increasing pockets of high levels of poverty without the presence of jobs have encouraged a deteriorating social climate in the inner cities. Wilson states the problem clearly, "The consequences of high neighborhood joblessness are more devastating than those of high neighborhood poverty. A neighborhood in which people are poor but employed is different from a neighborhood in which people are poor and jobless. Many of today's problems in the inner city ghetto neighborhoods—crime, family dissolution, welfare, low levels of social organization and so on—are fundamentally a consequence of the disappearance of work" (1996, xiii). Poverty appears to remain even when the economy improves because new jobs do not develop in inner-city areas. As a result, the presence of high levels of poverty may have become a permanent feature of the inner city.

The Globalization of Cities

If one accepts the logic of the post-World War II economy of cities, one might predict the end of the concentrated central city. If computers and high-speed telephones can connect people throughout the globe and make transactions without face-to-face contact, why does one need a central city? Why shouldn't every firm locate closest to open space where commuting costs are lower and the negative traits of cities are less? Shouldn't all cities be edge cities with the old central city simply one among several nodes?

The downtowns of many American cities reflect this assumption. Central cities in St. Louis, Detroit, and Philadelphia have lost population and contain many blocks of vacant land. Major businesses tend to locate on the periphery of these cities. The outlying portions of these and many cities are more prosperous than the central city.

Yet, a close look at some of our major cities reveals that the central city has become more concentrated, filled with newer buildings, and the center of more concerted activity than ever before. Downtown Los Angeles, Dallas, and New York City, for example, have added significant new commercial and residential buildings in recent years. They appear to be centers of major economic activity and supporting commercial and entertainment centers are prospering. Miami has become a major managerial and administrative center over the last few years. Large firms have expanded their Miami offices and located them in the city center (Sassen 1994: 80). The central city has become an important center for trade with Latin America and the Caribbean.

Why are some cities defying the logic of the new economy and creating dense, vibrant central cities? The answer is found in the emergence of an international urban economy. The cities with new downtowns and increased central city investment have become what Sassen terms "global cities." As the economy has become increasingly international, multinational corporations and international financial institutions have taken on added importance. Multinational corporations produce and sell products throughout the world. They rely on financial transactions that coordinate money flows in different currencies and with investments in various countries. The organization of this financial system is very complicated and requires the coordination of numerous institutions in different countries.

Organizations of such complexity require that complex decisions be made in a short time frame. Securities markets in various countries must be coordinated, laws and customs of different countries need to be compared, and money in different systems must be accounted for. Sassen argues that face-to-face interactions of many different kinds of industries and services are needed to efficiently coordinate such a system. In her words, "The accounting firm can service its clients at a distance, but the nature of its service depends on proximity to specialists, lawyers and programmers. Moreover, concentration arises out of the needs and expectations of the people likely to be employed in these high-skill jobs and the attraction of the amenities and life-styles that large urban centers can offer" (1994: 66).

Central cities, then, expand as the city becomes enmeshed in the international economy. Major multinational firms will locate there because they can interact with supporting organizations that assist their ability to interact with the international market. Therefore, one finds law and accounting firms, translators, international banks, and security traders located in the city center because all may need to interact with one another in short periods of time to complete international transactions. Supporting restaurants and entertainment activities thrive in this environment since many people with high salaries are working long hours in the central city. Much money changes hands in this process, which leads to an enhanced economy.

Large cities are not the only ones able to participate in the global economy. The case of Miami is an example. Sassen argues that Miami was well positioned to take advantage of the emerging markets in Latin America. She points out that the growth of the Cuban enclave supported the internationalization of the city by creating a pool of bilingual managers and entrepreneurs skilled in international business. This resource gave the city an edge in the competition for Latin trade (1994: 82). Other cities with significant upwardly mobile immigrant populations can therefore become potential global cities. The key may be in developing a critical mass of support facilities and sufficient office space to accommodate international corporations and support facilities.

What happens to cities that are not a part of the global economy? According to Sassen, they are less likely to develop a strong city center and less likely to prosper. Firms with a regional or local market are more likely to locate on the city's periphery.

Sassen notes that there have been sharp increases in socioeconomic and spatial inequities within major cities of the developed world (1993: 99). Increases in poverty throughout the developed world, she argues, is also a consequence of the global economy. Unskilled and semi-skilled labor now competes with labor costs internationally. Since American labor is comparatively more expensive than labor in many other countries, wages for these positions will decline. She concludes that "(T)he overall result is a tendency toward increased economic polarization" (1993: 117). Those who are a part of the skilled end of the global economy expand their wealth because they become central players in larger markets. Those on the periphery must compete with similar services in other nations, which means their wages are likely to decrease. One should expect, therefore, rich cities and poor cities and increasing differences of wealth within the city.

The Clinton Years: Did Economic Prosperity Improve the City?

The Clinton years are described as a time of significant economic growth and prosperity. Most indicators of economic well-being throughout the nation showed significant improvement; unemployment declined significantly, job growth increased, many left their welfare roles, and significant decreases in crime were recorded. How has this prosperity affected cities and suburbs? Generally conditions in both have improved, but in many ways the differences between city, suburb, Frost Belt and Sun Belt also increased.

Much of the job growth in the 1990s occurred in high-tech industries, and those grew 30 percent faster in the suburbs than in the central cities. The five largest cities were affected differently by changes in job growth in the 1990s. New York City experienced an increase of 4.6 percent, while its suburbs increased but one percent. Los Angeles City, on the other hand, actually lost 5.8 percent of its jobs, while the Los Angeles suburbs gained 6.9 percent. The greatest difference occurred in Philadelphia, where the central city gained a scant .5 percent while the suburbs gained 11 percent. Unemployment generally declined in cities and suburbs, but large differences between city and suburb remained (U.S. Department of Housing and Urban Development 2000: 6–28). In conclusion, a prosperous economy improves economic conditions in city and suburb, but differences between the two remain unchanged.

SUMMARY

American cities changed significantly in the 1950s:

- Suburban communities were created and became the popular destination for the White middle class.
- Technological changes, limited by the Depression and the war effort, encouraged the building of new homes, and the mass production of inexpensive automobiles made outlining areas feasible locations for new residents.
- Government policy encouraged this movement through new highways and loan supports for housing The changes happened quickly without a great deal of planning or direction.

At the same time, the decline of the southern economy and the positive view of life in the northern cities encouraged southern African Americans to move north. Poor Latinos from Mexico, Latin America, Puerto Rico, and Cuba also moved to the large cities. They migrated to the downtowns at the same time that changes in industrial production and government policies encouraged firms to locate in the suburbs. Discrimination and various government policies made it difficult for African Americans to move from the central city. By the 1960s, these changes encouraged significant differences in wealth and social opportunities.

The years from 1970 to the present saw these trends in city life continue as the city spread further into the countryside and central-city neighborhoods declined further. Other basic changes encouraged a very different kind of city:

- Changes in the industrial structure and the interests of industrialists and residents resulted in significantly different cities in the Frost Belt and the Sun Belt. Sun Belt cities generally were more prosperous, less crowded, and became the location of choice for newer, high-tech industries. Government policies, particularly defense spending, encouraged the growth of Sun Belt cities.
- Smaller cities throughout the country also increased in population and prominence.
- New immigrant groups migrated to the United States in large numbers and often settled in the city center.

- Substantial numbers of the minority population were able to move to the suburbs as government efforts to end discrimination limited the influence of housing discrimination.

- Those remaining in the central city and the new minority groups found employment possibilities and the social environment bleaker than in the earlier period. Concentrated pockets of poverty increased in central cities.

- Central cities that became a part of an international economy expanded and prospered. Globalization added wealth to many cities but also encouraged differences in wages and life styles. Both high and low salaries expanded with the advent of globalization.

In the industrial city, the welfare of all residents depended on a vital inner city where commerce, industry, and housing were closely interconnected. When wealth, jobs, and better housing developed outside the central city after the 1960s, the inner city lost much of its economic and social importance. As the poor and minority group members concentrated in the inner city, their problems increased. Because outlying areas now were economically independent of the inner city, suburbanites had little concern for the problems of the inner core. As urban areas matured, the economic health of the central city had little effect on the suburbs. Often, legally divided into separate cities, the residents of the suburbs had no legal obligation to deal with the problems of the inner city. Thus, the social and economic changes of the twentieth century changed the city from one where the health of all residents depended on the welfare of the city as a whole, to one where edge cities and suburbs could pursue their own goals, oblivious to the problems of the inner core.

REFERENCES

Abbott, Carl. *Urban America in the Modern Age: 1920 to Present.* Arlington Heights, Ill: Harlan Davidson, Inc., 1987.

Bartlett, Randall. 1988. *The Crisis of American Cities.* New York: M.E. Sharpe, Inc.

Bernard, Richard M., and Bradley Rice. 1983. Sunbelt Cities: *Politics ad Growth Since World War II.* Austin: University of Texas Press.

Bratt, Rachel G., Chester Hartman and Ann Meyerson. 1986. *Critical perspectives on Housing.* Philadelphia: Temple University Press.

Checkoway, Barry. 1986. "Large Builders, Federal Housing Programs, and Postwar Suburbanization" in Bratt, Rachel G., Chester Hartman and Ann Meyerson

Critical Perspectives on Housing. Philadelphia: Temple University Press.

Chudacoff, Howard P. 1975. *The Evolution of American Urban Society.* Englewood Cliffs, NJ: Prentice Hall, Inc.

Clay, Phillip L. 1979. "The process of Black Suburbanization." *Urban Affairs Quarterly* 14:4 (June) Sage Publications, Inc.

Donald, David Herbert. 1995. *Lincoln.* New York: Harper Touchstone.

Dreiser, Theodore. 1945. *The Titan.* Cleveland: The World Publishing Company.

Garreau, Joel. 1991. *Edge City: Life on the New Frontier.* New York: Doubleday.

Glaab, Charles N., and A. Theodore Brown. 1967. *A History of Urban*

America. New York: MacMillan and Company.

Halberstam, David. 1993. *The Fifties.* New York: Villard Books.

Halberstam, David. 1986. *The Reckoning.* New York: William Morrow and Company.

Howe, Irving. 1976. *World of Our Fathers: The Journey of the East European Jews to America and the Life they Found and Made.* New York: Harcourt Brace Jovanovich.

Jackson, Kenneth T. 1985. *Crabgrass Frontier: The Suburbanization of the United States.* New York: Oxford University Press.

Judd, Dennis R., and Todd Swanstron. 1998. *City Politics: Private Power and Public Policy.* New York: Longman.

Kasarda, John D. 1993. "Cities as Places Where People Live and Work: Urban Change and Neighborhood Distress," in Henry G. Cisneros, ed. *Interwoven Destinies: Cities and Nation.* New York: Norton.

Kweit, Robert W., and Mary Grisez Kweit. 1990. *People and Politics in Urban America.* Pacific Grove, CA: Brooks/Cole Publishing Company.

Lemann, Nicholas. 1991. *The Promised Land: The Great Black Migration and How It Changed America.* New York: Vintage Books.

Orfield, Gary. 1985. "Ghettoization and Its Alternatives" in Paul E. Peterson ed. *The New Urban Reality.*

Washington: The Brookings Institution..

Rybizynski, Witold. 1995. *City Life: Urban Expectations in a New World.* New York: Scribner.

Sassen, Saskia. 1994. *Cities in a World Economy.* Thousand Oaks, CA. Pine Forge Press.

Soja, Edward W., and Allen J. Scott. 1993. "Introduction to Los Angeles City and Region in Scott and Soja, eds. *The City: Los Angeles and Urban Theory at the End of the Twentieth Century.* Berkeley: University of California Press.

Spear, Alan H. 1967. *Black Chicago: The Making of a Negro Ghetto.* Chicago: University of Chicago Press.

Sugrue, Thomas J. 1996. *The Origins of the Urban Crisis: Race and Inequality in Postwar Detroit.* Princeton, NJ: Princeton University Press.

Tabb, William K., and Larry Sowers, eds. 1984. *Marxism and the Metropolis: New Perspectives in Urban Political Economy.* New York: Oxford University Press.

Wade, Richard C. 1971. *Cities in American Life.* New York: Houghton Mifflin.

Waldinger, Roger, and Mehdi Bozorgmehr, eds. 1996. *Ethnic Los Angeles.* New York: Russell Sage Foundation.

Wilson, William Julius. 1997. *When Work Disappears: The World of the New Urban Poor.* New York: Alfred A. Knopf.

Chapter Three

Conflicting Theories
of American
Urban Government

Political direction is needed to overcome the problems associated with the paradox of urban governance. So many governments, yet common problems; can the leaders of our local governments respond to the common problems of urban areas? Some of the problems of governance are related to how we choose to organize city governments. This chapter is concerned with how representatives are elected, the distribution of authority between elected and appointed officials, and the influence of career administrators and politicians. We call these matters *structures of government*. When citizens address these concerns they are dealing with very basic political questions not unlike the kinds of decisions that were made when the United States was founded. When city officials and citizens decide whether to give more or less influence to those elected in small districts or those elected citywide, they are dealing with questions similar to those that concerned those who founded the nation.

Americans organize urban governments in many different ways. All levels of government are involved. Some problems are more directly the concern of the federal or state government; others are the province of local governments. Some cities are organized around strong, elected mayors who work as the chief executive, while others elect city councils that share executive power with elected mayors. In some cities, the people elect part-time city councils and delegate many of the day to day tasks of running government to an appointed official. Chicago has a city council of more than 50 members; Anaheim voters elect five.

Community and neighborhood groups play an important role in Portland and San Antonio; other cities don't have such councils. State and federal laws and court decisions restrict the power of cities in many areas, but have less influence in others.

Why this confusing array of government types? Why do we rely on various levels of government to run our cities? The reasons are imbedded in our history. Since the founding of the country in 1776, conflicting principles of government have defined our urban areas. James Madison, one of the principal authors of the Constitution, argued for a system of checks and balances with emphasis on national institutions. Thomas Jefferson saw governmental strength in strong local governments with citizen participation. From these two giants of American government came conflicting principles about how best to run a government.

A third historical influence is traced to the era of industrialization. The *urban machine,* or boss system, was common in many of our cities in the first part of the twentieth century. It centralized power in the hands of a single person or a closed group of influentials who supplied city services in return for support of dominant interest groups. Many accused the system of corruption and worked to eliminate it. Our present day governments are often designed to rid the city of the supposed evils of the urban machine. Thus, like the Madisonian and Jeffersonian systems, present day government can be understood as a response to the characteristics of the urban machine.

This chapter examines these three influences on the structure of government in American cities. This includes how people are elected and appointed and the powers given to various parties. It also involves how we determine which level of government will be responsible for a particular service. Some responsibilities are given primarily to those at the local level. The police are a good example of this. Even though there are state and federal police forces, local government is the primary provider of police services. Other services are more a State or federal responsibility. Environmental protection and motor vehicle licensing are examples of this; the former more a federal responsibility, the latter largely a state service. We can understand the vast array of governments only through knowledge of the ideas that influence our thinking.

THE FOUNDING FATHERS
AND URBAN GOVERNMENT

DEALING WITH POLLUTERS

In the summer of 1990, Wichita, Kansas, officials faced a serious problem. The Kansas Department of Health and Environment, acting on behalf of the federal Environmental Protection Agency, reported that the center of town was located on top of a huge underground lake of cancer-causing contaminants. The chemicals in the lake had been deposited years ago by city industries. The pollutants were located above the city's water

(continued)

(continued)

supply, which meant the water would become contaminated unless measures were taken to drain the pollutants.

The cost of the cleanup efforts was estimated at as much as $20 million and the lake would take years to drain. The city was experiencing economic problems as it was. They had embarked on an expensive project to improve public facilities with the hope of attracting new industries to bolster their declining tax base. The country was also in a recession.

On top of these problems, the courts had recently ruled that a lender might be liable for the pollution costs of its clients. Thus, the banks in Kansas feared that the costs of the cleanup could be placed partially on their backs. Upon hearing of the problem, the banks in town halted most lending to interests in the city center.

City officials were faced with a very serious dilemma. Failing to act meant that residents and firms could sue the city for damages. The city would be eligible for funds from the federal government to help pay the costs, but if the federal government became directly involved, the city would be labeled formally as a serious polluter, and new businesses would be discouraged from locating there. Further, use of federal funds entailed additional costs of supervision and legal expenses. To cleanup the lake themselves, however, involved raising taxes significanlty, also discouraging new investments. City officials had to act quickly. If they waited, the Environmental Protection Agency would publicly place them on a list of major polluters and impose sanctions on them. Would anyone want to move to Wichita knowing that the federal government had so labeled the city?

Fearing the imposition of sanctions from the central government, local government and businesses got together on a plan that dealt with the problems. City officials assumed responsibility for draining the pollutants and devised a taxing plan. The plan required special state legislation to create a taxing district and ultimate approval from the Kansas Department of Health and Environment.

SOURCE: Susan Rosegrant, "Wichita Confronts Contamination," in Richard J. Stillman *Public Administration: Concepts and Cases, 6th ed.* (Boston: Houghton Mifflin Company, 1996).

TURNING PUBLIC HOUSING AROUND

The Kenilworth-Parkside development in northeast Washington, D.C. is a public housing project that was in serious decline in 1980. Drugs were purchased openly on the premises, and violence was so common that bulletproof barriers were placed around the main office. Residents often went without heat, rubbish was picked up infrequently, and rats infested the buildings. Kimi Gray, a single mother living in the project, was fed up with these conditions and decided to do something about them.

Gray and some of her neighbors petitioned the mayor to let them manage the project themselves. After much foot dragging, the mayor agreed. The tenants wrote their own constitution and created the Kenilworth-Parkside Resident Management Corporation. David Osborne and Ted Gaebler (1992), in their best selling book *Reinventing Government: How the Entrepreneurial Spirit is Transforming the Public Sector: From Schoolhouse to Statehouse, City Hall to the Pentagon,* describe what followed:

The Kenilworth-Parkside Management Corporation hired and trained residents to manage the property and do the maintenance. They held monthly meetings of all tenants. . . . Believing that peer pressure was the key to changing their environment, they set up fines for violating the rules—littering, loitering in the hallways, sitting on fences, not cutting your grass. They created a system of elected building captains and court captains to enforce them. They started mandatory Sunday classes to teach housekeeping, budgeting, home repair and parenting. Also they required mothers who enrolled their children in day-care center to work, attend school or get job training.

Based on the results of a needs survey, the Resident Management Corporation created an after-school homework and tutorial program for kids whose mothers worked full-time. They set up courses to help adults get their high school degrees; contracted with a doctor and a dentist to set up part-time office hours and make house calls at the development; set up an employment office to help people find training and jobs; and began to create their businesses to keep money and jobs within the community.

The first was a shop to replace windows, screens and doors, owned by a young man who could neither read nor count. In return for a start-up loan, from the residents council, he trained ten students, who went on to market their skills elsewhere in Washington. The board fired the garbage collection service and contracted with another young man on condition that he hire Kenilworth-Parkside residents. . . .

Perhaps the worst problem in Kenilworth-Parkside was drugs. Every evening hundreds of dealers lined Quarles Street. Many of the worst offenders lived at Kenilworth, but the police were reluctant to enter the neighborhood because residents were hostile. Mothers kept their children barricaded indoors.

Kimi called a meeting and invited the police. At first most residents stayed home, afraid to be seen as snitches. Kimi and the few residents who attended asked for foot patrols in Kenilworth. They suggested a temporary station- trailer on the grounds. The police agreed.

"By putting guys over there on a regular basis, they began slowly to develop a sense of trust in us" says Sergeant Robert L. Proiut Jr. "And they began to give us information . . . and now it's gotten to the point where we have mothers that have sons that if they're wanted for something, they'll pick up the phone and call us."

In 1986 the accounting firm of Coopers & Lybrand released an audit of Kenilworth-Parkside. During the first four years of tenant management, it reported rent collections increased 77 percent—seven times the increase at public housing citywide. Vacancy rates fell from 18 percent—then the citywide average—to 5.4 percent. The Resident Management Corporation helped at least 132 residents get off welfare; it hired 10 as staff and 92 to rent the businesses it started, while its employment office found training and jobs for 30 more. Overall, Coopers & Lybrand concluded that four years of resident management had saved the city at least $785,000. If trends continue, over the next six years, it would save $3.7 million more—and the federal government would reap additional savings.

SOURCE: David Osborne and Ted Gaelder, *Reinventing Government: How the Entrepreneurial Spirit is Transforming the Public Sector: From Schoolhouse to Statehouse, City House to the Pentagon.* (New York: Addison Wesley, 1992).

These cases demonstrate different ways in which our governments confront public problems. In the first case, an agency of the federal government, the Environmental Protection Agency (EPA), locates a problem and controls the solution. Legislation at the state and federal level has defined the problems and delegated implementation to specific agencies. While local officials have an influence on the solution to the problem, officials of higher levels of government must be satisfied. Local governments must comply with the concerns of the courts and the federal government. Legislation has given officials at the EPA the power to impose costs on local governments. A successful solution to the problem occurs because local residents know that the courts can impose a course of action that will have a negative effect on the town. It is assumed here that a just resolution to the problem requires a high level of influence from a large central government.

In the second case, allowing citizens in a small apartment complex to make decisions led to a much better resolution to the problems than was the case when a larger government had decision-making responsibility. Giving the residents authority over the housing complex led them to assume greater responsibility over their lives. The problems of the project became less serious because the residents assumed control. Here, the better solution was to let the smallest level of government assume major responsibility.

Is one approach superior to the other? This debate is embedded in our history and goes back as far as the thoughts of James Madison and Thomas Jefferson. As we will see, the conflict comes back to us frequently when changes in the organization of governments are proposed. To understand the different perspectives, we need to look closely at these early writings.

James Madison and the Evils of Faction

James Madison is the major author of the Constitution of 1789, which still frames our government. The American Revolution had been fought to free the country from a strong, centralized government. Yet the first constitution, the Articles of Confederation, led to significant instability and unrest. Those who gathered to write the new Constitution wanted to retain individual freedom but also create a government that was strong enough to provide some degree of central direction and control. The result was a compromise of interests generally based on ideas articulated by Madison, Hamilton, and Jay in a series of newspaper articles known as the Federalist Papers.

This dilemma confronted the Founders: Can individual freedom be maintained yet the government be strong enough to respond to the needs of the emerging common society? A central economy had developed that needed a common currency and the ability to enforce rules of commerce and trade. There had been public unrest creating a desire for greater governmental control of unruly citizens. A concern over foreign enemies implied the need for a defense system. Yet the states had a degree of independence that most wanted to preserve.

Did the protection of freedom require small governments? Was the solution to locate government power as close to the average citizen as possible? Madison worried about personal freedom when power was given to very small governments. In his opinion, *factions,* small groups of people acting against the interests of others, were more likely to gain power when the government was small.

Similar dangers were present in large governments if a particular class or group of individuals gained control. Legislators, meeting in isolation from the public, could tyrannize the masses. Madison always worried about the negative side of people. If given the opportunity, he believed some people always would take advantage of power for their own ends. In drafting the Constitution, he hoped to create a government that could prevent control by factions but still be able to act in the national interest.

Madison's solution is most clearly discussed in Federalist #10 and #51, required reading for an understanding of the American system. Madison began in a very elementary way by saying that governments have many purposes, but to him, the most important goal was to control the "violence of faction." By faction, he meant "a number of citizens who are united and actuated by some common impulse or passion or interest, adverse to the rights of other citizens, or to the permanent and aggregate interests of the community" (1787:77). Factions, according to Madison, are innate to man. One can eliminate them only by eliminating individual freedom. Thus, controlling the *effects* of faction was the only option open to Constitutional framers.

Federalist #10 discusses two ways in which the Constitution acts to control the evils of faction. A system of *checks and balances* whereby different parts of the government, elected and appointed in different ways, must agree before any law is passed. With many different groups involved, the chance of a small group of like-minded men controlling the outcome is reduced. Therefore, Madison advocated a Senate and a House of Representatives, one elected by the white male property owners in small districts, and the other appointed by state legislatures. He proposed a President selected by an electoral college, and a Supreme Court appointed by the President and confirmed by the Senate. Consequently, government action required the assent of people chosen in very different ways.

A second control of factions occurred if election districts covered a large territory with a diverse population. Factions were less likely to control the outcome if the district included several communities and a larger territory. ". . . as each representative is chosen by a greater number of citizens in the large than in the small republic, it will be more difficult for unworthy candidates to practice with success the vicious arts by which elections are too often carried out; and the suffrages of the people being more free, will likely be certain in men who possess the most attractive merit and the most diffusive and established characters" (Madison 1787:60). Madison argued that greater diversity of opinion in the governing body would result. "Extend the sphere and you take in a greater variety of parties and interests; you make it less probable that a majority of the whole will have a common motive to invade the rights of other citizens; or if such common motive exists, it will be more difficult for all who feel it to discover their strength and to act in unison with each other" (Madison 1787:83).

Madison saw *great danger* then *in small local governments* with a high degree of citizen participation. ". . . (I)t may be concluded that a pure democracy, by which I mean a society consisting of a small number of citizens who assemble and administer the government in person can admit no cure for the mischiefs of faction" (Madison 1787: 58). To Madison, a government physically close to the people, run by one's friends and neighbors, was not desirable. He felt that such a government would become a government of factions and those on the losing end were in danger of losing their freedom.

But could such a government act efficiently? Wouldn't there be great delays in getting laws passed? Couldn't disgruntled legislators prevent actions? Indeed they could, but Madison felt the gain in personal freedom was worth the loss in speed and efficiency. Referring to the proposed Constitution, he argued "(I)t may clog the administration; it may convulse the society but it will be unable to mask and execute its violence under the forms of the Constitution" (Madison 1787: 80). Madison had *little concern for the efficiency of government*. He hoped government would have very limited powers and influence on society. Preservation of freedom through the checks and balances system was more important to him than the speed and efficiency of the government. However, he favored a strong central government tempered by checks and balances within the governing structure and active state governments.

Madison's notion of government can be succinctly summarized:

- He feared most the influence of factions; like-minded people determined to press their will against the interests of others. To Madison factions were part of man's nature. They could not be destroying liberty.

- Government must control the effects of factions. This could best be done through a system of checks and balances and by electing representatives over a larger territory.

- Madison's view of man and government was pessimistic. The goals of government were to control man's baser instincts, and government was designed to do only that which was necessary.

- Madison placed much faith in structures of government, laws, and administrative organizations to prevent factions from influencing policy. Local governments are to be feared because factions are more likely to form in a small territory.

Thomas Jefferson: A Positive Role
for Local Government

Thomas Jefferson was an optimist. "We hold these truths to be self evident," he stated in the Declaration of Independence, "that all men are created equal, that they are endowed by their creator with certain unalienable rights, that among these are life, liberty and the pursuit of happiness." To Jefferson, a proper government could assist in that pursuit.

Jefferson had a *positive view of the average citizen*. A government of the average man was nothing to be feared. "If experience be called for, appeal to that of our fifteen or twenty governments for forty years and show me where the people have done half the mischief in these forty years, that a single despot would have done in a single year; or show half the riots and rebellions, the crimes and the punishments, which have taken place in a single nation, under kingly government, during the same period. The true foundation of republican government is the equal right of every citizen, in his person and property and in their management." (Jefferson 1984a: 1398). The right kind of government would encourage the positive traits of the average citizen and teach him how to be a better citizen. Jefferson saw in government the opportunity to improve people. Through education, and most importantly through a structure of government that encouraged participation and understanding of others, man could be perfected. Government was a vehicle not only for the making of societal decisions, but also to help people better understand others and to gain knowledge of the concerns for society.

Jefferson did worry about the potential tyranny of elected officials; the conspiratorial efforts of small groups of elected officials. Gather together a group of officials and detach them from the people, and you create a faction that will act against the interests of the common man. Thus, the problem for Jefferson was how to create a government that can make common decisions without detaching those decisions from the average citizen. *His solution was a system of government that was very decentralized and dominated by small governing units.*

Jefferson hoped to divide the country into small governmental units called *wards,* five by seven miles in area, a distance small enough for all to gather at a central meeting place within a day's horse ride. Wards were to be the primary unit of government.

> Divide the country into wards of such size that every citizen can attend when called on and act in person. Ascribe to them the government of their wards in all things related to themselves exclusively. A justice, chosen by themselves in each, a constable, a military company, a patrol, a school, the care of their own poor, their portion of the public road, the choice of one or more jurors to serve in some court and the delivery, within the wards of their own votes for all elective officers of higher sphere will relieve the county administration of nearly all its business, will have it done better, and by making each citizen an acting member of the government, and in the offices nearest and most interesting to him, will attach him by his strongest feelings to the independence of the country, and its republican constitution. . . . These wards. . . are the vital principal of their governments, and have proved themselves the wisest invention ever devised by the wit of man for perfect exercise of self government, and for its preservation. (Jefferson 1984A: 1399)

Jefferson most feared the elected representative who moved from the people and joined factions with his fellow legislators. A government of small wards would protect society from tyranny because "where every man is a sharer in the direction of his ward-republic, or of some of the higher ones, and feels that he is a participator in the government of affairs, not merely at an election one day of the year, but every day; when there shall not be a man in the State who will both be a member of some of its council, great or small, he will let the heart be torn out of his body sooner than his power be rested from him by a Caesar or a Bonaparte" (Jefferson 1984B: 1380). With the Land Ordinances of 1785 and 1787, he provided for the division of land into townships, providing 160-acre plots to be sold at auction. Land was also provided for local schools and public buildings (Hughes 1987: 90–1). Jefferson hoped that land would remain in the hands of local farmers; the Act prevented land taxes by the federal government. Thus, through ownership of property, and small democratic units of government, a tolerant public was preserved.

Jefferson's perspective then can be succinctly summarized:

- Jefferson's government was founded on an optimistic view of man. He feared the leaders more than the masses.

- He opposed large governments with selected representatives because delegates detached from the public may tyrannize the masses.

- He placed great faith in the right kind of governmental structure. Small, participative local governments would do more than govern properly, they would also create good people.

- Government was limited to those matters that local citizens could agree on.

Comparing Jefferson and Madison:
Our Diverse and Conflicting Legacy

Madison and Jefferson leave us with a conflicting legacy. One is an optimist about man, the other a pessimist. One values large governments, the other small units. One sees representatives as wise and trusting, the other fears representatives and finds more wisdom in the average person. They did agree on certain fundamental principles that also frame our discussion of urban politics. Both agreed that government should be limited in scope, though Jefferson saw a broader role for government in education and political socialization, and both placed great faith in structures of government. The properly designed government in both cases was thought to lead to the good society. Table 3.1 summarizes the two perspectives.

Returning to our two cases, we can see that the method of each draws support from a different source. Madison would bless the proponents of the legislation that permitted the EPA to force Wichita officials to devise a plan to rid

Table 3.1 Comparison of Madisonian and Jeffersonian Government

	MADISON	**JEFFERSON**
Source of tyranny	Factions	Representation
Nature of man	Pessimistic	Optimistic
Dominant government	National	Local
Role of government	Limited	Limited
Purpose of government	Control factions	Create good citizens

Thomas Jefferson advocated that government was small and locally elected. Yet he wanted these governments to perform many important tasks for the citizens.

© Bettmann/Corbis

the community of its underground lake. Without strong enforcement tools from the federal government, it is unlikely that Wichita officials would have voluntarily taxed themselves to clean up the mess. The federal government represented a broader constituency that could consider more than the immediate economic problems of the city. They could act to preserve the long-term health of the citizens. The courts, as potential intervenors, could prevent either level of government from injuring the citizens. The complex relations among the various governments undoubtedly delayed action on the problem. Such delays were worth the merits of finding a proper solution to the problem.

Jefferson, however, would take great pride in the efforts of Kimi Gray and her neighbors. Though inexperienced and poorly educated, they could act on the root causes of their problems in ways that the best-trained federal bureaucrats could not. By taking over the housing project and creating self-governing units, the members learned a great deal about tolerance and understanding of one another and developed the courage to attack those who were causing the problem. The community and the residents are much improved as a consequence of the creation of ward level decision-making bodies.

Americans are left with two traditions of government as they seek to deal with the problems of an urban society. As we will see, throughout history, policymakers draw on elements of both to seek better ways of dealing with public problems. Can the two be combined, or can a middle ground be found? Some argue that the presence of open lands and westward expansion permitted Americans to reconcile both perspectives. The central government encouraged the development of the west most pointedly through the subsidization of the railroads following the Civil War (see Ambrose 2000) and later with massive reclamation projects. At the expense of nature, Native Americans, and perhaps eastern and midwestern cities, the west became a place for those who were encouraged by the Jeffersonian ideal. Thus, government could promote rugged individualism and suspicion of a central government while allowing significant public investment in the westward movement.

THE PRACTICE OF GOVERNMENT: CITY GOVERNMENT AND THE AGE OF INDUSTRIALIZATION

The practice of government contrasts the Jeffersonian and Madisonian traditions with the reality of life in our cities. Structures of government are, in part, the result of political tradition and partially a response to the social and economic needs of leaders and residents. The immense changes in the social and economic environment of cities in the age of industrialization placed new pressures on cities for greater public services. The result was a unique political form, the urban machine; it has been a source of enjoyment, fear, and controversy ever since. The urban machine was a practical response to the political problems of its day; it was not the creation of men reflecting on the good life. Therefore, we need to look at the kind of government that preceded it and the conditions that led to a governmental change.

Government in the walking city was generally very limited, relying often on volunteers and informal relations among the citizens. Expenses were minimal; New York City was run with a $1.00 per person budget in 1910 (Kantor and David 1984: 72). Most argue that the commercial elite dominated the city. The broader functions that cities did perform were those that enhanced the commercial development of cities. City officials were often extensively involved in canal building and influencing the location of railroad lines. Beyond that, early cities emphasized public order and protecting personal property (Kantor and David 1984: 34).

In the years following the Civil War, cities developed the means to create stronger governments. In many cities, new charters were passed centralizing authority in the mayor's office and providing the means for a broader array of governmental services. Voting rights also expanded in this period to include non–property owners and women. In some cities, centralized government and strong urban mayors emerged (Bridges 1984).

The era of industrialization presented immense challenges to cities. Large industries required better roads, harbors, railroads, and canals. The immigrant population created new challenges to public order. People were crowded together in dense, compact, ethnic neighborhoods, each with different customs and languages. Sanitation, clean water, and public health and recreation took on much greater importance. As pointed out in Chapter 1, concentration of population and a complex technology requires significant increases in government.

The problem was compounded by a lack of concern on the part of the federal government. The federal system separated state government from the national system. The national party systems were dominated by rural and small-town elites who were often horrified by what they saw in the cities. For this reason there was little sentiment in Washington to respond to the problems of the cities.

How could one create a political system then that would connect the diverse and separate ethnic neighborhood? The service demand was very great; thus, large governments were required. The diversity of citizenry meant that connections had to be made to those speaking different languages. The demands from the citizen would also be broad because they came from different cultures with different traditions and practices. Such citizens owed their primary allegiance to their group rather than the city or society as a whole. The *urban machine* was a solution to this very difficult problem.

The urban machine has its supporters and critics. Few are neutral about it. Though it has been gone from most cities for nearly 100 years, it remains a source of concern to city officials today. Often I have been told by city officials that a small tinkering with the city charter, say the election of city council members in districts rather than citywide, or the privatization of some city services, will inevitably lead to "the boss system." Many city officials remain in fear of a resurgence of the urban machine. The boss system was more than a reality, it left an imprint on people's thinking that affects our thinking about government structures today. Thus, an understanding of governmental structures requires knowledge of the urban machine.

Foot Soldiers of the Machine: The Precinct Captains

The urban machine began with organizations of local neighborhoods, called precincts. Since votes were required to elect city leaders, those who could organize a precinct and get people to vote for particular candidates became very useful. These *precinct captains* were the backbone of the machine. They were responsible for a small neighborhood, generally no more than 400 people. If they worked successfully, direct contact was established with most voters and the result of the election could be determined. Good precinct captains could convince voters to change candidates, and even parties (Gosnell 1937: 53).

Why would voters follow the wishes of precinct captains? Largely because they were connected to the running of city government through links to *ward bosses* and ultimately to the person at the center of the organization, the *boss*. Precinct captains often had access to material benefits; free beer on election day, Christmas baskets for the poor, leniency toward those arrested, and even jobs and contracts with the city government.

As government expanded to meet the needs of the changing city, new employees were needed. Linguistic and cultural differences in the new populations required public servants with the ability to communicate with the new residents.

The new residents wanted influence over police officers, firefighters, and teachers. The precinct captain often played a role in selecting these people or in putting pressure on them. Obviously the precinct captain proposed people who had helped win elections.

Businesses in the precinct required government assistance. Some needed permits to operate; others required new roads, sewers, and water connections. The precinct captain was often the intermediary between these businesses and those who granted permits and supplied services. Fees for these services could be extracted.

Precinct captains who had the respect of their superiors were in a position to get concessions from government officials. Effective precinct captains could obtain personal favors for constituents in trouble. One of Gosnell's informants, a veteran Chicago precinct captain, states the activities of the job well:

> When anyone gets into trouble with the law-petty thieving, trouble with a relief investigator, or when he loses his job or is about to be evicted, or when a kid gets in with a bad gang and starts staying out all night, in cases like this it is not the relief agency or the social welfare agency that the harassed voter goes to, but rather to the precinct captain who stands in with the law, who will not talk down to him but will treat him as a friend in need, and who is waiting for him in the local tavern or in the ward headquarters where there is a full-time secretary who knows just who can handle the situation. (1937: 70)

THE WORK OF A SUCCESSFUL PRECINCT CAPTAIN

To be an effective precinct captain, or ward heeler as they were sometimes called, required hard work and great skill. Manipulating the election was a major duty that often required ingenuity. Dedication to the urban machine often involved sacrifice of personal relations because the machine demanded ultimate loyalty. Below is a description of the activities of one Boston ward heeler who went on to become a successful mayor of Boston. He was John F. Kennedy's grandfather.

Fitzgerald long remembered the pride he felt when the boss first designated him a "heeler" for the ward, one of the chosen few whose responsibility it was to ensure that only the "right" party members attended the local meetings designed to choose the delegates for the nominating conventions. Each year, in early September, the boss drew up a checklist of the voters in the ward who were fixed on the right side; it was these men, the heelers, who were dispatched to round up voters from their homes and their saloons on primary day. If the heelers did their job well, the proceedings took little time, as the hand-picked meeting invariably supported the boss's slate of delegates. But if a group of outsiders appeared at the door, the heelers were responsible either to prevent their entry or, failing that, to conduct a second roundup, this time of "the personators," the men who were willing to "vote the cemetery." This last task was the one Fitzgerald relished the most, for, as he liked to boast, time was of the essence and since he was still the fastest runner in the North End he was able "to round up more dead people in a shorter time than any other heeler."

So long as the boss's slate of delegates was kept intact, the process of choosing the nominees for office—for the city Common Council, the state legislature and the Congress—was entirely automatic. Since it was the city committee's practice to order the names of the candidates on the ballot in the same sequence in which their nominating papers were filed, it was in the interest of each ward leader—there were twenty-two at the time—to see to it that *his* candidates filed the papers first. More than any other practice during this era, this one, the rewarding of the first group through the door, produced the most absurd demands on the heelers. But this was Fitzgerald's world, and he accepted each challenge with the delight of a natural competitor whose exploits grew legendary as time went by. It was said that on one occasion, while a large gathering of a rival leader's forces were keeping an all-night vigil at the front door of the city committee headquarters, Fitzgerald climbed up a tree and came down through a skylight. And on another occasion it was reported that he managed to persuade the night janitor of the building to exchange roles with him, so that on the morning of the filing day he was able to present himself, the nominating papers in the pocket of his janitor's uniform, at the office of the city committee before the doors to the building were even opened.

As a reward for filling the post heeler so well, Fitzgerald was advanced to the speakers' bureau, where he joined a small group of men selected by the boss to give rousing speeches on behalf of the boss's nominees. The boss himself was not a man who felt comfortable speaking before public, but he was brilliant at turning the talent of others to his own account. And from the first time he heard the young Irishman speak, despite the slight lisp that stayed with Fitzgerald all his life, Keany took the measure of his extraordinary capacity as an orator. In an age when the people looked to politics for their entertainment and when campaigns resembled carnivals—with kerosene torches, spangled banners, marching parades and colorful speeches—Fitzgerald's dramatic presentation and vigorous movements touched all the proper chords. So effective was "little Fitzie," as he came to be called, not only in arousing his audiences but in getting to the best street corners first (every night there was a struggle to see which speakers could set up their soapboxes and portable platforms in the most populous places), that the boss rapidly advanced him to the speakers, whose job it was to infiltrate the meetings of the enemy and then, by heckling, wit and strength of voice, undermine the opponent and turn the audience in favor of the boss's man.

Through his far-ranging apprenticeship, Fitzgerald was treated to a view of the ward system at every phrase of its development—from the days of its planting, when the boss distributed his assistance to families in the district, through its cultivation at the primary, the convention and the campaign, to its harvesting when the elections finally took place and the boss reaped his rewards. It was during this final phase that Johnny came up against the hardest test of his early political education.

On the day before the elections Keany told Fitzgerald he wanted him to be a checker at the precinct headquarters at the Eliot School. It was the checker's job to sit where the voters deposited their marked ballots into the ballot box and determine exactly how each voter voted. In those days—before the requirements of the Australian system of secrecy—when

(continued)

(continued)

each party still printed its own ballots, there were several ways to determine how each voter was voting. First of all, the checker could determine which party's ticket the voter was using by noting the shade of the ballot he slipped into the box. Although Massachusetts had passed a law in the early 1870s prescribing that all ballots be printed on plain paper and without any mark to distinguish one party's ballot from another, the parties had skillfully evaded the law by using different shades of white, ranging from shiny white to cream.

In a district that was heavily Democratic as Fitzgerald's, however, this simple question of party loyalty was less important than the more elaborate test of whether every Democrat had voted exactly the way the boss had instructed. If, as it sometimes happened, there were two men, the boss's man and the rival candidate, running for the same office, the ballots had to be closely inspected to discern which one the voter had chosen. But the checkers had their ways—beginning with the distribution of pencils so hard that all the Xs came through to the surface in a pattern which the checker could interpret as the folded ballot was slipping through the rollers.

In the days before this particular election in 1888, an undercurrent of opposition had arisen. It happened that one of the boss's nominees for the Common Council was an aggressive man who had a reputation for unbridled arrogance and abusing power. There was talk in the street that some of the North Enders were going to defy the boss on this one and vote for a rival boss's candidate. Having heard these rumors, Keany was determined to catch the defectors early in the day so that reports of their swift and heavy punishment could be turned back on the streets as a warning to the rest of the voters.

With Keany, revenge was not taken in anger, it was simply his method of politics: These men had already bound themselves to him by accepting his favors; all he asked in return was their vote. Perhaps this blustery fellow was not the best candidate; if so, the boss would discard him the next time around. But for now, loyalty demanded that all his men rally around his candidates, including the objectionable ones.

So it was that Keany put his most trusted men on duty with instructions to identify the defectors as they slipped their ballots into the box by a raise of the arm which notified a gang of waiting heelers to retaliate. In some instances, the punishment could be administered immediately: If the defector had a city job or one supplied by the boss, he would be told on the spot that he was fired. With others, the web took longer to spin; but no one escaped the boss's wrath: A rebellious landlord would return to his tenement to find a group of investigators from the city's Health Department responding to complaints about the sanitary conditions of his buildings; a defecting saloon keeper would receive a hefty fine from the police for having stayed open after hours; an unfaithful merchant would be boycotted. And everyone would understand that all of these actions were the result of one man's word.

For himself, Fitzgerald had no trouble with the system. Harsh as the punishment seemed, it was only the corollary of the assistance Keany provided. But when the day of the balloting dawned, there arose for the faithful Fitzgerald an agonizing dilemma. It chanced that one of the men who had threatened to vote against the boss's candidate—based on a scuffle at the docks in which he lost the use of one of his eyes—was the uncle of the newsboy Fred, the friend and companion of Fitzgerald's youth. After young Fred's death, his paternal uncle had come to live with the family in the North End, where Keany had found him a steady job on the docks. A loyal man who was willing to work hard, he had done well by his dead brother's family, with whom Fitzgerald had kept in close touch. But on this occasion, when he saw the big man approach the precinct booth, Fitzgerald dropped his head; he knew the pride and independence of the family and feared the worst. As the uncle picked up his ballot, he said nothing; he merely glanced at Fitzgerald, a glance Fitzgerald would remember all his life.

Years later, Fitzgerald recalled that as he turned the rollers and discovered the uncle's X beside the rival name, he became conscious of a loud throbbing in his heart. He knew that if he turned the man in, all would be lost for Fred's family. Yet he felt that his first loyalty had to be to Matt Keany. To desert Keany was to lose everything he'd been working for since his father's death. But try as he might, he could never block from his mind the sight of the boss's heelers as they swarmed about the uncle to let him know that his job at the docks had vanished and that there was nothing else in the city he was qualified to do.

The reward for Fitzgerald's faithfulness came several months later when the boss secured for him a position in the Customs House which not only allowed him to work at Boston Harbor but also left him plenty of time to continue his political education. And the job had an additional benefit: Since a clerkship in the Customs House provided a substantial sum of $1,500 a year plus benefits, Fitzgerald was finally able to think of marrying the beautiful Josie Hannon, the girl with whom he had been in love since the first day they met.

Source: From Doris Kearns Goodwin, *The Fitzgeralds and the Kennedys* (New York: Simon and Schuster Inc., 1987), 73–6.

Major Fitzgerald as a young man and successful precinct captain.

© Corbis

Boss Tweed and his friends controlled the finances of New York City in the 1870s. Great public works were built but corruption was common.

© Bettmann/Corbis

Ward Bosses: The Center of Ethnic Power

At the next level of the hierarchy are the *ward bosses,* as they were often called. Ward bosses supervised the work of several precinct captains, and were responsible for connections between government and business in a large area of the city. Generally, council districts were drawn to contain one major ethnic or racial group. The ward boss became the group's spokesman to the outside world and represented it in the running of the government. In some cities, they were the most powerful politicians. The relationship between the ward bosses and the boss was often one of conflict since the boss needed the support of a majority of the ward bosses to act. Since the ward boss spoke the language of the ward residents and understood their customs and practices, the boss often had to tend to the wishes of the ward boss to gain his support.

Gosnell argues that Chicago ward bosses were extremely powerful people. They were members of committees that selected most of the prominent officials in the city including judges, members of the University Board of Regents, and the committees that selected members of the national nominating conventions and most local offices. They selected people for the city jobs in their wards and influenced the awarding of contracts. They could extract contributions from those needing the protection of the police to pursue illicit activities. They guarded their prerogatives carefully and resisted any encroachment on their territory (1937: 44).

The power of the ward bosses was apparent when other groups tried to encroach upon it. An important source of power to the ward bosses was the ability to draw their own election districts that contained their supporters. When the Kiwanis Club of Chicago, a respected civic organization, studied the drawing of election districts and proposed that changes be made to create districts equal in population, the author of the proposal received the following from his ward boss:

> Dear Sir:
> I am in receipt of a letter which you have forwarded to a member of the Kiwanis club.
> In this letter you state that a conference has been arranged with Mr. Cermak [the mayor] and Mr. Busch on a proposed plan of redistricting wards. I am told by the Kiwanis Club of my ward that you have a proposed plan to redistrict my ward by putting it in a neighboring ward.
> Let me tell you that you have as much chance of doing this as Ford has of being Mayor of Palestine.
> I am one of the members of a committee of five of the City Council who will redistrict Chicago and I suggest that if you want anything to say about redistricting my ward or any other ward you had better run for Alderman and if you are elected, you will have the right to redistrict by virtue of the people's votes.
> There is too much of usurping of the rights of the people-elected officials, and I know I voice the sentiments of every Alderman on the City Council when I say to you, Hands Off. (Gosnell 1937: 32)

Ward bosses prided themselves on being both close to the people but also able to extract funds from the financial community. They were intermediaries between those in daily contact with the voters and the boss who coordinated the political organization with business and other levels of government. One of the more articulate and colorful of the ward bosses was George Washington Plunkitt, a ward boss in New York in the first part of the twentieth century. Much of Plunkitt's money came to him through what he termed "honest graft." Here is an example:

> Supposing there is a new bridge they're going to build. I get tipped off and I buy up as much property as I can that has to be taken for approaches. I sell at my own price later on and drop more money in the bank.
>
> Wouldn't you? It's just like looking ahead in Wall Street or in the coffee or cotton market. It's honest graft, and I'm looking for it every day of the year. I will tell you quite frankly that I've got a good lot of it, too. (Riordan 1963: 4)

Plunkitt viewed himself as a dedicated politician who worked long hours to help the poor while helping himself. He described his job as follows:

> No other politician in New York or elsewhere is exactly like the Tammany district leader or works as he does. As a rule he has no business or occupation other than politics. He plays politics every day and night in the year and his headquarters bear the inscription "never closed."
>
> He is always obliging. He will go to the police courts to put in a good word for the drunks and disorderlies or pay their fines if a good word is not effective. He will attend christenings, weddings and funerals. He will feed the hungry and help to bury the dead.
>
> He seeks direct contact with the people and does them good turns when he can, and relies on their not forgetting him on election day. His heart is always in his work, too, for his subsistence depends on the results. (Riordan 1963: 91)

The Boss: The Captain of the Machine

At the center of the urban machine was *the boss.* The boss coordinated a coalition of ward bosses and provided the link between the precinct and ward organization and the world outside. This included local businesses, state and national officials, and various illicit businesses. Major public works projects that spanned ward boundaries were controlled by the bosses. Bosses often had great influence over state and national officials elected from within the city through their power over nominations and campaign funds. They were very visible people with strong personal followings.

Much of the power of the bosses resulted from their control of city finances. None exerted this power more blatantly than Boss Tweed of New York in the 1870s. Tweed used his influence over the city council and state legislature to obtain a new charter for the city, giving the mayor expanded powers of

*"Can we move our lunch up to noon? I've got to
be at City Hall by two to be arrested."*

© The New Yorker Collection 1999 Lee Lorenz from cartoonbank.com. All Rights Reserved.

appointment and creating a Board of Audit to handle the paying of all city bills. By manipulating the financial system, Tweed and his friends siphoned millions of dollars from the city budget (Chudacoff 1975: 136–7). With oversight by others eliminated, Tweed and his friends could manipulate city finance for their own benefit. Tweed bought controlling interest in a printing company and then directed all city business to that company. Office supplies were purchased from another Tweed company. In 1870, that company was paid $3 million, including $10,000 for a few ink bottles, six reams of paper and several boxes of rubber bands (Mohl 1985: 94).

Bosses were also builders and were responsible for most of the major improvements in city life. Central Park and the Brooklyn Bridge were built by the Tweed administration. Machine politicians coordinated the vast expanse of parks and museums that remain Chicago's hallmark. Given the fragmentation of neighborhoods and the lack of central authority in the structure of most city governments, these huge public projects remain as significant accomplishments.

While the image of the boss handed to us from the popular press is one of corruption and evil, some bosses were known as reformers, and others simply kept order among the various ward bosses. Zane L. Miller, for instance, de-

scribes the boss of Cincinnati in the early 1900s as a clever manager who created an orderly administration in a setting where disorder had been the pattern.
"Paradoxically, Cox and his machine were produced by, fed on and ultimately
helped dispel the spectacular disorder which engulfed Cincinnati in the late
nineteenth century and threatened the very survival of the democratic process"
(Miller 1968: 176).

What were the bosses like? What were their goals and interests? Arnold
Rogow and Harold Lasswell analyzed the backgrounds and actions of over 30
urban bosses who held power in major cities from 1870 to 1930. They argue
that there were two kinds of bosses, each with different values and motives.
The *game politician* became a boss because of his love for the game of politics.
He did not necessarily desire to make money from the system. The game
politician's goals were the honor of the job and the opportunity to manipulate people. The outcome of the battle was more important to him than the
issues involved, and he derived satisfaction from winning, no matter the
means used.

The game politician was born to an upper-class family with fathers who
were important in business circles. He was often an aloof person with many acquaintances but few friends and few interests outside of politics. His home life
mirrored his professional life, as he was loyal to his family but spent little time
with them. His lack of material interests, however, did not preclude the use of
corruption. Winning dominated the thoughts of the game politician, and he
was willing to use all the resources at his disposal in order to win. His goals extended beyond the city—he coveted higher office and sought to influence state
and federal officials.

The *gain politician,* on the other hand, was involved in politics for money.
He pursued opportunities that expanded the financial resources of his family
and friends and had little interest in goals that had no financial rewards. At the
same time, the gain politician was a generous man. He rewarded his family,
friends, followers, and the less fortunate, and donated large amounts of money
to charities and churches. Though his goal was financial reward, he often did
not become wealthy. His personality was quite different from the game politician. These bosses came from lower-class families, they were close to their wife
and children, and spent much time with their families. They were outgoing and
well liked by friends and acquaintances, and they had a number of close personal friends in whom to confide their inner-most thoughts (Rogow and Lasswell 1963: 45–54).

Following Rogow and Lasswell's analysis, bosses had significant freedom
to define their roles. Some used the power of the office to become influential nationally and advance certain policy goals. Others used it to gain and distribute wealth. Their positions were by no means secure. They could be
unseated by a coalition of the ward leaders, and frequently were. Bosses also
were attacked by newspapers, upper-class interests, and disgruntled favor
seekers. Thus, while the rewards were often great, the position was frequently
a very insecure one.

MAX WEBER ON THE BOSS SYSTEM

Max Weber (1864–1920), distinguished German author and social critic, is considered by many to be the father of modern sociology. He was fascinated by the organization of the emerging industrial society, and in his many writings he tried to describe the essence of the social processes he observed. We still look to him today to construct models of the social world.

Weber toured the United States in 1904, and became particularly fascinated with the urban machine. The selection that follows is his attempt to describe the common features of the urban boss. He was intrigued by what he saw in our cities and accepted much of it as a natural response to the problems of a changing society, but worried about its negative traits. Weber saw the need for more efficient and extensive delivery of urban services and wondered if those responsible for managing government would be controlled by representatives of the people. He saw the machine system as an important link between the public and the production of government services, but wasn't entirely happy with what he saw. This selection is one of the more thoughtful analyses of the boss system, viewed at the height of its influence.

Who is the boss? He is a political capitalist entrepreneur who on his own account and at his own risk provides votes. He may have established his first relations as a lawyer or a saloonkeeper or as a proprietor of similar establishments, or perhaps as a creditor. From here he spins his threads out until he is able to control a certain number of votes. When he has come this far he establishes contact with the neighboring bosses, and through zeal, skill, and above all discretion, he attracts the attention of those who have already further advanced in the career, and then he climbs. The boss is indispensable to the organization of the party and the organization is centralized in his hands. He substantially provides the financial means. How does he get them? Well, partly by the contributions of the members, and especially by taxing the salaries of those officials who came into office through him and his party. Furthermore, there are bribes and tips. He who wishes to trespass with impunity one of the many laws needs the boss's connivance and must pay for it; or else he will get into trouble. But this alone is not enough to accumulate the necessary capital for political enterprises. The boss is indispensable as the direct recipient of the money of great financial magnates, who would not entrust their money for election purposes to a paid party official, or to anyone else giving public account of his affairs. The boss, with his judicious discretion in financial matters, is the natural man for those capitalist circles who finance the election. The typical boss is an absolutely sober man. He does not seek social honor the professional is despised in respectable society. He seeks power alone, power as a source of money, but also power for power's sake. In contrast to the English leader, the American boss works in the dark. He is not heard speaking in public; he suggests to the speaker what they must say in expedient fashion. He himself, however, keeps silent.

The boss has no firm political principles; he is completely unprincipled in attitude and asks merely: What will capture votes? Frequently he is a rather poorly educated man. But as a rule he leads an inoffensive and correct private life. In his political morals, however, he naturally adjusts to the average ethical standards of political conduct, as a great many of us also may have done during the hoarding period in the field of economic ethics. That as a professional politician the boss is socially despised does not worry him. That he personally does not attain high federal offices, and does not wish to do so, has the frequent advantage that extra-party intellects, thus notables, may come into candidacy when the bosses believe they will have great appeal value at the polls. Hence the same old party notables do not run again and again, as is the case in Germany. Thus the structure of these unprincipled parties with their socially despised power-holders has aided able men to attain the presidency—men who with us never would have come to the top. To be sure, the bosses resist an outsider who might jeopardize their sources of money and power. Yet in the competitive struggle to win the favor of the voters, the bosses frequently have had to condescend and accept candidates known to be opponents of corruption.

SOURCE: From "Politics as a Vocation," From *Max Weber: Essays in Sociology*, in H. H. Gerth and C. Wright Mills Copyright © 1968 by Oxford University Press, Inc.

Analyzing the Urban Machine

Figure 3.1 summarizes the operation of the urban machine. Arrows indicate places where transactions between parties take place. Double arrows occur when an exchange takes place between machine members. Voters, for instance, support the machine candidate and receive services in return; baskets at Christmas time, help in getting a job, or simply the feeling that the ward boss and the boss represent them. Other groups receive more tangible rewards. Business groups receive preferential treatment for contracts and licenses. Gutterbock argues that support from the business community was easy to obtain. Business, like the machine, operated on the profit motive, and tends to cooperate with an organization that will protect its interests. Control of regulatory and law enforcement agencies by the successful machine makes it possible for businesses to receive illegal benefit with little risk of penalty (1980: 4).

Illicit businesses organize gambling, prostitution, narcotics sales, and other activities defined as illegal by the dominant Anglo society. Many of these activities and goods were an accepted part of the culture of various ethnic groups and were demanded by the residents. In that way, illicit businesses satisfy needs of the groups but their operation is defined as illegal by the larger society. The boss system can offer them protection from prosecution in return for financial support and assistance at the polls. Gosnell (1937) argues that these groups were among the most loyal constituents of the machine.

In a great metropolitan community like Chicago, the gambling privileges are perhaps the most important of all privileges at the command of the political machine. In the great cities of the United States, where there are many persons with liberal views on gambling, prostitution, drinking, and other human diversions, the existence of a powerful underworld, with its alliances and business men and machine politicians, may be taken for granted. Gambling kings, bookmakers, panderers, thieves, bootleggers, racketeers, and other hoodlums enjoy extraordinary immunity from

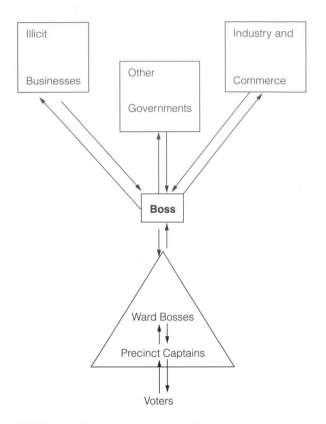

FIGURE 3.1 The operation of the urban machine.

interference on the part of the law-enforcing agencies. These outlaws realize that freedom from restraint depends upon how useful they can make themselves to the politicians. When asked to make campaign contributions or produce results upon election day, the leaders of the underworld can hardly refuse. If they do, their places will be promptly raided by law-enforcing authorities.

Not only are the contributions from the underworld interests an important item in the campaign funds of the dominant party, but the services of the underworld personnel are also significant. When word is passed down from the gangster chiefs, all proprietors of gambling houses and speakeasies, burglars, pick-pockets, pimps, prostitutes, fences, and their like are whipped into line (Gosnell 1937: 42).

State and local governments can support the machine through funds and the passage of laws. They can potentially control the urban machine through investigations and the actions of their employees. Machines are a source of support for elected officials at other levels of government. The powerful machines could place their own people in state and federal legislatures and nominating conventions, and they could help finance political campaigns. The Daley machine in Chicago, at the height of its power, controlled major blocks of legislators at both the state and federal level and thus could extract its wishes from those governments (see Chapter 5). Weaker machines and those in smaller cities, however, had much less influence at the state and federal level.

The urban machine, as described, is fundamentally a business operation where funds are obtained for services offered. Strong ward organizations could extract favors from the bosses. The bosses could respond to the ward leaders with money from businesses, other governments, and illicit trade. Bosses were in competition with other potential bosses and tried to satisfy the interests of as many of their constituents as possible. Hence, much money came in, but much went out.

Opinions differ on the profitability of the machine. There are reports of vast fortunes obtained by ward leaders and bosses. At the same time, bosses were often deposed if the ward bosses thought that another boss could provide them with better service. Scholars debate the extent to which the urban machine operated in a competitive market with little profit accruing to the boss, as (see Miller 1968: 110).

The urban machine as described in the previous paragraph is referred to frequently as an *economic model*. The machine is seen as a business that takes in contributions in return for services. It operates similar to a private business. Businesses have customers who are analogous to voters in the machine. A business produces goods and services, while the machine city produces services and privileges. All parties within the machine benefited from the system. The poor received charity and, in many cases, entry-level jobs. Public works projects supported businesses and permitted commerce and industry to operate. Illicit businesses provided services demanded by the public and secured a profit (Merton 1968; Banfield and Wilson 1963; Glazer and Moynihan 1963).

More recent scholars question the extent to which all aspects of the urban machine are explained by this model. Shefter (1976) looked closely at the New York machine over a number of years and found the machine dominated by conflicts among leaders rather than profits. While votes and contributions were important to the machine, it stayed in power because the leaders could build a centralized organization. Those that could organize the machine properly and form coalitions with major players succeeded. This made the role of voters less important. Erie compared the operation of Irish machines in eight cities over a 100-year period. He argues that one must make a distinction between recent immigrants and those who are second generation or more. Older immigrant groups tend to be incorporated into machines, but newer groups are often excluded (1988: 9–12; see also Gosnell 1937). Those who have looked at African American influence within the urban machine argue that racial biases prevented African Americans from achieving significant benefits in spite of significant electoral support (Grimshaw 1982: 42–3). Grimshaw and others have argued that the Daley machine in Chicago could not contain conflicts between African Americans and White ethnic groups.

The machine was never a smooth running business. There were always tensions among immigrant groups, many of whom had long histories of antagonism with one another. Conflicts among leaders led often to instability. As people matured and entered the middle class, the minor benefits that were attributed to the precinct leader became less and less important. When machine supporters moved to the suburbs, the machine's hold on the voters declined. Nonetheless, it remained the dominant form of government in most American cities for several decades and provided urban services that were badly needed to a society where agreement among contending groups was difficult to obtain.

SUMMARY: AMERICAN URBAN GOVERNMENT—A CONFLICT OF IDEAS

This chapter argues that conflicting ideas and practices describe the structure of American local government. Madison and Jefferson present us with very different ways of approaching government structure. The machine in practice describes another approach. Thus, when Americans approach the organization of government, they are faced with competing traditions.

- The Madisonian tradition looks to large governments and leaders elected from large districts who hold a broader view of the concerns of society. Madison would favor a system where those who are trained in leadership and politics emerge from a competitive system. He looks to checks and balances within the structure of government to protect the interests of citizens and groups. Thus, leaders must contend with divided power and the need to obtain agreement from diverse groups to accomplish their goals.

- Jefferson places his faith in small governments where the average citizen can participate. He favors the values of the public and fears leaders who are detached from the local community.

- The urban machine demonstrates that political entrepreneurs got things done when they were given the authority to run their organizations. Given the importance of the right to vote and charters that give central leaders significant authority, diverse groups and interests could be coordinated and policies carried out even when people and groups are very different. However, machine politicians often had little concern for fiscal efficiency and their attachment to the less savory elements in society raised ethical concerns.

The next chapter will look at changes that followed the urban machine era. The reaction to the excesses of the urban machine brought forth a major reform effort in the early part of the twentieth century that resulted in the development of common structures of government in many cities. Reaction to some of the problems of reform government, however, has caused some to look back at the positive features of the machine. We will see that current urban government politics and management incorporates principles from all three of these traditions.

REFERENCES

Ambrose, Stephen E. 2000. *Nothing Like It In The World: The Men who Built the Transcontinental Railroad.* 1863–1869 New York: Simon and Schuster.

Banfield, Edward, and James Q. Wilson 1963. *City Politics.* Cambridge, MA: Harvard University Press.

Bridges, Amy. 1984. *A City in the Republic.* Cambridge, MA: Cambridge University Press.

Chudacoff, Howard P. 1975. *The Evolution of American Urban Society.* Englewood Cliffs, NJ: Prentice-Hall.

Erie, Steven P. 1988. *Rainbows End: The Irish-Americans and the Dilemmas of Urban Machines, 1840–1985.* Berkeley, CA: University of California Press.

Gerth, H. H., and C. Wright Mills. 1958. *From Max Weber: Essays in Sociology.* New York: Oxford University Press.

Glazer, Nathan, and Daniel Patrick Moynihan. 1963. *Beyond the Melting Pot.* Cambridge, MA: MIT Press:

Gosnell, Harold. 1937. *Machine Politics Chicago Model.* Chicago: University of Chicago Press.

Grimshaw, William J. 1982. *Bitter Fruit: Black Politics and the Chicago Machine, 1935–1991.* Chicago: Prentice Hall.

Gutterbock, Thomas A. 1980. *Machine Politics in Transition: Party and Community in Chicago.* Chicago: University of Chicago Press

Jefferson, Thomas. 1984A. To Samiel Kerchival in *Writings.* Washington, D.C.: Literary Classics of the United States Inc.

Ibid. 1984B To Joseph L. Cabell

Kantor, Paul, and Stephen David. 1984. *The Dependent City: The Changing Political Economy of Urban America.* Glenview, Ill: Little Brown.

Kearns, Doris Goodwin. 1987. *The Fitzgeralds and the Kennedys.* New York: Simon and Schuster.

Madison, James. 1787. "Number 10–The Same Subject Continued." In *The Federalist.* New York: The Modern Library.

Merton, Robert K. 1968. *Social Theory and Social Structure.* New York: The Free Press.

Miller, Zane. 1968. *Boss Cox's Cincinnati: Urban Politics in the Progressive Era.* New York: Oxford University Press

Mohl, Raymond. 1985. *The New City: Urban America in the Industrial Age.* Arlington Heights, IL: Harlan Davidson Inc.

Osborne, David, and Ted Gaebler. 1992. *Reinventing Government: How the Entrepreneurial Spirit is Transforming the Public Sector: From Schoolhouse to Statehouse, City Hall to the Pentagon.* New York: Addison Wesley.

Riordan, William L. 1963. *Plunkitt of Tammany Hall: A Series of Plain Talks on Very Practical Politics.* New York: E. P. Dutton.

Rogow, Arnold A., and Harold D. Lasswell. 1963. *Power, Corruption and Rectitude.* Englewood Cliffs, NJ: Prentice-Hall.

Shefter, Martin. 1976. "The Emergence of the Political Machine: An Alternative View." In *Theoretical Perspectives in Urban Politics,* edited by Willis Hawley et al. Englewood Cliffs, NJ: Prentice Hall

Stillman, Richard J. 1996. *Public Administration: Concepts and Cases.* Boston: Houghton Mifflin Company.

Chapter Four

Organizing the Government of Today

We saw, in Chapter 3 that the social and economic structure of cities changed radically following World War II. Industry and commerce moved to the outer edges of the city and much of the White middle and working class located in the new subdivisions of suburbia, leaving the central city to the poor and newer migrants. The urban machine was built on strong ethnic neighborhoods and centralized control of the party machinery and the services of government. As social and economic conditions changed, the traditional machine either had to adapt to a new setting or be replaced by another governing system. In many of our urban areas, a very different kind of government emerged during the twentieth century. In others, the machine changed its structure and method of operation to accommodate a different environment.

This chapter looks at the major way in which many of our city governments changed to accommodate new ideas of governance and the different social and economic setting of twentieth-century America. We discuss the influence of the Progressive movement on the structure and operation of urban governments in this chapter. Many governments changed their structure of government to conform to progressive ideas.

In what ways are today's governments different than during the machine era? Most jobs today are obtained through neutral civil service procedures that emphasize the candidate's qualifications rather than his or her political connections. Appointed professional administrators hold powerful positions in most cities and exert a strong influence on city decisions. Smaller city councils with limited powers are elected rather than a large group chosen in wards. Political parties rarely determine the selection of candidates. Obviously, fundamental changes took place. This chapter examines the causes and the results of what we refer to today as reform structures of government.

Reform came to the cities as part of a political movement referred to as the Progressive movement. The progressive reforms changed the kind of people who govern our cities and also brought in new values and ideas. The machine was replaced not just by different leaders, but also by a set of ideas about how government should be organized. This chapter examines the impact of progressive reforms on cities. We begin by looking at the progressive ideas themselves since the changes that occurred were a consequence of these notions of good governance. The movement influenced law as well as practice. The chapter looks at legal changes in the relationship between cities, states, and the federal government and will examine the practice of government in reformed systems. Lastly, we look closely at the reform that had the greatest impact on cities; the council-manager form of government. Council-manager government became the major governmental form by the middle of the twentieth century. It also most fully embodies the principles of the Progressive movement. Thus, a close look at council-manager government tells us much about the positive and negative traits of progressive reforms.

THE PROGRESSIVE MOVEMENT AND THE EVILS OF THE MACHINE

Theodore Roosevelt hated urban machines. As a young politician, he attacked the power and corruption of the urban bosses. As a writer and thoughtful critic of the American system, his opposition to the boss system was incorporated into a new philosophy of government. His flamboyant career as cowboy, war hero, devoted family man, explorer, and author led to immense personal popularity and encouraged the adoption of the ideas that buttressed his concern for the governing of cities.

Roosevelt's major political opponent on the national scene, Woodrow Wilson, shared many of the same ideas of governance. Roosevelt and Wilson dominated politics from the beginning of the twentieth century until the end of World War I. The ideas of these two giants of American politics encouraged the popularity of a set of ideas that significantly changed the practice of urban government.

THEODORE ROOSEVELT ON URBAN REFORM

Theodore Roosevelt lived the life of a reform politician. Following a brief stint as a state legislator, he was appointed to the federal Civil Service Commission and then served as the police commissioner of New York City. In these two positions he applied some of the principles that would later be institutionalized in reform era changes in government.

In the following excerpts from his autobiography, you will read the words of a man who worked directly with the problems of machine government. Several aspects of the Progressive movement are apparent. Roosevelt opposed patronage or political appointments (sometimes referred to as the 'spoils system') and saw great value in appointing public administrators through examination rather than political influence. He argued that responsible government occurred when policy was made by elected officials and clearly delegated to appointed officers. He was critical of the prominent features of Madisonian government, separation of powers and checks and balances, because clear lines of responsibility are avoided.

As you read, reflect upon the discussion of the urban machine in the previous chapter. What problems of machine government most bothered Roosevelt? How would machine politicians like Mr. Plunkitt respond to Roosevelt?

The use of government offices as patronage is a handicap difficult to overestimate from the standpoint of those who strive to get good government. Any effort for reform of any sort, National, State or municipal results in the reformers immediately finding themselves face to face with an organized band of drilled mercenaries who are paid out of the public chest to train themselves with such skill that ordinarily good citizens when

they meet them at the polls are in much the position of militia matched against regular troops. Yet these citizens themselves support and pay their opponents in such a way that they are drilled to overthrow the very men who support them. Civil Service reform is designed primarily to give the average American citizen a fair chance in politics and to give this citizen the same weight in politics that the "ward heeler" has.

Under the spoils system a man is appointed to an ordinary clerical or ministerial position in the municipal, Federal or State government not primarily because he is expected to be a good servant, but because he has rendered help to some big boss or to the henchmen of some big boss. His stay in office depends not on how he performs service but upon how he retains his influence in the party. They know every twist and turn, no matter how intricate in the politics of their wards, and when election day comes the ordinary citizen who has merely the interest that all good men, all decent citizens, should have in political life, find himself as helpless before these men as if he were a solitary volunteer in the presence of a band of drilled mercenaries on the field of battle. The large number of men who believe vaguely in good are pitted against the smaller but still large number of men whose interest it often becomes to act very concretely and actively for evil; and it is small wonder that the struggle is doubtful.

I do not blame them in the least. I blame us, the people. For we ought to make it clear as a bell that the business of serving the people in one of the ordinary ministerial Government positions, which have nothing to do with deciding the policy of the Government, should have no necessary connection with the management of primaries, of caucuses, and of nominating conventions. As a result of our wrong thinking and suppineness, we American citizens tend to breed men whose interests in government matters are often adverse to ours, who are thoroughly drilled, thoroughly organized, who make their livelihood out of politics.

In most positions the "division of powers theory" works unmitigated mischief. The only way to get good service is to give somebody power to render it, facing the fact that power which will enable the man to do his job well will also necessarily enable him to do it ill if he is the wrong kind of man. What is normally needed is the concentration in the hands or one man or of a very small body of men of ample power to enable him or them to do the work that is necessary; and then the division of means to hold these men fully responsible for the exercise of that power by the people. This of course means that if the people are willing to see power misused, it will be misused. But it also means that if we hold, the people are fit for self-government—we will get good government. I do not contend that my theory will automatically bring good government. I do contend that it will enable us to get as good government as we deserve and that the other way will not.

SOURCE: From Theodore Roosevelt, *An Autobiography*, (New York: The MacMillan Company, 1913).

Origins of the Progressive Movement

Leaders like Roosevelt and Wilson campaigned for office on a new set of ideas and values. New ideas become important in politics only if there are stresses within the old political order. Unless there are dissatisfied people and groups, new ideas are not likely to influence the political system. In the early part of the twentieth century, many strains in the political and economic order were present. We will look at some of these.

Where were the potential sources of support for a new movement? Firstly, in any government some people are excluded from power, a limited amount of resources are at the disposal of the leadership group. Thus all supporters do not receive the rewards they feel they are entitled to. Machines were always unstable; some people and groups were always excluded from power. Frequently those out of power became supporters of a new boss and formed a coalition with various ward leaders. However, some groups rarely were able to gain influence. Such groups were potential sources of support for those who wanted to overthrow the boss system.

Secondly, descendents of the landed elites who had controlled cities before the age of industrialization, were excluded from the machine and appalled by what they saw. The big city bosses had little in common with the traditional elite who had independent sources of wealth and the values associated with the traditional privileged elite. Though increasingly becoming a minority, as immigration increased, the descendents of those with wealth in the early years of the country saw themselves as representatives of true American values. Members of the middle class, particularly professional and clergy, were another source of opposition because they, too, felt excluded from new sources of power and wealth. Hofstadter states their concerns most clearly:

> The newly rich, the grandiosely or corruptly rich, the masters of the great corporations were bypassing men of the Mugwump type—the old gentry, the merchants of long standing, the small manufacturers, the established professional men, the civic leaders of an earlier era. In scores of cities and hundreds of towns, particularly in the East, but also in the nation at large, the old family, college educated class that had deep ancestoral roots in local communities and often owned family businesses that had traditions of political leadership, belonged to the patriotic societies and the best clubs, staffed the governing board of philanthropic and cultural institutions and led the movement for civic betterment, were being overshadowed and edged aside in the making of basic political and economic decisions. In their personal careers as in their community activities, they found themselves checked, hampered and over-ridden by the agents of the new corporations, the corruptors of legislatures, the buyers of franchises, the allies of the political bosses. (1955: 137)

Lastly, some business leaders and citizens were critical of the ability of the machine to provide public services effectively. The machine encouraged narrow favors to ward oriented concerns. It was less skilled in developing services that were designed for the general benefit of the community. These included efficient transportation and water systems, linkages to national markets, and modern health systems. As the city matured, more interests became concerned with these more general problems and thus were critical of the urban machine.

The Progressive movement united these different groups and interests. It is hard to define because it encompasses people as different as Roosevelt and Wilson, and a variety of political movements that often seem contradictory in their philosophy. The movement consisted of several related ideas discussed over the next several pages. Crusading journalists and authors referred to today as the "muckrakers" provided the important link between these ideas and the average middle-class person. Newspapers and magazines increased significantly in circulation during the late 1800s. Writers such as Jack London, Upton Sinclair, and Lincoln Steffens investigated the ills of society and wrote graphic articles and books that became immensely popular. Innovations in paper production and printing reduced the cost of printed material and citizens, looking for a link to the changing society, became avid readers (Hofstadter 1955: 187). All this allowed the ideas of the Progressive movement to be transmitted quickly to an audience eager to grapple with the problems of a rapidly changing society.

We will examine the progressive approach to politics as it was used to change local governments. Four central ideas influenced the change in government. First was a philosophy of *pragmatic optimism* of man, generally and particularly the ability of man to alter his environment. A second influence was *scientific management,* a movement within the field of business that developed techniques of efficient organization. Thirdly, progressive proponents stressed common values among the public rather than specific ethnic or religious attachments. We refer to this as the search for the *public interest* rather than private interests. Lastly, progressive ideas advocated a *government of elites* rather than the masses. It favored government controlled by those of better education and with private sector accomplishments.

Pragmatic Optimism

Many of the best minds of the nineteenth century opposed government involvement in the social and economic problems of the city. Society worked best, they felt, if people competed with one another for jobs, income, and positions in society. Government actions to promote various social ends disturbed the natural competitive systems that would ultimately lead to a better society. In other words, the evils that appeared in cities were useful to society because they permitted the more fit members to advance through competition among people and groups. For this, they tolerated the squalor of the city and the corruption of the big city bosses.

This point of view received intellectual support through an extension of the writings of the much revered scientist Charles Darwin who argued that competition among species led to adaptations to their environment, and ultimately to more advanced forms of life. *Social Darwinists,* as these authors were called, felt that competition among men led to the survival of the fittest. Government assistance to help the less fortunate or control questionable practices of public officials was opposed because it disturbed the natural order of competition.

Even millionaires, proponents argued, should not be restricted because their wealth was a consequence of competition and it encouraged others to compete. William Grant Sumner, considered the leading social Darwinist thinker in the late nineteenth century, defended wealth accumulation. He argued that millionaires be regarded as the naturally selected agents of society for certain work. "They get high wages and live in luxury, but the bargain is a good one for society. There is the intensest (sic.) competition for their place and occupation. This assures us that all who are competent for this function will be employed, so that the costs will be reduced to the lowest terms" (Hofstadter 1955: 58).

Progressive thinkers, on the other hand, held to a belief in the ability of man to attack the problems of the day by changing the rules. They believed that structures of government, new laws, and government controls of undesirable practices could improve society. Government, they felt, could have a positive impact on the economy and social life; the job of government was to improve society through its actions. Though progressive thinkers generally held negative views about the skills and values of the average person, they shared with Jefferson an optimism about man and his ability to remake society through knowledge, analysis, and careful thought. Thus, they were opponents of social Darwinism; arguing that laws and good people could improve society.

Progressives proposed child labor laws and public health regulations, for example, as ways to improve society by regulating the economy. They advocated changes in local government to rid society of the perceived evils of the urban

The Fresno, California, City Hall conveys an image of modern technology and a sense of openness often lacking in older public buildings. Designed by noted architect Arthur Erickson and completed in 1987, it anchors a 12 block mall and civic plaza including a larger courthouse, library and state and federal buildings. According to the architect, it is intended as a civil and elegant monument for a progressive city, acting both as needed government office space and a forum for public events.

© Robert Holmes/Corbis

machine and increase the efficiency of service delivery. Government actions, they believed, could improve the economy and lead to a more just society.

Typical of the pragmatic spirit was Richard S. Childs, a businessman and entrepreneur who is credited with the creation of the council-manager form of government, which was the most successful of the many changes proposed for restructuring local governments. To Childs, man used his knowledge and research to change society the way an architect approaches his craft:

> In the past we have approached the people as a pagan approached the waterfall—to worship and peer around for nymphs. We must today approach the people as the mill builder approaches the waterfall—open-eyed, unafraid, expecting no miracle. Measuring its capacity, making allowance for its variations and irreverently guaging its limitations in order that our mill shall not exceed them.
>
> In considering the people thus we need not become cynics. A cat may look at a queen and a student of the American political panorama may apply a steel tape to the people and develop a discriminating admiration. (1952: 4–5)

To Childs, the right laws, the proper structure of government, and the use of science and technology could improve society in the interests of everybody.

The Philadelphia City Hall built in 1875 is the largest municipal building in the United States today, larger in fact than the U.S. Capital. Its many columns and ornate statures convey a sense of grandeur un-matched by other civic buildings. At 510 feet high, the largest and tallest masonry building in the world, it dominates the city's downtown.

© Michael Cerone/Superstock

Changes in rules and regulations would lead to changes in people's behavior, and these, in turn, would improve society.

Scientific Management

Proponents of scientific management argued that the analytical study of management practices could produce techniques that would significantly improve society. The pragmatic perspective led them to study organizations, searching for better methods. Fredrick Taylor, a business man, analyzed the work of assembly line employees and deduced procedures that, if followed, improved the production system. He measured the details of the workplace, where the worker held a shovel, and how many steps were required to lift and carry materials. From these studies, the most efficient techniques were deduced. The goals were to maximize effort and improve the output of the organization.

If the way in which an individual works could be analyzed to improve production, couldn't one use these ideas to produce better management? Organization theorists expanded on Taylor's ideas by examining the lines of authority, budgeting techniques, and ways of evaluating personnel. They proposed that a scientifically constructed organization could produce the best form of management. Certain common principles for constructing an organization could be learned and applied to all work groups. James D. Mooney, an industrialist closely associated with the movement, stated this perspective most succinctly:

The vast present day units of industrial organization are products of one creating factor, namely the technology of mass production and this technology, born of the industrial revolution, has been almost exclusively an evolution of the last century. In contrast, other major forms of human organization—the state, the church, the army—are as old as human history itself. Yet if we examine the structure of these forms of organization, we shall find that, however diverse their purposes, the underlying principles of organization are ever the same.

The point here is that a principle if it is to be truly such, must of necessity be universal in its own sphere and such it is with the principles of organization. A principle if it is truly such is a universal and a universal cannot be borrowed. It simply has a way of applying itself and this is ever true by whatever name we may call it. If we can but recognize a principle when we see it, it is a simple matter to identify and coordinate what, for present purposes . . . I have called principles of industrial organization. (1937: 92)

Applied to government, these ideas supplied hope that public organizations could be made to operate efficiently and effectively if knowledgeable people applied principles of good organization practice. Techniques of worker efficiency and organization developed elsewhere could be applied directly to public organizations, and problems could be solved through analysis and evaluation. Wilson, in a famous essay titled "The Study of Public Administration," expanded on this perspective arguing that, under proper supervision, techniques from societies very different than ours could be borrowed.

When we study administrative systems in France and Germany, knowing that we are in search of political principles, we need not care a peppercorn for the constitutional or political reasons why Frenchmen or Germans give for their practices when explaining them to us. If I see a murderous fellow sharpening a knife cleverly, I can borrow his way of sharpening the knife without borrowing his probable intentions to commit murder with it. We can thus scrutinize the anatomy of foreign governments without fear of getting any of our diseases into our veins; dissect alien systems without apprehension of blood poisoning. (1887, in Shafritz and Hyde 1997: 25)

Wilson looked at public administration practices in Europe and liked what he saw. French and German governments seemed more innovative and efficient than ours. Applying the perspective of scientific management, he proposed that the management principles used elsewhere could be readily applied in the United States.

Scientific management is an application of the pragmatic spirit. If man could improve society by changing the operations of government, scientific management provided techniques to analyze society and deduce principles of preferred action. Employees recruited for their skills and trained in the techniques of management could create a more effective public service.

The Public Interest

The progressives saw difficulties with the goals and incentives of participants in the boss system. Policy in the machine was the sum of numerous private interests; there was little concern for the interests of the city as a whole. A well-run city, however, required centrally directed projects and policies. Large public works projects, water and sewer systems, and coordinated highways, would benefit the entire community. These projects were in the public interest because they improved the city without considering specific benefits to individual citizens.

Ward-oriented politicians were more concerned with winning votes and finding jobs for their supporters. Progressives referred to this practice as pursuing the "private interest." A system run on ward-oriented benefits alone would fail to deal effectively with the aggregate concerns of the city. To reformers, then, the whole was different than the sum of the parts. Some policies could not be handled well by those whose main goal was the interests of a specific community or ethnic or racial group.

Some reformers argued that ward-based politicians, by demanding group-based services and rewards, prevented an objective and impartial policy process. By demanding a "share of the pie," ward politicians turned decisions that could be objectively determined into partisan debate. Progressives wanted elected officials who were not bound by a system of short-term rewards. The right kind of structure could encourage officials who pursued the public interest. Representatives who could act in the public interest were capable of analytically deciding policies that, in the past, had been partisanly determined. "There is no Republican or Democratic way to pave streets," reformers frequently said.

Three political scientists, Stone, Price, and Stone articulate this perspective as they reflect upon differences they saw between the machine government and the newer, reformed cities. They reached these conclusions after examining some of the early reform governments in the 1930s:

> The idea that various groups ought to have representation on the council to look after their interests overlooks what is usually the most important issue of municipal politics. In many cities, the great issue and the greatest conflict of interest was between those who supported a system of partisan patronage and those who demanded impartial administration. The interests of any social or economic group may often be more greatly affected by the quality of administration of non-controversial municipal policies than by the decision—one way or another—of the controversial issues. The competition of municipal political faction did little in those cities to bring democratic control of policies. On the other hand, it did a great deal to destroy the prestige of local government and to subordinate its fundamental purpose of community service to factional interests. (1940: 241–2)

To a large extent, the difference between pubic interest and private interest was a reflection on two different value systems represented by the older Anglo-Saxon citizens and the newer immigrant groups. Hofstadter states that the

Yankee-Protestant political tradition ". . . assumed and demanded the constant disinterested activity of citizens in public affairs, argued that political life ought to be run in accordance with general principles and abstract laws apart from and superior to personal needs, and expressed a common feeling that government should be in good part an effort to moralize the lives of individuals while economic life should be intimately related to the stimulation and development of individual character." The immigrant system, he argued, "took for granted that the political life of the individual would arise out of family needs. Interpreted political and civic relations chiefly in terms of personal obligations, and placed strong personal loyalty above the allegiance to abstract codes of laws and morals" (1955: 9). Progressives proposed changes in the political organization of cities, hoping that those with "Yankee-Protestant values" would supplant immigrant-based politicians.

A Government of Elites

Many progressives argued that the government of cities would improve only if the right kind of people were running it. The "right people" were generally those who shared the Yankee-Anglo value system and understood modern science and technology. Cities, to some, were not really governments; they were corporations created to produce public services. They needed oversight by those who understood the business, not necessarily the average person.

Andrew D. White, the first president of Cornell University, represents this perspective. He argued that voting for some local positions should be restricted to those who owned property because only they had a real stake in the community. He maintained that the city, unlike other levels of government, was really a corporation.

> The work of a city being the creation and control of city property, it should logically be managed as a piece of property by those who have created it, have title to it, or a real substantial part of it, and who can therefore feel strongly their duty to it. Under our theory, that a city is a political body, a crowd of illiterate peasants, freshly raked in from Irish bogs or Bohemian mines or Italian robber nests, may exercise virtual control. How such men govern cities, we know too well; as a rule they are not alive even to their own most direct interests. (1890: 272)

He saw German cities where members of the upper class were appointed to policy-making positions in cities and hoped that our cities could someday be so well governed.

Reform governments gave the electorate fewer choices and frequently eliminated the rewards that encouraged many to seek public office. While principles of efficiency and realization of the public interest influenced their thinking, the result often was control of government by those of wealth. The aim was to emulate the business corporation. City councils were meant to represent the better educated, well-informed sector of society.

CHANGING STRUCTURES
OF GOVERNMENT

Progressives who were concerned about local governments wanted to alter government structures, the way in which council persons were elected, and the powers of elected and appointed officials. These changes required new state laws that encouraged changes in the organization of local governments. Thus initially, much progressive concern was focused at the state level.

Cities legally have always been controlled by state law, but the oversight of state legislation and judicial rulings increased in the late 1800s as judges became leery of the actions of city governments (Buckwalter 1982: 399–406). In 1872, Judge John Dillon proposed what continues to be the leading interpretation of the powers of cities and the state. Dillon states:

> It is a general and undisputed proposition of law that a municipal corporation possess and can exercise the following powers and no others; First those granted in express words; second those necessarily or fairly interpreted in or incidental to the powers expressly granted and third, those essential to the accomplishment of declared objectives and purposes of the corporation; not simply convenient, but indispensable. (Dillon 1872, in Frug 1980: 53–4)

Thus, following Dillon's rule, cities are limited by the power of the states. State laws can alter rulings of city councils and mayors. Cities must conform to state rulings, and they have weak standing in court if they choose to challenge state law.

Dillon's rule reflects the thinking of the Progressive movement. Cities, Dillon argued, were not managed by those "best fitted by their intelligence, business experience, capacity and moral character." Their management was often "both unwise and extravagant" (Dillon 1872, in Frug 1980: 56–7). His solution was judicial supervision of city actions, a principle that remains in most states today. State judges, then, asserted authority over cities to correct the evils of the machine and encourage progressive governments.

> Judges viewed themselves as guardians of the "better" values in American society against what they perceived as the sins of the city. Just as evangelical reformers raised the specter of homeless boys adrift in the city without the moorings of Protestant Faith and discipline, so American judges viewed the wastefulness and heedlessness of municipal action as a symptom of a moral breakdown of government. Both urban reformers and judicial activists saw the city as a challenge to republican values. For the reformers, institutions like the Sunday School and the YMCA, which recreated discipline and order of the rural family and of small-town America, were all that kept the urban young from a dissolute and degrading existence. For judges, judicial intervention was all that restrained corrupt city governments that had lost all sense of republican virtue. (Hartog 1983: 222)

Thus, intervention into the actions of cities was needed to prevent city officials from acting contrary to the moral values represented by the judicial profession.

Cities, however, were often given some degree of independence from state law through the granting of *home rule* by the states. Home rule gives cities the power to initiate actions within the boundaries described by state law, and it often grants them an area of autonomy from state control. Once granted home rule by the state, the city was permitted to develop a charter—a legal document that spells out the rules and regulations of the structure of government. The drafting of new city charters became a major vehicle for progressive reform in the twentieth century. It was supported by judges because reform charters were seen as a way of limiting the power of urban machines and expanding the influence of those with the "right" values.

Progressives believed that serious changes in government action were a result of changes in the city charter. City charters describe the make up of the governing bodies, the powers of various office holders, the drawing of election districts, and the powers of the various elected bodies. Charters are granted by state legislatures or they are options permitted by home rule legislation. Commonly, states permit cities to adopt home rule statutes that permit then to enact laws of their own that do not conflict with state statutes.

Since the progressives placed great faith in structural changes, many of their concerns dealt with how people were elected and appointed in cities. Charter provisions incorporated many of their important concerns. New charters could construct city councils and mayors with different powers, alter the size and composition of an election district, define the relationship between elected and appointed official, and determine how appointed officials were selected. Thus, most of the progressive platform could be realized through changes in the city charter.

In the machine-run cities, existing charters created city councils that were large in number and often with two legislative houses, mirroring the U.S. Constitution. City councils were given most of the legislative powers and had great influence in appointing administrators. We refer to this structure of government as the *weak mayor system*. As demonstrated in Figure 4.1, power is divided between mayor and council with administrators reporting to each. Candidates were selected by a partisan ballot. Home rule, with oversight from the courts and the state legislature, gave progressives the opportunity to change city charters and implement structures of government compatible with the goals of the movement. The National Municipal League (NML), an organization of progressive interests formed in 1894 from progressive organizations in several cities, developed a national program to change city charters (Stewart 1950: 28). The NML became an influential organization of public officials and academics aligned with the Progressive movement. They proposed changes in city charters and assisted reform groups in securing their adoption. Their endorsement of a new form of government had a pronounced effect on changes in charters throughout the country.

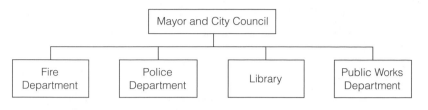

FIGURE 4.1 Weak Mayor Government

In the early years of the NML, different kinds of structural changes were proposed. The *strong mayor government* was the first new structure endorsed by the NML in 1894. The *commission government* (1911) and the *council-manager government* (1916) followed. All three of these forms remain in today's cities, but the success of the various structures was influenced by the NML endorsement and activities.

The Strong Mayor Form of Government

The strength of the council in most machine-run cities forced the mayor to depend on bargains with ward leaders to run the city. Mayors had to get council approval for most important decisions. Since the council was selected partisanly in ethnically based wards, policy required that mayors provide benefits to particular ward-based interests. Opponents of the bosses argued that this structure encouraged corruption and prevented cities from working toward the *public interest*. Thus, the first reform proposal was a strong mayor form of government. Strong mayor charters centralized the administrative authority of government in the office of the mayor and gave the mayor the authority to hire department heads and develop the city budget. The council's duties were restricted to general oversight of the administration, confirming appointments, approving the budget, and setting general policy. Mayors also had the right to veto council actions. Similar to other levels of government, vetoes could be overridden by the council. A civil service system was a frequent addition to mayor-council governments. The strong mayor system was designed to more clearly tie public authority to citywide concerns and give the mayor greater authority to implement policy.

Figure 4.2 diagrams the typical strong mayor government. It differs from the weak mayor system by placing city departments under the direct control of the mayor and it limits the number of elected officials. A frequent addition to the strong mayor system was a city council smaller in size, fewer elected administrators, and a decrease in the pay of city council members. In this system, it is assumed that the mayor is chief administrator as well as a legislator. He is expected to supply central direction to the administrative departments.

The difference between strong and weak mayoral systems is one of extent. Pure types of either government do not exist, and there are many variations that fall in between these two models of organization. When charters of

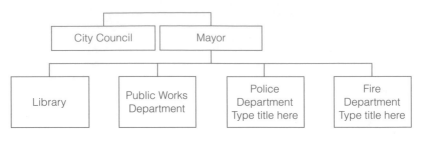

FIGURE 4.2 Strong Mayor Government

mayor–council cities are revised, the major issues generally revolve around how much power to allot the mayor or the council. The recent experience of charter revision in Los Angeles dramatizes the kinds of political conflict that frequently revolve around charter reform in large cities. The charter in place prior to the revision was an example of a weak mayor charter. Power was divided between the mayor, the city council, and several appointed commissions with direct control over many major city departments. Historically, mayors had complained of the difficulties of carrying out policy in such a dispersed system, yet city council members, city administrators, and many important interest groups were very comfortable with the existing system. Thus, when the mayor proposed a charter commission, the city council followed with one of its own. Each proposed a charter that maximized their influence. The two commissions finally formed a common committee and proposed a compromise charter that was ultimately approved by the two commissions and the voters in June of 1999. The approved charter changed the authority from one where the mayor had few powers to one where he or she can now appoint department heads and exercise some direct administrative authority over departments. The charter would best be described as a compromise between a strong mayor and weak mayor system.

The Commission Form of Government

A devastating hurricane nearly destroyed Galveston Texas in 1900. Businessmen in the city who had lost confidence in the city government used the crisis to convince state legislators to radically change the form of government. Galveston's new charter, known as the commission form of government, was credited with returning the city to solvency. Interest in commission government rapidly spread, initially to the larger cities in Texas, and then throughout the country. By 1922, nearly 500 cities had adopted the plan (Rice 1977: 53). Included were many large and medium-sized cities: Dallas, Houston, Fort Worth, and El Paso, Texas; Des Moines, Iowa; Salt Lake City, Utah; Columbia, South Carolina; and Glendale, Riverside, San Diego, and Oakland, California were among the early adopters of the commission plan (Rice 1977: 114–25). At the height of its use, the commission plan was found in all parts of the country and

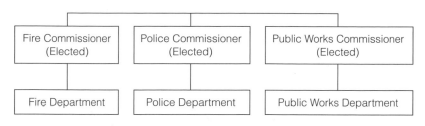

FIGURE 4.3 Commission Government

in cities of all sizes with the exception of the very large central cities of the east and midwest.

The commission form of government centralized authority in a small number of elected department heads who served both as the administrative heads of their organizations and as the city council. Thus, a police chief, public works chief, and parks and recreation chief were elected and functioned both as the head of their department and as the city council (see Figure 4.3). The council was non-partisan and elected at large.

In spite of its apparent success, reformers were often critical of the commission plan. Critics argued that the absence of control by a council representing general city interests led to difficulties in developing policies in keeping with the public interest (Knocke 1982: 1315). They were also concerned about the professional direction that was provided by elected department heads. Early commission winners rarely seemed to be those who understood the professional and technical details of the bureaucracies they were elected to oversee (Rice 1977).

The Council-Manager Government

The council-manager plan (Figure 4.4) appeared first in Staughton, Virginia, in 1908, and praise for the plan from leading progressives and business interests came almost immediately. Influential members of the NML preferred it to the commission form, in spite of the latter's apparent success, and recommended it as the preferred form of city government in the 1916 model charter (Stewart 1950: 75). Most saw it as a perfection of the progressive ideal and a necessary transition to a better form of government. As explained in an editorial in the *National Municipal Review*, the journal of the NML, "Historically the commission plan proved to be a transition device between the over-complicated check and balance system of the nineteenth century and the modern simple council-manager plan" (Rice 1977: 100).

Numerous adoptions of the council-manager plan followed in a brief time period. In less than 50 years, it became the most common form of government in the United States. While more popular in newer cities, suburbs, and in the south and west, the plan's appeal spanned the country and today includes cities

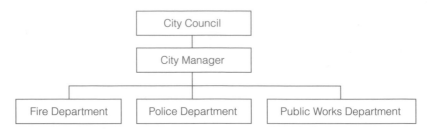

FIGURE 4.4 Council-Manager Government

of all sizes throughout the country. Commission governments declined significantly, most adopting the council-manager charter, and when new cities were created, they were likely to adopt the council-manager structure. Many mayor-council cities also changed their charters to the council-manager plan. Few cities with reform structures changed to mayor–council systems.

What was this revolutionary form of government? Richard S. Childs was one of the founders of the council-manager plan and became its chief advocate over a 50-year period. Childs described the features of the plan as follows:

> All of the powers of the city are vested in a single small board of elected representatives, usually called the council with five or seven members.
>
> The council hires from anywhere in the country a City Manager who holds office at the council's pleasure. The council can replace him at any time for any reason.
>
> The city manager serves full time, appoints and supervises the heads of all operating departments, prepares and submits the annual budget, attends council meetings without a vote and brings in much of the business. Like a superintendent of schools under the elective school board! (sic.)
>
> There is no mayor in the old sense as chief administrator. The council selects its chairman from its own membership. The chairman retains his vote but has no veto or other powers and is commonly called "mayor."
>
> Elections of Council are non-partisan and preferably at large rather than by wards so that every voter has the right to vote for all of the governing board.
>
> There are no elective officers since separate election of a treasurer, attorney, city clerk etc. . . . would impair the discipline and teamwork of the administration by manager. (1952: 22)

How does Child's proposal reflect progressive principles? The emphasis on changes in structure leading to changes in government operation and policy links it directly to *pragmatic optimism*. A new city charter reflecting the council-manager plan was expected to bring forth significant changes in all aspects of government. The *public interest* was realized through at-large elections and a small city council. By eliminating wards and parties, city council members were expected to be concerned only with the broader goals of the city as a whole.

The mayor in a council-manager government was expected to be a member of the council and usually selected by a vote of council members rather than the public. He or she was meant to be first among equals and have no more power and influence than other council members. *Scientific management* guided the council-manager plan by vesting authority in the city manager who was a municipal expert recruited for his knowledge and management skills. Managers were expected to have no political ties to the community and frequently worked in another city prior to their appointment as manager. The reform was meant to be a *government of elites.* The selection of council and manager was designed to attract people with certain kinds of knowledge and values. The manager was expected to be a trained professional, while the council position was attractive only to those with the time and interest to accept a position that was expected to be part-time and poorly paid. Proponents, like Childs, had enlightened businessmen in mind.

All of this shows that the council-manager form was a close approximation of the progressive ideal. How well have these governments worked? Does the practice of progressive government approach the ideal? Next, we will examine what is known about the practice of government in council-manager cities. In the process, we should gain insights into the practice of government in general. *Today most Americans are governed by a progressive government.* Even those cities that retain the weak mayor form of government subscribe to most of the progressive platform. Most positions today are awarded through civil service procedures, contracts are usually awarded by competitive bidding rather than patronage, and changes in government management generally add more progressive features to the existing system. Thus, an understanding of the practice of council-manager government reflects the overall changes in public management.

REFORM GOVERNMENTS: HAVE THEY
MADE A DIFFERENCE?

The numerous adoptions of reform governments provide analysts with years of experience in the operation of the application of progressive principles. How well have these principles really worked? Do we have better government as a consequence of the progressive reforms? What kinds of interests are served when a city changes from one structure to another? Social scientists comparisons of various characteristics of reformed and unreformed cities provide a body of knowledge that tells us much about the extent to which progressive reforms have met their objectives.

The literature examines these questions:

- Whom does the council represent? When council members are elected at-large and on a non-partisan ballot, do they represent the division of the population as well as in non-reformed cities? Council members in reformed cities are supposed to represent the public interest rather than narrower, private concerns. Is that really the case?

- Is policy and administration clearly divided between the council and the city manager in council-manager cities? Do council members limit their activities to the making of policy? Do city managers restrict their activities to "administration?"

- Does the structure of government influence public policy? Do reform governments operate more efficiently than mayor-council systems? Do spending patterns favor the public interest rather than private interests in reform governments?

Partisan debate has focused on these questions. Critics of the council-manager plan argue that the structure of the council and the social backgrounds of city managers favor the upper class. Proponents, on the other hand, see it as the most democratic of governments. Fortunately, we do have a body of social science research that attempts to collect unbiased data that lends itself to testing how the council-manager plan has operated in practice. This literature is summarized in the following paragraphs to permit us to reflect on the accomplishments and the problems of the application of the progressive ideal. It does not answer all of the questions, and it, too, is the subject of criticism, but it does bring a degree of objectivity into the debate.

ANALYZING CITY GOVERNMENT

The purpose of social science analysis is to look at problems in an objective and detached way. The concerns raised about the operation of the council-manager plan lend themselves to objective study. Many council-manager governments are present, and data about their characteristics is relatively easy to collect. In this section, we will look at several studies that have examined groups of cities to determine the answers to the questions listed in the previous section.

Two different techniques are employed to examine the impact of organizational structure on city outcomes. Some scholars collect information from a sample of cities throughout the country. This permits them to examine the relationship between city charters and various environmental or political factors. The survey provides a snapshot of city conditions from which the reason for changes that appear can be inferred. If we know the structure of government (mayor-council, commission, council-manager) and the ethnicity of the city council, we can see if different ethnic patterns are present in different kinds of cities. Statistical measures can tell us if the patterns we see are essentially random, or if they are so different that they are unlikely to occur by chance. If the patterns are unlikely to occur randomly, we can infer that they may be related to the governmental structure. Examples of this method are the studies of Karnig and Welch (1980), Welch and Bledsoe (1988), and MacManus (1978).

Other studies look at a smaller group of cities over time and examine the changes that take place before and after some important occurrence. Some of the studies discussed next examine changes in the city following a change in the charter (for example to council-manager form from mayor-council form).

By examining these cities over time, the impact of charter changes can be isolated. After the charter changed, for instance, analysts can see if the ethnic complexion of the council changed. The participants can be asked if the change in the charter affected their decision to run for the council. Examples of this approach are Heilig and Mundt (1984), Polinard et al (1994), and Saltzstein (1974).

The second method permits the analyst to examine the changes that occur in more detail. The disadvantage is that this is difficult to do with a large number of cities. Thus, it provides more depth of study, but a more narrow group from which to study.

We will look at comparisons of reformed and unreformed governments through both of these methods to gain an understanding of the success of the progressive ideal in American governments.

REPRESENTATION
AND REFORM GOVERNMENTS

Machine governments tied racial, ethnic, and neighborhood groups into the running of city government. Critics of machines argued that the result was inefficiency and a concern for the particular interests of groups rather than the public interest. Reform governments represent the public differently than mayor-council cities. Electing a small number of council members at-large and paying them as part-time employees should attract a different kind of council member or mayor. Has this really been the case? We will look at the results of empirical research that has examined these issues. All of the works cited are the result of systematic surveys or analyses of a large group of cities.

Four questions are examined in the literature:

1. Do reform councils favor the interests of those in the upper or middle classes at the expense of the lower class? Some argue that the plan was founded in part to further the interests of the upper class. Has that, in fact, been the case?

2. Are members of minority groups represented as well in reformed cities as they are in unreformed cities? The council-manager plan was designed to represent the public interest rather than localized private interests. In practice, has this meant that racial and ethnic minorities are not represented as well?

3. Do patterns of women's representation on city councils and mayoral positions differ in different types of governments?

4. Does the structure of government affect the relationship between the public and the elected? Do those elected at-large concentrate their concerns on citywide matters? Do those elected in districts pay more attention to district or neighborhood concerns?

A city council meeting in Santa Monica, California. In most modern city halls like this one, the public sits close to the council and the council members are not on elevated platforms. The goal is a less formal atmosphere and closer collaboration between citizens and elected officials.

© David Young-Wolf/PhotoEdit

Class

Two major studies examined the difference between income and education levels of council members in at-large elections and district elections. Welch and Bledsoe surveyed city council members nationally. Their data indicated that council members in at-large and non-partisan elections tended to be people with higher family incomes and a higher level of education. This finding remained while controlling for factors such as population size, median income, region, and ethnicity (1988: 46). Heilig and Mundt looked closely at 11 large cities that changed their election structure from at-large elections to election in districts. Thus, they were able to examine the impact of changing the election system over time. They found that upper classes were more likely to be represented in at-large systems. However, districts did not necessarily result in an increase in lower status or lower-class council members (1984: 64; see also Bridges 1997: 107).

Race and Ethnicity

Several scholars have looked at whether at-large elections affect the representation of African Americans and Latinos. Most of these studies conclude that African Americans fare much better in district elections. Karnig and Welch (1980), using a sample of cities over 25,000 where at least 10 percent of the population was African American, found that district elections favored African

American candidates (see also Robinson and Dye 1978; Karnig 1979; Engstrom and McDonald 1981; and Davidson and Korbel 1981). Heilig and Mundt (1984), examining cities that changed their charters over time, concluded that African American representation increased when the city changed from at-large to district representation. Welch surveyed cities in 1988, and found that at-large elections continued to under-represent African Americans though the difference in representational equity was less in this survey than in their earlier survey (Welch 1990).

Latinos The literature contains fewer studies of the impact of structures of local government on Latino representation. Polinard and his colleagues (1994) looked at the effect of changes in election districts on several Texas cities over time. They argue that the change to a district form of elections did result in the election of more Mexican Americans. More mixed findings come from surveys by Welch (1990) and MacManus (1978). These authors argue that the concentration of the Latino population may explain the different findings. In cities where Latinos are geographically concentrated, district elections result in more representation. Where they are dispersed, district elections were associated with under representation of Latinos.

Women A small but sophisticated literature has looked at representation of women in city government and examined whether structural characteristics of cities affect representation. Welch and Karnig (1987) found that women were actually favored in at-large elections, though the effect was quite small. Darcy, Welch, and Clark (1987) summarized data from several sources and concluded that structure of government had little impact on the presence of female office holders. Both of these sources suggest that women office holders are more common when salaries of office are less.

The Public Connection

Reform proponents expected city council members to be more concerned with citywide policy and less interested in responding to direct citizen pressure. Analyses of council members attitudes and actions confirm these expected differences in council members elected in districts and at-large. Analysts have surveyed city council members in cities with district elections and those where candidates are elected at-large. Generally, council members elected in districts focus more on neighborhood concerns than city wide matters and spend more time on service to constituents (Welch and Bledsoe 1988). Others report that district elected members receive more support from neighborhood groups than do those elected at-large (Polinard et al 1994: 93) and receive more requests for assistance (Heilig and Mundt 1984: 91).

Critics of reform structures argued that voter interest would decline in reformed cities because the link between the elected and the public is less direct. Ward-based machine systems connected rewards to the voter with the career of the city council member. The restricted power of elected officials, at-large elections, and restrictions on patronage may serve to limit the rewards for electoral support. Supporters of reform argued that voters would remain interested in local government because government would more effectively deal with city problems.

Evidence supports the arguments of the critics of reform government. Comparisons of voting turnout in reformed and unreformed cities nationally reveal that turnout is significantly lower in cities with the council-manager or commission plan (at-large elections or non-partisan elections) (Alford and Lee 1968; see also Bridges 1997: 128–9). Frequently, these differences are quite striking; Lee reports that the median proportion of adults voting was 50 percent in mayor-council cities, 38 percent in commission cities, and a meager 27 percent in council-manager cities (Lee 1963: 83; see also Bridges 1997: 130). This data was collected in the 1960s when reformed cities tended to be middle and upper class suburbs with populations that, in their social characteristics, normally turnout in higher numbers than central cities and cities with lower-class populations.

More recently published analyses find lower turnout in reformed cities. Bridges compared turnout in large reformed cities with those in machine descendent cities from 1947 to 1963, and, again, the differences are dramatic. "In

New York City Mayor Michael Bloomberg working with his staff inside the New York City Hall.

AP/Wide World Photos

Phoenix, Albuquerque and Dallas average turnout was below 20 percent over the whole period (and only 10.8 percent in Dallas), while New York, Chicago and New Haven averaged respectively 43.6 percent, 54.3 percent and 57.3 percent of adult voting in municipal elections" (1997: 132). She also reports that elections are less competitive in reformed cities (34). Heilig and Mundt report lower turnout in cities that switched to at-large elections, but less consistent patterns in those that shifted to district elections (1984: 76–80). Dye (1985: 298) and Karnig and Williams (1985) supply more recent data on turnout in cities with reformed and unreformed characteristics. Both studies find a significantly lower turnout in council–manager than in mayor–council cities.

Bridges also argues that turnout in large reform cities favors the upper class. She analyzed voting results for city council candidates in Austin, Phoenix, and Albuquerque in 1960. In each city, citywide turnout was low but much higher in affluent areas. In big city reform environments, she argues, the cost of mounting citywide campaigns and the requirement of gaining more than half of the votes cast in the whole city proved insurmountable barriers to most challengers, particularly if they were less well-off (1997: 107).

Together, these studies give us a picture of governments that are less directly connected to the public and weakly attached to major racial, ethnic, and neighborhood groups. Compared to the machine, reform governments seem to be less responsive to the needs and demands of the people. The machine system, by connecting the public to government, integrated citizens into the political system. Reform governments loosened this connection. Thus, in our zeal for efficient government with a focus on the general good, we may have loosened the link between the citizen and government.

SEPARATING POLICY
AND ADMINISTRATION:
COUNCIL-MANAGEMENT GOVERNMENT

POLICY-MAKING

Council-manager government is premised on a separation of policy-making and administration. The task of the council is to make policy, and the job of the manager is to carry that policy out efficiently. The progressives argued that good policy resulted when the two major functions were separated. From the early days of the manager plan, however, this seemingly neat division of roles was rarely found in practice. Leonard White, writing in one of the first books to look closely at city managers, pointed out that:

> Many managers by virtue of the wisdom and appropriateness of their recommendations acquire an actual leadership and dominance in the determination of pubic policy. This is accomplished with no desire on their part to outshine the council or to wrest from them their prerogatives, but develops solely on account of the superior ability to plan

and to for-see possessed by the manager. . . . Some managers still think of themselves in the role of the chief figure in the town with which they are connected and insist on the acceptance of their program at the cost of resignation. . . . Observation of managers at work leads the writer to the conviction that many, if not, most managers do in fact possess the initiative in most matters of policy. One manager, who is careful to avoid any appearance of pushing himself forwards, frankly said that 99 percent of council business originated with him or with officials under his control. . . The office of the city manager has become the great center of initiating and proposing (but not deciding) public policies as well as the sole responsible center of administration. (White 1927: 208–10)

Councils, similarly, were less competent and aggressive than originally intended. White adds:

The inability of the council to bring forward and to retain in the councils men of ability and vision and aggressiveness is one of the most serious weaknesses of all forms of municipal government, including the council-manager plan. . . . The contrast between a continuous and an intermittent, not to say casual contact with city affairs also helps explain the tendency toward domination of the manager in all phases of city affairs. The manager is on the job every day, some add every night; the council in smaller cities meets every two weeks for a couple of hours. The mayor is more constantly in attendance but chiefly to sign official papers. . . . The manager comes then to personify city government rather than the council or mayor. (1927: 229)

Early case studies verified the tension White perceived in the council-manager plan. Councils often deferred to the managers on policy questions, and managers willingly moved in to the vacuum and became proponents of policy as well as implementers (see also Stone, Price and Stone 1940). The International City Manager's Association debated the proper role of the manager often and eventually changed their code of ethics to reflect the position of city manager as a community leader as well as administrator.

Tensions, however, were common in cities when the manager assumed a dominant role in community decision making. City councils, of course, are elected to make policy and are ultimately responsible for the results. Surveys of council members and managers indicate that they disagree on the proper role for the city manager in policy-making. Kweder surveyed councils and managers in North Carolina and found that the two groups differed on the role of the manager in policy-making. City council members tended to assume that the manager was not involved in policy, while managers believed that policy-making was an important part of their job (1965). Loveridge surveyed numerous council members and managers in the San Francisco Bay area and found greater conflict between the two bodies than did Kweder. Managers in these cities desired to be active in policy but were often limited by the council. Managers resolved this conflict by restricting innovations to areas of policy where there is less public controversy (1968, in Gertzog ed. 1970: 271–89; see also

Stinchcombe 1969). Consequently, changes in government were limited to areas where the city council had less interest.

Tension is evident in studies of turnover in the city manager position. The tenure of many city managers averages around five years though many managers stay in the same community for many years. While turnover of managers is partially explained by movement to a better position, retirement, or illness, significant numbers of managers leave because of conflicts with the council. Whitaker and DeHoog followed the careers of 133 city managers in Florida, 33 of which left their positions during the time of the study. Conflict with the council accounted for about half of this turnover (1991: in Fredrickson ed. 1995: 143; see also Kammerer et al 1968).

Others see the relationship between council and manager as different from that of the founders, but still one that accommodates the concerns of both

---

POLICY-MAKING IN COUNCIL-MANAGER CITIES

In City A, a small Houston suburb, city council meetings lasted about 15 minutes. The Council endorsed the manager's proposals, handled the legal requirements of the office, and quit for the night. In City B, a suburb of similar size, city council meetings often lasted from 7:00 P.M. until 1:00 A.M. Every item was a matter of intense discussion between council members, city staff, and the public. The manager rarely spoke at the meetings and seemed to be an assistant to the mayor and council. Why such a difference in very similar communities? The reason, I have argued, is a different role for the city manager. This role varies in different communities at different points in time.

Why are there such large differences in the role of the city manager? When councils want major changes in their city, they look to a manager who will take the lead. Some managers are very comfortable assuming a strong leadership position within the city. He or she becomes the source for new ideas; policies follow from his or her initiation. However, at other times, the council wants to set the agenda and make the major decisions. These councils want a manager with a lower profile. When the city changes managers, they are often deciding the kind of leadership

and direction they want from the manager.

I looked closely at the policy-making process in four Texas suburbs and interviewed all managers and council members over a five-year period. The interactions between council and a manager could readily be divided into those with a dominant council and manager who looked to the council for policy guidance and those where the manager dominated policy as well as management. Over time, one pattern followed the other in each community; that is, the manager dominated policy for awhile, then was replaced by a less dominant manager and the council became more active.

This pattern was a result of fundamental tensions within the council-manager plan. Councils often want to make policy but discover that they don't have the time or skills to do it well, so they hire a manager who will take the lead in policy matters. However, eventually the council, either because of electoral turnover or a change in thinking, desires to be more active in policy matters. The manager is usually fired or leaves at that point, and he or she is replaced by a less-dominant manager. A few years later, the cycle repeats itself (Saltzstein 1974: 275–88).

democratic government and efficient administration. Svara has looked closely at both managers and city council members in a variety of cities. His studies confirm that policy and administration cannot be neatly divided between council and manager and he sees tensions in their respective roles. He argues that there is a clearer division of function if one broadens the meaning of both policy and administration. Rather than two categories, he suggests there are really four. Most generally there is the *mission* of the community, a general set of goals that is predominantly in the purview of the council. Secondly, there is the area of *policy* where the mission is related to specific goals and actions. The manager and the council frequently share decisions in this concern. Thirdly, there is the area of *administration* where the terms of policy are converted into specific actions. Here, the manager takes the lead but the council exerts some influence. Finally, there is the area of *management,* in which the manager dominates with little direction or interference from the council. The curved line in Figure 4.5 depicts the influence that each party is likely to have in these

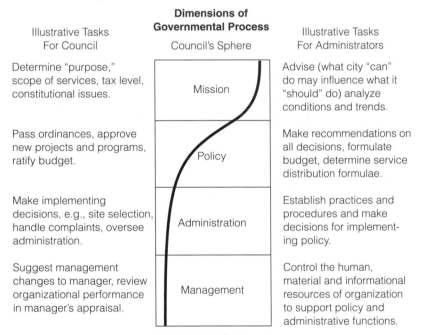

Illustrative Tasks For Council	**Dimensions of Governmental Process** Council's Sphere	Illustrative Tasks For Administrators
Determine "purpose," scope of services, tax level, constitutional issues.	Mission	Advise (what city "can" do may influence what it "should" do) analyze conditions and trends.
Pass ordinances, approve new projects and programs, ratify budget.	Policy	Make recommendations on all decisions, formulate budget, determine service distribution formulae.
Make implementing decisions, e.g., site selection, handle complaints, oversee administration.	Administration	Establish practices and procedures and make decisions for implementing policy.
Suggest management changes to manager, review organizational performance in manager's appraisal.	Management	Control the human, material and informational resources of organization to support policy and administrative functions.

Manager's Sphere

The curved line suggests the division between the Council's and the Manager's spheres of activity, with the Council to the *left* and the manager to the *right* of the line.

The division presented is intended to roughly approximate a "proper" degree of separation and sharing.

FIGURE 4.5   Mission-Management separation with shared responsibility for Policy and Administration.

Form James H. Svara, "Dichotomy and Duality: Reconceptualizing the relationship between Policy and Administration in Council-Manager Cities," in *Ideal and Practice in Council-Manager Government,* 2nd Ed., George H. Frederickson, ed.

four areas. On the left is the council's influence, with the manager's influence on the right. Svara maintains that the shape of the curve will change over time and vary in different communities. The contour of the curve will always be the same. Mission is dominantly the sphere of the council and management is the dominant sphere of the manager. There will be differences of opinion as to the role of each party in the middle two categories (1985).

Everybody who has looked at council-manager government finds that managers exert an important role in the making of policy. How can we reconcile an appointed official as a policymaker with our democratic traditions, particularly when that official is selected for his skills and knowledge in managing rather than policy-making? Some argue that city managers, through their values and commitment to the public service, represent the views of the citizen and act in the better interests of the community. The training and socialization of city managers includes more than running public services efficiently. Managers are committed to finding out what is in the public interest, promoting constitutional government, and acting ethically. Nalbandian argues that:

> Managers as idealists are committed not only to an employment relationship as a vehicle for accountability but also to an understanding of and commitment to a broader array of community values which include but are not focused only on efficiency and the practical justification for responsiveness. Commitment to a broader range of community values than expressed in the governing body provides another source of professional authority for managers *and* for city/county management as a profession. (1991: 167)

As city managers influence decisions, they take into consideration the better interests of the community and the democratic traditions of the nation. They act as surrogate representatives of the public through their professional training and ethical commitment to their profession.

Some suggest that council-manager governments need to expand the role of the council, particularly in larger cities, to incorporate more diverse portions of the public into city decisions. A council with greater expertise and closer ties to the sectors of the community may be better able to provide policy guidance to the manager, permitting the manager to concentrate on policy implementation. In larger cities, it is common for some city council members to be elected in districts, to have a separately elected mayor, for mayor and council to be paid more, and for the council and mayor to have significant staff assistance (Newell and Ammons 1995: 65). All of these changes diverge from the original council-manager plan as envisioned by Childs. The council in these cities is taking on some of the qualities of councils in machine cities. They are a stronger policy-making body and they have personal resources at their disposal. Newell and Ammons surveyed municipal executives and looked closely at differences in the manager's job when the councils incorporated more of the unreformed characteristics. They found that, as the council becomes a more powerful body, the manager concentrates more on management rather than policy-making. Thus, as the council gains strength, the manager concentrates on management and less on policy-making.

Svara examined council manager relations in 31 cities with a population larger than 200,000. He found more active councils but reasonable accommodations between managers and councils.

> Council members are active proponents of policies to solve current problems. City managers are extensively involved in developing broad-range, long-term and city-wide proposals as well as continuing to be very active in proposing middle range policies. There is much closer scrutiny of the details of manager's proposals and policy decisions by the council and policy decision by the council are often provisional and temporary with requirements that the manager check back to report on progress and get additional guidance. In the administrative realm, council members emphasize the ombudsman role . . . whereas the city managers stress making systems work better. In management, the council promotes change in management methods e.g. more privatization and wants a hand in or to be informed in advance about key decisions. Beyond appraising the manager they would want to know more and have more impact on management below the level of the manager. (1999: 51; see also Morgan and Watson 1999: 438–53)

Therefore, in larger cities, formally and informally, structures and practices change to overcome some of the difficulties of progressive governments. City councils formally take on some of the characteristics of machine-era councils; election in wards, some staff support that may be a minor form of patronage, and more active intervention in government. Informally, city managers, mayors, and city councils coordinate their efforts providing the council and mayor with more policy responsibilities, permitting the manager to concentrate more on management.

STRUCTURE, EFFICIENCY, AND PUBLIC POLICY

The proponents of council-manager government assumed that a change in structure would alter what government does. They expected council-manager governments to operate more efficiently than mayor-council governments. They also expected government services would focus on the general good of the community rather than the needs of particular sections or neighborhoods. Critics of the council-manager plan argued that reform governments would serve the interests of the upper classes rather than the general population and would generally be less aggressive in pursuit of new projects and policies. Now, we will look at the results of empirical research that deals with these questions. Are council-manager governments more efficient than mayor-council governments? Do council-manager governments spend public money differently or pursue different public policy initiatives than mayor-council governments?

Does the Structure of Government Affect Efficiency?

Most assume that council-manager governments operate more efficiently than do mayor-council governments. Managers are hired because of their knowledge and experience running city governments. City functions are centralized under the manager's direction, which should mean that efficient use of resources is an important value in council–manager governments.

Systematic evidence of greater efficiency in council–manager governments is absent from research literature. There is much impressionistic and case study evidence of efficient and innovative management in council–manager governments. The book *Reinventing Government,* for example, is filled with examples of innovative and efficient programs implemented by city managers (Osborne and Gaebler 1992). City managers also speak of the importance of efficiency in their daily practice (see Harlow 1981). Much of the literature of the International City Management Association addresses the importance of innovative and efficient practice among city managers (see Newell and Ammons 1995).

REINVENTING GOVERNMENT

Concern for efficiency and responsiveness in local governments, usually the topic of rather esoteric management texts, became the focus of a best-selling book *Reinventing Government How the Entrepreneurial Spirit Is Transforming the Public Sector From Schoolhouse to Statehouse, City Hall to the Pentagon* (Osborne and Gaebler 1992). The authors, David Osborne, an accomplished journalist, and Ted Gaebler, a veteran city manager, discuss in a lively fashion how governments could be recast to more effectively accomplish public goals. Unique to the book is a belief that modern managers could revamp government to connect citizens to government and radically improve organizational efficiency. The book's influence was immediate and widespread. No city manager or public administration student can ignore it.

Central to the authors' thesis is the adoption of private sector management techniques to government. They propose that outputs of government be carefully measured and managers be held accountable for policy outputs. To give managers the tools needed to meet these goals, they argue that many of the rules and regulations that limit managers discretion be discarded. Privatization of many important government programs are seen as a way of accomplishing public goals more efficiently. They propose that neighborhood groups be incorporated into the policy-making and management of government resources through innovations like neighborhood watch programs, community-based policing, and neighborhood school councils.

The authors draw on the accomplishments of many city managers to make their case. The view of the urban executive promoted by the book is that of an entrepreneur who actively promotes public projects using this new battery of techniques and practices with fewer limits on his or her discretion. Elements of the original council-manager plan are evident in the book; the manager and council act to promote the public interest through innovative projects and new techniques. The view is also one of a dominant and powerful city executive who actively coordinates elected officials, neighborhood groups, and the private sector. Therefore, it is a view of urban management that allows for significant innovation from the manager.

The Structure of Government and Public Policy

The effect of reform government on public policies is addressed frequently in the literature using systematic social science techniques. Two general hypotheses are addressed in this literature. Some propose that reform governments are less likely to respond to the demands and needs of various sectors of the population. Leaders in reform governments, they argue, are less closely related to the needs and demands of the public. At-large elections and the lack of a popularly elected executive limits the impact that demands from the public will be translated into public policies. Thus, hypothesized here is a less direct connection between demands from the public and policies adopted by governments.

A second group of studies looks at large-scale innovations in governments and hypothesizes that council-manager governments will be less likely to pursue these because they lack the political strength of a mayor-council system. Mayors in a mayor-council government will be more likely to mobilize support in the community and in the private sector for large redevelopment projects, for instance, because they have stronger ties to community interests and place a higher value on community mobilization than officials in council-manager cities would.

Are Reform Governments Less Responsive
to Community Interests?

Several social scientists have looked at this question by systematically examining spending patterns of a sample of cities and correlating spending with various social and economic characteristics. Then, by controlling for the structure of government, they test to see if the relationship between the nature of the community—its ethnicity, poverty, distribution of wealth, and local government spending—is different in council-manager as opposed to mayor-council cities. It is assumed that a close correlation between community characteristics and spending indicates that the elected decision makers are responding to the interests of the public.

The findings of these studies are ambiguous and offer little consensus on the issue. Lineberry and Fowler began this line of inquiry by examining correlations between city spending and taxing and a vast array of community characteristics. They found that spending and taxing were less closely related to city characteristics in reformed cities (1967: 291).

Lineberry and Fowler's conclusions have drawn support from more recent analyses of national samples of cities. Mladenka found that the correlation between African American representation on the city council and employment of African Americans in the city government was significantly greater in mayor-council cities than in council-manager cities (1989; see also Stein 1986). G. H. Saltzstein found links between female mayors and increases in female employment in mayor-council cities, but not in council-manager cities (1986). Sharp analyzed economic development policies in cities and found that that these efforts and indicators of community distress were more closely related in council-manager cities than in mayor-council cities (1991). Thus, the link between community needs and public policy was more direct in mayor council cities.

Other studies challenge the relationship between structure and public policies. Morgan and Pelissero examined expenditure patterns in 11 cities that had changed their charters from mayor-council to council-manager and compared them with similar cities that had retained the mayor-council system. They found no conclusive evidence of changes in spending patterns in the cities that adopted a council-manager charter (1980). Clark found that political structure was unrelated to urban renewal and general city expenditures (1968; see also Leibert 1974), and G. H. Saltzstein concluded that government structure exerted little influence on the relationship between the presence of black mayors and various indicators of police responsiveness (1989).

Does Structure Affect the City's Ability to Implement Large Projects?

Major redevelopment efforts, the attraction of new industries, and community action programs often require leadership skills and community connections among elected officials. Some argue that mayor-council governments are more successful in these projects because the political leaders are closer to the public and have more time and resources to devote to politics.

Several authors have systematically examined the presence of such projects and expenditures devoted to them in a large number of cities. All conclude that mayor-council cities are more involved in these policies than are council-manager cities. Feiock and Clingermayer (1988) examined the adoption of several different economic development projects in a national sample of cities. They controlled for a wide variety of characteristics and found that the structure of government remained an important predictor of economic development activity. Council-manager governments generally were less involved than were mayor-council governments. O'M Bowman examined economic development activity among a large number of southeastern cities. She found that cities with reform structures generally were less aggressive than were mayor-council cities (1988; see also Kuo 1973, and Aiken and Alford 1970A, 1970B).

RUNNING THE CITY: THE VIEWS OF TWO CITY MANAGERS

Following are two descriptions of the practice of council manager government written by veteran city managers. They reveal much about the practice of council manager government. In the first, Richard G. Simmons demonstrates the importance of efficiency to the management profession. As city manager he was willing to take serious personal risks to improve the operation of a basic city service. In the second, Thomas F. Maxwell also stresses the importance of efficiency and his understanding of techniques of management as he approached the manager's position in University City, Missouri. His feelings about the

(continued)

(continued)

city council tell us a bit about the kind of representative system city managers desired. Do his views suggest to us the conditions under which the council-manager plan works best?

Garbage, Garbage, Who Hauls the Garbage?
Richard G. Simmons

In West Palm Beach, Florida, commercial garbage—from restaurants, stores, hotels, businesses, and office buildings—was collected both by the city and by private collectors. Each had their own customers. This meant that we knew only our customers and that the private collectors knew only theirs. We would drive a truck up to two containers and empty one, and a private collector would drive a truck up to get the other one. And I guessed that many people didn't pay the commercial collection fee to anyone.

We did an evaluation of this system and found that economies could be gained by having one operator collect all the commercial garbage. Of course, the private collectors felt strongly that either the city or an individual should not interfere with free enterprise. I felt equally strong that either the city or an individual should be the sole collector. Either could do it more cheaply than under the present system.

To get around the free-enterprise argument, I proposed to put the commercial collection out to competitive bids and solicit the three largest companies in the nation to bid, along with the local private collectors. One of the local private collectors who

had a piece of the action in our city refused to bid but kept feeding the commission information about problems the major companies were having. All the allegations were unsupported. As a consequence, I implemented my proposal, recommending to the city commission that we accept the lowest bid by a private individual or firm and award the winner a contract for collecting all commercial garbage.

One evening I received a call from the principal of the small private collector, who told me that I would be a ghost in a year if I pursued this recommendation. I reported this to the police department in the event something happened, and they made an investigation of this company. The police chief urged me to be exceedingly careful, because these people had direct Mafia connections. For the next month or so it was a common joke around city hall that the interns would take turns starting my car in the morning.

I am happy to say that nothing came of the threat. The commission decided that the city would not be involved with private contractors, that the city would do all the commercial collection. And my guess proved correct: We found that more than four hundred commercial concerns were paying no garbage-collection fee at all. Not only were we able to improve the efficiency of the operation, but we were also able to eliminate the inequity of having some pay and some not.

Reorganizing A "Before-and-After" Picture
Thomas F. Maxwell

University City had no slums, no organized criminal element, limited services, high property values, and low property taxes. From the city's founding, municipal affairs had been run by part-time mayors and a city council.

A coalition of outstanding community leaders and the League of Women Voters promoted the council-manager plan, which was adopted in a low voter turnout. The plan was not actively opposed except by a local weekly newspaper, which was a one-man operation. The editor was vicious in his opposition to the plan and to me when I arrived as city manager. During my entire three-year tenure, he referred to me as a "Pendergast politician," although he well knew that the administration I worked for in Kansas City was the one that had destroyed the Pendergast machine.

The newly elected city council was composed of top grade people. Four of the seven members, including the mayor, were successful St. Louis lawyers. The council met twice a month, and the council members were paid $10 per meeting. The new charter was a city manager's dream.

When I arrived in University City, the city had no budgetary system, no classification and compensation plan for employees, no central purchasing, no established lines of responsibility (not even an organizational chart!), and no central executive control. Each department head ran his little empire as he saw fit on whatever appropriations he could persuade the council to give him.

There was no civil-service plan. Employee pay rates were disgracefully low and, consequently, municipal services were inferior. Many of the city employees lived in St. Louis because they could not afford to live in University City.

The public works, finance, health, police, and fire departments were sadly neglected. In contrast, there was an excellent park commission. It received all the money it wanted because it was composed of prominent citizens. Also, there was a library commission which operated under the same circumstances.

In three years, without outside consultant help, I established an accounting and budgetary system that won the Municipal Finance Officers Association's Achievement Award. Also, I prepared a complete compensation and classification plan, established a civil-service commission, obtained new zoning and building codes, increased employees' salaries substantially, and reduced taxes. When I left at the end of that time, the city had a sound, well-organized and amply financed government. A move to abandon the council-manager form of government obtained so little support that the dissidents did not carry the question to a vote. The entire council was reelected by a four-to-one margin over a slate that advocated abandoning the council-manager plan.

SOURCE: From Leroy F. Harlow ed. *Servants of All: Professional Management in City Government* (Provo UT: Brigham Young University Press, 1981): 255–6, 264–5

We have summarized much of what we know about the practice of council-manager government. Has it accomplished its goals? Are citizens better off today as a result of the council-manager plan? Our conclusions must be tentative, given the limits of the research process, but several inferences can be drawn. *Most would agree that local government today is more honest and efficient than in the machine era.* City managers are by and large well trained and committed to improving the operation of government. Civil service systems and merit hiring have improved the quality of public employees. Our governments generate higher-quality public services and progressive reforms are, in part, responsible for this. Fair and equal treatment of the citizens by government has certainly improved as progressive reforms have become more common.

However, progressive governments generate less citizen interest and are less likely to represent the diversity of the community in its elected body. Voting turnout is significantly lower in reformed cities, and members of minority groups are less likely to be elected. This may mean that today's governments are less likely to respond to different demands for services. "Better government," then, may be gained at the cost of less connection between the citizen and government. As we will see in Chapter 9, linking citizen to governments has become a major social concern that goes beyond the running of local governments.

PROGRESSIVE GOVERNMENT:
A SUMMARY

This chapter has examined the theory and practice of progressive government, the dominant philosophy of government in the twentieth century. Progressivism was initially a philosophy of governmental reform rooted in three ideas:

- *Pragmatic optimism.* The belief that man could change the rules, regulations, and laws of government through reason and analysis and improve the quality of government.

- *Scientific management.* The belief that principles of management can be scientifically determined and would lead to an improved society through science and analysis.

- *The public interest.* The belief that there are policies that improve the well-being of everybody that are different from those that focus on the desires of particular groups or interests. These policies can be realized through a structure that promotes certain kinds of people to policy-making positions.

A program of action to change the structure of government follows from each of these ideas. The ideas received popular support that led to new forms of government. Progressive ideas radically changed many governments; progressive principles influenced all governments. Analysis of these progressive governments suggests strengths and weaknesses that dominate local government at the end of the twentieth century:

- Local government today is less corrupt and probably more efficient than at the end of the nineteenth century.

- Governments are less closely tied to the public than in the earlier era. Voting turnout has decreased, and representation of different groups and interests in society is less. Representation of interests in elected bodies seems to have less influence on public policy.

As we look ahead to other chapters of the book, these two conclusions point to problems that will be addressed. Can we maintain the virtues of reform government—impartial management, efficient service delivery, and the application of science to public problems—while we address the need to more closely relate the decisions of government to the needs and wishes of the citizens?

REFERENCES

Aiken, Michael, and Robert R. Alford. 1970A. "Community Structure and Innovation: The Case of Public Housing." *American Political Science Review 64* (September): 843–64.

Aiken, Michael, and Robert R. Alford. 1970B. "Community Structure and innovation: The Case of Urban Renewal." *American Sociological Review 35* (August): 340–62.

Alford, Robert P., and Eugene C. Lee. 1968. "Voting Turnout in American Cities." *American Political Science Review.* 62: 796–813.

Ammons, David N., and Charldean Newell. 1989. *City Executives: Leadership Roles, Work Characteristics, and Time Management.* Albany, NY: State University of New York Press.

Bridges, Amy. 1997. *Morning Glories: Municipal Reform in the Southwest.* Princeton, NJ: Princeton University Press.

Buckwalter, Doyle W. 1982. "Dillon's Rule in the 1980's: Who's in Charge of Local Affairs?" *National Civic Review* (September): 399–406.

Childs, Richard S. 1952. *Civic Victories: The Story of an Unfinished Revolution.* New York: Harper.

Clark, Terry N. 1968. "Community Structure, Decision Making, Budget Expenditures and Urban renewal in 51 American Communities." *American Sociological Review 33* (August): 576–93.

Darcy, R., Susan Welch, and Janet Clark. 1987. *Women, Elections and Representation.* New York: Longman Inc.

Davidson, Chandler, and George Korbel. 1981. "At-large elections and Minority-Group Representation; A Reexamination of Historical and Contemporary Evidence." *The Journal of Politics 43,* no. 4 (November): 982–1005.

Dillon, John. 1872. "Dillon's Law." In Frug, Gerald E. 1980. *Local Government Law,* San Francisco: West Publishers Inc., 1980.

Dye, Thomas R. 1985. *Politics in States and Communities.* 5th ed. Englewood Cliffs, NJ: Prentice-Hall Inc.

Engstrom, Richard L., and Michael D. McDonald. 1981. "The Election of Blacks to City Councils: Clarifying the Impact of Electoral Arrangements on the Seats/Population Relationship." *The American Political Science Review 77,* no. 4 (June): 344–54.

Feiock, Richard C., and James Clingermayer. 1988. "Municipal Representation, Executive Power and Economic Development Policy." *Policy Studies Journal 15* (December): 211–30.

Frug, Gerald E. 1980. "The City as a Legal Concept" *Harvard Law Review,* no. 6 (April): 1062–1154.

Gertzog, Irwin N. ed. 1970. *Readings in State and Local Government.* Englewood Cliffs, NJ: Prentice Hall.

Hartog, Herndrik.1983. *Public Property and Private Property: The Corporation on the City of New York in American Law, 1730–1870.* Chapel Hill, NC: The University of North Carolina Press.

Harlow, LeRoy ed. 1981. *Servants of All: Professional Management of City Government.* Salt Lake City: Brigham Young University Press.

Heilig, Peggy, and Robert J. Mundt. 1984. *Your Voice in City Hall: The Politics, Procedures and Policies of District Representation.* Albany, NY: State University of New York Press.

Hofstadter, Richard. 1955. *Social Darwinism in American Thought.* New York: George Braziller Inc.

Kammerer, Gladys M., Charles D. Farris, John DeGrove, and Alfred D. Clubok 1968. *City Managers in Politics: An Analysis of Manager Tenure and Termination.* Jacksonville, FL: The Miller Press.

Karnig, Albert. 1979. "Slack Resources and City Council Representation." *The Journal of Politics 41,* no. 1 (June): 134–46.

Karnig, Albert K., and B. Oliver Williams. 1985. "Municipal Voter Participation: Trends and Correlates." In *Public Policy Across States and Communities,* edited by Dennis R. Judd. Greenwich, CN: JAI Press.

Karnig, Albert. 1981. *Black Representation and Urban Policy.* Chicago: University of Chicago Press.

Karnig, Albert, and Susan Welch. 1980. *Black Representation and Urban Policy.* Chicago: University of Chicago Press.

Knocke, David. 1982. "The Spread of Municipal Reform: Temporal, Spatial and Social Dynamics." *American Sociological Review 87,* no. 6 (May): 1314–39

Kuo, Wen. 1973. "Mayoral Influence in Urban Policy Making." *American Journal of Sociology 79* (November): 620–38.

Kweder, James B. 1965. *The Roes of the Manager, Mayor, and Councilman in Policy Making.* Chapel Hill, NC: Institute of Government, University of Carolina.

Lee, Eugene C. 1963. "City elections: A Statistical Profile" in Orin Nolting and David S. Arnold, eds. *Municipal Yearbook.* Chicago: International City Managers Association.

Leibert, Roland J. 1974. "Municipal Functions. Structure and Expenditures: A Reanalysis of Recent Research." *Social Science Quarterly 54* (March): 117–24.

Lineberry, Robert L., and Edmund P. Fowler. 1967. "Reformism and Public Policy in American Cities." *American Political Science Review 61* (September): 701–16.

Loveridge, Ronald O. 1968 "The City Manager in Legislative Politics." *Polity 1* (Winter): 214–36.

MacManus, Susan S. 1978. "City Council Election Procedures and Minority Representation: Are They Related?" *Social Science Quarterly 59:* 153–61.

Mladenka, Kenneth R. 1989. "Blacks and Hispanics in Urban Politics." *American Political Science Review 83* (March): 167–91.

Morgan, David R., and John P. Pelissero. 1980. "Urban Policy: Does Political Structure Matter?" *American Political Science Review 74* (June): 999–1006.

Morgan, David R., and Sheilah S. Watson. 1999. "Policy Leadership in Council-Manager Cities: Comparing Mayor and Manager." *Public Administration Review 53* (September/October): 438–53.

Mooney, James D. 1937. "The Principles of Organization." In *Papers on the Science of Administration,* edited by Luther Gullick. New York: Institute of Public Administration.

Nalbandian, John. 1991. *Professionalism in Local Government: Transformation in the Roles. Responsibilities, and Values of City Managers.* San Francisco: Jossey Bass Publishers.

Newell, Charldean, James Ammons, and David N. Ammons. 1995. "City Managers Roles in a Changing Environment." In *Ideal and Practice in Council Manager Cities,* edited by H. George Fredrickson. Washington: The International City Management Association.

O'M Bowman, Ann. 1988. "Competition for Economic Development Among Southwestern Cities." *Urban Affairs Quarterly 23* (June): 511–27.

Osborne, David, and Ted Gaebler. 1992. *Reinventing Government: How the Entrepreneurial Spirit is Transforming the Public Sector from School House to Statehouse, City Hall to the Pentagon.* Reading, MA: Addison Wesley.

Polinard. J. L., Robert Wrinkle, Tomas Longoria, and Norman E. Binder. 1994. *Electoral Structure and Urban Policy: The Impact on Mexican America Communities.* Armouk, NY: M. E. Sharpe.

Rice, Bradley E. 1977. *Progressive Cities: The Commission Government Movement in America, 1901–1920.* Austin, TX: University of Texas Press.

Robinson, Theodore, and Thomas R. Dye. 1978. "Reformism and Black Representation in City Councils." *Social Science Quarterly 52* (March): 941–5.

Roosevelt, Theodore. 1913. *An Autobiography.* New York: The Macmillan Company.

Saltzstein, Alan L. 1974. "City Managers and City Councils: Perceptions of the Division of Authority." *Western Political Quarterly 28* (June): 275–88.

Saltzstein, Grace Hall. 1989. "Black Mayors and Police Policies." *The Journal of Politics 51* (August): 525–44.

Saltzstein, Grace Hall. 1986. "Female Mayors and Women in Municipal Jobs." *American Journal of Political Science 30* (February): 140–64.

Sharp, Elaine. 1991. "Institutional Manifestations of Accessibility and Urban Economic Development." *The Western Political Quarterly 44* (March 1991): 129–48.

Stein, Lana. 1986. "Representative Government: Minorities and Municipal Workforce" *Journal of Politics.* 48 (June): 694–713.

Stewart, Frank Mann. 1950. *A Half Century of Municipal Reform: The History of the National Municipal League.* Berkeley, CA: University of California Press.

Stinchcombe. Jean L. 1969. *Reform and Reaction in City Politics in Toledo.* Belmont, CA: Wadsworth Publishing Co.

Stone, Harold A., Don K. Price, and Kathryn H. Stone. 1940. *City Manager Government in the United States.* Chicago: Public Administration Service.

Svara, James H. 1985. "Dichotomy and Duality: Reconceptualizing the Relationship Between Policy and Administration." *Public Administration Review 45* (January/February): 219–35.

Svara, James H. 1999. "The Shifting Boundaries Between Elected Officials and City Managers in Large Council-Manager Cities." *Public Administration Review 59,* no. 1 (January/February): 44–53.

Welch, Susan, and Timothy Bledsoe. 1988. *Urban Reform and Its Consequences.* Chicago: University of Chicago Press.

Welch, Susan, and Albert K. Karnig. 1987. "Correlates of Female Office Holding in City Politics." *The Journal of Politics 4* (May): 478–91.

Welch, Susan. 1990. "The Impact of At-large Elections on the Representation of Blacks and Hispanics." *The Journal of Politics 52* (November): 1049–76.

Whitaker, Gordon P., and Ruth Hoogland DeHoog. "City Managers Under Fire: How Conflict Leads to Turnover." In *Ideal and Practice in Council Manager Cities,* edited by H. George Frederickson. Washington, D.C.: The International City Management Association; 142–56.

White, Andrew D. 1890. "Municipal Affairs are Not Political." In *Urban Government: A Reader in Administration and Politics,* edited by Edward C. Banfield. New York: The Free Press, 1969.

White, Leonard D. 1927. *The City Manager.* New York: Greenwood Press Publishers.

Wilson, Woodrow 1987. "The Study of Administration" in Jay M. Shafritz and Albert C. Hyde, eds. *Classics in Public Administration 1997.* Fort Worth: Harcourt-Brace.

Chapter Five

The Making
and Unmaking
of Federal Urban Policy

Since the 1960s, every administration in Washington at one point in time or another has talked about developing a cohesive national urban policy that responds to critical urban problems. Like the search for the holy grail or the Fountain of Youth, these efforts have borne little fruit. Although the glittering skylines and the new commercial complexes in many cities often make us feel good, and indeed should make us feel good, they hide the fact that almost one-half of all America's poor now live in cities. They also blur the fact that since 1960, cities have become home to increasing numbers of chronically poor, mostly minorities, whose chances to participate in the American dream are marginal at best and impossible at worst. They divert us from the fact that the numbers of homeless now walking the streets searching for shelter are at all-time highs. Finally they mute the fact that for far too many city dwellers, discrimination, crime, violence and drugs have become part of everyday urban life. (Kaplan 1995: 622)

We see the influence of the federal government throughout this book. I mentioned in an earlier chapter the Federal Housing Authority, which financed the suburban explosion of the 1950s, and the interstate highway system that encouraged the dominance of the automobile. We also saw how the war effort during World War II limited the development of cities and forced factories to produce war machinery rather than consumption goods. All of these are programs that have been approved by Congress and the president with rather clear purposes in mind, and they have had a pronounced effect on how our cities have grown and developed. They authorized the spending of federal tax dollars to deal with specific city problems, but some affected society in ways not necessarily intended by the sponsors. The FHA program, for instance, provided much housing, but discriminated against African Americans, and federally funded highways displaced urban neighborhoods, often with out compensation.

Since the middle of the twentieth century, the role of the federal government in urban matters has been extensive, often dominant. Many look to the federal government to overcome the paradox of urban government mentioned in the first chapter. As the problems of urbanization increase and more government programs and funding are required, many think it is the job of the federal government to step in. Perhaps the federal government should supply funding for the increased cost of government attributed to urbanization? The need to coordinate actions of the numerous governments on our metropolitan regions may logically be a federal responsibility since the central government is expected to deal with the overall problems of the society. The federal government potentially has the resources to make a significant difference in urban policy.

However, the role of the federal government in urban concerns has always been controversial. Americans are not at ease with federal government influence in the business of cities. Many feel local governments are designed to deal with the problems of cities. Both Madison and Jefferson questioned an active role for the federal government in domestic concerns.

This chapter will look closely at how the federal government has operated in American cities. We will look at what the influence of the federal government has been and various ways in which it has been organized.

The purpose of the federal government is to develop policies that deal with national problems as defined by Congress and the president. Our cities should benefit from federal policies but many critics, like Marshall Kaplan, a former government official, feel cities aren't well served by Washington. He is troubled by our inability to clearly define a federal urban policy in spite of spending significant sums on various urban-related matters.

We begin the chapter by defining what an urban policy should be. The rest of the chapter looks at the practice of federal policies over time. The way in which Americans divide authority among the levels of government has much to do with the way in which the federal government must operate in cities. Thus, our second task is to discuss the meaning of the federal system and the peculiar features it requires of the three levels of government.

The federal government influences cities through many very different policies. Some, like public housing or funds for mass transit, are defined as primarily urban programs. Others, such as the deduction of mortgage payments from one's income taxes or the placement of military installations, are designed to pursue other goals but their influence on cities may be major. We will look at the variety of federal policies that influence urban areas.

The federal government also uses different techniques to affect urban areas. These range from directly providing services (building roads, for example) to providing funds to local governments for general purposes, to requiring state and local governments to conform to their directives. These techniques will be described and analyzed.

Lastly, the federal government has used different approaches and programs to influence urban areas over time. The interest of the federal government has expanded and contracted throughout our recent history. An understanding of how these different programs have operated is gained through our third task, an understanding of the history of federal urban programs.

As you read this chapter, try to keep the following general concerns and questions in mind:

- What is an urban policy? What should it be? How do actual urban policies differ from what you think an urban policy should be?

- How does the federal government influence what goes on in cities? How effective are these tools?

- How has federal urban policy changed over time to meet new concerns and interests?

- Can federal urban policy effectively overcome the difficulties posed by the paradox of urban governance?

AN URBAN POLICY: WHAT SHOULD IT BE?

All administrations come to Washington wanting to implement a new urban policy. Often, concerns for urban areas are a prominent part of political campaigns. During the last campaign, President Bush talked extensively about the role of faith-based organizations, the use of vouchers in education and housing, and the need to involve local citizens in governmental programs. Certainly this was seen as at least an outline of a strategy to improve life in cities, yet few agree on the components of an urban policy.

Most of us understand what is meant by a foreign policy. It preserves American interests abroad, promotes world peace, and assists our allies in the world community. A defense policy protects the country against foreign aggression. An agriculture policy is created to improve agricultural production and protect the interests of farmers.

An urban policy is harder to define. It emphasizes the common problems of cities and residents in urban areas that can be influenced by government. City residents, however, are a diverse group who want different things from their government. Urban governments provide a wide array of services that are used more by some residents than others. As we have seen, cities bring very different kinds of people together with different concerns and interests. Yet there are a series of common problems that all big cities face and these should be the focus of an urban policy.

Urban policies are government activities that aid all members of an urban community. They may provide particular benefits to some citizens, but the impact of the policies makes the urban area operate more effectively. They improve the life of all. Three common concerns of all city residents should be the focus of an urban policy:

1. Effective urban areas coordinate housing, commerce, and the location of jobs; what noted scholar Anthony Downs refers to as "spatial efficiency" (1995: 132). Cities work best when there is efficient movement of goods and people. All residents benefit if people and goods are connected in less time and with less cost. People are more productive if they can get to and from work, shopping areas, and home quickly. Industries operate more efficiently if goods rapidly move in and out of the places of production. Therefore, policies that encourage coordination benefit all residents. Such policies may include improved transportation systems; land use planning that encourages concentrations of business, commerce, and homes; or measures that make living in most parts of the city safe and attractive.

2. Effective urban areas implement public policies that promote the health and welfare of citizens by controlling the hazards of city life. Policies that curtail air and water pollution, make the streets safe, and efficiently eliminate waste benefit all citizens.

3. Unequal distributions of opportunities and wealth, if they lead to unproductive citizens and disruptive behavior, contribute to the ineffectiveness of the urban area. Thus, policies aimed at providing opportunities for the poor, and expanding their skills, will contribute to the betterment of the urban area.

Urban policies then should coordinate decisions and the use of resources that span city boundaries. They should promote the health and welfare of all city residents by limiting the negative byproducts of city life and they should work to assist the underprivileged to become more productive citizens.

A federal urban policy incorporating these concerns, however, is difficult for Americans to promote. We are uncertain where federal responsibility begins and ends. Should these problems be left to state and local governments and individuals, or does the federal government have a unique role? These concerns are also related, often quite directly, to other policies. Making citizens more productive, for example, involves education policies. Housing and transportation policies are an important component of measures to expand the economy, another area of policy. The closing of military bases is a defense concern, but it often has a very profound impact on certain cities.

A wide range of programs influence urban policy. Some are central to the interests of urban policy-makers, others are related in a secondary way. Central to urban matters are policies dealing with public housing, urban renewal, and industrial development. The Federal Department of Housing and Urban Development (HUD) is responsible for these concerns and has become the focus for urban policies in the federal government. Other policies are also quite important to urban interests. These include transportation, crime control, welfare, and public health. Lastly, there are other policies that significantly impact urban

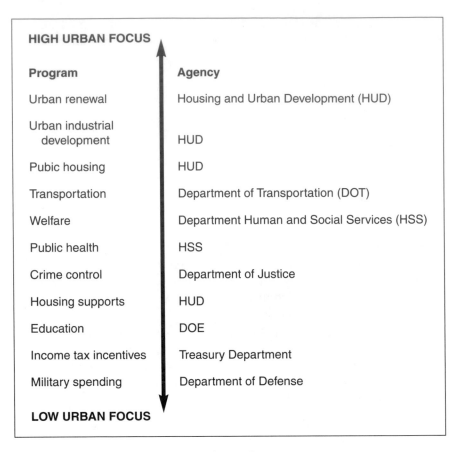

FIGURE 5.1 Federal Urban Programs and Agencies

matters, but urban policy is not the primary focus of the agency. These include education, taxing policy, and military policy. Figure 5.1 arranges various policies according to the degree to which they are urban in nature. The placing of programs on the continuum is somewhat arbitrary. You may wish to decide for yourself the most appropriate place to put your favorite concern. Notice that many different government agencies are involved in this chart. Agencies within the same department of the cabinet are also located in different places.

THE ORGANIZATION OF GOVERNMENT AND URBAN POLICY

When the economy is in trouble, the Federal Reserve Board changes interest rates, and Congress alters spending and taxing policy. Other levels of government play no direct role in these decisions because the Constitution specifically gives this power to the federal government. In urban matters, however, the authority of the federal government is less clearly defined, and actions are not as directly or easily undertaken. Why is this the case? The reasons are related to the structure of government and the relationship between the central government and the states, the organization of Congress and the executive branch, and the unique position of local governments within the federal system.

The Constitutional Structure of Federalism

The Constitution began as a political bargain between autonomous states that were connected to a weak central government under the Articles of Confederation. Strengthening the central government required that the new constitution ensure significant autonomy for the states. The result was **Federalism,** a solution to the problem of uniting different governments with a central government that still preserves the rights of individual states. Federalism is defined as "a governmental system that includes a central government and at least one major sub-national tier of governments; that assigns significant substantive powers to both levels initially by the provisions of a written constitution; and that succeeds over time in sustaining a territorial division of powers by judicial, operational representation and political means" (Walker 1995: 20). The important point to emphasize is the legal rights of the states in a federal system. States can challenge acts of Congress and receive significant support in the courts because of key Constitutional provisions.

The national government is given only those functions explicitly stated in the Constitution. Madison maintained that "the proposed government cannot be deemed a *national* one; since its jurisdiction extends to certain enumerated objects only, and leaves to the several States a residuary and inviolable sovereignty over all other objects" (1937: 249). Though the powers of the national government have broadened over the years through interpretations of several amendments, the principle of state supremacy in certain matters remains.

Local governments, as we saw in the preceding chapter, have no Constitutional role and, through Dillon's rule, are treated as wards of the state. Jeffersonian tradition, as discussed in Chapter 2, provides some support for the influence of local units in an urban policy. Proponents of some urban policies can draw on the Jeffersonian perspective to grant local governments an important role in urban policy. Local governments, however, remain constitutionally weak in a federal system.

Congress and Urban Policy

Historically, Congress initiates policy proposals. This appears to be even more likely in urban matters where the policy itself is less likely to be directly a part of a presidential initiative (Cleaveland 1969: 355). When clear policy proposals from the executive are lacking, Congress often initiates policy. The organization of Congress and the dynamics of the legislative process tell us a great deal about how urban matters are dealt with in our national government.

Several features of Congress affect the kind of urban measures that ultimately become law. The most important decision-making bodies in Congress are committees and sub-committees of small groups of Congressmen

(Davidson and Oleszak 2000: 197). Here, legislation is written and the oversight of executive agencies occurs. Agreement on proposals in committees usually proceeds to the floor of Congress where it is directly voted on. Thus, how committees are organized significantly influences the nature of legislation.

Urban concerns are hindered because, unlike many other policies, there is no standing urban committee. Housing bills, for instance, will be referred to the Banking and Financial Services Committee, transportation issues are discussed in the Transportation and Infrastructure Committee, and Food Stamp measures are produced in the Agriculture Committee. As legislation proceeds, urban advocates must compete with other interests within the committees. Housing interests, for example, face committee members whose main interest is the banking system or the savings and loan industry. Interests in mass transit share a committee, Transportation and Infrastructure, with those concerned with the interstate highway system and major infrastructure projects such as dams and office buildings. This committee is a major source for projects that Congressmen can use to demonstrate their value to their district (sometimes we call these pork). All congressmen want to return home with tangible evidence of their influence. Therefore, recently the Transportation and Infrastructure Committee received requests for nearly 1,500 projects from about 90 percent of the House districts (Davidson and Oleszek 2000: 360). With such diverse concerns confronting committee members, transportation policy becomes a secondary concern for the members.

Congressmen rely on supportive members of the federal bureaucracy to assist them in preparing legislation. Thus, administrators in the Department of Agriculture work with Congressmen to prepare bills and inform them of the concerns of the agricultural community. Urban interests, again, face a splintered focus within the Executive Branch that mirrors the organizations of Congress. While the Department of Housing and Urban Development is the major federal agency concerned with urban problems, transportation concerns remain housed in the Department of Transportation. Welfare and most social services are administered by the Department of Health and Human Services, and the Food Stamp program is located in the Department of Agriculture. Therefore, aid in developing a coherent policy is lacking, and urban legislators must work with a variety of administrators and cabinet members.

Critics have pointed out for decades that Congress favors rural interests, reflecting the anti-urban bias that has historically been a part of American culture and the representation systems that over-represent rural areas. Powerful positions in Congress accrue to those with the most seniority. This system favors so-called safe districts where one party habitually wins the election. Historically, those districts tended to be rural and southern. The biases of Congress favored small town and rural origins until the 1970s. Reforms since then have altered the balance somewhat by awarding high committee positions in ways other than seniority. At the same time, some inner city congressmen have achieved seniority as many of these districts have become safe districts as well. None the less, the bias remains. Urban legislation is frequently compromised to avoid being viewed as a "big city" bill (Cleaveland 1969: 362).

The Economics of Divided Government

Some levels of government may be better suited for some kinds of policies than others. Does the size and breadth of the federal government, for instance, dictate that certain kinds of policies are likely to be promoted? Likewise, local governments are often small and competitive with one another. Do these conditions make them better suited for other kinds of policies? Some have argued that the location of government within the federal system leads to definite policy preferences. If that is so, we can expect certain kinds of policies to be preferred at one level but opposed at another. Smooth working relations are less likely if location within the system influences policy preferences.

Peterson maintains that the resources of government within the federal system affect the kind of policies it pursues. He argues that one can divide all policies into three groups (1981). *Redistributive* policies are those that distribute resources to the less fortunate. Welfare, food stamps, and low income housing programs are redistributive policies. These measures aid the lower class at the expense of the general taxpayer. *Allocational* policies are those that produce policies roughly equal to the population. Park systems, police services, and waste removal are examples of allocational policies. Third, are *developmental* policies. These policies enhance the economic position of a government in its competition with other governments. Providing tax breaks for local industries, removing low-income housing to produce a shopping mall, and building a football stadium at taxpayers' expense to attract a National Football League team are examples of developmental policies. The goal of developmental policies is to increase the tax resources of the community.

Peterson argues that different levels of government emphasize different combinations of these three policies. Local governments emphasize developmental policies. When communities compete for resources with other communities, the central concern of policymakers is gaining an economic advantage over other communities. Thus, redevelopment, taxing policies, and pursuit of interests that will increase tax receipts are the main concerns of the government. Such cities avoid redistributive policies. City officials will oppose shelters for the homeless, aid to those out of work, and medical assistance of the indigent because these policies deter the city from attracting better taxpayers. New firms, he argues, will not locate in a city where homeless people are visible and service providers for the less fortunate must share the central business district with corporate officials. Distributive policies are supported by cities to the extent to which they assist developmental policies. For example, a good school system is supported if firms are attracted to the city because of the schools. School systems will pursue those policies that make their schools appear to be attractive to new investors. Police funding is supported if it is perceived that safe streets will assist the city in attracting higher-yield taxpayers.

The federal government, on the other hand, is in a much less competitive position with other governments. With the exception of major pieces of trade legislation, most federal legislation is proposed within the context of a single national government that does not face significant competition from others.

For this reason, concerns for redistribution will not automatically face opposition in Congress—in fact, Peterson argues that only the federal government will support them. Thus, one would expect the federal government to promote welfare policies, aid for the homeless, and public housing. This, of course, doesn't mean that they always will; as we will see the support for redistributional policies within the federal government has varied significantly over time.

States occupy a midway position between cities and the federal government in these matters. Large states may feel less competitive pressures from other states and will pursue redistributive policies. Small states, however, may be very concerned with increasing tax resources and, therefore, pursue developmental policies. (See Table 5.1.)

Peterson's typology is not without its critics. Authors object to the limited view it implies as common among local government officials. They point to cities like Santa Monica, California, Burlington, Vermont, and Hartford, Connecticut, as cities where political organization brought a liberal coalition to power that was concerned about redistribution (Clavel 1986; Kann 1986). Others find that liberal coalitions can win elections in cities and distribute benefits to their supporters, many of whom are poor (Browning, Marshall and Tabb, 1984; Sonenshein 1993). Nonetheless, the basic argument seems to describe city policies in urban areas with significant numbers of cities and a taxing policy that distributes tax money where it is earned. Few deny that concern for redistribution in this society is the domain of the federal government. While some states have pioneered in health and welfare reform and implemented significant redistributional policies, the major policies that aid the poor emanate from the federal government.

What does Peterson's argument suggest for the role of the federal government and federal programs? His theory leads one to assume that interest in redistribution can be expected primarily at the federal level and that assistance in administering redistributive programs is not readily assumed by local officials. Partnership is logical in developmental policies where local officials should be eager to work with federal officials, assuming that their city can benefit economically from that cooperation. Local governments will welcome most forms of aid for distributive policies, but desire to control the administration of the aid. Funds for law enforcement are welcome, therefore, as long as the local police department controls the administration of the funds. If too many strings are attached to the funds, that is, if the federal government insists on enforcing specific details of policy implementation, local governments will resist.

Table 5.1 Peterson's Typology of Government Policies

POLICY	EXAMPLE	MAJOR GOVERNMENT
Redistributive	Welfare, public housing	Federal
Distributive	Police, fire, parks	All levels
Developmental	Redevelopment, industrial tax breaks, stadiums	Local

Thus, the problems associated with the paradox of urban governance are apparent again. Local governments welcome federal assistance in certain policies but resist it in others. Their competitive position dictates conflict with some components of a federal urban policy and support of others. The kind of policy, therefore, determines the degree to which a partnership among governments is possible.

HOW THE FEDERAL GOVERNMENT INFLUENCES URBAN MATTERS

The federal government rarely finances and administers urban programs. The legal position of the state within the federal system and American traditions of local government assume that local governments deliver primary services. Commonly, aid is made available to local governments and they may accept it subject to conditions stipulated by legislation. The stipulations are frequently referred to as *strings* attached to the aid. Cities that accept federal transportation funds, for example, must develop detailed plans for the use of the funds, and legislation may require that these plans include concern for air quality. Thus, the influence of the federal government in urban matters involves more than specific spending programs.

Over the years, the federal government has implemented many different kinds of federal urban programs. In the following paragraphs, we look at the various kinds of measures employed by the federal government to influence city growth and development.

Federally Administered Programs

Some urban programs are financed and administered by the federal government. In these programs, legislation is passed that delegates to federal agencies the power to directly plan and administer the program. The Army Corp of Engineers, for instance, builds ports, flood control dams, and levees in urban areas. Some elements of the national park system operate within cities.

Categorical Grants

Categorical grants are aid programs in which Congress designates specific purposes for which the funds are to be used. Legislators define a specific need and write legislation to ensure that the recipient governments will use the funds for that purpose only. Federal level administrators also audit the spending of the money to make certain that the intent of Congress is followed. To the recipient of the aid, the enforcement of the details of the legislation and the auditing are frequently referred to as *red tape,* or the attachment of strings to the measures. Many local officials find these intrusive and burdensome.

For some categorical grants, the recipient submits specific, individual applications in the form and at the times indicated by the grantor. Local officials desiring such a grant must become aware of the rules and regulations that govern the particular grant and make an application for the funds. They are likely to be competing with other jurisdictions for these funds, and the federal agency responsible for the disbursement can choose among the applications. Frequently, a matching of funds according to an established formula is expected of the recipient agency, which means local governments must fund a portion of a program with their own money in order to receive federal dollars.

Legislation for airport, highway, and hospital construction are examples of categorical grants. Congress stipulates requirements for use of the funds in considerable detail. Construction standards, the use of specific materials, and the location of the facilities are often written in the legislation. In the case of interstate highways, for example, state governments were required to pay 10 percent of the cost with the federal grant paying for the remaining 90 percent.

National Purpose Grants

Legislation in the 1960s produced a much broader form of categorical grants we will refer to as National Purpose Grants. Rather than aiding states to accomplish specific purposes, these grants were designed to accomplish broad national goals. Written into the legislation were general goals like the following:

> The Congress declares that the maintenance of the national economy at a high level is vital to the best interests of the United States but that some communities are suffering substantial and persistent unemployment; that such unemployment and underemployment cause hardship to many individuals and their families and detract from the national welfare by wasting vital human resources. (Area Redevelopment Act)

> The Congress hereby finds and declares that improving the quality of urban life is the most critical domestic problem facing the United States.

> The Congress further finds and declares that cities of all sizes, do not have adequate resources to deal effectively with the critical problems facing them and that Federal assistance in addition to that now authorized . . . is essential to enable cities to plan, develop and conduct programs. (Demonstration Cities and Metropolitan Development Act) (Sundquist 1969: 4)

Funds for these grants are appropriated for general purposes and delegated to federal agencies for disbursement. Potential recipients apply for these funds in a manner similar to the categorical funds. However, the funds can be used for broad purposes allowing the recipients to propose a wide variety of potential uses for the money within the scope of the title of the Act. Federal officials are then given significantly more discretion as to how this money is to be spent. The Model Cities Program, the Manpower Development and Training Act, and the acts mentioned in the previous quotes are examples of national purpose grants.

Revenue Sharing

Another approach is simply to share revenue from the federal government with cities or states with no particular obligation on the part of the recipient. Revenue sharing disperses federal funds according to a formula stipulated in the legislation. General Revenue Sharing is an example of this kind of grant that was designed to distribute federal funds to a wider array of governments than was the case in categorical or national purpose grants and to restrict the control of federal administrators. The role of the federal government is to disburse payments and receive reports on disbursement from local governments.

Block Grants

Block grants represent a compromise between categorical grants and revenue sharing. The legislation appropriates funds for general purposes such as community development, employment, or education. The legislation stipulates the amount that each recipient will receive, giving federal officials very little discretion over the amount of money each government receives.

Potential recipients, however, must apply for the funds and describe in detail how those funds would be used. Legislation dictates certain specific requirements. For example, recipients of Community Development Act funds must maintain acceptable housing and zoning codes. Federal officials review the applications and have the power to reject an application, but they have no discretion over the amount of funds received once the application has been approved.

Similar to revenue sharing, block grants disperse the funds broadly to a wide variety of cities. Some control is exercised over its disbursement both within the words of the legislation and on the part of federal officials. Examples of block grants are the Community Development Act, the Comprehensive Employment and Training Act, and the Safe Streets Act.

Loan Supports

Federal legislation influences urban areas through acts that provide support for loans to individual and groups. The funds permit the federal government to assume the risk of default on the loans. Thus, the recipients earn a lower interest rate and payments can be spread out over a longer number of years than would be the case if the loan was secured on the private market. Conditions can be placed on the recipients to ensure that the goals of the legislation are met.

FHA and VA loans discussed in Chapter 3, and other more recent federal housing programs, are examples of loan support programs. Prospective homeowners who met the qualifications of the program, veterans of World War II in the case of VA loans, and those below an income threshold in the case of the FHA, received low-interest loans for the purchase of housing. Private lenders advanced the loans for a lower rate, knowing that the federal government would assume the loss in the event that the recipient could not make his or her payments.

The Tax System

The structure of the tax system has many direct effects on the city. The Federal Tax Code permits homeowners to deduct mortgage interest and property taxes from their income taxes. Such provisions encourage home ownership and, in tandem with loan supports, have subsidized new suburban homes. Other provisions of the Tax Code encouraged new industrial and commercial investment at the expense of the renovation of older structures.

Other uses of the tax system have aided the inner city and the working poor. The Earned Income Tax Credit provides income tax relief to lower-income workers. Enterprise zone legislation has granted tax relief to industries locating in areas of low unemployment.

Mandates

All of the programs described attempt to accomplish federal objectives by giving the recipient something they want in return: funds for projects, tax breaks, or loan supports. Other programs treat the recipients more as subjects than partners; they employ the stick rather than the carrot. These programs, called mandates, require compliance with legislative goals and use federal enforcement or the fear of loss of funds to gain compliance (Advisory Commission on Intergovernmental Relations 1978: 7–10).

A variety of legal and fiscal techniques have been employed to encourage acceptance of regulatory standards, or mandates. These include *direct orders, cross cutting requirements, crossover sanctions,* and *partial pre-emptions.*

Direct orders are legislative commands that must be complied with under threat of prosecution. The Equal Employment Act of 1972 bars discrimination by state and local governments and the Marine Protection and Sanctuaries Act prohibits cities from dumping sewerage in the oceans. Those damaged by government actions or the federal government can sue local governments and the courts can order cities to comply.

Crosscutting requirements originate in legislation designed to further national goals in all aid programs. Recipients of federal grants, for instance, must not exclude participants on the ground of race, color, or national origin as stipulated in the Civil Rights Act of 1964. Similar requirements were enacted to protect the handicapped and the elderly. Others require environmental and historical impact statements in all grants. The purpose of crosscutting requirements is to accomplish certain national goals across all federal programs. The federal system makes it difficult for the federal government to order state governments to do certain things. It is legally easier to require matters as a consequence of accepting the funds.

Crossover sanctions impose federal fiscal sanctions in one program or activity to influence state and local policy in another. For example, the Highway Beautification Act of 1965 permits the Department of Transportation to withhold 10 percent of a state's highway construction funds if it does not comply with billboard control requirements, states that fail to pass laws requiring motorcycle riders to wear helmets face loss of highway funds, and cities that are not able to reduce air pollution face the possible loss of several kinds of federal funds.

Partial preemptions permit the federal government to take over a function of state or local government if the goals of legislation are not met. The Clean Air Act of 1970, for instance, sets air quality standards, and states are expected to devise implementation plans to meet those standards. The Federal Environmental Protection Agency, however, can impose standards and enforcement policies on cities if it feels that state rules are insufficient.

Mandates have few friends among state and local government officials. Many perceive them as imposing costs without proper compensation. *Unfunded mandates* is the term frequently applied by state and local officials. Congress granted some relief from the costs of mandates with the Unfunded Mandates Act of 1989. The act does not prohibit unfunded mandates but makes it more difficult to impose them, and it assumes an obligation on the federal government's part to fund the costs.

Location Effects

Where the federal government chooses to locate facilities has had a pronounced effect on cities. Beginning with the war effort in the 1940s, much of the defense spending has been located in the south and southwest. This trend accelerated in the post-war years. From 1950 to 1976, Judd and Swanstrom report that total defense employment increased by 35 percent in the Sun Belt but declined by 3 percent in the northeast (1994: 257). Defense spending expanded the economies of Sun Belt cities; but cities in the northeast, however were negatively impacted.

The decline in defense spending in recent years has, of course hurt the economy of many cities, particularly in California. Thus, the power of the federal government to influence cities extends to areas that seem to be unrelated to urban concerns.

Devolution

Devolution is defined as the transfer of programs from the federal government to the states often with controls or requirements that must be met and some degree of oversight by federal agencies. The welfare reform of 1996 is an example of devolution. Control of the welfare program was transferred primarily from the federal government to the states. The Federal government, however, remains the major provider of funds and stipulates certain requirements for their use. For example, the federal act stipulates that recipients may stay on welfare no longer than five years, and that convicted drug felons are ineligible for aid. Thus, Congress reserves the right to directly influence the program in areas of central concern to its members. Within the stipulated boundaries, states can establish their own programs.

The welfare reform act also rewards states for meeting performance goals, another unique feature of this act. States that reduce their welfare rolls by a prescribed amount receive additional funds from the federal government.

THE RISE AND FALL
OF FEDERAL URBAN POLICY

Urban policy in the twentieth century is the combination of many different programs using all the various tools discussed previously. Many kinds of programs are part of urban policy: housing, transportation, redevelopment, manpower training, and education. It is a complex mix, often working in different directions, with conflicting effects on the city. Politics is often a part of urban policy, and those concerned with the kind of aid that is given are often active in the political arena. Each administration uses the form as well as the amount of urban related funds to reward their supporters. Changes in federal aid are usually a response to major elections. We will look at the recent history of federal urban policy. As we proceed on this journey, ask yourself several questions:

- How do the social and economic conditions of the city, discussed in Chapter 3, influence the kind of federal urban policy that occurs?
- Do political changes and conditions influence the use of the various tools described in the preceding section?
- What groups or interests gain the most from the various combinations of policies at different points in time?

The Beginning of Urban Policy: The New Deal

We begin with the New Deal—that burst of government activism following the Great Depression under the direction of President Franklin D. Roosevelt. With many people out-of-work and several cities bankrupt, the Roosevelt administration created numerous new government programs and agencies to revive the economy and aid the needy.

To get people back to work, government-supported jobs were created through the Works Progress Administration (WPA). The WPA funded numerous projects ranging from schools, water systems, and roads to park maintenance and the writing of city histories. Most of these programs were categorical grants to states or local governments. Often, WPA employees were placed under the supervision of city employees. The WPA projects are the earliest examples of federal-city joint programs (Gelfand 1975: 65). They created direct relations between cities and the federal government, often bypassing the State.

The 1935 Social Security Act provided old age pensions and cash assistance for children in families without breadwinners. This program, of course, was the precursor to Aid to Dependent Children, or welfare. Work relief programs for the unemployed and social insurance were also provided by this act. Most of these programs were state-administered with much of the support coming from the federal government.

Government support for housing began with the Housing Act of 1937. The Act established the Federal Housing Authority (FHA), which was to become a major contributor to the suburban expansion of the 1950s (see Chapter 2). Government built and managed public housing, administered by local authorities, was the primary focus of the FHA during the pre-World War II years.

New Deal programs brought a new relationship to the cities. Federal programs for specific projects were implemented with cooperation from city officials. Mayors, congressmen, and administrators in the executive branch formed alliances for the first time. The purpose of most programs was to invigorate the economy and put people to work. The impact of the programs, however, led city officials to look to the federal government as a part of the city policy-making process.

The Post-War Period: 1945–1960

National domestic policy immediately following World War II was dominated by the needs of returning servicemen, the conversion of the economy from war production to domestic needs, and the military needs of the cold war period.

As discussed in Chapter 2, government policies encouraged the movement of many to the suburbs. Federal housing and transportation policies were instrumental in changing the organization of urban areas. Housing policies subsidized new suburban developments and the interstate system aided the new suburban residents and industries.

As neighborhoods in the central city deteriorated, policymakers looked to the federal government to develop policies to bring sources of wealth back to the central city. The vehicle was **urban renewal,** a federal program that gradually emerged from changes in the public housing program. The Housing Act of 1937 permitted local authorities to buy degraded property to build public housing with federal funds. Through a succession of housing acts, this program was transformed to a large-scale program to renew the central city through a variety of changes in land use. The definition of slum was broadened to include property that was not necessarily blighted but could be brought to a higher use through government action. Changes in the definition of the intended use of the land expanded to include projects that would increase the economic health of the city.

Urban renewal permitted government to buy land through *eminent domain,* the taking of private property for general governmental purposes. The Constitution requires just compensation for property acquisition, but eminent domain permitted the condemnation of property and judicial determination of its value to the former property owner if necessary. The program also provided federal funds for the cost of land acquisition, but no funds for construction and development. It was assumed that once the property was cleared and improvements in place, the private market could produce new uses for the land.

Thus, the urban renewal program permitted city officials to take over significant amounts of land, provide new public improvements, and sell the land for use as up-scale apartments, commercial centers, or industrial locations (Sanders 1980: 103). City mayors and business leaders saw the program as a way of returning wealth to the city. As Frieden and Kaplan state "In essence, cities were using urban renewal to refurbish the central business district, build housing for middle- and upper-income families, and bolster their property tax base" (1975: 23). Urban renewal legislation combined economic growth with assistance to the poor, but in the minds of city officials, it became a developmental policy. Concerns for the poor were often forgotten in their zeal to increase the economic health of the city.

Urban renewal efforts often failed to meet their objectives. Land was cleared, but incentives were often insufficient to entice wealthier residents and entrepreneurs to locate in the city rather than the suburbs. Frequently, older housing units were bought, improvements implemented, but the properties remained vacant. The consequences for the poor were often disastrous as relocation payments were minimal and alternative housing was of lower quality than their previous home. City actions often destroyed the social fabric of ethnic neighborhoods, which is so vital to the cohesion of our cities (see Chapter 3).

Critics spoke with loud voices as the problems of the program came to light in city after city. "In the pursuit of high sounding objectives as saving the central city and revitalizing old neighborhoods urban renewal was evicting the poor and doing little to relocate them" stated Kaplan, a former high-level HUD official, and Frieden, a distinguished urban studies professor (1975: 19). Greer, a noted sociologist, provided a most stinging commentary following a careful examination of many urban renewal programs. "At a cost of more than a billion the Urban Renewal Administration has succeeded in materially reducing the supply of low cost housing in American cities" (1965: 3). Herbert Gans characterized the problem as a failure to think through the aims and goals of the problem clearly:

> Suppose that the government decided that jalopies were a menace to public safety and blight on the beauty of our highways, and therefore took them away from their drivers. Suppose then that to replenish the supply of automobiles, it gave these drivers a hundred dollars each to buy a good used car and also made special grants to General Motors, Ford and Chrysler to lower the cost—although not necessarily the price—of Cadillacs, Lincolns and Imperials by a few hundred dollars. Absurd though it may sound, I have described with only slight poetic license, the first fifteen years of a federal program called urban renewal. (in Bellush and Hausknecht 1967: 465)

Some of this criticism may have been hasty. Sanders points out that the positive results from urban renewal often took years to realize since there was frequently a lag between land acquisition and construction. When looked at over a number of years, more housing was replaced than the early critics found. Sanders also notes that the federal government did respond to the concerns of these critics. In 1967, federal officials redefined the program with an emphasis on social concerns, and they limited the discretion of local officials. The result was an increased emphasis on rehabilitation and preservation of existing housing units, less destruction of neighborhoods, and an increase in low- and moderate-income housing (1980: 112).

As this period ended, urban policy was in disarray as conflicting goals were pursued through federal programs. Highway funds and market supports worked to encourage suburban development while public housing and urban renewal attempted to bring people back to the central city. Urban renewal efforts had spent vast sums of money, but the central city deteriorated. Critics blamed the deteriorating central city on federal efforts encouraged by local leaders. The quality of life in the central cities became an important issue in the presidential campaigns of 1960 and 1964.

The Kennedy-Johnson Years: Attacking the Problems of Poverty and the Inner City

John F. Kennedy was elected president in 1960, following a campaign emphasizing government activism and public investment in domestic policy. Kennedy's assassination and the landslide election of Lyndon Johnson in 1964, were viewed as a strengthened mandate for a much larger federal presence in the concerns of city governments and a more direct interest in the poor. The Department of Housing and Urban Development was created in 1965 to coordinate an urban presence by the federal government. Legislation followed stating a clear federal purpose and mandating direction of the program to federal agencies. These programs, of course, are those referred to as national purpose grants in the previous section.

The aim of these programs was to fund and manage a diverse array of efforts that contributed to the goal of the legislation. The Model Cities Program was the major such program aimed at dealing with the problems of the inner city. President Johnson thought of the program as the primary means of improving life in the central city. In his words:

> To be effective, concerted attacks on city problems must be planned by the cities themselves. The new model cities program is now the *primary* incentive provided by the Federal Government to accomplish this objective. Special grants will be made to help transform entire blighted areas into attractive, useful neighborhoods. To receive grants cities must:
>
> - Develop imaginative and comprehensive plans of action; and
> - Enlist Federal, State, local and private resources in a concerted effort to bring their plans to fruition. (Sundquist 1969: 79)

Public housing projects were built with the best of intentions but many were unable to create the social networks of the traditional lower density city block. Hence social conditions often deteriorated and some, as in the picture here, had to be demolished.

AP/Wide World Photos

Funds could be spent on physical improvements, housing, transportation, education, manpower development, and slum clearance. Federal agencies were the major decision makers. Potential users of the funds were expected to apply to federal agencies for support. Federal policymakers were given the authority to select among the applications.

The programs were also designed to respond to the problems of urban renewal. To some critics, urban renewal failed because it was unconcerned with the residents of the city, particularly those in the neighborhoods affected by urban renewal projects. Jane Jacobs, a journalist and social critic, argued that urban renewal proponents failed to understand that the strength of the city rested on groups of people with commitments to their immediate surroundings. Planners, she maintained, were concerned only with higher tax yields and luring suburbanites back to the city, and the people in the slums were forgotten. "To overcome slums, we must regard slum dwellers as people, capable of understanding and acting upon their own self interests, which they certainly are. We need to discern, respect and build upon the forces for regeneration that exist in slums themselves and that demonstrably work in real cities. This is far from patronizing people into a better life and it is far from what is today" (1961: 271).

Jacobs' immensely popular book challenged the view of most city planners and urban renewal officials at the time. Professionals had assumed that they could speak for the better interests of the city. If this meant destroying neighborhoods for the better economic health of the urban area, the goal was worth pursuing. Jacobs challenged this premise, and the failure of urban renewal strengthened her case enormously.

Following from her concern, new programs required that the wishes of residents were to be an important part of the decision-making process in each project. To some degree, the program was created to politically change city neighborhoods by empowering the residents. Councils composed of affected residents were elected and given the authority to review recommended programs. Representation of the poor in many of these programs was required, so the federal agency established election districts and oversaw the voting process. Council members were paid and met regularly to review proposals and oversee implementation. It was hoped that the program would improve political awareness and knowledge while working to improve social and economic conditions. The programs also permitted flexibility in the selection of service providers. Thus, non-profit agencies, churches, and universities were often recipients of program funds.

Unlike federal efforts in prior years, these programs were selective rather than inclusive. The Model Cities Program was designed to fund a concentrated attack on the problems of a small number of inner cities. Initially, proponents wanted to fund only three cities, but in obtaining congressional approval, the number of cities was expanded and the resulting money in each city was reduced. The aim was to concentrate funding in areas of greatest need. Thus, many cities applied for the funds, but a small number were actually chosen.

Concerns for urban transportation also received increased federal interest in these years. The interstate highway system had improved the efficiency of automobile transportation, but those living in central cities were forced to depend on deteriorating busses and mass transit systems. Beginning in 1964, with the Urban Mass Transit Act, funds were provided to build mass transit systems.

Consequently, the number of grants and the amount of funds allotted to urban concerns increased significantly from 1964 to 1968. The number of grants available in 1962 had nearly tripled by 1967, and federal assistance in dollar terms more than doubled between 1963 and 1969 rising from 7.7 percent to 11 percent of all federal budget outlays (Advisory Commission on Intergovernmental Relation 1978: 27). The targeted nature of the programs meant that some cities received many more funds than others.

The changes in federal efforts to aid cities can be summarized as follows:

- The programs were *federally centered*. Federal legislation and the actions of federal administrators directed these programs.

- An attempt was made to bypass city hall and develop new decision-making bodies in neighborhoods through efforts at citizen participation.

- Funds were concentrated in cities of greatest need. Thus, all cities did not receive funding and some received considerably more than others.

The Nixon Years: Spreading the Funds to a Different Constituency

Richard Nixon's campaign for the presidency in 1968 focused, in part, on perceived problems with the federal aid process. He argued that domestic programs were overly bureaucratic, too centralized in Washington, and too concentrated in the large cities. The role of the federal government in city policies, he maintained, should be one of writing checks. Elected officials, not Washington bureaucrats, were in the best position to determine how that money should be spent.

These arguments hit a responsive chord among parts of the electorate. Nixon won large majorities in the expanding suburbs and small towns, and was endorsed by big city mayors such as Richard Lugar in Indianapolis and Sam Yorty of Los Angeles, who felt excluded from the Kennedy-Johnson era programs and objected to the participatory requirements.

THE POLITICS OF REVENUE SHARING

To Richard Nixon, and to most presidents, federal aid to state and local governments is politics. Nixon's revenue sharing proposal follows as it relates to his 1972 campaign for the presidency.

In his state of the union address, Nixon declared, "The time has now come in America to reverse the flow of power and resources from the States and communities to Washington, and start power and resources flowing back from Washington to the States and communities and, more important, to the people all across America." He proposed to do this by sending $5 billion per year to the states as a kind

(continued)

(continued)

of tax rebate, with no strings attached—the states could spend the money as they chose. More dramatic was his proposal to take $10 billion out of existing aid programs, which required spending for this or that designated purpose, usually to help the poor and minorities, and leave it to the states to decide how to spend it.

Nixon called it a revolutionary program. The Democrats called it a counterrevolution. Nixon's claim was that the state and local governments, being closer to the people, could better decide how to spend the people's money. The Democrats' charge was that the middle- and upper-class whites who controlled state and local government would use the money to reduce their own property taxes, pave suburban roads, build new airports, and leave the inner cities to rot.

Whether or not it was good government was a debatable point. That it was good politics for Nixon could not be argued. Win or lose on this one with Congress, revenue sharing gave Nixon a strong domestic claim for the 1972 campaign, at least with the suburban, small-town, and rural homeowning Silent Majority. Revenue sharing appealed to their disgust with the performance of government, to their outrage that they paid high taxes to support giveaway programs for the poor, to their fear that if property taxes kept rising they would soon be driven from the ranks of homeowners.

Nixon's appeals to the suburbs were direct and unashamed. He described property taxes as the most "unfair, unpopular, and fastest-rising of all taxes," and promised that adoption of revenue sharing would lead to a 30 percent reduction in property taxes. He also pledged that he would not use federal leverage to force local communities to accept low- and moderate-income housing against their wishes (by law, federally funded housing had to be integrated housing).

SOURCE: Stephen E. Ambrose, *Nixon: The Triumph of a Politician: 1962–1972* (New York: Simon & Schuster, Inc., 1981), 432–3.

Appearing simultaneously with Nixon's election were important criticisms of the Kennedy and Johnson programs. Implementing participation of the residents in the distribution of funds proved to be difficult in many cities. Big city mayors often opposed or tried to curtail the influence of these groups. In cities where the participatory bodies were taken seriously, less money was distributed and there were frequent delays in the implementation process. Greenstone and Peterson concluded that in machine cities, like Chicago, aid was distributed quickly but the participatory bodies had little influence on its distribution. In reform cities, like Los Angeles and New York, federal administrators partially realized the goals of increasing citizen participation, but at the cost of many delays and less actual funding (Greenstone and Peterson 1968, 1973). Moynihan examined the attempts at citizen participation in the Great Society programs and found them ridden with conflict, disorganized, and often dominated by an unrepresentative few. The problem, he concluded, was misguided theories and assumptions that meaningful participation could be easily produced. "The Government" he concluded, "did not know what it was doing" (1969: 170).

Another group of critics looked at program implementation and argued that the complexity of managing intergovernmental programs with the in-

President Richard Nixon signs legislation creating General Revenue Sharing. With this Act, urban aid was spread throughout the nation and no longer concentrated on the areas of greatest need.

© Bettmann/Corbis

volvement of several governments and citizens led to delays and waste. The title of Pressman and Wildavsky's study of the implementation of employment programs expresses their findings as well: *Implementation: How Great Expectations in Washington Are Dashed in Oakland or Why It's amazing that Federal Programs Work at all This Being a Saga of the Economic Development Administration as Told by Two Sympathetic Observers Who Seek to Build Morals on Ruined Hopes.* The program they examined was designed as a concentrated effort to expand job opportunities for the poor. The technical details of administering the program, however, proved to be more difficult and time-consuming than the supporters had ever dreamed they would be (1984: 6). They conclude that federally directed intergovernmental programs with several goals and the need to coordinate other governments and private employers are doomed to fail. They are simply too complex.

The Nixon Administration and Congress responded with a new series of domestic programs. General Revenue Sharing (GRS), approved in 1972, provided federal funds to all cities based on a formula written directly by Congress. The formula itself was ultimately a complex one based partially on population, but also favoring small towns and rural areas over large cities. All cities received GRS automatically, subject only to minimal audits by the federal government.

A second change in federal urban policy in the Nixon years was the development of *block grants.* To simplify the administration of federal programs and distribute the funds more broadly, Nixon proposed that categorical grants be collapsed into several common funding categories. Urban Renewal and Model

Cities funds, for instance, would now become part of a larger Community Development Act. Other block grants emerged for Criminal Justice, Health, and Manpower programs. Legislation provided general guidelines for the use of the funds and required detailed applications from the recipient agencies outlining proposed uses of the funds and indicating conformance with congressional intent. Once the proposal was accepted by the federal agency, the recipient was entitled to the money subject to auditing by the federal government.

The role of the federal government in block grants was less than it was in categorical grants. Federal authorities had no control over the amount of money received, but they could enforce restrictions that were a part of the legislation, and they made certain that the funds were spent for the intended purpose. Through interpretations of the legislation, federal officials were able to limit participation of some cities from the program. Houston, for instance, received no Community Development Act funds for many years because the city refused to adopt zoning and building ordinances. Thus, block grants are best viewed as programs with the features of both revenue sharing and categorical grants. Like revenue sharing, the amount of money received was determined by a legislative formula. Similar to categorical grants, restrictions were placed on the use of the money, and recipients had to develop specific plans for the use of the money. Federal officials maintained some control over the use of the funds, but could not affect the amount of money spent in each city.

Housing policy also changed significantly in the Nixon years. Prior federal housing policies provided market supports for the middle class through the FHA and VA programs and government-financed public housing for the poor. The latter was operated by local housing authorities, with most of the money coming from the federal government. Both of these efforts were the subject of criticism by the late 1960s.

Initially public housing was meant to provide homes for diverse people of various income levels, aiding them to eventual home ownership. Local prejudice and limited resources, however, led to a concentration of housing units in the inner city, and deteriorating housing quality. Many proponents of public housing assumed that new structures with modern services would encourage public housing residents to develop a sense of ownership in the projects, resulting in a healthy living environment. Therefore, multi-story, high-rise units were constructed, replacing lower-density older buildings. Housing specialists assumed that new units were preferred living quarters, ignoring the fact that the social structure of the neighborhood was destroyed when high-rise housing projects replaced older structures. To many, central city projects were also seen as a way of keeping the minorities within the central cities rather than face the conflict that might ensue if minorities moved to the suburbs.

The central city housing projects, however, rarely produced viable neighborhoods. Neglect, mismanagement, and social decay resulted in slum conditions within the projects themselves. The problems became most visible in the early 1970s when the city of St. Louis destroyed the Pruit-Igloe housing project less than 20 years after it was built. The newsreel of the building imploding became a symbol of the failure of public housing. By the late 1960s, public housing was considered a failed program.

FHA–VA subsidies remained the staple of support for the private market but were of less help to the working class as housing prices rose in the 1960s. Nearly 9 out of 10 FHA–VA loans went to those of middle income or above (Henig 1985: 180). As pointed out previously, FHA–VA loans discriminated against African Americans and emphasized new suburban homes rather than inner city apartments or older houses, which left the working class to receive little from housing policies. Public housing had become the location of those at the bottom of the social ladder, while the price of housing kept the working class out of the market in spite of the price support programs.

Nixon-era housing policies were aimed at both of these concerns. In 1973, Nixon suspended all new construction of public housing. In its place, Congress passed the Housing and Community Development Act of 1974. This act radically altered the focus and nature of public housing and remains the centerpiece of present day federal housing efforts. Rather than build housing for the poor, the Act provides aid for lower income citizens to supplement private rental payments. Eligible participants, those with incomes below a given threshold, receive a housing voucher that can be used to pay a portion of their rent. The owner of eligible rental units then receives money in the amount of the voucher from the federal government. A second government program offers developers low-interest loans for housing units that house lower-income residents. The hope was that the private market would prove to be a more efficient way of providing housing. By broadening eligibility, the hope was that subsidized units would be scattered throughout the community.

All of the Nixon-era initiatives discussed so far broadened aid to suburban and non-metropolitan areas. A decidedly different pattern occurred in transportation policy. Post World War II programs had emphasized freeway construction connecting suburbs and central cities and linking cities. The Nixon years saw significant increases in aid for mass transit systems in large urban areas and a relative decrease in aid for highways. The Federal Highway Act of 1973, and subsequent additions to it, changed the focus of transportation aid from highway construction to mass transit. Mass transit obligations increased from $108 million in 1970, to over $3.2 billion in 1978. Aid was received for operating assistance as well as capital expenditures and was concentrated in the 10 largest metropolitan areas of the country.

The Nixon Presidency also encouraged the control of environmental hazards in cities. The Clean Air Act of 1970 and the establishment of the Environmental Protection Agency (EPA) initiated federal concern for air quality in cities. The 1977 Amendments to the Clean Air Act established the beginnings of what would become regional enforcement of air quality standards in many cities. States with urban areas that failed to meet federal air quality standards were required to develop plans to bring the areas into conformance. Consequently, many urban areas created Air Quality Management Districts—regional agencies with the power to control environmental contaminants.

Engine exhaust and industrial emissions are the major sources of urban air pollution. Therefore, plans to improve the quality of the air require controlling industrial emissions and reducing the amount of automobile and truck traffic. Air quality management districts were given authority to fine industries that violated state emission guidelines. Reductions in mobile sources of pollution, those produced by trucks and automobiles, are influenced primarily by land use decisions, transportation planning, and changes in individual habits. Air quality management districts were given some influence over land use decisions and regional transportation plans and they offered incentives to industries and governments to encourage car pooling, bicycling, and public transportation usage.

In summary, the Nixon years were times of significant change in the structure of federal urban programs.

- The focus of federal programs changed from the poor of the inner city to the middle and working classes throughout the country.

- Urban programs assisted all cities regardless of need or interest.

- Spending on urban matters increased radically. Federal grants, as a proportion of state and local expenditures, rose from 18 percent in 1968 to over 24 percent in 1975. Total aid to state and local governments increased from $13 billion in 1967 to over $50 billion in 1975.

- Through environmental and transportation policies, new urban problems were addressed.

The Carter Years: A Brief Return to Urban Policy

President Carter's election in 1976 signaled a return to an urban policy oriented on the inner city. He gathered urban policy experts in an attempt to develop a series of programs designed to improve life in the inner city. The resulting proposals focused on economic development and job creation as well as the revitalization of distressed neighborhoods. The administration initiated Urban Development Action Grants (UDAG), a focused block grant program aimed at large, deprived inner cities to expand economic development and provide jobs.

Political and economic problems, however, all but eliminated the Carter program. Inflation and recession in the late 1970s and the tax revolt, an initiative movement that limited taxes in many states, led Congress to become increasingly concerned about the level of federal spending. Starting in 1978, the federal government began a retreat from spending on domestic policies that continues today (see graphic demonstration of this in Figure 5.2).

The Reagan and Bush Years: Urban Programs in Retreat

Ronald Reagan's election in 1980 brought forth another major change in urban policy. Reagan's campaign emphasized the role of the private sector and the need to decrease taxation and government regulation. His supporters assumed that the health of cities would improve with an expansion of the private

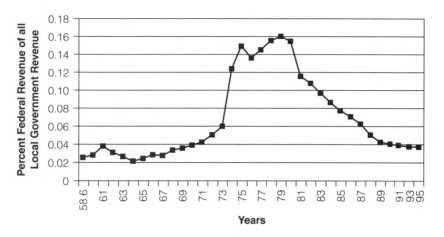

FIGURE 5.2 Revenue from Federal Government as a Percent of All
Local Government Revenue, 1957–1992

economy. Less government meant that the private market could employ more
people and produce more goods. In the process, the poor as well as the rich
would benefit.

For urban programs, Reagan's approach dictated massive cuts in spending
programs and less influence by the federal government. Thus, significant cuts were
made in spending for urban programs. HUD programs alone decreased in funding from a high of $57 billion in 1978 to a low of $9 billion in 1989 (Stoesz 1996:
89). Aid from all federal sources to cities over 300,000 dropped by 35 percent
from $5.2 billion in 1980 to $3.4 billion in 1989. Federal aid to cities as a percent of city revenue dropped from 23 percent in 1980 to 11.6 percent in 1986.

The approach also restructured the organization of federal aid to cities.
Revenue sharing ended in 1986, and many categorical grants were eliminated
entirely while others were folded in to several new block grant programs. Tar-
geting of funds to poorer cities was virtually eliminated (Kaplan 1995: 669).
The Department of Housing and Urban Development ceased to be a prominent federal agency. President Reagan, it is said, failed to recognize his Secretary of Housing and Urban development at a gathering of local officials,
confusing him with one of the mayors.

As the recession of the 1990s spread across the country, cities faced extreme
hardships. With high unemployment and the added burdens of expenses related
to AIDS, the widespread use of crack cocaine, and increases in crime, needs for
city services expanded greatly but the decline in federal aid and the recession
reduced revenues radically.

Efforts to stimulate the private sector during the Reagan and Bush years
met with limited success. Changes in the tax code and the 1981 tax cuts placed
more money in the hands of urban dwellers and may have encouraged investors
and developers in central cities (Kaplan 1995: 671). These changes and local
redevelopment efforts stimulated new building activity in many central cities. *Enterprise zones* were the major urban innovation proposed by both administrations.

An enterprise zone is an area within the city of high unemployment where taxes are reduced for firms willing to locate there. In return for lower taxes, the firms are required to hire the unemployed from the area. It is designed as a private sector alternative to urban renewal or other forms of direct government activity. Several states implemented them but partisan differences prevented them from becoming a national reality during the Reagan and Bush administrations.

Transportation funding and policy changed significantly during the Bush administration. The Inter-modal Surface Transportation Efficiency Act (ISTEA), approved by President Bush in 1991, radically reorganized the structure of transportation policy and added significant funding to transportation programs. The act replaced a largely federal and state program of categorical grants with a block grant process that gives significant authority to metropolitan planning agencies to develop integrated transportation programs for their region. Significant public input in project selection was also required for the first time. The legislation contained a major increase in transportation funding, guaranteeing $151 billion over a six-year period.

With the exception of transportation, these were years of significant retrenchment of federal urban policies, graphically demonstrated in Figure 5.2. Cities had received 16 percent of their revenue from the federal government in 1977, by 1992, federal assistance had been reduced to 4.7 percent of local revenues. For the poorer cities, the decline in federal support was significantly greater (Eisinger 1998: 310). Critics maintain that the loss of federal funds, coupled with an economic downturn and little additional help from states, resulted in significant service declines in most large cities (Eisinger 1998).

The Clinton Years: Many Urban Policies

The Clinton years can be viewed as a renewal of concern for the urban policies of the 1960s, an expansion of the Reagan agenda, or as an attempt to chart a new kind of federal urban policy. Indeed, elements suggesting all three are represented in the policies that were put into practice. Some new urban initiatives are reminiscent of the Kennedy-Johnson years. Welfare reform, the major change in urban policy, is considered by many to be an extension of the conservative agenda. The Welfare Reform Act, however, contains many unique features that suggest a pattern that may be copied in other new policies.

Two major new urban programs were implemented by the Clinton administration. The *empowerment zone* program combines elements of the enterprise zone with features of the Model Cities program. It requires residents of poverty-stricken communities to be involved in developing revitalization plans. The legislation permits tax breaks for industries locating in the zones and $3.5 billion for various community services. The program is a competitive one with officials from HUD selecting the better proposals.

The ISTEA was revised and significantly expanded in 1998 as the *Transportation Equity Act for the 21st Century* (TEA-21). The bill appropriated $217 billion over another six-year period, making it in one of the largest public works bills in the nation's history. The bill also expands the flexibility of state and local officials to determine spending priorities.

The Personal Responsibility and Work Opportunity Act: The Beginning of a New Federalism?

The welfare reform of 1996, the Personal Responsibility and Work Opportunity Act (PRWORA), radically changed welfare policy and may be the beginning of a different chapter in federal state and local relations. While not technically a piece of urban legislation, since historically welfare was a state and federal program, the program's impact on life in the city and on future programs is so significant that a close look at the policy and this important change is warranted. It represents a very different way of defining federal, state, and local government relations.

Federal welfare efforts began in the Roosevelt years as aid to dependent children only. In 1950, it was expanded to include mothers as well as children and given the title Aid to Families with Dependent Children (AFDC). This change secured the program as an *entitlement,* which meant that all mothers and children eligible for the program would receive aid. Declines in the inner-city economy and the increase in single parents in the 1950s and 1960s led to an increase in the number of people who qualified for AFDC.

While AFDC was never a large part of the federal budget, always less than 1 percent of the total, it became a source of frustration as life in the inner city deteriorated and the numbers receiving assistance increased. Conservatives clamored for an end to the program, while liberals saw it as necessary to prevent unrest and provide minimum protection for deprived children. Feasible alternatives also seemed to either increase costs or promote values that made some people uncomfortable. Nixon, for instance, proposed replacing welfare with a guaranteed income for the very poor. Conservatives thought it discouraged the search for work, while liberals disliked it because it did not provide personal assistance to welfare clients.

The Family Support Act of 1987, a major revision of AFDC, permitted experimentation with different kinds of welfare programs by states. Several states successfully implemented work requirements with various kinds of support services. These experiments suggested that changes in the welfare programs were feasible and that states could successfully take responsibility for implementation.

As governor of Arkansas, Clinton had frequently taken positions in opposition to many Democratic Party colleagues on welfare reform. Running for President in 1992, he pledged to "end welfare as we know it." Thus, welfare reform was expected to be an important part of the Clinton agenda. Politically, however, it became more difficult for him to realize this goal in a way compatible with his party since the Republicans carried both houses of Congress in 1994, with a platform that included an end to welfare entitlements and significant state control of the policy. At the same time, Clinton's health care initiative had failed, and he was running for reelection and needed significant domestic accomplishments. Much discussion and negotiation ensued between the White House and Congress over the outlines of new welfare legislation. Clinton vetoed two congressional proposals, but ultimately agreed to the Personal Responsibility and Work Opportunity Reconciliation Act (PRWORA), a series of measures approved by Congress in the summer of 1996 (see Figure 5.3). The bill radically overhauled welfare but, as one would expect in an environment of conflict and time pressures, the resulting law mixed various policy positions and practices.

A review of these provisions suggests that several policy tools are being used. The program *is fundamentally state-dominated* since each state must set up its own program with little or no direction from the central government. State laws will be the governing document for the policies and significant variations in programs are clearly encouraged. States have created very different welfare programs as a consequence. Benefit levels, sanctions against those who fail to find work, and support facilities for those in the program vary significantly (Cashins 1999: 60). The bill has been described as *devolution* because it removes authority from the federal government and gives it to the states.

Congress still specifies certain policies that states must carry out. Unmarried parents must live at home or in group homes, convicted drug felons cannot receive aid (presumably those convicted of other felonies remain eligible), each client can receive aid for no more than five years, and the states cannot reduce

---

THE MAJOR PROVISIONS OF PRWORA ARE:

- It ends the federal guarantee of providing checks to all eligible families and creates a maximum lifetime limit of five years for the receipt of benefits.
- It establishes state goals for bringing clients in to the workforce and rewards states that meet the goals.
- It denies benefits to convicted drug felons.
- It requires states to set up registries to track the status of child support orders.
- It makes legal immigrants ineligible for Supplemental Social Insurance and food stamps unless they become citizens. (This provision was later modified.)
- It requires unmarried parents on welfare to live at home or in group homes.
- It requires states to maintain 80 percent of the 1994 funding levels.
- It permits states to exempt up to 20 percent of the caseload from the five-year limit.
- It permits states to perform drug tests on clients.

FIGURE 5.3 The Major Provisions of PRWORA

spending on welfare more than the specified amount. Obviously, some direct control from the federal government remains in areas of particular concern to various members of Congress. In these provisions, the federal government is independently setting policy.

PRWORA also establishes a series of *incentives to encourage, but not require, state action*. States are rewarded with additional funds if they meet work participation rates and reduce illegitimacy, for instance, because those are goals established by Congress. Previous aid programs either provided funds based on a congressionally established formula (GRS, Community Development Act), or money was extended based on a proposed course of action (Model Cities, various categorical grants). In this program, one may receive additional funds as components of the program are completed, based on actual performance.

Thus, the program mixes central and local control and uses both prohibitions and incentives to affect state behavior. It both centralizes and decentralizes. It permits experimentation in service delivery but requires that certain standards be met. It is a new model of policy-making in a federal system.

The Future of Devolution

Legislative proposals and campaign pronouncements suggest that devolution may be the future for federal urban policies. Proposals to develop similar programs in education, criminal justice, homelessness aid, and housing, have been seriously discussed. Some states are now providing bonus payments to schools, for instance, where performance standards are met and threatening to take over districts when performance declines. What can we expect from an urban policy of devolution?

Analysts see positive and negative features of a devolved system. Many are inspired by the initial results of welfare reform. Nationally, caseloads have declined by 50 percent with some states experiencing much greater success. The bonus payments and the required spending limits have resulted in increased attention to those who remain on the rolls. State and local governments have implemented new kinds of programs, front line welfare workers have successfully made the transition from regulators to service providers, and clients have responded positively to work requirements and welfare limits (Nathan and Gais 1999: 64; Quint 1999). It appears that a devolved system may release new initiatives from state and local systems and produce better results.

Others are concerned about the long-run implications of a system that places ultimate responsibility for redistributive programs at the state and local level where developmental policies are dominant. Some government officials fear that more generous benefits will induce the poor to move to their areas, leading some states to work to reduce benefits to limit the number of participants (Peterson and Rom 1999).

When the economy no longer generates jobs, and state tax bases decline, job placement of those on welfare becomes difficult, but states will receive less money per client. Will states continue to implement the goals of the legislation when there is greater competition for program resources? Many states now are reducing welfare benefits and imposing rigorous sanctions against clients. More states may do so as the economy declines. The problems caused by those out of work turn into mounting costs for the cities, which city programs will shoulder alone. Thus, unless the federal government mandates spending levels or provides sufficient performance bonuses, the program may become one that offers increasingly less assistance to the poor.

Currently the Act requires minimal evaluation of state and local programs. States are not expected to monitor those who leave the welfare rolls, for instance. Therefore, we have limited knowledge of the success of the programs in accomplishing their goals. There is little incentive for states to carry out evaluations without directions to do so from the federal government.

Some people are concerned that devolving responsibility for programs without providing sufficient resources ultimately affects the ability of local officials to truly represent the interests of their constituents. If city officials are given responsibility without sufficient funds, fiscal management rather than policy advocacy becomes their dominant concern. The search for resources and the efficient management of programs rather than the advocacy of constituent interests dominates their public life. Eisinger states the problem well: "By increasingly forcing local leaders to make do with less intergovernmental aid and by making them husband what resources can be raised locally, the New Federal Order has placed a premium on local public management skills and discouraged grand visions of social and racial reform" (1998: 319).

★ ★ ★

Urban policy in the Clinton years, then, was one of conflicting signals:

- A renewed interest in the central city is apparent in the adoption of new programs, but small changes in funding have occurred.

- Welfare reform may have established a new form of federal aid— devolution. State control, with federal influence, through requirements and incentives best describes the welfare program. Its effect on the poor and the social structure of the city remains to be seen.

THE GEORGE W. BUSH YEARS: WHAT CAN WE EXPECT?

As I write, the urban policies of the George W. Bush administration remain in the formative stages. Yet the contours of urban policy can certainly be inferred from the election returns themselves, the new President's cabinet appointments, some policy pronouncements and a few pieces of legislation. The following comments are only speculative in nature.

Election returns suggest that the new president should have limited concern for the inner city. Central cities by and large did not support the Republican candidate. He also did poorly among African Americans, particularly those who live in the inner city. Even big city Republican mayors like Richard Riordan in Los Angeles and Rudolph Guiliani in New York City, while supportive of the new president, were not seen as a major part of his campaign. New urban initiatives were rarely mentioned by either candidate.

George W. Bush has talked frequently of the use of faith-based organizations in the administration of certain federal programs. Federal grants have been received by such organizations in the past, and the new president seems committed to expanding their use. Can religions and church-based organizations run programs more efficiently and effectively? Can they do so without disturbing the balance between church and state? These concerns will be interesting to watch.

Bush made education reform a central part of his campaign and his first legislative initiative. Legislation he supported provides that states with funds to improve education; states, in turn expected to implement measures of performance, and aid may be withdrawn if the standards are not met. More extensive use of vouchers for education and housing policies were frequently discussed in the campaign. Though omitted from legislation. Following September 11, aid for domestic security assisted local police departments and funds to assist New York City were approved.

The influence of Democrats in Congress, however, should lead to compromise on many of these policies. Given the closeness of the election and the success of many Democratic Senators, the outcome of the legislative struggle for urban matters is very hard to predict. Stay tuned!

CONCLUSION: THE FEDERAL GOVERNMENT AND THE PARADOX

We began this text with the paradox of urban governance. Urbanism requires more government power, yet Americans insist on dividing power. Some look to the federal government as that part of the political system where the paradox can be overcome. Urban policy created by the federal government is an attempt to make common decisions for an urban area and supply the needed power and resources to carry it out. However, we find that the federal government rarely fulfills this goal.

- The federal government does not speak with a united voice. It consists of a splintered Congress and administration when it comes to urban matters. Urban policies are often subordinate to other concerns. There has been significant disagreement within all administrations as to the need for a consistent urban policy.

- The place of cities within the federal system makes it difficult for the federal government to have a sustained influence in the major policy areas of concern to urban problems. Local governments are primarily concerned with developmental policies—those that will increase their own resources. They are often hostile to redistributive policies because they feel that these may limit their ability to acquire new resources. Thus, the cooperation between local and federal governments depends on the kind of policy pursued.

- Federal urban policy is closely related to politics. Presidents attempt to use urban policy to award their supporters, therefore, the kind of urban aid varies in different administrations and has risen and fallen over time.

Figure 5.3 graphically demonstrates the variations in the amount of urban aid. In the 50-year time span, one can readily see that urban aid has risen and fallen in dramatic fashion, reflecting different policy prescriptions undertaken at different times.

- Federal urban policies are related to dominant ideas in different time periods. Cooperation defined public management in the Roosevelt years, when federal-city relations were referred to as *cooperative federalism*. Common interests between government officials at all levels were assumed, and federal programs were designed to encourage cooperation and mutual adjustment. The Kennedy-Johnson years were described as a time when the federal government was the major partner and was expected to lead the society. In the Reagan years, pre-eminence was assumed by the private sector, and domestic policy was advanced through fewer constraints on businesses and lower taxes. The present time is typified by a devolution best described as one of federal direction but local implementation. Today, policy guidance occurs through incentives based on output measurement and direct proscriptions.

Thus, the Federal government's influence in urban matters varies by policy and over time. The attention of national leaders is rarely fixed on urban concerns. Mayors, city managers, and city activists must consider the federal government as one among many sources of influence and resources as they attempt to manage city problems. In the next chapter, we examine how city officials in different cities and contexts make policy within the complex environment of the contemporary city.

REFERENCES

Advisory Commission on Intergovernmental Relations. 1978. *The Development of Categorical Assistance.* Washington: Advisory Commission on Intergovernmental Relations.

Ambrose, Stephen E. 1981. *Nixon: The Triumph of a Politician 1962–1972.* New York: Simon and Schuster.

Bellush, Jewel, and Murray Hausknecht, eds. 1967. *Urban Renewal: People, Politics and Planning: A Reader on the Political Controversies and Sociological Realities of Revitalizing the American City.* Garden City, NJ: Anchor Books.

Browning, Rufus M., Dale Rogers Marshall, David H. Tabb. 1984. *Protest Is Not Enough: The Struggle of Blacks and Hispanics for Equality in Urban Politics.* Berkeley, CA: University of California Press.

Cashins, Cheryll D. 1999. "Federalism, Welfare Reform and the Minority Poor: Accounting for the Tyranny of State Majorities." *Columbia Law Review 99* (April).

Clavel, Pierre. 1986. *The Progressive City: Planning and Participation, 1969–1984.* New Brunswick, NJ: Rutgers University Press.

Cleaveland, Fredric N. 1969. *Congress and Urban Problems.* Washington D.C.: The Brookings Institution.

Davidson, Roger H., and Walter J. Oleszek. 2000. *Congress and Its Members.* Washington D.C.: Congressional Quarterly Press.

Downs, Anthony. 1995. "HUD's Basic Mission and Some of Their Key Implications." *Cityscape: A Journal of*

Policy Development and Research 1 (September).

Eisinger, Peter. 1998. "City Politics in an Era of Federal Devolution." *Urban Affairs Review* 33:1 (January): 308–25.

Frieden, Bernard J., and Marshall Kaplan. 1975. *The Politics of Neglect: Urban Aid from Model Cities to Revenue Sharing.* Cambridge, MA: M.I.T. Press.

Gelfand, Mark I. 1975. *A Nation of Cities: The Federal Government and Urban America, 1933–1965.* New York: Oxford University Press.

Greenstone, J. David, and Paul E. Peterson. 1973. *Race and Authority in Urban Politics.* New York: Russell Sage Foundation.

Greer, Scott. 1965. *Urban Renewal and American Cities.* Indianapolis: The Bobbs-Merrill Company Inc.

Henig, Jeffrey R. 1985. *Public Policy & Federalism: Issues in State and Local Politics.* New York: St. Martins Press.

Jacobs, Jane. 1961. *The Death and Life of Great American Cities.* New York: Random House.

Judd, Dennis R., and Todd Swanstrom. 1994. *City Politics: Private Power and Public Policy.* New York: HarperCollins College Publishers.

Kann, Mark E. 1986. *Middle Class Radicalism in Santa Monica.* Philadelphia: Temple University Press.

Kaplan, Marshall. 1975. *The Politics of Neglect: Urban Aid from Model Cities to Revenue Sharing.* Boston: The MIT Press.

Kaplan, Marshall. 1995. "Urban Policy: An Uneven Past, an Uncertain Future." *Urban Affairs Quarterly* 30 (May): 662–79.

Madison, John. 1937. "Federalist Number 47." In *The Federalist,* edited by Alexander Hamilton, John Jay, and James Madison. New York: The Modern Library.

Moynihan, Daniel P. 1969. *Maximum Feasible Misunderstanding: Community Action on the War on Poverty.* New York: The Free Press.

Nathan, Richard P., and Thomas L. Gais. 1999. *Implementing the Personal Responsibility Act of 1996: A First Look.* Albany, NY. The Nelson Rockefeller Institute of Government.

Peterson, Paul E. 1981. *City Limits.* Chicago: University of Chicago Press.

Peterson, Paul E. and Mark C. Rom. 1990. *Welfare Magnets: A New Case for a National Standard.* Washington, D.C. The Brookings Institution.

Pressman, Jeffrey L., and Aaron Wildavsky. 1984. *Implementation: How Great Expectations in Washington are Dashed in Oakland or Why It's Amazing that Federal Programs Work at all This Being the Saga of the Economic Development Administration as told by Two Sympathetic Observers Who Seek to Build Morals on a Foundation of Ruined Hopes.* Berkeley, CA: University of California Press.

Quint, Janet, Kathryn Edin, Maria L. Buck, Barbara Fink, Yolanda C. Padilla, Olis Simmons-Hewitt, and Mary Eustace Valmont. 1999. *Big Cities and Welfare Reform: Early Implementation and Ethnographic Finding from the Project on Devolution and Urban Change.* Manpower Demonstration Research Corporation. http://www.mdrc.org.

Sanders, Heywood T. 1980. "Urban Renewal and the Revitalized City: A Reconsideration of Recent History." In *Urban Revitalization,* edited by Donald B. Rosenthal. Beverly Hills, CA: Sage Publications.

Sonenshein, Raphael. 1993. *Politics in Black and White: Race and Power in Los Angeles.* Princeton, NJ: Princeton University Press.

Sundquist, James L. 1969. *Making Federalism Work: A Study of Program Coordination at the Community Level.* Washington, D.C.: The Brookings Institution.

Walker, David B. 1995. *The Rebirth of Federalism: Slouching Toward Washington.* Washington, D.C.: CQ Press.

Chapter Six

Power and Leadership
in the American City

Yet how do you govern a city where everyone thinks he or she is the best and can do it better than you? You do it by conveying that you are giving it everything you have, and you demonstrate that what you are doing is what they would be doing if they were in your place. You become their hand on the wheel of government. People want to touch you, praise you, harangue you, love you and hate you. And as Mayor you must be able to accept it all and at the same time not become overwhelmed by the praise or overcome by the abuse—Edward I. Koch, former mayor of New York (Koch and Rauch 1985: 458)

Previous chapters have pointed out that:

- Resources and people have migrated to outlying areas leaving the central cities with serious problems.
- Americans lack a tradition of strong local government.
- Authority in urban areas is usually dispersed among numerous local governments.
- Governmental structures in urban areas divide power among numerous elected and appointed officials.
- The federal government does not consistently concern itself with urban matters and when it does, rarely speaks and acts with a united voice.

Taking all this into consideration, it is surprising that our local governments accomplish anything. Yet we know that in many of our cities, politicians and administrators lead. They pull citizens and businesses together to revitalize old downtowns, energize police departments, and build new schools. How do these public leaders overcome the many impediments to active leadership in our cities? When they do so are they able to lead with the interests of the average citizen in mind? These are the concerns we will address in this chapter.

The focus of this chapter is *power,* a primary concept in political science, but one that is mysteriously difficult to define and measure. We will define power as "The capacity of one actor to do something affecting another actor which changes the probable pattern of specific future events" (Polsby 1963: 3). Most would accept this as a reasonable definition. Using it as a way of measuring power, however, is fraught with unanswered questions and controversy.

Here are some of the important considerations that surround discussions of defining and measuring power. Ask yourself how they fit with your knowledge of power in your community.

- Is power exercised only when orders are given, received, and acted upon?

- Perhaps, but others will argue that when orders are given, those not present are really issuing the orders to the actual participants. In their opinion, those behind the scenes, the powerful business leaders or wealthy landowners, are the real power wielders.

- Or perhaps when decisions are made, those making the decisions are assuming they represent someone behind the scenes? Orders are never given, but the decision makers assume that they are acting in the interests of others. Mayor Koch (quoted at the opening of the chapter) hopes that people think that he is acting in their interest when he exercises power, but is he actually representing the powerful landowners while appearing to be the delegate of the average citizen?

- Then again, if the rules of the game of politics discriminate against your group, perhaps others have power over you.

For decades, authors have tried to define and measure power with only limited success. The issue is so important for an understanding of how urban areas operate politically, however, that the attempt to understand power is needed even if we can't reach definitive conclusions about it. This chapter looks closely at how social scientists have defined and measured power. We then turn to several cases that discuss how actual urban decision makers have used power to change life in our cities. Our goal is an understanding of how power has been defined and measured and an understanding of how it is actually exercised.

WHAT WE KNOW ABOUT POWER
IN AMERICAN CITIES

Power as Reputation

Philosophers and political scientists have talked about power for centuries. A sociologist named Floyd Hunter, however, was the first person to try to measure power in local community in a systematic way. Hunter's goal was to determine

the holders of power in a city he referred to as "Regional City" to protect the
anonymity of his sources. (We know today that the city is Atlanta.) He sought
to identify the people who had the greatest influence on city policy.

To find city leaders, Hunter used the *reputational method*. Following is
Hunter's summary of how he approaches the study:

> The leaders selected for the study were secured from lists of leading civic,
> professional and fraternal organizations. Governmental personnel, business
> leaders and "society" and "wealth" personnel were suggested by various
> sources. The lists of more than 175 persons were rated by "judges" who
> selected by mutual choice the top forty persons in the total listings. These
> forty were the object of study and investigation in Regional City. . . .In
> the interviews, Regional City leaders were asked to choose the top ten
> leaders from the basic list of forty. (1953: 65)

Hunter was asking a large group of people who they thought were powerful people. In turn, those labeled as power wielders were asked who they
thought were powerful people. He was interested in the size of the powerful
groups and the issues in which they were influential. Did the informants see a
small group with influence in all areas of public policy or a large number of diverse groups? Were those thought to be influential in one policy also of importance in another? He was also concerned about the backgrounds of those
thought to be powerful. Were they elected officials, businessmen, those from
higher levels of government? He hoped that the study would tell him something about kind of leadership in communities. The results from Regional City
could then be generalized into a broader theory of power in communities.

Hunter found a small number of people's names occurred again and again
in the interviews. Most informants perceived a similar set of people as powerful in all matters of public policy. Most of these people were members of the
business community; residents of companies, chairmen of boards, or professional positions of some prestige (1953: 75). Thus Hunter concluded that power
in Regional City was held by a "power elite" of members of the business community. These were people who knew one another and interacted with each
other regularly.

Figure 6.1, drawn from Hunter's work, represents his view of the power
structure. He sees a small group of people largely drawn from the private sector involved in the primary decisions for all important public projects. This is
represented by the pyramid in the center of the drawing. Others in the lower
pyramids take part in the implementation of projects, but defer to the power
elite when important questions are raised. Here is Hunter's description of how
a public project comes about in Regional City:

> A policy committee is formed. . . . Such a policy committee would more
> than likely grow out of a series of informal meetings and it might be
> related to a project that has been in the discussion agenda of many
> associations for months, even years. But the time has arrived for action.
> Money must be raised through private subscription or taxation. A site

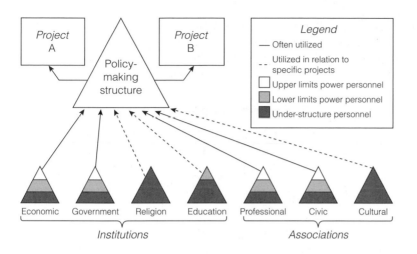

FIGURE 6.1 Generalized Pattern of Policy Committee Formation Utilizing Institutional and Associational Structures.

selected, and contracts let. . . . The selection of the policy committee will fall largely to the men of power in the community. They will likely be businessmen in one or more of the large business establishments. Mutual choices will be agreed upon for committee membership. In the early stages of policy formation there will be a few men who make the basic decisions. As the project is trimmed, pared, and shaped into manageable proportions there will be a recognition that the committee should be enlarged. Top-ranking organizations and institutional personnel will then be selected by the original members to augment their numbers. . . . The civic associations and the formalized institutions will next be drawn in to certain phases of planning and initiation of the project on a community-wide basis. (1953: 93)

Hunter concluded that a small group of wealthy businessmen and professionals controlled the policy-making process in Regional City. Through use of their resources, and to some extent fear and intimidation, this group dominated policy-making in all issue areas and controlled access to policy-making circles. Their goals were to maintain power and prevent significant change in policy. Hunter states, "When new policy is laid down it must be consistent with the general scheme of old policy and should not radically change basic assignments of settled policy. This does not mean that structural alignments do not undergo drastic overhauling on occasion, but consistency is a prime virtue which must not be passed over lightly, so that the basic equilibrium in the social systems of the community may undergo as little disruption as possible" (1953: 209).

We call Hunter's perspective the *elitist approach* to the study of power. Hunter assumes that one's reputation for power is an indication of the actual use of power. He does not, however, actually test this. It is assumed that those surveyed are reflecting upon the actual use of power. He also assumes that the perceptions of his interviewees indicate if the power elite acts as a cohesive group. Again, this conclusion is based on perceptions of power rather than actual examinations of power.

The Decisional Approach

The findings of Hunter were troubling to political scientists. If a power elite of businessmen actually control major policy decisions in cities, the democratic nature of city government is seriously called into question. Most in the discipline had viewed power in government as the interplay of diverse interests. Hunter was saying that small, unrepresentative groups made most of the important decisions.

Concern about the reputational method of power research led Robert Dahl and his associates to embark on a major study of the government of the city of New Haven, culminating in the publication of *Who Governs? Democracy and Power in an American City,* in 1961. The study flatly contradicted Hunter's work in method and conclusions and set the groundwork for years of serious conflict.

Dahl premised his study on a different definition of power. He assumed that there was a difference between perceptions of power and the actual use of power in making decisions. He argued that perceptions of power really had little to do with its actual use. The rich in New Haven, for example, may have access to great wealth and power but may choose to use it in ways unrelated to the running of the city. Likewise, reputations for power were of little value unless the reputed leader chose to exert influence. Unless power was actually being used, it wasn't really power, according to Dahl.

To study power, then, one must rely on the "careful examination of a series of concrete decisions" (Dahl 1961). The aim was to study specific outcomes in order to determine who actually prevails in community decision making (Polsby 1963: 113). In the New Haven study, three issue areas; public education, urban renewal, and party nominations were selected for detailed study. These three areas were chosen because they included important community-wide decisions.

Dahl and his students carried out a complex strategy to study decision making within these three areas. They compiled lists of people formally connected with decision making in each area. These people were then interviewed to ascertain which particular issue they thought was crucial. Those decisions were then analyzed in detail using interviews and public documents. Judgments were then made as to whom had exercised power over the decision studied (Ricci 1971: 131).

The analysis revealed that those involved in the cases were a political elite, unrepresentative of the population as a whole. Thus, similar to Hunter, Dahl concluded that the key decision makers were better educated, wealthier, and of higher social status than the average citizen. However, other traits of the leadership group led Dahl to question the conclusions of the reputational method. The power group in Dahl's study contained few economic and social notables of the city. Power holders, he argued, were a separate political class interested in group activities and the political process.

Dahl also concluded that influence among the leaders was specialized. Individuals influential in one sector of public activity tended not to be influential in another (1961: 169). Those involved in urban renewal, for instance, were different from those considered influential in public education. He found little overlap across the three issue areas.

The defined leaders bore little resemblance to Hunter's power elite. They tended to be middle class; in fact, he found them more similar to the average voter than the social and economic notables. However, they differed from the average voter in their interest in public affairs and their propensity to join organized groups (1961: 169–74). They were best described as a separate political class, motivated by public service and active in social and political groups.

Dahl also argued that the use of political resources was, in his words, *noncumulative,* which means that political resources come in many forms. These include money, control of jobs, knowledge and expertise, popularity, etc. Some people possess more of these than do others, but the total is widely distributed and those with much of one kind do not necessarily control other resources. Consequently, power is widely distributed among many different kinds of people.

Lastly, Dahl argued that most of the citizens of New Haven were not involved in politics, but they had an indirect influence on the decision-making process through the attitudes of the leaders. Leaders were aware of the potential power of the voters and tailored their actions to comply with their perception of the public's needs. Leaders were also committed to democratic norms and values, and these attitudes required that the interests of the average citizen be heard.

The term *pluralist* is frequently attached to the work of Dahl and his followers. He concludes that the New Haven system is one of plural elites. The leaders constitute a diverse group, which tend to limit their activities to a specialized area of policy. They are predominately motivated by interest in particular policies and involvement in the political process. The diversity of their values and their commitment to represent the public and enforce rules of fair play are more important than any allegiance to the social and economic leaders. Thus, they are a plural array of interests with no single perspective or common approach to the making of decisions.

Comparing Pluralist and Elitist Studies of Community

The pluralist perspective contradicts every major idea advanced by Floyd Hunter and the proponents of the reputational or elitist approach. While the elitists maintain that there are few power holders in the city, pluralists maintain there are many. Pluralists find the power holders overtly visible while the elitists find them covert or hidden. Pluralist leaders are highly specialized in their interests and influence; elitists' scope of influence is general, spanning all major areas of decisions. Political resources for the pluralist are plentiful and can be acquired and used when one's interests are at stake. Homeowners in an area destined for urban renewal, for example, can organize and pressure the leaders to acquiesce if needed. In the elitist system, it is very difficult for the average citizen to acquire resources, and the organization of new interests is opposed by those in power.

Beliefs on issues from the pluralist perspective are diverse and competitive. Decision makers will differ on basic questions. From the elitist perspective, most leaders hold to the same beliefs—to advance the interests of the business class. Government to the pluralist is a neutral group that responds to organized interests and is sensitive to elections. To the elitist, government is the agent of the business class. Government officials respond to cures from business leaders and rarely support initiatives that do not have the blessing of the power elite. Pluralists see the political system as one that is constantly changing—those with merit gain access to the system. Leaders make incremental changes to accommodate new groups and interests, and over time, new groups gain access to leadership positions and the policy-making process accommodates the emerging interests. To the elitist, the elites protect their interests and resist change. Table 6.1 graphically contrasts the pluralist and elitist perspectives.

The Debate Expands

Following publication of Dahl's book, disciples of both Dahl and Hunter proceeded to study other communities. Each method was employed in different settings with slight variations (see Hawley and Svara 1972 for summaries). Generally, the method used seemed to predict the results. Those examining decisions following the pluralist approach usually found that power was widely distributed, while those examining perceptions of power discovered a power elite. The method ruled even in communities where previous researchers had used the other approach. Thus, Jennings (1964) went to Atlanta, examined de-

Table 6.1 Distinguishing Contrasts between Pluralism and Elitism

ITEMS	PLURALISM	ELITISM
Number of power holders	Potentially many	Few
Visibility	Overt	Covert integration
Scope of influence	Highly specialized	Very general
Political resources	Slack, unequal, noncumulative resources can be used, if interests at stake	Very difficult for average citizen to acquire; numerous obstacles to mobilize
Beliefs on issues	Competitive	Consensual
Role of government	Neutral but more responsive to mobilized interests/ electorate	Agents of privileged place of business
Probabilities of changing	Social class structure weak; those with merit gain access to power, incremental changes	Elites protect/promote strong ruling elite interests; thereby face and resist dramatic changes

cisions and found pluralism, while Domhoff (1977) looked at New Haven using the reputational method and found a power elite. Much debate took place in scholarly journals and at professional conferences trying to prove the superiority of one or the other method. Ultimately, the conflict was never resolved. Power defined as perceptions and as involvement in decisions are likely to be two different concepts, each with a claim on the true meaning of power.

Later, several noteworthy studies examined a larger number of cities and used elements of both approaches. These studies helped analysts realize that there was merit in both approaches as well as problems with the limited questions raised by studies of a small number of cities. These works changed the focus of power research from "who governs?" to what difference does it make when various kinds of power structures are present? These authors asked, for example, if cities with greater diversity among the influential spent city money differently or responded more clearly to the interests of groups of citizens. Most noteworthy among these are the studies by Agger, Goldrich, and Swanstrom (1964) and Clark (1971). Both of these studies demonstrate that elitism and pluralism may be useful in comparing cities and explaining differences in community policies and practices, and in explaining community differences.

Agger et al. exhaustively analyzed power structures and policies in four small- and medium-sized communities in two regions over a 15-year period. The findings are derived from detailed cases of community decisions and random samples of leaders and the public. The data permits the making of comparative judgments about the nature of power in the communities and the changes that occurred over time. They also looked closely at the belief systems or ideologies of the participants to test the proposition that differing values among leaders affect the distribution of power.

Power, they found, was also related to the extent to which local politics is open to all citizens. In some communities, illegitimate sanctions blocked efforts of citizens to gain influence. Citizens in these cities feared loss of jobs or protection from the police if the wishes of the leaders were challenged. In others, citizens had a weak sense of electoral potency, that is, they felt they had little say in the selection of elected officials.

The work of Agger et al. provided a rich base of information that permitted an assessment of both approaches to the study of power. Like the pluralists, they found that elections and local office holders were important, independent sources of power, and they criticized the elitists for underplaying the role of elections and the political system as independent forces in decision making. They saw the election process as a source of change in these communities.

However, the analysis of illegitimate sanctions and electoral potency lends support to elitist perspectives. In some of the communities at various points in time, an elite ruled partially through intimidation and control of economic and political power. The richness of their work points to an important time dimension in community power, because over time, the power structures of these communities changed generally in the direction of a more pluralistic system.

Clark (1971) and Clark and Ferguson (1983) expanded the comparative evaluation of power significantly by measuring the distribution of power in large numbers of cities and using this measure to analyze whether differences in the concentration of power affected city spending patterns. In each community, 11 strategically placed informants were interviewed concerning the number of actors involved in decisions in four issue areas; urban renewal, the election of the mayor, air pollution, and anti–poverty programs.

These researchers found that more decentralized power structures were associated with greater budget expenditures and a larger urban renewal program. Apparently when power is more broadly distributed, decision makers hear more demands for public expenditures, and they respond by increasing the budget.

Similar to Agger et al., Clark's work points to the value of examining the distribution of power as it influences the ongoing operation of government. The use of a large number of cities permits comparison of the influence of different power structures on government decisions. Thus, they were able to look more concretely at the kind of differences that various power structures make on policy.

A Return to the Problem of Power: Systemic Power

Analysts and practitioners continue to be fascinated by the notion of community power in spite of the difficulties of measuring it. Many felt pluralists, in their zeal to defend their method, neglected obvious examples of influence that could not be observed. Accepting the pluralist belief that power occurs only in overt interactions seemed to mask what most feel to be an important "other face" of power. An influential book by Bachrach and Baratz (1970) proposed that power had two faces; the overt face as defined by the pluralists and apparent in the making of decisions, and a hidden face where power was exercised without direct interaction among policymakers. They tried to give more substance to the second face of power by emphasizing the importance of nondecisions, the ability of those in power to set the agenda of discussion and thereby eliminate concerns of those outside of the centers of influence. They also emphasized the "mobilization of bias," or the presence of values within the leadership group that defined certain kinds of issues as legitimate and others as illegitimate. Pluralists responded by arguing that one cannot measure matters like nondecisions, and if they can't be measured, perhaps they do not exist.

Clarence Stone, however, remained troubled by what he saw as continuing upper-class influence in community decision making in spite of increasingly broader representation by diverse groups. As minority representatives gained influence in cities and the poor became a larger proportion of the city population, one would expect greater influence of minorities and the poor. As he looked at policy-making in cities, however, this didn't seem to be the case. Other concerns, imbedded in the way in which leaders operate, seemed to give an advantage to upper-class and business interests in spite of changes in the city's population. The influence of the upper class wasn't explained by willful conduct on the part of the business class or obvious biases against challenging groups. Elected leaders seemed to encourage upper-class influence. Mayor

Richard Daley, the political boss of Chicago in the 1950s and 1960s, on assuming office with the electoral support of the working class, wrote three or
four of Chicago's major business leaders asking them to list the things they felt
he should do. The poor in parts of the community at the same time had engaged in protests, voter registration drives, and other visible forms of political
activity. Yet the businessmen were able to gain access to the mayor with little
effort, and the wishes of the protesters, many of whom had voted for Daley,
were neglected (Stone 1980: 981).

Stone proposed that Daley's actions are explained by the needs of governmental officials to accomplish public goals, and the limits on government's
ability to act on public problems without the support of influential members
of the community. Major changes in cities require resources and support of
certain key groups. Local governments, as has been pointed out, are relatively
weak actors. If the officials' goals include acquiring property, raising new
sources of funds, or changing the use of land, support must be gained in the
community. Agreements must be reached between property owners and public officials and interest groups must be convinced of the merits of the project. Major changes in public policy require the support and cooperation of
those outside of city hall.

How does one gain this kind of support? A shrewd public official must look
for the groups and people who can help him acquire these resources. Stone
identifies three kinds of resources that are particularly relevant to community
decision making:

1. *Economic position.* Those with greater wealth and command of major
   economic enterprises can aid in acquiring funds for public projects.

2. *Associational position.* Those who command people through civic
   associations, professional groups, or trade associations have access to large
   numbers of people and can influence the members' support of public
   projects.

3. *Social position and life style.* Some people in every city enjoy high esteem
   and status within the community. Others listen to them and look up to
   them as people whose opinions matter. The support of these people for
   proposed public projects aids their approval by larger groups of people.
   (1980: 983)

Those who possess all three of these resources are likely to be found among
the upper class. They have access to money, they are more likely to be the leaders of associations, and they are frequently perceived as people of higher status.
Thus, the elected official, regardless of political positions or the interests that
were raised in the campaign, turns to big businesses and the upper class when
he or she wants to get major projects implemented.

Stone calls this notion of power *systemic power,* and defines it as "the circumstance that office holders (regardless of personal background, nature of
electoral support, network of association etc.) are by virtue of their position,

more situationally dependent on some interests rather than others." Systemic power, he adds, ". . . Involves no overt attempt to influence the context of decision making. It lies in the imperatives of the situation and requires no elite group engaged in changing or maintaining institutions, procedures or norms" (1980: 981–2). Power, then, is not a consequence of pressure from the elites or the result of interactions among contending parties—it is brought about at the instigation of public officials. In the need to get their aims accomplished, public officials are drawn to the upper class.

The experience of Maynard Jackson, mayor of Atlanta from 1973 to 1981, demonstrates the importance of systemic power. Historically the largely white business community had dominated politics in Atlanta. Jackson's election promised to bring forth an administration independent of the traditional sources of influence. He was Atlanta's first African American mayor and enjoyed a very high level of support within the African American community. Jackson had been a proponent of newly emerging neighborhood organizations of grass roots volunteers and had won their support. A new city charter provided for district elections for the first time. Consequently a council evenly split between Whites and Blacks, with significantly less support from the business community, was elected in place of a largely White business-dominated body. Jackson himself was an articulate, polished, and intelligent person with the ability to reach out to new groups and interests. Thus, all the pieces for a progressive, anti-establishment regime appeared to be in place.

However, Jackson had great difficulty pulling a progressive coalition together. Differences among the coalition partners prevented the development of a common agenda. At the same time, the business elite became wary of the new regime, and the press encouraged public concerns through a series of critical articles.

Ultimately, Jackson made peace with the business community and promoted many common projects. In the process, he became less attentive to the electorally potent neighborhood movement and the large Black middle class (Stone 1989: 95). The realities of systemic power ultimately forced Jackson to back away from the coalition that elected him and coalesce with the united business community. Stone states the dilemma clearly:

> As mayor, Jackson's bold assertion of a reform agenda was based upon the assumption that he had a popular mandate to lead in that direction. After all, he was a capable exerciser of formal authority of the office, and, as a popular leader, he was able to mobilize mass support. *But he lacked command of the informal system of cooperation that was so important in the civic life of Atlanta.*
>
> The powers of the office of mayor enabled him to do some things, such as alter the leadership of the police department. But a broad agenda of action would require support from several sectors of the community and from the state government as well. To pursue economic development, Jackson would need business cooperation and in seeking it, he operated from a distinct disadvantage. His constituency was loose-knit and had to

be mobilized issue by issue. By contrast the Atlanta business community was highly cohesive and it controlled key resources that enabled it to facilitate a variety of projects. Moreover, the business elite operated from multiple points of strength that made it a formidable adversary. Jackson was pulled inevitably toward accommodation. (1989: 95)

EXAMINING BIG CITY POWER

Systemic power focuses the inquiry on the actions of leaders. The center of the analysis is the public leader. His/her actions are examined and from them conclusions are reached concerning the factors that influence actions. Systemic power also allows us to look at sources of power within the political system and in the larger community. This unites the central concerns of the elitist and pluralist perspectives since elitists looked to the private sector to the exclusion of the public, and pluralists concentrated on governmental decision making.

Power is examined through attempts to gather the resources needed to act. The limited power of the city requires that leaders interact with potential allies to acquire the resources and public support needed to bring forth changes. We will look closely at the work of three political leaders in our largest cities: New York, Chicago, and Los Angeles. In each case, we will examine how the leader searched for sources of support and ultimately developed a coalition to bring forth significant changes in city policy. The cases allow us to examine how leaders organize and use potential resources available to leaders and understand the extent to which they are limited by the constraints on actions. As a prelude, the sources of power and the constraints will be described.

Factors Influencing a City Leader's Power   Previous chapters mentioned several sources of power available to city leaders. Leaders and their opposition work with these sources or conditions of influence. Power results from the leader's ability to use these resources and minimize the effects of constraints on power. As we look at the case studies, evaluate how each leader works with these concerns:

1. *Political structures.* Some cities give mayors significant authority; others limit the power of the mayor. Some cities have strong, independent city councils, others have weak councils. In some cities, the legacy of the urban machine encourages strength in the mayor's office. In others, reform traditions institutionalize delegation of authority to civil servants and career administrators.

2. *Federal and state government.* As we have seen, state and federal governments have been a source of money and support at different times. Leaders can exert influence on state and federal programs to accomplish their goals. They can propose legislation and influence the distribution of funds.

3. *The private sector.* The Atlanta case demonstrated the important role of private-sector interests in a leader's success. To bring about changes in

land use and encourage industrial and commercial growth, the support of business interests is essential.

4. *Organized citizens.* Political organizations, neighborhood groups, organized labor, and citizens organized around a particular interest or concern can be potential allies for a leader. They help him or her get elected and they can support and aid in implementing policies.

5. *The bureaucracy.* Elected leaders often are unable to command city employees. Generally, they are organized and are holders of expertise and experience that can be a source of support or opposition to a leader.

6. *Changing economic structures.* As resources have moved to suburban and outlining areas, cities are faced with less income for a progressively poorer population.

7. *Controls on bureaucratic influence.* Legal changes limit the ability of mayors to control employees through patronage and gain private-sector support through preferential contracts. Laws requiring public access to city decisions and open proceedings limit the ability of leaders to covertly reward and punish people and groups.

8. *Vigilant press.* Active, aggressive reporting limits the ability of leaders to act secretly.

9. *Resource limitations.* Citizen groups and state legislators frequently act to limit city resources. The tax revolt of the 1970s, for example, placed limits on the ability of city officials to raise revenue. State legislatures in many states require state action to increase revenue.

10. *Governmental fragmentation.* With numerous governments spanning the urban area, and valuable resources often contained in small governments, big city mayors lack the resources and the jurisdiction to deal with many urban problems.

LOS ANGELES: MAYOR TOM BRADLEY ENERGIZES THE POLICY-MAKING PROCESS

We turn first to Los Angeles and the efforts of Mayor Tom Bradley to put together a coalition of African Americans, liberal Whites, and elements of the business community. His success demonstrates that through sustained effort and the right kind of person, a decentralized political system can be organized to carry out centrally directed programs. We will look briefly at some of the characteristics of the Los Angeles setting that are relevant to Bradley's success. Then, we will chronicle the years prior to Bradley's election as mayor and trace the elements of his successful coalition. In conclusion, we will focus on the problems the Bradley regime experienced in its later years. As the case unfolds, keep in mind the general properties of successful regimes and the discussion of the nature of power in cities.

The mayor of a major city is a chief executive, its major ambassador and a primary influence on the international position of the city. Mayor Tom Bradley of Los Angeles entertains Britain's Queen Elizabeth.

AP/Wide World Photos

The Los Angeles Setting

Los Angeles is the nation's second largest city with a population of over three million, nestled within an urban area of well over eight million. The city is the major government, but by no means the only important center within a huge urban area covering over 500 square miles. Most analysts describe Los Angeles as more decentralized and fragmented than other large cities (see Fogelson 1967).

The city's position as a major American city is a relatively recent one. In 1900, when New York and Chicago were major metropolitan centers of several million people, Los Angeles contained but 102,000. Migration to Los Angeles increased significantly throughout the twentieth century, but was most marked after World War II. The city is a product of the more recent changes in the industrial structure, discussed in Chapter 3.

Migrants to Los Angeles were more likely to be second-generation American citizens than recent immigrants. In the early years, therefore, the city never had a strong immigrant-centered social structure conducive to the development of the urban machine. The city grew with the automobile so houses and apartments tended to spread out beyond the city center, creating lower densities. The central city, while always important and the focus of government, never became the concentrated area of commerce and employment that one finds in older cities.

The racial and ethnic composition of the city sets it apart from large cities in other regions. Latinos are the

(continued)

(continued)

major ethnic group and their numbers have increased significantly in recent years. From 1970 to 1990, the Latino population increased from 18.4 percent of the city total to 40 percent. African Americans constitute 14 percent of the 1990 population, an increase from 10.8 percent in 1970. While segregation of other groups has always been significant, the structure of the city and the space available allowed both groups more living options than did Chicago or New York.

Reform political institutions have always been common in Los Angeles. Like most California cities, elections have always been non-partisan, and party organizations have played little part in the election process. Civil service has always been extensive, leaving few patronage appointments for the mayor. The structure of government delegates significant power to the city council and to appointed commissions that have direct control over some city departments. Therefore, legally, the mayor's position has been less powerful than is common in other big cities, and city councils can frequently over-rule the mayor on policy questions. The commissions tend to limit mayoral influence in several important areas such as public works and the police. Thus, Los Angeles mayors come to office with little direct authority to make significant changes in policy.

Historically, mayors were considered tools of the business community. Banfield and Wilson, for instance, noted that:

> (I)n Los Angeles, the selection of a candidate to represent the important downtown and commercial interests is made after a series of meetings in which are brought together the spokesmen of the metropolitan press, the larger manufacturing and utility companies and the banks, department stores and other

leading interests. *The Los Angeles Times* has often taken the lead in arranging such meetings. Campaign funds are raised almost entirely from corporate gifts by executives of large corporations. A public relations firm is hired to conduct the campaign. It is given a budget, told in a general way what issues are important, and left to manage the campaign as it thinks best. (1963)

Yet governmental accomplishments were significant. Major city-sponsored water systems permitted the city to develop, and a modern harbor was built through the foresight of city officials. The city prided itself on efficient and professional public management.

Political History Prior to Bradley

Historically, the city of Los Angeles was dominated by reform-minded politicians with close ties to the business community. Representation of minority groups on the city council and in government positions generally was limited. Bradley's immediate predecessor, Sam Yorty, mayor from 1961 to 1973, was the first to break the pattern of subservience to the business class. Yorty's early career was best-described as working-class populist. He had been elected to Congress as a democrat, and his advocacy of a single container for garbage collection rather than the separation of recyclables was largely responsible for his landslide victory in 1961, over an incumbent supported by the business elite. The issue was a symbol for a candidate who would represent the average person against the concerns of the business class.

Yorty's perspective on the world seemed to change significantly when a major civil disturbance in 1965, known today as the Watts Riot, occurred in south central Los Angeles. The events were the first major civil disturbance of the 1960s. Over $183 million in property damage occurred and 53 people were killed. The riots disturbed the generally tranquil view of the city, and suddenly placed the mayor in the national spotlight. In Senate hearings following the riots, perhaps unfairly, Yorty became the symbol of the elected official who had little concern for the welfare of deprived citizens as he defensively supported his position as one with little influence over city policies. The Kennedy administration interpreted his views as an explanation for the inattention of cities to the plight of the poor.

In 1963, three African Americans, among them Tom Bradley, were elected to the 15-member city council. Bradley, a former athlete at UCLA and former police officer, had become active in local liberal politics. This activity put him in contact with members of the largely Jewish west side political organization that was to form the basis for his coalition when he ran for mayor. He and other liberals on the council saw the Watts Riot as an opportunity to forge a consensus for more direct intervention by the city in economic and social concerns. The federal government was providing significant funds to cities (see Chapter 5), but the Yorty administration was not interested in receiving them. Bradley and his allies on the council pursued these funds as council projects, often challenging the Yorty administration to be more aggressive with the federal government. He also became active in city concerns nationally, becoming the first non-mayor to serve as vice president of the National League of Cities in 1963.

Bradley challenged Yorty for the mayor's position in 1968. The election became a bitterly divisive one following Bradley's strong showing in the primary election. Yorty's campaign heightened racial tensions in the city by claiming that much of the police force would resign if Bradley were elected. The appeal to people's fears led to another Yorty victory, but increased tensions between the more liberal council and an increasingly reactionary mayor.

Bradley, meanwhile, expanded his influence on the council and tried to create a liberal counter to the mayor within the council. At his initiation, the council formed the Board of Grants Administration, over Yorty's veto, to seek and coordinate federal funds.

In a 1973 electoral rematch against Yorty, Bradley focused on his ability to bring warring factions of the city together and to more aggressively seek federal funds to deal with the city's problems. He won the election easily.

The Bradley Coalition

Significant changes in numerous facets of city government occurred during Bradley's 20 years in the mayor's office (1973–1993). Federal aid increased radically; from under $100 million in 1972 to a high of $320 million in 1978. Through redevelopment, downtown was fundamentally rebuilt, changing it from an aging center of run-down buildings with little claim to being a real city center, to one with numerous stunning high rises housing the main offices of banks, insurance companies, businesses, and high-rent apartments. The port was modernized and new airport terminals were built, and investment expanded to other parts of the community, particularly the glitzy west side. The 1984 Olympics, spearheaded by Bradley, were an immense success and projected the image of a progressive Los Angeles around the globe.

Behind these efforts was a new coalition in city hall that formed the alliances necessary to bring forth these changes. How was Bradley able to pull off such a significant change in city policy? Several elements were

(continued)

(continued)

brought together under his leadership.

1. *The political coalition.* Bradley's early links with the Democratic Party and the westside community served as a source of political support. The result was strong electoral support in both communities, uniting groups that weren't always political allies.

2. *The support of the council.* As a prominent member of the city council for a number of years, Bradley had earned the respect of most members and the strong confidence of a majority. He solidified this connection by including the council members in the making of major decisions and delegating decisions within council districts to the council members. Thus, the conflict between council and mayor faded considerably during the Bradley years, and the council generally went along with his initiatives.

3. *Support of downtown business interests.* Downtown redevelopment plans were drawn up with the encouragement and direction of business interests. Important elements of the business community became strong supporters as redevelopment successfully gave taxing advantages to the business community.

4. *Organized labor.* Support from organized labor was secured through the building boom that proceeded from redevelopment projects. This extended the coalition's support into some sectors of the White working class.

5. *Control of federal funds.* Bradley maintained control of many of the federal funds within the mayor's office. This provided a source of direct funding for patronage appointments, and permitted personal control and credit for many of the projects.

6. *Commission appointments.* The Bradley Administration used the numerous commission appointments to reward supporters and broaden the decision-making structure. Significantly more women and minority appointments were made in the Bradley years.

7. *Community-based organizations.* Within many of the ethnic communities in Los Angeles were numerous community organizations that had assumed some responsibility for delivery of social services to less well-off populations. These organizations also served as important political organizations. Their power had been limited during the Yorty years, but Bradley decentralized some of the new federal grants to these organizations, making them partners in public service delivery. In turn, these organizations lent political support to the mayor.

8. *Support of council candidates.* Bradley used his personal influence to recruit and campaign for key council candidates. When elected, these council members were, of course, supportive of the mayor's initiatives.

9. *Leadership style.* Bradley's leadership style has been described as low key and non-ego driven. He was willing to give others credit for accomplishments that might be assumed by the mayor. He successfully cultivated an image of a hard-working, conservative person who had earned the mayor's office and was fundamentally decent. His image as a minority and a liberal was balanced by conservative principles and his background as a police officer.

Bill Boyarsky, a veteran *Los Angeles Times* reporter, described him in the following way:

Bradley was a tall, athletic looking man, possessed even in later years of his UCLA track star body. He talked little. Interviewing him was a chore. He was reserved and dignified, impeccably dressed. He had command presence. When he called me in to bawl me out about something I had written as *The Times* city hall reporter, I felt I was being hauled into the principal's office. (1980)

Bradley's leadership brought diverse parts of the community together to form a coalition that significantly changed the size of government in Los Angeles. The coalition survived through the influx of new money from federal funds, redevelopment, a generally positive business climate, and the ability to reach potential voters. Power shifted from the council and dispersed commissions to the mayor's office. At the height of its influence, the normally decentralized political system obtained considerably more central cohesion.

The Decline of the Bradley Coalition

The success of the coalition depended on public actions and financial support to diverse people. In the late 1970s, the means to keep the coalition together declined rather abruptly. The passage of the property tax limitation, Proposition 13 in 1978, drastically curtailed one of the major funding sources for the city and immediately reduced city income. The federal funding declines of the Carter and Reagan administrations followed, leaving the mayor's office without its major source of discretionary income.

At about the same time, tensions emerged between development interests, environmental interests, and those concerned with moderate-and low-income housing and traffic congestion. Bradley had moderated his pro-business stance in the mid 1980s to accommodate disaffected liberal interests. Housing for the poor and lower class expanded and became an important component of redevelopment, but tensions continued. As funding declined, however, it became more difficult to pursue business, environmental, and community interests simultaneously through downtown expansion. Many former supporters became vocal critics as the problems that follow business growth and economic expansion increased.

The one element of the bureaucracy Bradley never was able to influence was the police department. Conservative Police Chief Daryl Gates continued in office because of the generally positive image of the active efforts of community support groups in White middle-class areas and the department's positive professional image. Bradley, thus, had to co-exist with Gates, in spite of opposition to him within the African American community because of the power he seemed to wield. The two, however, scrapped frequently and were rarely on speaking terms. When community anger exploded following the failure to convict the officers involved in the beating of Rodney King, the lack of communication between the mayor and police chief's offices was sadly brought to light. The dramatization of the case split the community, fraying the Black-liberal coalitions (see Chapter 7).

Bradley served out his term, but the last five years lacked the strength and enthusiasm of the first 15. The city had changed with the influx of many new Latino and Asian residents, the movement of much of the middle class to the suburbs, and an expanding international business presence. If city hall were to play an important role in the life of the city, new coalition partners were needed.

SOURCE: The case is based on material found in Ainsworth, 1969; Saltzstein, Sonenshein, and Ostrow 1986; and Sonenshein 1993.

CHICAGO: RICHARD DALEY AND THE CHICAGO MACHINE: RENEWAL AND DECLINE

From 1955 to 1976, Richard Daley assumed more influence over the governmental system of Chicago than any mayor in modern political history. Under Daley, the city council became a rubber stamp for his policies; one critic compared it to the Supreme Soviet during the Stalin years. He earned the respect and support of the business community and the state and federal governments, and all contributed mightily to the machines coffers. Voters reelected Daley by wide margins every time he ran; he became a folk hero to many—a tough working class man who could get what he wanted from the educated elites.

Daley correctly understood the changes in urban society in the post-World War II era and adapted the traditional urban machine to meet these new conditions. His coalition eventually became the victim of further changes in urban life and his own actions. Thus, his time as mayor demonstrates how one can build an effective coalition and the forces that tear it apart.

Chicago and the Age of Industrialization

Chicago's rise to urban prominence was entirely the consequence of the age of industrialization from 1880 to 1920. In 1860, the city was a minor trading center of 100,000 people with little to distinguish it from other middlewestern cities. (Both St. Louis and Cincinnati were larger cities at that time.) The great fire of 1871 destroyed the central city leaving one-third of the population homeless, destroying 17,450 buildings and 73 miles of streets. Public officials accepted the aftermath of this devastation as a great challenge and rebuilt the city to meet the needs of a changing society. Swamps were drained, the central city redesigned,

and the river system expanded to connect the city's boat and barge traffic to the Mississippi. The new Chicago contained all the prerequisites of an industrial city in the early years of the twentieth century. Central railroad lines connected it to the Atlantic seaboard, and the widened Chicago River gave the city a direct link to the Mississippi and all points south. Iron ore from Minnesota could float down the lakes, while finished products could exit by rail and boat. With the addition of large numbers of unskilled but eager immigrants, all the ingredients for economic growth in the industrial era were present.

Chicago grew rapidly in the next 40 years to become the nation's second largest city. By 1930, over 33 million people lived within the city boundaries; more than two-thirds recent immigrants from eastern and central Europe who were attracted to the needs of heavy industry. With large ethnic populations and the governmental needs of an industrial society, the urban machine was the logical political response. (The description of the machine in Chapter 3, in fact, is based primarily on what is known of Chicago in the early twentieth century.) Immigrant groups lived in compact neighborhoods where their own customs and traditions were preserved. Political entrepreneurs connected the new residents with employers and government and ruled through tightly run wards controlled by clever ward politicians. Residents gained city jobs and received services if they helped get out the vote. A city council of 50 wards and a partisanly elected mayor with influence over all aspects of local government provided the means for a powerful urban machine. With over 30,000 patronage jobs and few controls over the letting of contracts and zoning decisions, government provided ample resources to the mayor and the ward leaders. Notorious connections with organized crime preserved local customs that may have been defined as illegal by the larger society and served as a source of funds for ward leaders and the central bosses. An aggressive business community with needs for public services was more than willing to make the necessary deals with machine leaders. Few members of the upper class had the time or interest in political reform. As pointed out in Chapter 3, machines provided governmental services in a society with little central unity. In Chicago, the prerequisites for a strong machine were all in place.

Richard Daley was born in 1902, in a working-class Irish neighborhood of Chicago less than a block from his residence as mayor. His parents were immigrants; his father worked in a steel mill. Daley was employed briefly in the stockyards, but gravitated toward politics as a precinct captain at the age of 21. He advanced up the machine ladder, first as a clerk to the city council, and later as a state representative and state senator. He also served briefly as the director of the Illinois Department of Finance.

Daley gained access to city leadership in 1953, through election as the chairman of the Cook County Democratic Committee. Historically, this committee controlled the recruitment of candidates to all city offices, and was vital to the operation of the machine system as a limit to the power of the mayor and city council. Mayors generally were beholden to the committee since it placed people in the critical city council positions. Daley ran successfully for mayor in 1955.

The Making of a New Coalition

The social and economic characteristics of the city were undergoing immense change as Daley assumed office. As much of the working class moved to the suburbs and immigration from Europe declined, the ethnic neighborhood became less significant in the life of the city. The sons and daughters of first-generation immigrants now spoke English and, through the war effort, became more a part of common American culture. New industries moved to the suburbs as the forces of change described in Chapter 3 took place. Suburban communities surround Chicago, and as residents and businesses moved, the city often lost resources.

At the same time, the collapse of the southern agricultural economy led many African Americans to venture north. Chicago became a primary destination because of its reputation as a major employer of unskilled laborers, a general environment of tolerance, and the presence of a small, comparatively successful Black community. The Chicago African American population increased from 322,000 in 1930 to 812,000 in 1960; becoming over one-fifth of the city's total. Most settled in the inner city and were restricted to a small number of clearly defined neighborhoods. As employment in heavy industry declined, many of the new residents slipped into poverty.

Social and economic change was pulling the machine apart. White ethnic neighborhoods now were less cohesive and many residents had moved to the suburbs; businesses were now larger, national in scope, with less need for unskilled labor; and the suburbs, with better air and truck connections, were the preferred industrial location. Public values were changing, too; supporters of reform were now more vocal, and concerns for professional management and opposition to the corruption of the machine were heard frequently. There was also an increase in racial tension as the Black population expanded. The old urban machine was poorly suited for the new Chicago.

(continued)

(continued)

Daley Responds to the New Chicago

Daley knew that leading Chicago required major changes in the traditional machine. Upon assuming office, he retained his position as Chair of the Democratic Central Committee, giving him direct control over the city council. Thus, no longer would the mayor be beholden to a coalition of the council. He convinced the state legislature to change laws, giving him the authority to control the city budget. With authority centralized, he implemented reforms in service delivery. Patronage appointments continued, and the ward leaders accepted Daley's command while retaining the ability to reward supporters. Daley could rely on the machine to win elections, but he was less beholden to ward leaders when distributing the spoils of office.

Daley foresaw further decline in the city's fortunes unless the business community could be persuaded to invest in the central city. Urban renewal seemed the obvious vehicle for retention of businesses in the downtown area, so he worked closely with the banking and business community to provide new locations for business interests. This required the condemnation of land, often destroying neighborhoods and lessening the tax burden on the new land uses. In return, business interests became supporters of the machine.

He also proposed and built elaborate facilities that were particularly important to the business community. A modern airport, new hospitals, a downtown university, and the largest convention facility in the country at the time were built under Daley's leadership. He oversaw the construction of massive freeways to accommodate traffic from the suburbs to downtown. The cultural community applauded the architectural designs of the new buildings and a major Picasso statue was placed in the civic center. The power of the machine permitted Daley to produce new buildings faster and with less bureaucratic hassle than occurred in other cities; in his words, Chicago was "the city that works."

Daley's skill in accommodating suburban interests was apparent in less dramatic innovations. Michigan Avenue is Chicago's most prominent boulevard, and one of the world's most beautiful urban streets. Turn of the century architectural landmarks, including Chicago Institute of Art, one of the world's best art museums, line the street and beautiful Lake Michigan is frequently in view. Michigan Avenue is the gateway to the downtown centers of commerce and industry and viewed daily by commuters on their way to work.

Each spring, the pavement of most northern cities is filled with holes from a long winter of freezes and snowplowing. Chicago's drivers drove home one spring evening, dodging large potholes and broken sections of asphalt, but the next morning, the same drivers traveled on a newly paved Michigan Avenue. Daley had lined up all the city's paving contractors and assigned them half a block, providing each with a set, generous price on the condition that the work be completed by morning. Competitive bids and public hearings were not necessary when Daley wanted something done.

Daley responded to concern for the quality of the public services by appointing key professionals to run many of the departments. When the newspapers reported on scandal in the police department, angering the forces of good government, Daley hired O.W. Wilson, then head of the Criminology School at the University of California, Berkeley, as the new police chief. When school quality became an issue, Benjamin Willis, another noted authority, was appointed school chief. Professional appointments served to dampen calls for more general reform. Thus, the patronage machine could continue with less criticism from reformers.

Daley viewed the increasing numbers of African Americans as similar to new immigrants in the old machine. He included African Americans in the machine, giving them places on the city council and other patronage positions. As the machine took hold, African Americans responded by supporting the machine at the polls with greater loyalty than other groups.

Daley's control over the election machinery and appointments to public office provided the means for influence at the state and federal levels. Chicago congressmen and state officers were cogs in the machine, reporting to the mayor. With a group of loyal supporters, he could extract favors from governors and even presidents. Kennedy's election in a very close race in 1960, for instance, was attributed to very high margins won in Chicago. From that time forward, while the Democrats were in office, Daley secured abundant federal funds and could control their use. Demands for citizen participation in the Kennedy-Johnson programs were ignored without reprisals from Washington D.C., and pressures for school integration of schools fell on deaf ears in Chicago, but federal money for education continued.

The last group whose support was needed, the White working class, was the most difficult to maintain. Fear of interracial integration and racial prejudice replaced need for the services of the machine as the dominant concern of White ethnic groups. As the number of African Americans increased, and their members tried to move into White ethnic areas, clashes became common. Daley was cross-pressured by the need to accommodate both groups. African Americans pressed for improved facilities, integrated schools, and the right to move beyond the crowded confines of the ghetto. The White working class groups feared

integration and pressed for continued segregation. Daley responded by building massive new public housing largely for African Americans within the confines of the ghetto areas. Lacking the social structure of the old neighborhoods, new projects quickly acquired all the negative traits of declining communities. The mayor approved a massive freeway to purposely create a wall between White and Black. He forestalled school integration by moving temporary classes, dubbed "Willis Wagons," onto existing largely African American school properties while schools in White areas went underutilized.

A tough police presence also helped to placate the concerns of the White working class. When abuses were brought to light, Daley blamed them on a few Communistic militants. Daley reminded his supporters of his background. His accent reflected his upbringing in an Irish home, and his frequent mispronunciations and inelegant phrases were perceived as signals to the White working class that he remained one of them.

The Machine Unravels

In the spring of 1967, Daley was at the height of his power. The voters re-elected him overwhelmingly; he carried all 50 wards. Other cities experienced major civil disturbances in the summer of 1965, but Chicago had been relatively quiet. Martin Luther King had come to town organizing marches and rallies. The marches were met by rock-throwing, White, working-class citizens. Daley met with King and seemed to defuse the anger, but King left without an agreement of major policy changes. Daley was one of the few mayors who remained strong in spite of the turmoil of the 1960s.

Soon, strains within the coalition came to the surface. King's assassination in April of 1968 triggered more serious civil disturbances. Daley responded by publicly ordering the police

(continued)

(continued)

Mayor Richard Daley in one of his least dignified moments, shouts his displeasure at the proceedings of the 1968 Democratic Party Convention.

© Bettmann/Corbis

department to shoot to kill arsonists and looters. Though he later recanted the phrase, it became a rallying point for the machine's critics and generated much negative publicity.

The next year the city hosted the National Convention of the Democratic Party. The primaries had been disorderly, conflict-ridden, and saddened significantly by the death of Robert Kennedy. Daley looked forward to the convention as his chance to visibly demonstrate that "Chicago worked." Members of the anti-war and civil rights movements occupied the city's parks and major rioting ensued when police and anti-war demonstrators clashed. When criticism of Daley's police tactics was raised on the Convention floor, Chicago's mayor was seen nationally shouting obscenities. To Daley's critics, the "city that works" wasn't working, and now there was some visible evidence.

The city's redevelopment efforts became a focus for neighborhood

criticism at roughly the same time. Neighborhood groups demanded participation, and organizers objected to the destruction of neighborhoods to make way for business and upper-class interests.

Daley's greatest challenge, however, was the African American community. As more Whites moved to the suburbs and the Black population increased, African Americans became an increasingly larger part of his electoral strength. In 1963, Daley actually lost a majority of the White vote, but won easily as a consequence of strong support in Black wards.

Gradually complaints of police abuse and conflicts over schools and housing fueled greater African American opposition to the mayor. The police raided the headquarters of the Black Panther Party in 1969, killing two well-known and respected youths. Subsequent investigations questioned the police version of the incident suggesting that those killed were unarmed. The incident became a rallying point for the machine's opponents, and by 1975, Black politicians openly rebelled against the Daley forces and won several key elections against candidates endorsed by Daley.

Daley won re-election in 1975 following the first real contested election since his initial victory in 1955. The relatively close election (Daley won 57 percent of the vote compared to over 70 percent in the previous two elections) was a sign of the decreased power of the machine. Black support had trailed off significantly, and though White support remained strong, Whites represented an increasingly smaller percent of the voters.

Indictments of several key Daley appointees tarnished his public image and provided fuel for reform candidates. Legal decisions lessened the number of patronage positions available to the machine, and they also forced the city to disperse public housing. Discrimination in the hiring of police officers led to a court order demanding that hiring practices be changed. Then, revenue sharing funds were impounded until some of these abuses were corrected. Obviously Daley's influence in state and federal circles had diminished, but he vowed to fight the attempt to change practices in the police department. Daley died in 1976, still the mayor, but no longer the leader of a powerful, successful coalition.

Source: This case is based on the following sources: Cohen and Taylor 2000; Klepner 1985; Lemann 1991; Miller 1996; O'Connor 1975; Orfield 1969; Rakove 1975; Royko 1971; and Snowiss 1966.

NEW YORK: ROBERT MOSES, POWER BEHIND THE SCENES

You've got to understand—every morning when the mayor comes to work there are a hundred problems that must be solved. And a lot of them are so big and complex that they just don't seem susceptible to solution. And when he asks guys for solutions, what happens? Most of them can't give him any. And those that do come up with solutions, the solutions are unrealistic or impractical—or just plain stupid. And those that do make sense—there's no money to finance them, but you give a problem to Moses and overnight he is back in front of you with a solution, all worked out down to the last detail, drafts of speeches you can give to explain it to the public, drafts of press releases for the newspapers, drafts of state laws you'll need to get passed, advice as to who should introduce new bills in the legislature and what committees to go to. Drafts of any City Council and Board of Estimate resolutions you'll need; if there are Constitutional questions involved, a list of relevant precedents—and a complete method of financing it all spelled out. He had solutions when no one else had solutions. A mayor *needs* a Robert Moses—Judge Jacob Lutsky, an advisor to several mayors of New York (quoted in 1975 Caro: 463)

We turn now to a man who never held elective office yet managed to single-handedly control much of the spending on capital improvements in the city of New York for a period of 40 years; from the depths of the Depression to the expansion of government in the 1950s and early 1960s. Most state and federal funds for the city flowed through the offices of Robert Moses. Parks, roads, mass

(continued)

(continued)

transit, and public housing were built by agencies he controlled. While visible in city matters, few realized the extent of his influence until the publication of a painstakingly detailed and fascinating biography by Robert Caro from which most of this discussion is drawn. Caro's picture of Moses is that of a man who appeared to serve city leaders tirelessly and deferentially, using his skills and charms to enhance the betterment of the city. Behind the façade was a man who ruthlessly garnered power to control an invisible empire and radically change the face of the city. At the height of his influence, mayors, bankers, and even governors came to Moses for help.

Moses' influence is more astounding when one considers the setting. New York City is led by one of the world's largest governments; its budget and payroll dwarf those of most states and many countries. New York City government combines all functions of civil government, schools, and even a large university system. It is governed by a separately elected, legally powerful mayor; a city council elected in wards; and until 1989, a second legislative body, the Board of Estimate, consisting of powerful elected borough presidents and several other elected officers. At the height of Moses' influence, the city employed over 150,000 people, including over 30,000 police officers, and had a budget exceeding $2 billion.

The city is also highly politicized by partisan elections and broad public interest in politics. Both machine and reform traditions are present and generally compete for elective office. Public administrators are organized through alliances with key professional and public interest groups and unions.

Most describe New York as a place that is ungovernable. Sayre and Kaufman, in the most thorough study of the city, argued that decision making was divided by functional specialized groups. Health decisions, for instance, were made by health administrators, health employees, and organizations representing key external groups such as doctors, nurses, and public health advocates. Police administrators, members of police unions, and interest groups concerned about law and order, made police decisions. Once key groups within one functional area agreed, the mayor and city council were unlikely to interfere. Thus, power was pluralized generally with no one group controlling all areas of policy, but within each policy area, key interests dominated decisions (Sayre and Kaufman 1960). Their analysis suggests that it would be very difficult for a mayor to wield influence. Yet Moses became powerful without the benefit of elective office.

The Career of Robert Moses

Moses began life with many advantages. His parents were wealthy and encouraged their intellectually gifted son to pursue the best possible education. He earned degrees from Yale and Oxford, then joined the Bureau of Municipal Research, a reform organization pioneering in the development and application of techniques of public administration. There he became a champion of reform management; developing techniques to evaluate employees based on their skills and work accomplishments and budgeting techniques that encouraged quantitative evaluations of city expenditures. A few years later, he extended his efforts to the state level as a member of the State Efficiency Commission. His efforts won the attention of Governor Al Smith who made Moses one of his major assistants in 1923, at the age of 35.

As the governor's aid, Moses focused his intelligence and energy on the techniques of state power. He learned to draft bills and evaluate the impact of legislative language. Smith rewarded him with the first of many commission appointments—head of the Long Island State Parks Commission in 1923. This would prove to be the beginning of the source of much of Moses' later influence. He drafted legislation creating commissions that were given authority to run specific services. Once enacted in law, Moses was frequently appointed as the commission's executive director. He then would hire a loyal and technically skilled staff, referred to as "Moses' men", who often stayed with him throughout their careers.

Through this power, Moses developed an elaborate park system in Long Island and later throughout the state. In 1932, when the federal government began funding public works projects to put people back to work, Moses was placed in charge of the State Emergency Public Works Commission that screened projects and became a conduit for federal funds. In 1933, he joined the City of New York administration as park commissioner, while retaining several of his state positions.

By 1934, Moses seemed destined for a major role in elective politics. He won the Republican nomination for governor. His lone try for elective office, however, led to one of the few major defeats of his long career. He proved to be a poor public speaker and frequently antagonized potential supporters and the press. He was soundly defeated.

Electoral defeat, however, did not dampen his energy and enthusiasm for political influence. As the federal government became a more important player, Moses convinced the legislature to create new districts to handle freeway construction, bridges, and later public housing. The pattern developed in the park efforts continued in this new area of concern; Moses was appointed the executive of the districts, and friends of his became the governing body.

The backbone of Moses' power was the creation of a new kind of government referred to as the *Authority.* We pointed out in Chapter 4 that special districts are a common form of local government designed to produce a single or limited number of governmental functions. The governments Moses controlled began as special districts. They were often given the authority to borrow money on the assumption that proceeds from the project would eventually pay off the debt. Thus, bridges were built and tolls were used to pay for the cost. Once the project was paid for, it was expected that the authority would no longer charge the toll. The bridges and tunnels under his direction were built as automobile ownership expanded, and money made by the tolls increased beyond the original expectations. Moses realized that this stream of income could then be used for other projects.

Authorities were also expected to be run similar to private businesses. Laws championed by Moses exempted his authorities from civil service rules and requirements for competitive bidding of contracts. He was permitted to make decisions secretly and his records were often shielded from the press. With the power to hire his own employees and award his supporters with contracts, he could get things done more quickly and with greater skill than other government agencies. He could pay his employees more, which helped him retain competent, skilled employees.

As the federal government expanded its involvement in urban matters in the post-World War II years, Moses was ready with a skilled staff, experience in managing major public works, and the ability to influence the legislatures and city councils to extend authority to him. Thus, public housing, urban renewal and interstate highway funds became a part of his empire. In 1945, he was appointed Coordinator of

(continued)

(continued)

Construction for the City—placing all federal funds in the city were under his influence. Caro estimated that in the 15 years following World War II, agencies controlled by Moses spent $4.5 billion while spending under the control of the city council and Board of Estimate totaled $3.75 billion.

If Moses were simply following the leadership of city officials in his efforts, one could view his work as that of a loyal city official with little independent influence. However, Caro points out that Moses had distinct policy goals and carried them out with little deference to others. The beautiful beaches he built on Long Island were purposely planned to discourage their use by African Americans and the poor. Bridges on the approaches to the beaches offered minimum clearance, preventing busses from traveling. He lowered the temperature of the pools, assuming that African Americans did not like cold water, and hired only White life guards on the better beaches. His slum clearance efforts destroyed minority neighborhoods, leaving White areas unaffected. Little concern was given to assisting those displaced by his projects, and public housing was meant to segregate African Americans and Latinos. The new housing units provided minimal amenities and rapidly deteriorated into worse slums than the neighborhoods that had been uprooted. Caro maintains that Moses systematically defeated every attempt to create a master plan that "might have enabled the city to develop on a rational, logical, unified pattern—defeated it until, when it was finally adopted, it was too late for it to do much good" (1974: 20). He attributes the decline of the city in the 1960s to Moses' influence. His work encouraged the degradation of the poor, the segregation of races, the decline of mass transit, and the rise of the suburbs. Others would point out that larger trends might be equally responsible for these results (see Kaufman 1975). As we have seen these same trends occurred in most cities. Undeniably, Moses work did little to counter the negative effects of Post World War II changes, and probably encouraged the forces that led to the decline of the central city.

Moses and Power: What Were the Keys to His Success?

Moses remained powerful well beyond the age when most of us retire. Only when confronted by Governor Rockefeller, who had the resources and confidence to act independently of Moses, did the strings of his empire begin to loosen. Yet in his late 70s he organized New York's World's Fair and remained a power to be reckoned with. Why was he able to exert such an influence? Caro identified four general sources of his power:

1. *Knowledge and skill.* Moses' career demonstrates that knowledge and skill by themselves can be sources of power and influence. Early in his career, he learned how government agencies work and thus how they can be influenced. His time in the state legislature taught him how bills were written and how clauses in legislative acts, unseen by those who propose them, can move authority and funds in prescribed ways. He also knew how to organize people to maximize their potential and gain the most from them. The organizations under his control could then out produce others. He was known as one who could get things done; hence, power was delegated to him.

2. *Personality.* Moses was gifted with multiple personalities that often could be changed to maximize his influence. He could be charming and ingratiating to those whom he wanted to influence. To some he was a charismatic leader; he was followed by those who saw him as one who

Robert Moses, directing one of the many large public works projects built during his time, with the city skyline in the background. Most of the major public projects built in the city in the 1950s and 1960s were in his control.

AP/Wide World Photos

knew the best course of action. At other times, he was ruthless; one to be feared. A wise aid or co-worker learned never to contradict Mr. Moses—careers were ruined when he was crossed. He was often arrogant to the point of bull headedness, and out of fear, respect, or a sense of his rightness, Moses got his way. He sweet-talked those whose support he needed, he demanded order from his staff, and rewarded those who performed. He dressed down his enemies publicly if that gained him support. Often he threatened to resign when he couldn't get his way, and others always backed down. He used all contours of his personality to accomplish his wishes.

3. *Image.* Moses effectively cultivated an image of a public regarding, selfless servant. His salary was always modest and he refused to live lavishly. He alluded frequently to his background in the reform movement, portraying himself as a public servant unattached to private interests. To the public, he was someone who could be trusted with public authority. Thus, politicians were willing to delegate power to him.

4. *Flexibility.* Though Moses had precise policy goals, he learned early in his career that one had to make

(continued)

(continued)

compromises to get ahead. For that reason, parkways curved around wealthy estates, and urban renewal avoided influential neighborhoods. While often stubborn and unyielding, he could give in when it seemed to be in his interest to do so, and he could give others credit for his accomplishments if power or respect could be gained as a consequence.

Who ruled New York in the Moses era? Was it a power elite or a pluralized group? Did the structure of community resources dictate an upper class advantage? Caro argues that the needs of the poor were hindered by Moses' efforts. His personal biases were elitist: Parks were for those who could take care of them and appreciate their value, and those who couldn't care for themselves consciously chose slums. While these were his personal values, they also coincided with those who could help him the most.

Moses knew that pleasing key interests was the key to his success. As a public official quoted by Caro states:

Each of these groups—bankers, union people, whatever—all had their own interests at heart, but Moses succeeded in combining all interests behind his own aims. He gave everybody involved in the political setup in this city whatever it was they wanted. Therefore they all had their own interest in seeing him succeed, The pressure that interest all added up was to a pressure that no one in the system could stand against, because it came from the system itself. (1974: 347)

As he pulled coalitions together, therefore, the participants were getting a piece of the action. Was the result Moses' own plan or the will of the participants? It is difficult to say. Like Bradley and Daley, Moses needed the support of community groups, but he faced these groups from a position of greater strength than did the other two.

SOURCE: This case is based on Caro 1974; Kaufman 1975; and Sayre and Kaufman 1960.

POWER IN THE AMERICAN CITY:
SUMMARY AND CONCLUSIONS

We began the chapter by examining approaches to the study of power. Social scientists spent decades looking for ways of measuring power with little success. Power remains central to an understanding of city politics, so the quest for understanding of power must continue though few will agree on its definition and measurement. We looked at case studies of power and influence in our three largest cities. These examples lack the precision and sophistication of earlier studies of power, yet they yield insights into the importance of power holding, and the impacts of different kinds of power are evident when we compare these three cases. Several general conclusions can be drawn from the cases:

1. *We find little evidence of either a power elite or a pluralist distribution of power.* None of those who study power in these three cases make mention of a covert elite that directs those in power. The relationship between business leaders and government officials may be one of government officials proposing access to government in return for political support rather than

business leaders using government officials to accomplish their personal goals. Both Daley and Bradley, for instance, sought out business leaders' assistance for downtown redevelopment. Prior to their efforts, business leaders were not necessarily interested in investing in the downtown.

Moses had control of so many resources that often the power elite came to him for support. Banks, for instance, competed for his favor because he had access to so much money. He would often mobilize the elites for his purposes. Hearing that the Metropolitan Opera performed in an inadequate building, that Fordham University desired a downtown campus, and that Carnegie Hall had notified the New York Philharmonic that their lease would not be renewed, Moses proposed what is now Lincoln Center. When the federal Department of Housing and Home Finance balked on providing federal funds, Moses called upon those with influence. Caro reports that, "Father McGinley and other key figures in the Catholic Archdiocese, key union leaders, key bankers, John D. Rockefeller, III himself—all were on the phone to Washington." Albert Cole, an HHFA key administrator, commented, "The amount of pressure put on was unbelievable. . . . He (Moses) just murdered me in there" (Caro 1974: 1016).

2. *We also find little evidence that those in power are representative of the broader population or consistently act in the interests of those not represented.* The concerns of the poor are rarely heard in these three cases. One can argue, perhaps, that Daley's downfall was the consequence of years of inattention to the problems of minorities in the inner city and the failure of the machine to incorporate their concerns. Bradley responded initially to the problems of those in the inner city, but had to balance their interests with those of the financial community. Moses had little concern for the problems of the lower class and acted to make their lives worse.

3. *All three cases support Stone's thesis that coalition leaders look up to the heads of businesses, associations, and high status members rather than downward to those with fewer organizational resources.* Both Bradley and Daley saw the need to include business and civic leaders in their coalitions. Yet unions and neighborhood organization were also prominent in all coalitions and proved to be influential.

4. *Power structures change.* Each case illustrates that the nature of power changes over time. New leaders come forth and pull together different elements of the community. The components of the leader's coalition also changes over time. Daley saw the need to include new elements of the business community that had not been a part of city politics when he took over the machine. Bradley's coalition included vastly different participants than did Yorty's. All three studies demonstrate that federal and state governments played a much larger role in city affairs in the late 1960s than they had previously. To be effective, however, the federal government had to be encouraged by local officials. They were not a prominent player in the Yorty administration even though funds were available.

5. *Leadership and skills make a difference.* The personal characteristics of leaders affect their ability to wield power. In all three of these cases,

knowledge and analysis is an important component of power. The Moses case is the clearest demonstration of this. His skill in understanding the nuances of legislation and in organizing his staff led directly to the power he was able to wield. Daley's understanding of machine politics helped him reorient the machine to meet changing conditions. Bradley's knowledge of the federal government and the contacts he had made as a city council member led to the acquisition of new resources as mayor.

All three expanded their influence as a consequence of their skills in dealing with people. Bradley's experience on the city council and the respect he maintained in the community and with council members permitted him to move the city into new policy areas. Daley's background, speaking style, and demeanor allowed him to maintain the respect of the White working class as he moved policy more in the direction of the business class. The many shades of Moses' personality could charm potential clients and force compliance on the part of subordinates. In all cases, then, personality and the skill in using one's individual characteristics were important components of power.

Power, then, is a resource that often pulls together the diverse sources of influence in an urban area. In the right conditions, leaders act to counteract the splintering of authority that typifies American cities. In our next chapter, we will look at a quality of life in our cities that further divides authority—urban violence.

POWER IN THE TWENTY-FIRST CENTURY CITY: A BRIEF LOOK AT THREE BIG CITY MAYORS

Present day mayors confront a different set of challenges than those featured in our cases. Public resources have changed; federal government resources have declined, states frequently limit property taxes, and the sources of wealth in many cities have migrated to the suburbs. The population is increasingly minority, and many cities have experienced an increase in immigrants. The keys to electoral success, therefore, are different. The global economy presents city officials with an international dimension. Multinational corporations and international firms are now major stake holders. How have current leaders adapted to a different environment? We will look briefly at today's mayors of our three case-study cities—New York, Los Angeles, and Chicago.

Elected in 1993 as a Republican and former city attorney and prosecutor, Rudolph Guiliani seemed ill-suited to be the mayor of a city with a large Democratic majority and a politically active Black and Latino population. His confrontational style and strong support for the police department often generated extreme hostility within the African American community. Yet as he ended his term as mayor in 2001, he can point to a string of important accomplishments and significant sources of support within the city.

"It's just Mayor Giuliani asking us to have a nice day."

© The New Yorker Collection 2000 Lee Lorenz from cartoonbank.com. All Rights Reserved.

Guiliani's style is in marked contrast to that of Bradley, Moses, and Daley. One journalist described him in this way:

> He is a divider, not a uniter. He demonizes anyone who disagrees with him as "idiotic." Or "crazy" or "silly" or "dangerous" or "jerky"... He is a beady-eyed, bully, a ruthless egomaniac, a world class control freak. He informed the media he was separating from his wife before he informed his wife. He ousted his star police commissioner for getting too much good publicity. He ran two supposedly independent school chancellors out of town for daring to question his absolute authority.... He crusaded against cab drivers, Legal Aid lawyers, bike messengers, hot dog venders, street artists, community gardeners. (Grunwald 2001: 30)

The author, however, then points out that he may be the most successful mayor in America. Changes in police policy have undoubtedly contributed to a drop in the crime rate and a decline of the fear of crime. The economy of the city boomed during his tenure, and many residents perceive a new sense of pride in the city. Critics begrudgingly admit that his gruff, no nonsense exterior and his theatrical efforts to focus on cultural values and civic pride often serve as a source of public support. Giuliani's successor is Michael Bloomberg, a wealthy white businessman.

Mayor Richard Daley of Chicago, son of the former mayor, has, to some extent, followed in his father's footsteps by promoting behind-the-scenes deals that have shored up support within the business community. Initially elected in 1989, and currently in his third term, his popularity within the city is now very broad. In 1999, he was re-elected with 73 percent of the vote. Daley is credited with improved public services and stronger ties within the minority community. Like his father, he wins points in the community at-large for dramatic public gestures—highways, a rebuilt airport, and reforms of public housing. His style is moderate and conciliatory. The term most frequently invoked when discussing Daley is "corporate." He tries to run city hall like a business.

Richard Riordan of Los Angeles was elected in 1993, his term ended in 2001. He is a millionaire businessman with close ties to the elite White establishment in the city. He financed his own campaigns, however, and thus acted with some degree of independence from major parties and significant interests in the community. Though fundamentally a conservative Republican, he supported President Clinton and maintained close ties with that administration. He won strong support among White voters, particularly in the San Fernando Valley, and was well liked by the business community. He governed the city somewhat at a distance and often conflicts with the city council, organized labor, and community interests. Yet Riordan accomplished much in his tenure; major public projects, a sports arena and subway, and a new city charter. One author describes him as "Mystery mayor. He's got 40,000 books. Friends all over town and a reputation and a soft touch. He is a risk taker and problem solver. He can be absent minded, inarticulate, contradictory and downright sloppy" (Fiore and Clifford 1993: 19).

Why have these three conservative White politicians succeeded as mayors of our largest cities at a time when the populations are increasingly minority? (James Hahn, also a white politician, succeeded Riordan.) Does their tenure indicate a change in the kind of leadership patterns in our cities?

Several common characteristics are related to their success:

- All three enjoy significant support within the White working class. Support among Whites, in fact, may be greater than in the past because of a need for White politicians to be united when faced with a larger minority electorate. The minority population is increasingly poor and often recent immigrants. While they constitute a majority of the population, they represent a smaller portion of the voters.

- All have also benefited from an improved economy and a major drop in the crime rate nationwide in the late 1990s. The downtowns of all three cities have experienced a building boom, aided by successful city-sponsored redevelopment efforts. Successful redevelopment has led to mayoral support from the business community.

- All three are also able to gain support among important elements in the minority community. Daley was initially opposed in the African American community, but now receives large majorities even when running against African American opponents; Riordan did rather well among Latino voters; his successor, Hahn gained strong support in the African-American Community and Guiliani was met with hostility from traditional African American interests, but often gained support from recent immigrant groups.

The divergent styles of these mayors may reflect the changes in the present-day city, as discussed in Chapter 2. Globalization of the business community means that leaders must search for different sources of power within the private sector rather than a clearly defined power elite. Diversity within the minority population provides many different avenues of public support for the mayor. Traditional sources of neighborhood influence, then, may not be as important because there has been significant movement in and out of traditionally stable neighborhoods. With the continuing movement of the middle class of all groups to the suburbs, coalitions within all groups may frequently change. Lastly, the resources that accrue naturally to the mayor's office are much less today. Declines in federal funds, controls on patronage, and the assertion of state authority require all mayors to seek increased support from the private sector. Stone's argument that mayors must look to private sources of influence to accomplish their goals may be even more important in the city of today.

Thus, public leadership faces new challenges when it tries to unite significant sectors of the city. Mayors must continually search for new groups and interests; they can't rely on the sources of power that the earlier mayors were able to use. Power is an ever-changing resource, and prospective leaders must constantly assess the sources of power.

The difficulties of our paradox of urban governance are apparent when we look at leadership within the city. Uniting diverse groups to overcome the division of authority within our urban areas is more difficult today as sources of power are more broadly dispersed, resources are less, and our city economies are part of an international system.

REFERENCES

Agger, Robert E., Daniel Goldrich, and Bert E. Swanson. 1964. *The Rulers and the Ruled: Political Power and Impotence in American Communities.* New York: John Wiley and Sons.

Ainsworth, Ed. 1969. *Maverick Mayor: A Biography of Sam Yorty, Mayor of Los Angeles.* Garden City, NJ: Doubleday & Company.

Bachrach, Peter, and Morton Baratz. 1970. *Power and Poverty: Theory and Practice.* New York: Oxford University Press.

Banfield, Edward C., and James Q. Wilson. 1963. *City Politics.* Cambridge, MA. Harvard University Press.

Boyarsky, Bill. 1980. "Bradley Has Done Much Despite His Shortcomings." *Los Angeles Times.* (September 9).

Caro, Robert A. 1974. *The Power Broker: Robert Moses and the Fall of New York.* New York: Alfred A. Knopf.

Clark, Terry N. 1971. "Community Structure, Decision-Making, Budget Expenditures and Urban Renewal in 51 American Communities." In *Community Politics: A Behavioral Approach,* edited by Charles N. Bonjean, Terry N. Clark and Robert L. Lineberry New York, the Free Press, 1971.

Clark, Terry Nichols, and Lorna Crowley Ferguson. 1983. *City Money: Political Processes, Fiscal Strain, and Retrenchment.* New York: Columbia University Press.

Cohen, Adam, and Elizabeth Taylor. 2000. *American Pharaoh: Mayor Richard J. Daley: His Battle for Chicago and the Nation.* Little, Brown & Co: Boston

Dahl, Robert A. 1948. "A Critique of the Ruling Elite Model." *American Political Science Review 53* (June): 463–69.

Dahl, Robert A. 1961. *Who Governs? Democracy and Power in an American City.* New Haven, CN: Yale University Press.

Domhoff, G. William. 1977. *Who Really Rules? New Haven and Community Power Reexamined.* New Brunswick, NY: Transaction Books.

Fiore, Faye, and Frank Clifford. 1993. "Mystery Mayor." *Los Angeles Times Magazine* (July 11).

Fogelson, Robert M. 1967. *The Fragmented Metropolis: Los Angeles, 1850–1930.* Berkeley, CA: University of California Press.

Grunwald, Michael. 2001. "Rudolph Giulani Means and Ends: Cruel to be Kind." *The New Republic* (January 15).

Hawley, Willis D., and James H. Svara. 1972. *The Study of Community Power: A Bibliographic Review.* Santa Barbara, CA. ABC CLIO Inc.

Hunter, Floyd. 1953. *Community Power Structure: A Study of Decision Makers.* Chapel Hill, N.C.: University of North Carolina Press.

Jennings, Kent M. 1964. *Community Influentials: The Elites of Atlanta.* Glencoe, IL: The Free Press.

Kaufman, Herbert. 1975. "Robert Moses: Charismatic Bureaucrat." *Political Science Quarterly.* 90:3 (Autumn) 521–38.

Kleppner, Paul. 1985. *Chicago Divided: The Making of a Black Mayor.* DeKalb, IL: Northern Illinois University Press.

Koch, Edward L., and William Rauch. 1985. *Mayor: An Autobiography.* New York: Warner Books.

Lemann, Nicholas. 1991. *The Promised Land: The Great Black Migration and How It Changed America.* New York: Vintage Books.

Miller. Ross. 1996. *Here's the Deal: The Buying and Selling of a Great American City.* New York: Alfred A. Knopf.

O'Connor, Len. 1975. *Clout: Mayor Daley and His City.* New York: Avon Books.

Orfield, Gary. 1969. *The Reconstruction of Southern Education: The Schools and the 1964 Civil Rights Act.* New York: Wiley-Interstate.

Polsby, Nelson W. 1963. *Community Power and Political Theory.* New Haven, CN: Yale University Press.

Rakove, Milton L. 1975. *Don't Make No Waves Don't Back No Losers: An Insider's Analysis of the Daley Machine.* Bloomington, IN: Indiana University Press.

Ricci, David. 1971. *Community Power and Democratic Theory: The Logic of Political Analysis.* New York: Random House.

Royko, Mike. 1971. *Boss: Richard J. Daley of Chicago.* New York: New American Library.

Sayre, Wallace S., and Herbert Kaufman. 1960. *Governing New York City: Politics in the Metropolis.* New York: Russell Sage Foundation.

Saltzstein, Alan L., Raphael Sonenshein, and Irving Ostrow. 1986. "Federal Grants and the City of Los Angeles: Implementing a More Centralized Local Political System." In Terry *Research in Urban Policy Volume Part 2,* edited by Terry Nichols Clark. Greenwich, CN: JAI Press.

Snowiss, Leo M. 1966. "Congressional Recruitment and Representation." *American Political Science Review 60* (September): 627–39.

Sonenshein, Raphael J. 1993. *Politics in Black and White: Race and Power in Los Angeles.* Princeton, NJ: Princeton University Press.

Stone, Clarence N. 1980. "Systemic Power in Community Decision Making: A Restatement of Stratification Theory." *American Political Science Review 74* (December): 978–90.

Stone, Clarence N. 1989. *Regime Power: Governing Atlanta, 1946–1988.* Lawrence, KA: University of Kansas Press.

Chapter Seven

Urban Riots
and Public Policy

The Los Angeles Riots of 1992

Throughout south Los Angeles, poor Latino residents joined their black neighbors in looting the hundreds of liquor stores and discount clothing outlets that lined Florence, Figeroa, Slauson and other thoroughfares. At the corner of Slauson and Vermont, hundreds of people ransacked the indoor Swap meet. Pregnant women emerged carrying boxes of diapers and baby food. It was clear, the protest over police abuse had become a poverty riot. Latino residents who had barely heard of Rodney King helped bend back security bars so they could loot at will. (59)

The deadliest part of Los Angeles Wednesday night was the heart of Watts. Far from the television cameras, as blazes roared through shops on the perimeter of the Nickerson Gardens housing project, police fired 188 rounds in firefights with snipers. "It was anarchy," said Lt. Michael Hillman of LAPD's Metro Division. "You had people running in the streets, looting, shooting at firefighters, shooting at the police. Total chaos." (63)

The violence was no longer confined to one area. Along every major thoroughfare running from Koreatown into south-central Los Angeles. Businesses were being sacked. With thick smoke clouding the air and car horns and burglar alarms blaring, looters swarmed dozens of stores seeing little fear of reprisal. Looter gridlock snarled parking lots and streets.

© David and Peter Turnley/Corbis

Carting off everything from guns to diapers, some people expressed fury over the King verdicts, but others went about their work in high spirits, seeming to enjoy the anarchy.

Scenes of the Los Angeles Riots of 1992 from The Los Angeles Times *"Understanding the Riots,"* The Los Angeles Times, *1992.*

The Watts Riot in Los Angeles, 1965

A 21-year-old Cornell University law student, Roy Calamaro, was driving a taxi for the Yellow Cab Co. during the summer months. Having been asleep during the day he knew nothing of the disturbance and had picked up a fare at International Airport. Coming along Imperial, he reached the intersection of Avalon. The light turned red; the white woman motorist ahead of him stopped. Rocks started splattering down on both vehicles but she refused to budge. She saw the police cars, she knew the law. As Calamaro frantically tried to maneuver around her, the door of his cab flew open, he was jerked out, a rock crushed his jaw, breaking it. A minute later the cab sat sitting on its top, wheels clawing the air like the feet of a helpless turtle.

When the three television men returned to their station wagon it was in flames, no police were in sight as the immediate vacinity seemed abandoned. As they stood, momentarily in shock, illuminated by flames, a barrage of rocks and bottles rained down behind them, like a phalanx of Indians following the arrows, the youths came rushing.

The police were moving east along Imperial, driving the people before them. Residents of the area were intermingled with spectators from all over the city who, coming upon the crowd, had parked their cars to watch. A girl in a bathing suit stood next to a man in a tuxedo, a wizened old preacher was going along waving a Bible high in the air.

The police made no distinction. "Get the hell out of here! Run!, nigger," an officer jabbed her with his baton.

She started to turn on him. Another policeman's gun was pointed at her belly. "You ever been pregnant with a bullet, girl?" he asked.

There was a crash of glass. Benton looked up to see a youth stepping through the plate glass window of a market, chug-a-lugging a fifth. Within fifteen minutes the area was aswarm with people, their arms loaded with groceries, some pushing overflowing shopping carts. As Benton tried to make his way to a telephone, the Bing and Yet Market which had been looted the night before, began turning red with fire. There were kids in the neighborhood who had a feud to settle with the owner because he kept a baseball bat behind the counter for self protection—there were a lot of feuds waiting settlement.

Scenes for the Watts Riot in Los Angeles, 1965, from Robert Conot, Rivers of Blood, Years of Darkness *(New York: Bantam Books 1967)*

The Newark Rebellion in 1967

Just after midnight two Molotov cocktails exploded high on the western wall of the precinct. A stream of fire curled fifty feet down the wall, flared for ten seconds and died. The people now numbered at least 500 on the street let out a gasp of excitement. Fear, or at least caution was apparent also as many retreated in to the darkness or behind the cars in the Hayes parking lot. . . .

Less than an hour after the bomb hit the precinct, the looting phase began. A group of twenty-five young people on 17th Avenue decided that the time was ripe to break into the stores. They ran up 17th toward Belmont as the word of their mission spread along the way. . . . People poured out from the project areas into liquor stores as the young people tore them open.

People voted with their feet to expropriate property to which they felt entitled. They were tearing up the stores with the trick contracts and installment plans. The second-hand televisions sets going for top quality prices, the phony scales, the inferior meat and vegetables. A common claim was: this is owed me. . . .

Police behavior became more and more violent as the looting expanded. The size of the rebellion was far too large for 1400 patrolmen. Their tactic seemed to be to drive at high speeds, with sirens whining, down major streets to the ghetto. Thus they were driving too fast for rock throwers while attempting to still slow the force.

Scenes for the Newark Riots of 1967, from Tom Hayden, Rebellion in Newark: Official Violence and Ghetto Response *(New York: Bantam Books, 1967).*

The Miami Riot of 1980

Late Sunday night . . . three more blacks were shot by white motorists driving through black areas. One of the victims, fourteen year old Andre Dawson had run after his sister, who had gone to the store on 3rd Avenue and 83rd Street despite her mother's warning to stay where she could call them both for the curfew. Suddenly what witnesses later said was a blue pickup truck or van raced down 83rd Street and three shots rang out. Two of the bullets struck Dawson in the head; he was dead on arrival at Jackson Memorial Hospital. At the same time Eugene Brown, forty-four, a cement finisher and father of three who liked to talk of the day he would open his own construction business, was driving two of his children and his wife, Rosie to a U-Totem store on 83rd Street at North Miami Avenue to get some orange juice. The store had been partially looted the previous night but was still open for business. While Brown waited in the car, the other three went toward the store. Shots were fired from what eyewitnesses think might have been a blue truck. Rosie ducked down behind her car. When she raised her head she saw her husband had been sitting there "with blood all over his mouth". She drove him to Jackson Hospital where he also was dead on arrival.

The MPD had set up a temporary command post at a firehouse on 46th Street and 14th Avenue, from which to launch missions to rescue people reportedly being beaten on 62nd Street, sixteen blocks away. However, the commander at the post, Captain Mahoney was having serious manpower problems. "We were really afraid at this point that we didn't have enough men to take charge of the situation," he says "and we didn't want that to get to the community." The result was that the police stayed hunkered down at the firehouse listening to the growing riot over their radios. They also started hearing reports of the crowds heading down to the rally that had been called at the Metro Justice Building.

"Here we are," recalls captain Mahoney "we're at this damn fire station. Everything's going to hell. Crowds throwing rocks and bottles, motorists trapped, people being beaten, reports of 'man down'. And when we're getting calls about huge crowds heading down to the meeting at the Justice Building. Now I'm really concerned and I'm saying to myself 'I'm just not prepared for anything else.'"

From Bruce Porter and Marvin Dunn, The Miami Riot of 1980: Crossing the Bounds. (Lexington, MA: Lexington Books 1984), 71–88.

INTRODUCTION

Urban riots are major disturbances involving many residents and significant police response that immobilize an area of the city for several hours and result in significant destruction and deaths. They happen infrequently in unpredictable ways in most of our major cities. Riots have occurred in our poorest cities, but also in some of the more prosperous settings. We have limited understanding of why and where they occur.

Common to urban riots is a breakdown of civil society. The ties that encourage us to act civilly to one another and respect property and public authority break down. Residents shoot deadly weapons at other residents and the police and firefighters; stores are broken into and looted and firebombed; the police attack demonstrators, and snipers fire at the police; large sections of the city are destroyed; and many are arrested and killed. Riots are precisely the opposite of good government.

Major urban unrest is the antithesis of pluralism as discussed in Chapter 4. Pluralists argue that major interests and concerns of society are heard by the political system and therefore grievances are generally addressed. If, however, urban violence is caused by people who are excluded from the political system or from the benefits of the society, questions are raised as to the ability of the system to represent major groups and interests. Thus, the presence of violence in cities may be a political crisis as well as a vast human tragedy. If many people rioted and the rioters were motivated by political questions, then the problem of violence becomes a basic political concern.

Riots do not occur in all cities and years go by without significant urban riots. From 1965 to 1967, major riots rocked most large cities and many small ones. Then few such disturbances were recorded until violence occurred in Miami in 1980. Years passed again until the Los Angeles riots of 1992, but that disturbance was the largest, bloodiest, and costliest of all. In 1999, a different kind of unrest took place in Seattle where a major international conference was halted by a serious demonstration. Many thought that the concerns of the 1960s riots had been addressed, but recent disturbances suggest that old problems have resurfaced. Or, are the recent disturbances of a different kind?

Why do major outbreaks of urban violence occur in American cities, and what are the consequences of our history of urban violence? This chapter will begin with a look at the history of major civil disturbances since 1960. The prevalence of violence in the 1960s permitted social scientists to examine the causes and consequences of these riots with the hope of developing a general understanding of why such disturbances occur. The second part of the chapter examines this literature. Most of this discussion is based on the disturbances of the 1960s. The disturbances of the 1980s and 1990s seem to follow different patterns than did the earlier riots. We conclude this chapter with a closer look at the Los Angeles riots of 1992.

RIOTS AND REBELLIONS: A BRIEF
HISTORY OF URBAN UNREST

Urban areas in this country have periodically been centers of unrest (see Brown 1969). Urban riots occurred as far back as the Colonial period. Historians point to major riots in the 1830s and 1840s in several cities and again with great frequency from 1913 to 1919. The poor housing and health conditions in the inner city, the presence of very different kinds of people living close together, and historical conflicts between various groups were assumed to provide the potential for urban riots. Specific events, elections, the draft, and labor disputes were frequent triggers for the disturbances. Brown argues that both the modern police department and the National Guard system began as responses to urban unrest. Thus, the present period may be a continuation of historical patterns of violence.

Contemporary riots trace their origin to the Civil Rights movement of the early 1960s. Serious disorder in 1963–1964 followed from peaceful demonstrations in several Southern cities. The most violent encounters took place in Birmingham, Alabama, where police dogs and cattle prods were used against peaceful demonstrators. At the same time, many cities remained calm in spite of triggering events that were well publicized—children were killed by bombs in an African-American Sunday school; White civil rights workers died, their bodies found in a cement grave, or openly shot on the highway. Demonstrators were jailed in large numbers, often in deplorable conditions, but few White southerners were convicted of obvious crimes. By then, television was a part of most American homes and the scenes of police whipping demonstrators and crowds of Whites taunting demonstrators with racial epitaphs were widely seen (Brown 1969).

Lyndon Johnson's election in 1964, led to the passage of the Civil Rights Act of 1964—the most far reaching civil rights legislation since reconstruction. The Voting Rights Act was passed the next year, protecting the rights of southern Blacks to engage in politics. The civil rights era encouraged feelings of optimism on the part of Black city residents. At the same time, the decline of the southern economy and the suburbanization of housing and industry brought with it an economic deterioration of the central city. The economic decline and hopes for a better life in the North sent rural Black citizens to eastern and midwestern cities. Discrimination and economic disadvantage forced minority residents to live in declining, overcrowded housing in the inner city (see Chapter 3). Thus, to Black city residents, the middle 1960s offered both hope and frustration as they became residents of northern and western urban areas.

The Watts Riot of 1965

The arrest of a young Black man in south-central Los Angeles on a hot August night triggered a night of rock throwing, beating of passing White motorists, and fires. Community leaders attempted to mediate the disputes the next day with little success. For the next 30 hours, residents looted and burned stores. With the police away, the looting spread to other parts of the city. Eventually, the National Guard was called and, after many delays, the guards tried to reclaim the streets, firing guns rather indiscriminately.

Order was finally restored by the police, the National Guard, and the army after the worst urban riot in over 20 years. Thirty-four people were killed, over

1,000 were severely injured, over 4,000 were arrested, and $40 million in property damage occurred.

The length, destruction, and ferocity of the Watts riot shocked the nation and led to much soul-searching in Los Angeles. Prior to the riot, south-central Los Angeles, while poor, appeared to be an area of contentment with low-density living in garden apartments and small detached homes. Few considered it a likely location for a major urban riot. Mayor Sam Yorty blamed the disturbance on poor responses from the National Guard and federal officials who had needlessly raised the hopes of the residents through promises of federal programs (Ainsworth 1966). These comments and his later testimony before Congress labeled him as an opponent of national liberals who saw the riot as an expression of poverty and inattention.

The Disturbances of 1967

The summer of 1966 saw urban disturbances continue in Chicago and Cleveland. Deaths occurred in both cities and, in Chicago, the National Guard was called up to patrol the streets.

Urban violence expanded significantly in the summer of 1967. Violence spread from one end of the country to the other; to large and small cities. Over 200 separate disorders occurred in 168 different cities. In total, over 18,000 people were arrested, 344 injured, and 82 were killed. Property damage was estimated at greater than $69 million dollars. The National Guard was called out 18 times and federal troops once. Over 32,000 National Guard and federal troops were involved in restoring order to the cities (United States Government 1968a: 156–65).

Riots in Newark over a three-day period killed 23 people. Hayden argues that the rioters focused their anger on White-owned stores and businesses, and few were intending to harm civilians or public buildings (1967: 30). The National Guard may have contributed to the mayhem. The Guard units were almost entirely White and racial epitaphs were commonly spoken. Nearly all of the dead were killed by police, state troopers, or guardsmen. Most charges against the dead were minor. Only one was alleged to be carrying a gun (1967: 50).

As reports of looting, sniping, and death spread, disturbances occurred in the nearby communities of Elizabeth, Jersey City, and Patterson. In the seemingly pleasant suburban community of Plainfield, a tree-lined, largely middle-class city of 45,000 people, a week of serious disturbances occurred. Looting was widespread, cars were overturned, and rock-throwing youths kept the police at bay. In the midst of the riot, demonstrators beat one officer to death (Report of the National Commission on Civil Disorders 1969: 75–84).

The most serious rioting occurred in Detroit, a politically liberal city with a sensitive White mayor and several Black elected officials. The disturbances lasted nearly a week and occurred over a large part of the central city. Arrests totaled over 7,200, requiring makeshift jails and numerous detention facilities

Troops patrol Detroit during the riots of 1967. Thirty of the forty-three people who died in Detroit during a week of rioting were killed by law enforcement officials.

© Bettmann/Corbis

so vast and disorganized that some were lost for days in the maze of different facilities. Forty-three persons were killed—30 by law enforcement officials. Over $45 million in property damage was recorded and 2,509 buildings burned, leaving 5,000 people homeless. Both National Guard and federal troops were required to bring order to the city (Report of the National Commission on Civil Disorders 1969: 84–112).

The Riots of 1968

The death of Dr. Martin Luther King, Jr., in April of 1968, triggered a new wave of urban violence. Major disruptions were recorded in 172 cities throughout the country. The rioting was particularly severe in Washington D.C. where 11 people were killed and fires raged over a broad area. A total of 43 persons were killed in all of these disturbances, and $58 million in property damage was reported (see Table 7.1). Significantly more were arrested; 27,000, compared with 18,800 in 1967. More National Guard and federal troops were also employed. All of the disturbances occurred in the eight days following Dr. King's death.

Together, the disturbances of 1967 and 1968 affected the lives of most Americans. It was reflected in the political rhetoric of the campaign of 1968 and at the Democratic Party convention in Chicago, where demonstrations and riots took the nation's attention away from the drama in the convention hall. As one commentator noted, "There is . . . substantial agreement that the 1960's riots confronted America with the greatest threat to public order since the

Table 7.1 Comparing Civil Disorder

	Watts, 1965	1967 (233 Disorders)	1968 (202 Disorders)	Los Angeles, 1992
Deaths	34	82	43	58
Injuries	1032	3400	3500	2383
Arrests	3952	18800	27000	17000
Property Damage	$183 Million	$69 Million	$58 Million	$758 Million

SOURCES: *Los Angeles Times*, May 11, 1992, and Riot Data Review, Lemberg Center for the Study Of Violence, August, 1968

dreadful industrial disputes of the late nineteenth century and early twentieth centuries" (Fogelson 1971: 5).

Miami, 1980

The outcome of a highly visible court case finding a police officer not guilty of the killing of two Black residents led to several days of rioting. The result was the bloodiest and most costly urban disturbance since 1968. Eighteen people were killed, over $80 million in property was destroyed, and 1,100 were arrested (Porter and Dunn 1984: 107–146).

During the 1980s, killings by the police or jury verdicts led to riots on four other occasions. No deaths, but extensive property damage and numerous arrests, occurred in each of these disturbances.

Los Angeles, 1992

The acquittal of the police officers involved in the beating of Rodney King triggered the nation's bloodiest and largest urban riots. The beating had been frequently broadcast on television, and the trial was covered in much detail by the print media and television. National figures, including President Bush, had expressed their disgust at the conduct of the officers. The acquittal had preceded another well-publicized trial where a Korean woman was given a probated sentence in the shooting death of a young African-American woman. The results of the King trial unleashed collective anger in the African American community that spread rapidly to members of the Latino community as well.

The disturbances lasted for five days and moved from an initial flash point near the original Watts riots throughout south-central Los Angeles into wealthier areas of West Los Angeles and Hollywood and suburban communities 30 miles away. Participation reflected the multiethnic fabric of the city. More Latinos than Blacks were arrested, and many of them were recent immigrants from Mexico and Central America. Korean businesses were frequent targets of the demonstrators, and many Koreans were seen armed on the roofs above their stores. Massive looting with little police control was visible to all on televised news. The disturbance rapidly spread to distant parts of the urban area.

Deaths in Los Angeles totaled 58—the most of any civil disturbance. Over 17,000 people were arrested, and property damage totaled over $785 million. Federal troops, the National Guard, and police and fire officers from numerous surrounding and distant communities were called into service.

Figure 7.1 compares the damage of the two Los Angeles-area riots, which occurred as largely isolated events, and the disturbances in many cities in 1967 and 1968. One notes immediately the severity of the Los Angeles riots of 1992. More were killed in that event than in all the rioting of 1968, and the property damage is much greater than the total of all the disasters in 1967 and 1968. The Watts riot, too, is severe in comparison with the events of 1967 and 1968, but a smaller riot than the Los Angeles disturbances of 1992.

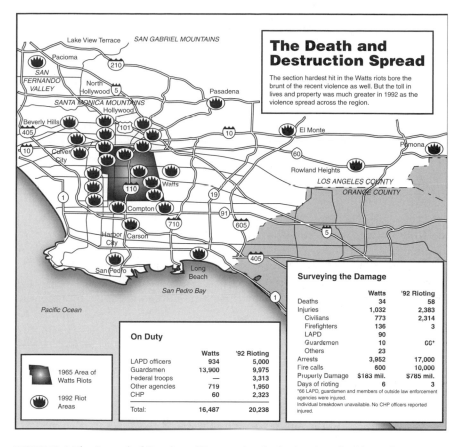

The Death and Destruction Spread

The section hardest hit in the Watts riots bore the brunt of the recent violence as well. But the toll in lives and property was much greater in 1992 as the violence spread across the region.

On Duty

	Watts	'92 Rioting
LAPD officers	934	5,000
Guardsmen	13,900	9,975
Federal troops	—	3,313
Other agencies	719	1,950
CHP	60	2,323
Total:	16,487	20,238

Surveying the Damage

	Watts	'92 Rioting
Deaths	34	58
Injuries	1,032	2,383
Civilians	773	2,314
Firefighters	136	3
LAPD	90	
Guardsmen	10	66*
Others	23	
Arrests	3,952	17,000
Fire calls	600	10,000
Property Damage	$183 mil.	$785 mil.
Days of rioting	6	3

*'66 LAPD, guardsmen and members of outside law enforcement agencies were injured.
Individual breakdown unavailable. No CHP officers reported injured.

1965 Area of Watts Riots

1992 Riot Areas

FIGURE 7.1 The Spread of Death and Destruction in the Los Angeles Riots of 1992.

Los Angeles Times, May 11, 1992. Used with permission.

Seattle, 1999

American cities have been comparatively free of violence since 1992. A 1999 disturbance in Seattle contained some of the elements of an urban riot; involvement of large numbers of people, the mobilization of the National Guard, and some commercial destruction. However, compared to other urban riots, the disturbances in Seattle in the fall of 1999 were quite mild. A peaceful protest of 30,000 to 40,000 people demonstrating against the Conference of the World Trade Organization was followed by burning and looting in the downtown area. The protesters took over at least five city intersections. They broke windows in several downtown businesses and vented rage at unoccupied police patrol cars, spray-painting them and slashing tires. Ultimately, the National Guard was called in and the protesters were disbursed. In all, 22 people were arrested and over $3 million in property damage was recorded.

The direct consequences were very minor compared to other urban riots, and they didn't appear to be related to the problems of urban life experienced by poor residents. Significant, however, was the result of the protests. The annual meeting of the World Trade Organization, a gathering of international leaders to establish common trading policies among nations, was disrupted and ultimately had to be cancelled. Thus, an urban protest directly impacted international concerns.

ANALYZING URBAN RIOTS

Riots are a serious concern for city officials and a frequent subject of social science research. Their sporadic occurrence and diversity, however, makes them difficult to analyze systematically. When they occur, hasty evaluations are often required and there is interest in taking immediate steps in order to prevent their reoccurrence. As they drop from view, however, social scientists turn their attention to other things. Thus, the literature on urban violence tends to be a response to specific recent events rather than thoughtful long-range studies of the problems that caused them. Nonetheless, there have been several attempts to look closely at the meaning and impact of urban riots. Analysts have examined three basic questions:

1. Why do riots occur?
2. Do riots and related disturbances have an influence on government policy?
3. Do the actions of the police, for example, encouraged rioters, and are riots encouraged by the failure of public officials to be properly prepared?

We will turn now to each of these questions.

Explaining the causes of riots leads one to raise very basic questions about people: Why do they act in seemingly irrational ways without concern for loss of life or incarceration? Why do normally peaceful people risk their lives, burn their neighborhoods, or loot and destroy the stores they regularly frequent?

Determining who riots and why becomes a reflection on the operation of the peaceful side of society as well. If one concludes that riots are the work of a small number of malcontents, the basic structure of society and the operation of government remains unchallenged, and the rioters are blamed. If one concludes that neglect on the part of industry and government caused some to riot, significant change in public policy to alleviate these causes should follow. If the rioters' aims are radical changes in the distribution of power, significant change in who runs powerful institutions is the only way of satisfying the rioters' concerns. If the problem is the behavior of public officials, those in power will be threatened. Given such divergence in policy proposals, it should come as no surprise that the conclusions of researchers have often been questioned and challenged. We will look at each of these explanations as reflected in the social science literature.

Rioting for Fun and Profit

Edward Banfield was the first contemporary writer to develop a systematic explanation for the urban riots. His influential and controversial book *The Unheavenly City,* first published in 1968, looked closely at the causes of the urban riots of the time. His explanation is related to assumptions of the American class structure and the relationship between social class and individual attitudes. Banfield argued that early socialization strongly influences behavior. He was particularly concerned about a group he defined as the *lower class* who live for the moment and have little concern for the future. They are present oriented, and impulse governs the behavior of the lower-class citizen: "(t)hings happen to him, he does not make them happen" (1968: 61).

Lower-class behavior is a consequence of a chaotic home life. Those who learn present-oriented behavior early in life will rarely change their attitudes. The lower class has little respect for the institutions of society that help people advance—for example, schools, job training, and self help programs. They live for the moment and see little value in working hard for a future they see as unpredictable and threatening. The presence of many people with lower-class attitudes, according to Banfield, increases the potential for riots that are mainly "for fun and profit" (1968: 211).

He argues that there are four types of riots. The *rampage* is an outbreak of high spirits. The instigators are young men "especially naturally restless, in search of excitement, thrills, action." The goal of the rioters are personal and selfish. They are out for a good time. The lifestyle and values of the lower-class person coincided with the goals of the rampage (1968: 213).

Secondly, there is the *foray* or *pillage*. Here the motive is primarily theft. Boys and young adults of the lower class are not the principal instigators, but they become enthusiastic participants. The goal of the rioters is short-run economic gain, or simply to secure goods that they would not otherwise be entitled to. The rioters here include the working class, a group motivated primarily by short-run economic gain, as well as the lower class.

The *outburst of righteous indignation* occurs when rioters are moved by indignation at what they regard, rightly or wrongly, as injustice (1968: 216). Riots of this kind, Banfield maintains, are always spontaneous. It is triggered by an incident of some sort and generally is leaderless. The lower class and working class will have no interest in the initial reason for the riot, but will join in if they can gain some goods and/or have a good time.

Lastly, the *demonstration* is advanced to promote a political ideology or cause. Demonstrations are organized by middle- and upper-middle-class persons, motivated by broader societal concerns, and rarely involve violence. Since the working and lower classes are present-oriented, they do not take part in demonstration riots.

Banfield argues that the riots of 1965 and 1967 were primarily rampages. They expanded as those interested in the foray or pillage joined them. Therefore, they had no broad social purpose and little support among the middle and upper classes. He points to attitudinal studies that conclude that African Americans at the time were "neither sunk in hopelessness not consumed with anger" (1968: 221). This meant that widespread acceptance of the riot as a political tool was lacking. Further, he argues that Los Angeles of 1964, and Detroit three years later, were poorly suited for purposeful riots. Watts, he argues, was a comparatively well-off area, and the incident that triggered the riot, the arrest of a drunk motorist, could hardly have aroused significant indignation. Similarly, he maintains that Detroit of 1967, was a city of relative prosperity with significant opportunities for African Americans. Again, the initial incident, the raid of an illegal drinking establishment, could not be a rallying point for those with broader social concerns. Arrests in Detroit were primarily related to looting, most of those arrested were young, and the pattern of destruction was what one would expect when the motive was pillaging (224).

Banfield concluded that the riots of the 1960s were carried out by people interested in a good time, joined by some who wanted to take a few things. As the riot spread, however, it acquired more supporters as the stealing of goods becomes easier to do and included a broader range of items. As it was viewed on television and given endorsement by some visible leaders, more and more people could rationalize their participation. Feelings of societal grievances or discrimination were added later only as members of the middle and upper classes looked back on the events. Such grievances had no meaning to the lower- and working-class people who participated. The riots were basically destructive events with no particular social purpose. They only made life miserable for the middle and upper classes, those that who saw positive values in saving for the future and attaining goals beyond fun and profit.

He argues then, that several conditions accelerate riots. Sensational television coverage enables the rioters to watch and respond to the movement of the police, spreads the tactics of the rioters to a broader audience, and encourages copycats. The daring of some of the rioters, Banfield blames on a lenient police and court system that lowers the punishment for those who are caught, and he is critical of elites who lend support to the cause of the rioters by blaming the riots on social conditions rather than lawless behavior.

The causes of riots, therefore, according to Banfield are a consequence of conditions in society that are unaffected by government policy to improve the lives of the poor. The supply of young, poorly socialized males, which is growing, provides an increasing support for potential riots. In earlier times, churches and urban machines influenced the behavior of the lower class and controlled deviants. As their influence has declined, the potential for rioting has increased. Thus, he concluded that there is likely to be more rioting in the cities, and it is naive to think that the funding of social programs will have much effect on the incidence or severity of riots. Present-oriented people are rarely influenced by governmental assistance.

Banfield is pessimistic about the ability of government policy to alter the causes of riots. He focuses on actions that might contain the lower classes. Programs aimed at providing better opportunities and improving the living conditions of those who riot will fall on deaf ears. The lower classes riot because it is what they want to do. They will refrain from this behavior only if the penal-

ties for taking part are more severe. Most people in the communities torn by
riots do not support the rioters' acts. Class position, according to Banfield, is
related to attitudes toward the future, and most people have some degree of future orientation. The rioters are often a very small minority who should be isolated from the rest of society.

The McCone Commission, formed by the State of California following the
Watts riots, supported much of Banfield's argument. As the first of many major
commissions to examine the riots, its conclusions were widely read and initially
influential. The commission, following considerable community testimony and
some investigation, accepted Banfield's conclusion that riots were caused by
those who were social deviants, misfits, and outcasts. Colloquially, it became
known as the riff-raff theory.

Fogelson summarizes their perspective and points to the policy implications
of the report:

> If the rioters were only a small group of unemployed, ill educated
> delinquent, juvenile and uprooted Negoes then the Los Angeles riots
> were less serious than the concern they aroused indicated. It follows, that
> the rioting was not only peripheral to the issues of Negro-white
> relations, but also manifest of problems of poverty, which, in American
> thought, is alterable rather than race which is, by contrast immutable. It
> also follows that the Los Angeles riots reflected not so much the social
> problems inherent in modern Negro ghettos as the personal disabilities of
> recent Negro newcomers. It follows further that the violent acts, the
> assaults, arson, and theft were not expressions of legitimate grievances and
> that they were in the words of the McCone Commission "formless, quite
> senseless" and by implications meaningless. Hence future riots could be
> prevented in south-central Los Angeles merely by elevating the riffraff
> without transforming the Negro ghetto—without in effect radically
> changing greater Los Angeles or seriously inconveniencing the white
> majority (1971: 348).

If we accept the perspective of the McCone Commission, the Los Angeles
riots were caused by the personal problems of the rioters. Conditions of society are not blamed, and there is little that policymakers can do to prevent such
events from occurring again. The perspective was quite comforting to city
leaders since it absolved them of all blame.

Riots as Social Protest

Federal agencies, universities, and foundations wanted to know why the 1960
era riots occurred and what could be done to prevent them. Social scientists
were given funds to examine the causes and results of the disturbances. The
"riff-raff" theory gave them a group of testable hypotheses. Did the rioters
match the profile described by Banfield? Were they small fringe groups within
the community or did they enjoy considerable support among those on the
sidelines? Did they have clear and logical reasons for their actions, or was it all

"fun and profit?" The riots raised basic questions that could be subjected to analysis by looking into the backgrounds of rioters and interviewing participants and bystanders.

Research institutes at the University of California, Los Angeles evaluated that city after the Watts riot, while others at the University of Michigan studied both Newark and Detroit after the riots. Both bodies of research came to similar conclusions. Firstly, they found that the extent of participation in the riots was much larger than initially stated. In all three disturbances, 10 to 20 percent of the residents were actively involved—the McCone Commission had pegged the participation at 2 percent. Secondly, they compared the rioters to a sample of the community members in general and found that their social and economic statistics were similar. Many of the rioters were employed, many had graduated from high school, and a sizeable percentage had never been arrested. Thirdly, the rioters were more likely to have grown up in the community and had families in the riot area. The riff-raff theory surmised that rioters were likely to be newer residents, recently moving to the community from the South without strong community ties. Lastly, attitudinal studies of the nonrioters indicated that many sympathized with the rioters and viewed the participants, if not as heroes, at least as those who were carrying out meaningful acts. The riff-raff theory assumed that the rioters would be viewed as outcasts by most community members.

Sears and McConahy, professors at UCLA, examined the attitudes and values of rioters and bystanders in the Watts riot, trying to see if the rioters perceived their actions as socially and politically meaningful. They questioned residents carefully, asking them about the meaning of their participation in the disturbances. Within the group involved in the riot, they found significant numbers they labeled as the "new urban blacks." They were described as under 30, native to Los Angeles, and better-educated than the average Watts resident. Many expressed strong racial identity, general political disaffection, and greater dissatisfaction with their own current occupation. Most felt that those Whites in power were unresponsive and indifferent to the interests of African Americans and uninterested in meeting the demands of social change. Yet they were optimistic about the future. The riot had increased their pride; their "image of blackness had become notably more positive over time" (1973: 195).

Aberbach and Walker, professors at the University of Michigan, surveyed Whites and Blacks in Detroit in 1967 and again in 1971. They also found significant support for the rioters among Blacks and an evolving ideology of "Black power" that also had significant support. Over two-thirds of the African Americans in the sample felt the riots were caused by people being treated badly. Nearly half of the Black sample expressed sympathy for the people who took part (Aberbach and Walker 1973: 71). Majorities of Blacks also felt that the riots had made the White community more aware of the problems of African Americans (59).

The Black power ideology includes the selection of a militant leader as a spokesman, sympathetic explanation of the 1967 riots, increasing skepticism about the quality of race relations, a strong racial identity, and growing concern over the treatment of African Americans in America. Proponents of Black power viewed the Detroit riots as a defining moment in the development of their values. About 30 percent of the Black sample were classified as Black power supporters. They tended to be young, among the better educated, most members had blue collar jobs, and their family incomes were higher than the average Black respondent (Aberbach and Walker 1973:103–48).

Both these studies found that the participants' values differed from those assumed by Banfield. Their actions were related to what they perceived as injustices in society, and there was significant bitterness about their lot in life. They saw the riots as an expression of this frustration, yet their hope for the future suggested that, with changes in opportunities and a lessening of perceived discrimination, they could become positive citizens.

The picture painted by these studies is one of a community at odds with the dominant White society. The community's more able young males are willing to risk their lives either out of a sense of futility or a feeling that violent acts will bring about change. Other community members often sympathize with the rioters and have similar hostility toward the White power structure. Most blame their deprived condition on discrimination and powerlessness. Thus, the rioters are not the riff-raff and the community is not at odds with their actions. It is the community itself that is adrift from the dominant White institutions.

Whites, however, tended to believe in the riff-raff theory. Sixty-eight percent of the Whites in the Detroit sample, for instance, felt that the reasons for the disorders were either "criminals did it" or "people wanted to take things." Eighty-two percent of the Whites expressed no sympathy for the rioters, compared to 54 percent of the Black sample. Whites, by and large, were opposed to policy proposals aimed at improving race relations if these policies impinged directly on neighborhoods, schools, or life styles (Aberbach and Walker 1973: 220)

The distance between Blacks and Whites on questions of trust in government and relations among races increased from 1967 to 1971. Detroit's African-American community became progressively more distrustful of government and angrier about racial discrimination, and the Anglo respondents expressed greater hostility toward African Americans. Both groups perceived that the other group was receiving greater benefits from the government.

President Johnson established the The National Advisory Commission on Civil Disorders, commonly known as the Kerner Commission. The commission's startling conclusion laid the major blame for the disturbances on the institutions of Anglo society. The introduction to their report became an often quoted statement that succinctly summarizes their work:

> The President of the United States established this Commission and
> directed us to answer three basic questions:
> What happened?
> Why did it happen?

What can be done to prevent it from happening again?
This is our conclusion: Our nation is moving toward two societies: one black, one white—separate and unequal. . . . What white Americans have never fully understood—but what the Negro can never forget—is that white society is deeply implicated in the ghetto. Elite institutions created it, white institutions maintain it, and white society condones it. (United States Government 1968a: 2)

Their policy recommendations called for significant investment in public facilities, education, and job creation aimed at closing the gap between promise and performance. The goal articulated by the commission was to "change the system of failure and frustration that now dominates the ghetto and weakens our society" (United States Government 1968a: 2).

Testing the Causes of Riots: Comparing
Riot and Non-Riot Cities

The Kerner Commission and Sears and McConahy paint a picture of communities where Black citizens perceive discrimination and poor treatment from White society. As a result, conditions in the city as viewed by the rioters may be linked to the rioters' behavior. One would assume that the degree of deprivation experienced by the minority community would be related to the propensity to riot. Riots occurred in some cities, but not in others. Perhaps the degree of deprivation in the community explains why riots occur.

Political Scientist James C. Davies examined explanations for rebellions throughout history, drawing on historical material in many societies and commentary on the nature of revolution and rebellion. Revolutions are most likely to occur, he argued, when a prolonged period of objective economic and social development is followed by short periods of sharp reversal (quoted in Gurr 1971: 52). Another Political Scientist, Ted Robert Gurr, argued that the hypothesis was applicable to urban riots as well. "The income of Negroes relative to whites of comparable education increased rapidly toward equality between 1940 and early 1950, but then began to decline so that by 1960, half the relative gains of the early period were lost. . . . Diminishing capabilities, evident in politicians reluctance to extend political rights and in irremediably economic decline, provided the background conditions necessary for the outbreak of violence" (1971: 54).

If the Davies thesis could be applied to the urban riots, differences in relative deprivation or changes in deprivation over time should explain why riots occurred in some cities rather than others. Those cities where riots occurred should be cities where African Americans' income, housing choices, and employment opportunities were significantly less than Whites in that city.

Several studies made such comparisons among a large number of cities. Downes compared the social and economic conditions of riot and non-riot cities and found that cities experiencing riots had higher unemployment rates, poor quality housing, and lower educational attainment. The intensity of the riots were also related to these conditions. He argued that these conditions together led to a riot when a certain aggregate threshold of deprivation occurred (1968). Morgan and Clark looked at the frequency, severity, and precipitating conditions of riots and also found that community conditions affected riot behavior. Inequality in housing, they concluded, coincided with increased riot behavior, though job inequality did not. Cities with higher grievances among Blacks were also associated with a higher level of disorder (1973).

Lieske examined disorder propensity in 119 cities with a wider range of indicators of potential causes of disorder. He found a complex relationship between the degree of social disorganization in the Black community, the social condition of urban Blacks, and the extent to which the city's institutional structures were open or closed (1978: 133). Racial violence was significantly greater in cities where opportunities for African American were somewhat more open: These were cities where the social status of Blacks approached Whites, and where Blacks were less racially segregated, and less segregation in schools. At the same time, disorder was more likely to occur where other forms of opportunity were more closed: These included cities that failed to recruit Black teachers in proportion to the Black population, and cities that reported higher levels of job discrimination. The study suggests that violence occurs where conditions for Blacks have improved somewhat, but the political system does not respond to the changes in the Black population.

Others, however, questioned the Davies-Gurr hypothesis, which stated that revolutions are most likely to occur when a prolonged period of objective economic and social development is followed by short periods of reversal. Spilerman (1971, 1976) also looked at large numbers of riot and non-riot cities. He found that the size of the African-American population and location in the North explained riot behavior to a greater extent than variables related to city conditions or deprivation of the minority community. He argued, therefore, that deprivation was a general occurrence. A critical mass of Blacks rather than the extent of their relative deprivation led to riots.

Downes and Morgan and Clark were also criticized for inferring individual traits from information about the city's population, the so called "ecological fallacy." Critics maintained that individual acts were difficult to infer by looking simply at aggregate city characteristics. Surveys of residents were a more direct way of determining a link between deprivation and riot behavior. Miller, Bolce, and Halligan used national surveys to determine if perceptions of relative deprivation were greater in the late 1960s when significant riot activity occurred (see also McPhail 1971). Grofman and Muller analyzed individual propensity toward violence and indicators of perceived deprivation in one city. Both studies found inconclusive evidence of a link between relative perceptions of deprivation and potential riot behavior. Lastly Rossi et al, as a part of the report of the national advisory commission on civil disorders surveyed teachers, police officers, merchants, political workers, and employers in riot and non-riot cities in 1967. Generally, they found few differences in attitudes. Those in riot cities did think that racial tensions were greater than in non-riot cities, and the quality of public leadership was rated higher in non-riot cities; but the differences were not great (United States Government 1968b: 103–43).

In various ways, these studies support a relationship between societal conditions in cities and the propensity to riot. Deprivation seems to be related to riot behavior, though it may not explain the cause of individual actions in riots areas. Since the size of the African American population and indicators of deprivation are interrelated, it is difficult to determine if the presence of a large Black population or deprivation is the major cause, but both indicators may be related to the same condition. One can infer from these studies that many in the African-American population in the inner cities hoped that conditions would improve as a consequence of the civil rights movement and the initial success of many of its members in the early 1950s. As ghetto conditions deteriorated in the 1960s and African Americans were excluded from the movement to the suburbs, disillusion resulted. The riots of the 1960s, then, were the consequence when initial hopes for a better life met with the reality of job losses, crowded conditions, and job and housing discrimination.

Riots and Public Policy: Do Urban Riots Affect Government Policies?

Several authors have argued that riots are purposeful activities. Their research concluded that the participants viewed their activities as a protest against government policies and that these views were supported by significant elements in the community. Government commissions, particularly the Kerner Commission, concluded that the rioters' grievances were serious and just. Significant new policy initiatives were proposed. Policies, however, are made by states, cities, counties, and several federal agencies operating under different pieces of legislation. Thus, the impact of riots on public policies depends on the responses of many different governments.

We will look at the extent to which governments responded to urban riots with policies aimed at controlling the negative effects of civil disturbances. Several social scientists have analyzed the impact of the riots on various public policies. Welfare policy has been subject to the most extensive analysis, and some have looked at changes in federal policies and at city budget expenditures.

Regulating the Poor: Do Changes in Welfare Policy Follow Civil Disturbances?

In 1971, Frances Fox Piven and Richard Cloward proposed a bold and provocative thesis. Looking at welfare policy historically, they argued that "(H)istorical evidence suggests that relief arrangements are initiated or expanded during the occasional outbreaks of civil disorder produced by mass unemployment and are then abolished or contracted when political stability is restored. . . . expansive relief policies are designed to mute civil disorder, and restrictive ones to reinforce work norms (1971:xiii). Welfare rolls expanded following the Great Depression and again in the late 1960s. In both cases, civil disorder preceded the increase and, according to the authors, led government officials to expand the rolls to quell the potential disorder. As order returned, welfare benefits were cut back. Thus they argue that welfare benefits are a means by which government controls the potential for civil disorder.

Piven and Cloward's work relies primarily on historical narrative and focuses on federal policy. Is it also predictive of state and local activities? Do state and local welfare policies expand following civil disturbances? Several social scientists have used Piven and Cloward's thesis to test the influence of riots on state and local government welfare policies.

Isaac and Kelly looked systematically at the impact of riot frequency and severity on welfare expenditures and the numbers of welfare recipients in all cities with at least 25,000 in population in 1960, and they examined national welfare expenditures over time to determine if in fact expenditures, numbers of recipients, and benefit levels increased following the urban riots. They found that racial insurgency did have expansive consequences at both levels (1981: 1374). With this evidence, they argued that welfare policy-making responds to social unrest rather than increases in wealth or pluralistic bargaining.

Jennings took issue with the boldness of Isaac and Kelly's findings, and reexamined their hypothesis with data from the same cities. He argued that the impact of riots must be placed within the broader context of public policy-making. Both economic need and community wealth, he argued also influence the level of extent of welfare benefits. His study qualifies Isaac and Kelly's conclusion; yet he agrees that riots had a significant effect on welfare policy (1983: 1232).

The most sophisticated look at this relationship is a recent study by Fording (1997). He concentrates on the impact of African American insurgency on state welfare rolls from 1962 to 1980, and controls for more potential influences than do the previous studies. These additional influences include the power of the Black community, societal demand for welfare, changes in federal legislation, economic capacity, and characteristics of the state political institutions. Fording is interested not only in the effect of insurrection but whether there are situations where insurrection is more effective.

Fording's conclusions support Piven and Cloward; riots precede expansion of welfare payments. Ideology, the level of unemployment, and benefit levels were the only other significant influences on welfare payments. He found that insurgency had the greatest influence whether the Black population was small or large. When the African-American percentage of the state population was between 9 and 25 percent, insurgency had a weaker effect on policy. He argued that where the percentage of the black population was small, White resistance to increases in welfare policy was low. When the African-American population was large, Blacks represent a significant voting block and use their political influence to increase benefits. Where African-American population was moderate, White opposition to increases diminished the influence of civil disturbances.

Through all these studies, the Piven and Cloward thesis has been subjected to rigorous analysis. Some of these findings qualify its impact (see also Albritton 1979), but the findings have held up surprisingly well. Thus, in the area of welfare policy, urban riots appear to influence the expansion of welfare expenditures.

Do Riots Influence Budgetary Decisions?

We assume that legislators respond to demands from their constituents for policy changes. If the riots were signs that minority communities were poorly served by governments or that local police and fire departments needed aid to prevent future disturbances, one would expect the governments to respond with increased aid and new programs. The response from political leaders, however, took many forms. Some viewed the riots as indications that the communities needed aid, but others argued that new spending programs could be viewed as rewards for bad behavior. Those who supported social service aid were not necessarily the same as the supporters of additional police expenditures. Therefore, the amount and kind of aid that followed the riots may have varied by the kind of aid and the political ideology of the legislators. Two studies analyzed the effect of the riots on spending decisions: Susan Welch analyzed the impact of the riots on spending decisions of local governments, and James Button looked at the effect of the riots on federal government programs. Both of these studies were quantitative in nature; they relied on actual budget data for a large number of cities and federal agencies.

Are local government budgetary allocations affected by riots? Welch examined budgetary allocations between 1965 and 1969 in all cities larger than 50,000 people. Her major concern was a comparison between cities experienced a riot and those that did not. She found that cities that experienced riots increased expenditures in those areas assumed to be the concern of those demanding control and punishment of the rioters. Police and fire expenditures significantly increased in these cities, even when controlling for social and economic differences. Cities that did not experience a riot generally did not increase police and fire spending, and there were no differences in expenditures for other governmental functions. Social expenditures designed to meet the needs of residents of the riot areas did not increase following a riot.

Button looked closely at the impact of the riots on aid from the federal government. His study looked closely at the amount of aid supplied from various government agencies over a 10-year period following the disturbances of 1967. He also interviewed federal officials to determine the goals of the aid process and the kinds of decisions that led to different forms of aid.

He found very different patterns of aid occurring in different agencies and at different points in time. Aid from the Office of Economic Opportunity (OEO), often referred to as the Poverty Program, was sensitive to the presence of riots. This office and its funding had been established as an independent agency during the Kennedy-Johnson years to assist deprived communities through programs designed to alleviate poverty by emphasizing economic opportunity that ranged from public works to employment and education. As a new agency with a rather general mandate, it was designed to respond to a wide variety of local problems through its own funding and through coordination of other federal programs. Budgetary allocations could respond to change because, as a new agency, past funding allocations had little influence.

Button found that OEO funding was very responsive to cities experiencing riots; it was more responsive than other programs he analyzed. Over 30 percent of the variation in per-capita expenditures, for instance, were accounted for by the presence of and severity of the riots.

The Department of Housing and Urban Development was formed in 1965 to deal primarily with the problems of the inner city. It was largely a consolidation of existing housing programs, so much of its budget was used to fund ongoing housing programs. Newer programs, like Model Cities and Urban Renewal (see Chapter 6), were also a part of its mission.

Button found that HUD's funding increased significantly following the riots and that in 1964–1965, riot cities received considerable increases in funds. From 1967 through 1969, however, a conservative backlash and concern about budget deficits curtailed much of the response to the riots. Riot characteristics overall had a moderate influence on total HUD expenditures in this later period. Contrary to expectations, Model Cities funding, a program that originated partly in response to the riots, was not affected by either the number or severity of the riots.

Another federal government program receiving significant resources to deal with urban problems was the Law Enforcement Assistance Administration (LEAA) in the Department of Justice. This program supplied significant grants to local police departments with special emphasis on increasing their riot control capacities (Button 1978: 138). Cities experiencing riots received significantly more LEAA funds than did non-riot cities with similar social characteristics (140).

Generally, Button found that the influence of riots on federal funding varied with the resources available, the ideology of those in power, and the sympathy for the rioters in the minds of the public. Cities experiencing riots benefited from federal social funding when episodes of violence were not so severe as to cause massive social or societal instability and the demands of the proponents were limited, specific, and clear to those in power. Riot cities, therefore, fared better from 1964 to 1965 because sympathetic politicians were in power and the fear of mass insurrection was not present. As riots spread to numerous cities in 1967, and the Nixon Administration was in power, social funding to riot cities declined. LEAA funding increased during the Nixon years because its use was in keeping with a law and order strategy.

Civil disturbances, then, do affect government policy. Expenditures for both social welfare and public safety respond to the presence and extent of civil unrest. Changes in policies appear to vary with community, agency, and level of government. Local governments are more likely to look for repressive measures, while the federal government appears to provide social aid. Peterson's federalism typology does seem to affect policy response (see Chapter 4), and the federal government responds to redistributive pressures. Local governments, dominated by concerns for development, will provide increased funds for the police if it is perceived that controlling disorder affects its ability to attract increased revenues.

Does Government Action Encourage Rioting?
Police and Official Behavior and Urban Violence

In addition to the causes mentioned previously, riots can also be influenced by the actions of government officials. The decisions of mayors and police chiefs affect the course that a riot may take. Some city officials effectively prepare for a riot and prevent its spread. Plans to appropriately use emergency powers, the ability to call on neighboring police departments, and state and federal officers can help to control bloodshed and property loss. Well-trained officers, the imposition of curfews, and the careful use of the National Guard and the military can also help to diffuse a riot.

However, the actions of public officials may also encourage rioters. Delays in getting officers in place, and officers who are poorly trained or who act on their own prejudices or misguided values can make the situation worse. Hayden blames the police and the military for much of the violence in Newark in 1967. He maintained "the evidence points to a military massacre and suppression in Newark rather than a two-sided war" (1967: 53). He pointed out that the American Civil Liberties union and several professors of constitutional law charged the police with engaging in a ". . . pattern of systematic violence, terror, abuse, intimidation and humiliation to keep Negroes second-class citizens" (1967: 53).

The Kerner Commission, while more measured, was also critical of police practices in many of the 1965 and 1966 riots. They accused the police of harassment in ghetto areas and pointed to surveys performed by the commission that indicate that the public believed that the police discriminate against ghetto residents and were often brutal. Reform of police policies and recruitment of more minority officers were among their strongest policy suggestions.

The National Commission in the Causes and Prevention of Violence, formed in 1967 to evaluated the causes of violence of that summer, also was critical of the police. Jerome Skolnick, the author of a portion of the report, claimed that the police response to mass protest resulted in ". . . a steady escalation of conflict, hostility and violence (1969: 289). He argued that poor training, low salaries, and inferior working conditions resulted in police forces that were unprepared for riot control. In Detroit, for example, control of the streets was split between inexperienced local police, National Guard troops, and trained and experienced paratroopers. The police and National Guard fired 2,000 rounds of ammunition, killing 30 persons, while the paratroopers fired but 201 rounds, killing only one person (1969: 258).

Since the late 1960s, however, great strides have been made in the recruitment, training, and intelligence of police officers. Minority representation on urban police departments was shockingly small at that time (see Report of the National Advisory Commission on Civil Disorders 1968: 321–2), and salaries were lower than any other professional occupation (see Skolnick 1969). Today, minority officers are common, salaries have been raised significantly, and riot control is a common part of the training of all officers. Many communities have experimented with community-based police officers who try to maintain close contact with community members and respond to their needs (to be discussed in Chapter 9).

Most assumed that the decline in urban violence was partially attributed to advances in police science and the recruitment of better police officers. A close look at the Los Angeles riot of 1992, however, raises questions about the preparedness of the police for the riot situation and the extent to which elected officials and the police chief acted to safeguard the community against the potential for riot.

THE LOS ANGELES RIOTS OF 1992: REBELLION, PROFIT, OR BAD MANAGEMENT?

Everyone who followed current events in 1992 has different images of the Los Angeles riots. The brutal beating of a young Black man, Rodney King, by several White, muscular members of the Los Angeles Police Department; the vicious beating of a White truck driver, Reginald Denney, by seemingly joyous Black young men; fires, destruction, and general mayhem occurring in the absence of the police; and residents looting stores freely and openly in front of television cameras. As was the case with the Watts riot, the country was surprised that Los Angeles was again the center of a major disorder. The city was supposed to be enjoying a renaissance. An interracial coalition rather than a White establishment governed the city, the downtown literally glistened with new buildings, and the city had hosted the 1984 Olympics, revealing to all that a "world city" had emerged.

Below the shiny setting, however, were a series of concerns—economic, interracial, and political—that set the stage for a different kind of riot. As the story is brought forth, reflect upon the explanation of other disturbances. How are the Los Angeles riots of 1992 a different kind of disturbance?

The "City of Angels" in 1992

The Los Angeles of 1992 seemed to be a different city from that of 1964. The city that appeared so divided racially was now governed by a coalition of African Americans, Latinos, and west-side liberals that had taken power from the White conservative establishment. A Black former police officer, Tom Bradley, governed as mayor with a supportive coalition of city council members (see Chapter 7). With the help of the federal government and clever use of expanded authority in redevelopment, downtown Los Angeles emerged as a true financial and entertainment center. Major buildings were added to the sky line, and a modern transit system was under construction. The city successfully hosted the 1984 Olympics, demonstrating to the world that Los Angeles was a city of beauty and charm. Logistically, the Olympics was a major feat of modern city management. Held on numerous sites and with limited public financial contribution, the Games dramatized a beautiful city that really seemed to work. Traffic jams, and clogged freeways, usually Los Angeles symbols, were rare. Viewers saw beautiful weather, clean beaches, and modern buildings and facilities.

The city had become multiethnic with concentrations of Blacks and Latinos near the city center, but much of the middle class of both groups by then lived in outlining parts of the city and in the suburbs (Morrison and Lowry 1994: 19). Other new groups from throughout the world settled in various parts of the metropolitan area. Thus, the Los Angeles of 1992 had become truly multiethnic, and would have a non–Anglo majority early in the next century. Increasing prosperity, improvements in the education system, and affirmative action seemed to be leading Los Angeles in the direction of significant mobility for all groups.

Signs of trouble, however, lay beneath the surface. The recession of the early 1990s was particularly severe in Los Angeles. Aerospace industry declines added to the steep industrial downturn. New industries more frequently located in outlining and suburban areas, leaving central Los Angeles with large numbers of unemployed. It is estimated that at the time of the riots over 50,000 young unemployed males living in south-central Los Angeles had been unemployed for some time and had little hope of future employment (Morrison and Lowry 1994: 35–6).

New immigrant groups moved to south-central Los Angeles, replacing the African Americans who were able to move out. Many of the new immigrants were first generation Latinos from rural Mexico and Central America; by 1990, Latinos made up the majority of south-central Los Angeles (Bobo et al, 1994: 103). As refugees from third-world countries, they were willing to work for extremely low wages and accepted jobs with poor working conditions. New Asian groups often brought some financial resources with them and commonly invested in the small stores that served the area though, generally, they lived elsewhere. African Americans, then, were caught in an economic squeeze. Thus, potential for racial conflict between minority groups, as much as between African Americans and Whites, smoldered beneath the surface.

The Prelude to the Riot

Riots are always triggered by incidents. The riots of 1992 can be viewed as a response to four vividly publicized events; the Rodney King beating, the acquittal of the police officers involved, the shooting of an innocent young Black woman, and the trial that gave her killer a probated sentence. The King verdict triggered the riot, but without the vivid tape of his beating, the trial probably would not have attracted significant attention. The second incident, while less publicized nationally, reinforced a perception of an unfair system to significant elements in the African American community.

The King beating occurred in the night of March 3, 1991. Following a long automobile chase, several officers were videotaped gruesomely beating Mr. King, and the tape was played frequently on television. The actions of the officers widely condemned by the newspapers, Mayor Bradley, and even President George Bush.

Thirteen days later, Latasha Harlins, a fifteen-year-old high school freshman entered a south-central area convenience store to purchase a bottle of orange juice. She placed the juice in her back pack and approached the counter with two dollars in her hand. An argument and physical struggle ensued between Harlins and Soon Ja Du, the 49-year-old Korean woman who owned the store. Du fired the gun at the retreating Harlins, hitting her in the back of her head and killing her instantly. The Harlins case was also publicized on television news and in the press.

Through much of that spring, public conflict between Mayor Bradley and Police Chief Daryl Gates dominated the news. Police Chiefs in Los Angeles traditionally operate rather independently of the mayor. An appointed Police Commission, rather than the mayor and city council, supervise day-to-day activities of the force. California law protects police chiefs from being fired by elected officials without cause. Chiefs in Los Angeles also enjoy significant support within certain segments of society and Gates was adept at generating a positive image, particularly among the Anglo working and middle classes. Thus, while Bradley frequently criticized Gates, he had learned to accept the limits of his authority over the chief.

Following the King incident, Bradley appointed a commission to investigate the incident, giving it broad powers to look into the management of the LAPD. The commission's report, released in July of 1991, was very damaging to the once vaunted police force. It included recorded tapes with racist overtones, evidence that a handful of individuals labeled "problem officers" were allowed to work despite complaints of excessive use of force, and severe criticism of Gates's management style (Cannon 1997: 140). Bradley felt the charges so damaging that he asked for Gates's resignation.

Gates's position then became involved in much political jockeying between his supporters and those of the mayor. The police commission responded to the mayor's request by placing Gates on administrative leave with pay. The city council, in turn, reinstated Gates. The turmoil publicly dramatized the conflict between the two men and broadened the focus of concern from the welfare of Mr. King to the managing of the police department.

Two events that increased tensions in the Black community occurred on November 15, 1991. Soon Ja Do was found guilty of killing Latasha Harlins but given a probated sentence requiring no time in jail. The trial of Rodney King's attackers was moved to Simi Valley, a suburban area on the edge of the metropolitan area that was largely Anglo and the home of many LAPD officers. The change of venue was viewed in the Black community as an attempt to acquit the officers. Together, the events led many to wonder whether an African American get a fair trial in Los Angeles.

The trial of the officers in the King beating lasted many months and was again well-publicized in the media. The jury was sequestered in April 23, 1992, and on April 29th, a verdict was reached, but the announcement was delayed for two hours to assist the police in preparation of possible disturbances. The officers were acquitted of all charges.

The Riot Process

When word of the verdict quickly spread, disturbances developed in south-central Los Angeles. As pictures of rock-throwing mobs and sounds of gunfire were heard, television reporters pointed out that the police were nowhere in sight. The vicious beating of truck driver Denney was seen on television as was his rescue by some courageous African-American bystanders.

The riot rapidly spread to other parts of south-central Los Angeles, and the police withdrew. Massive looting of stores was seen on television. Fires broke out; the fire fighters, lacking police escorts, often had to retreat from the burning buildings as shots were fired on them. Incidents also began to occur miles away from south-central Los Angeles such as in Hollywood and in some of the suburban communities. The National Guard was called to restore order the next day, but their appearance was delayed due to lack of preparation and logistical problems (that is, several hours were lost when ammunition could not be found).

By Sunday, May 4, order was restored after five days of violence. Fifty-four people had died, 2,328 were treated for injuries, and over $900 million in property damage was recorded. It was the costliest, longest, and, in area, the largest of all twentieth century civil disturbances.

Where Were the Police?

Important social and economic conditions might have induced Los Angeles citizens to riot. The setting in the early 1990s was similar to the conditions for rebellion proposed by earlier by James Davies—a prolonged period of objective economic and social development followed by short periods of sharp reversal. Specific incidents that would encourage the rebellion were obviously present. The well-publicized incidents and trials were likely to increase underlying tensions between restless groups and the police and among the groups themselves.

One would expect, then, that Los Angeles officials would have prepared for trouble as the King trial progressed and would put a detailed plan into action as the time for the verdict approached. A closer look at the actions of the mayor, police chief, and key officers gives one a picture of a city very poorly prepared to deal with the potential disorder and seemingly unconcerned. Two hours after the verdict was announced, while mayhem was brewing in south-central Los Angeles, Chief Gates left his office early in the evening to attend a fundraiser in Brentwood (20 miles from the riot center), and two-thirds of the police captains were attending a retreat in Ventura, 80 miles away.

Officers on the scene of the riot seemed confused and unprepared. Cannon quotes Lieutenant Michael Moulin, the ranking officer on the scene. "I found utter chaos. . . . The officers were being subjected to bricks, to huge pieces of concrete, to boards, to flying objects. . . . Most of the police officers had no helmets. They had no bullet proof vests, no tear gas, no face shields" (1997: 287).

Sensing the disorganization of his troops, Moulin ordered a pullout of the area. Cannon suggests that the retreat led to a loss of control of the riot area. From that point on, the police spent their time reacting to ever increasing levels of violence. Once they lost control of the flashpoint, they retreated and waited for more than 45 minutes. The delay prevented them from successfully cordoning off the riot area, and the communication system frequently malfunctioned leaving officers uncertain what they should do. Thus, the riot spread.

Matters did not improve when the National Guard was called the next day. State law required that other police units be employed before the guards were called. Therefore, the use of the guards had to be cleared with the sheriff and the California Highway Patrol. They, too, appeared to be unprepared. There were delays in deployment and long waits for their ammunition to arrive.

The heart of the problem seemed to be conflicts between Bradley and Gates. The two had not spoken in 13 months. Both were embroiled in Bradley's attempt to oust the chief.

A blue-ribbon commission investigated the riots and found that no meaningful preparation for the specific coordination with county, state, and federal authorities had occurred; indeed, no event-specific planning within the LAPD itself. The commission report makes clear that both Bradley and Gates had the authority to prepare and to mobilize for a riot, but they failed to do so. The mayor possessed broad emergency powers but failed to exercise his own emergency authority. The chief was empowered to arrange, with local governments and state and federal agencies, cooperation and mutual aid during a local emergency. When it was necessary to call on other troops, the chief found himself unprepared. The National Guard appeared only after Governor Pete Wilson inquired about the need and ordered them to the city (Cannon 1997: 265).

Why the Los Angeles Riots of 1992?

Did they happen for fun and profit? Yes, there was indeed some of that. The looters were having a good time, and many took part to get desired goods. It was rumored that some came from as far away as Orange County. It is difficult to find social explanations for the large numbers of Latinos that were involved, for instance, as the trials and precipitating incidents did not involve Latinos. Most Latino politicians expressed little concern for the issues that led up to the violence, and some praised their communities for remaining quiet while the riots occurred. Sociologist Leo Estrada argues that the participation of recent Central American immigrants may reflect a fear that consumer goods will not be available following a disturbance, a frequent happening in similar Latin American disturbances (Cannon 1997: 350).

Were there grievances against a social and economic system that once seemed to be promoting advancement? Certainly. With so many unemployed and an influx of new competitors, frustration was undoubtedly high. Korean stores seemed to be a particular target; an obvious sign of interethnic furor (Morrison and Lowry 1994: 19).

But how large would the riot have been had the mayor, the police chief, the officers, and the emergency preparedness system worked?

CONCLUSIONS: WHAT DO WE KNOW
ABOUT URBAN RIOTS?

We have looked at the recent history of urban riots and studies of the causes and consequences of riots. Major civil disturbances occur frequently in American cities, but their incidence is sporadic and unpredictable: We have periods of many riots, followed by many quiet years. If the Los Angeles riot of 1992 is indicative of future disturbances, riots with much loss of life and destruction of property are possible. Why will riots continue and their severity increase, and what can be done to lessen their occurrence? I close with a few speculative conclusions.

The potential for violence in cities is always present because American cities are locations where different racial and ethnic groups come to the city and struggle for advancement. The new groups face a society where wealth is unevenly distributed by groups and by territory. American cities tend to concentrate the poor and the recent immigrants in the same location. Frequently, areas where the poor live are crowded and opportunities for advancement are limited, making dissatisfaction and conflict over resources and territory likely.

Improvements in social and economic opportunities for the poor decrease the likelihood of riots but do not eliminate it. As Davies and others have pointed out, reversals of fortune after times of relative plenty may lead people to riot. The Los Angeles riots also revealed that Banfield's much discredited theory may explain some of the behavior during riots. Some people join disturbances for fun and profit; tensions between groups can be unrelated to social and economic conditions; and emotions are stirred by events such as trials and arrests.

Thus, public officials must always work to eliminate potential causes of unrest, but be prepared for the possibility of disturbances. The relative calm in most cities since 1967 is probably the consequence of better communication with residents, increased opportunities for minorities in public agencies, and improved training in dispute resolution and riot mobilization. In many ways, our efforts to prevent riots have been successful.

Several new features of contemporary society, however, increase the potential for civil disturbances. People are much more closely connected as a consequence of advances in communication. Television brings the news into everybody's home, and local news has increased the speed and depth with which local events are covered. People and groups are interconnected through cell phones and the Internet. For example, residents gathered at each intersection as O. J. Simpson's white Ford Bronco slowly crossed the city; the crowds in Seattle were mobilized quickly large through cell phone and Internet contact; and during the Los Angeles riots, television news was on the scene sooner than were the police. Thus, rapid response by law enforcement officials becomes more important today than it was a few years ago.

The large increase in the availability of guns, the presence of weapons of much greater destructive power, and the decrease in the cost of weapons means that rioters potentially can cause much greater damage, and the police need to be prepared with similarly advanced weapons. In the 1965 and 1967 riots, weapons in the hands of rioters were limited and much less dangerous than the arms available to potential rioters today.

City officials must be prepared for civil disturbances both by greater sensitivity to the problems of those living in deprived communities and by developing careful plans for dealing with riots when they occur.

REFERENCES

Aberbach, Joel D., and Jack L. Walker. 1973. *Race in the City.* Boston: Little Brown.

Ainsworth, Ed. 1966. *Maverick Mayor: A Biography of Sam Yorty of Los Angeles.* Garden City, NY: Doubleday and Company.

Albritton, Robert B. 1979. "Social Amelioration through Mass Insurgency? A Reexamination of the Piven and Cloward Thesis." *The American Political Science Review 73:* 1003–11.

Banfield, Edward C. 1968. *The Unheavenly City.* Boston: Little Brown.

Brown, Richard Maxwell. 1969. "Historical Patterns of Political Violence in the United States." *The History of Violence in America: A Report of the National Commission in the Causes and Prevention of Violence,* edited by Hugh Davis Graham and Ted Robert Gurr. New York: Bantam Books

Bobo, Lawrence, Camille L. Zubrinsky, James H. Johnson, and Melvin L. Oliver. 1994. "Public Opinion Before and After the Spring of Discontent." In *The Los Angeles Riots: Lessons for the Urban Future,* edited by Mark Baldassare. Boulder: Westview Press.

Button, James. 1978. *Black Violence: Political Impact of the 1960s Riots.* Princeton, NJ: Princeton University Press.

Cannon, Lou. 1997. *Official Negligence: How Rodney King and the Riots Changed Los Angeles and the LAPD.* New York: Times Books.

Conot, Robert. 1967. *Rivers of Blood, Years of Darkness.* New York: Bantam Books.

Crosby, Faye. 1979. "Relative Depravation Revisited: A Response to Miller, Bolce and Halligan." *The American Political Science Review 73:* 103–12.

Downes, Bryan T. 1968. "Social and Political Characteristics of Riot Cities: A Comparative Study." *Social Science Quarterly* 49 (December) 504–20.

Eisinger, Peter. 1973. "The Conditions of Protest Behavior in American Cities." *The American Political Science Review 67:* 11–28.

Feagin, Joe R., and Harlan Hahn. 1973. *Ghetto Revolts: The Politics of Violence in American Cities.* New York: MacMillan Publishers Inc.

Fogelson, Robert M. 1971. *Violence as Protest: a Study of Riots and Ghettos.* Garden City, NY: Doubleday and Company.

Fording, Richard C. 1997. "The Conditional Effect of Violence as a Political Tactic: Mass Insurgency, Welfare Generosity, and Electoral Context in American States." *American Journal of Political Science 41:* 1–29.

Grofman, Bernard N., and Edward N. Muller. 1973. "The Strange Case of Relative Gratification and Potential for Political Violence: The V-Curve Hypothesis." *The American Political Science Review 63:* 514–39.

Gurr, Ted Robert. 1971. *Why Men Rebel.* Princeton NJ: Princeton University Press.

Hayden, Tom. 1967. *Rebellion in Newark: Official Violence and Ghetto Response.* New York: Vintage Books.

Isaac, Larry, and William R. Kelly. 1981. "Radical Insurgency, the State and

Welfare Expansion: Local and National Evidence form the Postwar United States." *American Journal of Sociology* 86: 1348–86.

Jennings, Edward T. Jr. 1983. "Racial Insurgency, the State and Welfare Expansion: A Critical Comment and Reanalysis." *American Journal of Sociology* 88: 1220–36.

Lemberg Center for the Study of Violence. 1968. "Aftermath of the King Assassination." *Riot Data Review.* Number 2.

Lieske, Joel A. 1978. "The Condition of Racial Violence in American Cities: A Developmental Synthesis." *The American Political Science Review* 72: 1324–40.

Los Angeles Times. 1992. *Understanding the Riots.* Los Angeles: Los Angeles Times.

McPhail, Clark. 1971. "Civil Disorder Participation: A Critical Examination of Recent Research." *American Sociological Review* 36: 1058–73.

Miller, Abraham H., Louis Bolce, and Mark Halligan. 1977. "The J-Curve and the Black Urban Riots: An Empirical Test of Progressive Relative Deprivation Theory." *The American Political Science Review* 71: 964–82.

Morgan, William R., and Terry Nichols Clark. 1973. "The Causes of Racial Disorders: A Grievance-Level Explanation." *American Sociological Review* 38: 611–24.

Morrison, Peter A., and Ira S. Lowry. 1994. "A Riot of Color: The Demographic Setting." In *The Los Angeles Riots: Lessons for the Urban Future,* edited by Mark Baldassare. Boulder: Westview.

Piven, Frances Fox, and Richard Cloward. 1971. *Regulating the Poor: The Functions of Public Welfare.* New York: Vintage Books.

Piven, Frances Fox, and Richard Cloward. 1979. "Social Amelioration through Mass *Insurgency?* Electoral Instability. Civil Disorder and Relief Rises: A Reply to Albritton." *American Political Science Review* 73: 1012–19

Porter, Bruce, and Marvin Dunn. 1984. *The Miami Riot of 1980.* Lexington, MA: Lexington Books.

Sears, David P., and John B. McConahay. 1973. *The Politics of Violence: The New Urban Blacks and the Watts Riot.* Boston: Houghton-Mufflin.

Sharp, Elaine, and Steven Maynard-Moody. 1991. "Theories of the Local Welfare Role." *American Journal of Political Science* 35: 934–50.

Skolnick, Jerome. 1969. *The Politics of Protest.* New York: Simon and Schuster.

Spilerman, Seymour. 1971. "The Causes of Racial Disturbances: Tests of an Explanation." *American Sociological Review* 36: 427–42.

Spilerman, Seymour. 1976. "Structural Characteristics and the Severity of Racial Disorders." *American Sociological Review* 41: 771–93.

United States Government. 1968a. *Report of the National Advisory Commission in Civil Disorders.* New York: Bantam Books.

United States Government. 1968b. *Supplemental Studies for the National Advisory Commission on Civil Disorders.* New York: Fredrick A. Praeger, Publishers.

PART II

Changing America's Urban Areas

Chapter Eight

Can Citizens Control Urban Governance?

The Elusive Search for Social Capital

> What Americans *do* hunger for is more control over matters that affect their lives: public safety, their children's schools, the developers who want to change their neighborhoods. They care so much about these things, in fact, that many of them devote precious hours every week to volunteer work in the schools, on neighborhood watches, or in community organizations. It is precisely here that participatory democracy is becoming real within American governments. (Osborne and Gaebler 1992: 74)

Democracy requires a connection between citizens and government. We saw in Chapter 3 that two different conceptions of political participation define American democracy. Pluralists, drawing on Madison's theories, proposed a limited but nonetheless important role for the participation of the average citizen. While Madison had a dim view of the abilities of the public as a major player in political decisions, he felt that broadly based political participation served as an important check on the power of leaders. Jefferson, on the other hand, viewed participation in government as extremely important. Direct involvement by all citizens in government preserved the democratic system and promoted norms of tolerance.

At several places in this book, we have noted that many of our cities operate with limited public participation. Many of those who study power in communities conclude that those with money and associational ties exert a disproportionate influence on city decisions (Chapter 6). Our discussion of voting in cities revealed that turnout is generally low and public choices are limited. At-large districts, non-partisanship, and poorly paid elective positions discourage competition and a diverse selection of candidates (Chapter 4). Institutional changes during the Reform Era severed the connection among ethnic groups and government encouraged by the urban machine. The machine brought many citizens in close contact with government; reform governments detached government from the citizen. Reform governments today are the most common political system, and the link between the citizen and local government has deteriorated. Did we lose something very important with the spread of reform institutions? Many critics think we did.

Can we resolve the paradox of urban governance without a strong link between the citizen and its elected officials? Leaders who perceive and will act on the common interests of a region are necessary if the paradox is dealt with. Can we expect these leaders to emerge if the public is not aware of their common problems and influential in the actions of the leaders? Recently, some have become more concerned about the weak connection between citizens and governing decisions throughout our society. Robert Putnam decries the decline in what he terms "social capital" defined as ". . . connections among individuals— social networks, norms of reciprocity and trustworthiness—that enable participants to act together more effectively" (1995: 664). Social capital is the glue that holds society together. It begins with social connections in one's neighborhood, church, or recreational activities. If effective, it connects these groups with those that link people and groups to government, campaigns for political office, interest groups that try to influence government policy, and major professional organizations, trade associations, and unions. Social capital involves the assumption of mutual obligations on the people's part. Favors done for you will be reciprocated, and consequently people will feel positively toward one another and be willing to work on another's behalf. The famed philosopher Yogi Berra stated the concern well: "If you don't go to somebody's funeral, they won't go to yours" (quoted in Putnam 2000: 20).

Putnam is worried about the decline in social capital among individuals in the last third of the twentieth century. Voting, group membership, and trusting attitudes toward others all have declined since 1960. He argues that we are losing the interconnectedness among people, organizations, and government that tied the elements of our society together. His book, *Bowling Alone,* refers to the decline in league bowling, a dominant form of recreation in the 1950s, but today of minor significance even to bowlers. Bowling Alone, he argues, is a symptom of a larger problem for society; it symbolizes a nation of disconnected people. Social capital has historically been the way in which individuals are linked to wider social concerns and it is related to many of the positive features of life; mutual support, cooperation, trust, and institutional effectiveness (2000: 22). Are we a truly participative society if the extent of social capital is very low? Without connections among people, can we deal with the problems we face as a society?

William Julius Wilson worries that the poor in our most deprived areas are disadvantaged by the declining links between jobs and successful people. He studied the social and economic life of residents of the poorest sections of inner city Chicago and described these areas as follows:

> Neighborhoods that offer few legitimate employment opportunities, inadequate job information networks, and poor schools lead to the disappearance of work. That is, where jobs are scarce, where people rarely if ever have the opportunity to help their friends and neighbors find jobs, and where there is a disruptive or degraded school life purporting to prepare youngsters for eventual participation in the workforce, many people eventually lose their feelings of connectedness to work in the formal economy; they no longer expect work to be regular, and a regulating force in their lives. (1997: 52–3)

Both job opportunities and people with successful careers have left the inner city in recent years leaving behind a community dominated by the unemployed. Without positive role models and connections to the workplace, residents of these communities have few opportunities for success. While he doesn't use the term "social capital," the problem he poses is similar to that raised by Putnam. When people lack connections with one another and with the institutions that control the societal resources, they are unable to obtain the aid and support necessary to succeed.

If the findings of Wilson and Putnam are accurate, limited social capital signifies major problems for urban society. The lack of interconnectedness between citizens, business, and government can affect the efficiency of government, the life chances of the poor, and the degree of social trust. Should local governments try to do something about declining social capital? That is the central question discussed in this chapter. Public efforts to increase social capital have been a part of city policy for some time, and private efforts to organize and revitalize neighborhoods have always been common in some cities. This chapter looks closely at government and private actions in cities aimed at improving the connections between citizens and government. These efforts include:

- Enhanced community participation through the creation of community or neighborhood councils.

- Encouragement of community-based organizations; private, non-profit organizations that invite community participation and administer public programs.

- Community-based policing where the police become an agent for connecting the citizens to government.

- Internet democracy where cities and citizens use new electronic technology to connect citizens to government.

In examining these efforts, we will reflect on the problems posed by Putnam and Wilson, and review what is known about whether the measures listed have improved the stock of social capital. We will ask if the actions of citizens and governments can correct the problems caused by the decline of social capital.

SOCIAL CAPITAL: THE CONDITION
AND THE PROBLEM

A mother of six children who recently moved with her husband and children from suburban Detroit to Jerusalem described one reason for doing so the greater freedom her children had in Jerusalem. She felt safe in letting her eight year old take the six year old across town to school on the city bus and felt her children to be safe playing without supervision in a city park, neither of which she felt she was able to do where she lived before.

The reason for this difference can be described as a difference in social capital available in Jerusalem and suburban Detroit. In Jerusalem the normative structure ensures that unattended children will be "looked after" by adults in the vicinity, while no such normative structure exists in most metropolitan areas of the United States. One can say that families have available to them in Jerusalem social capital that does not exist in metropolitan areas of the United States. (Coleman 1988: 99)

The woman in the previous example perceives a difference in the connections among people in suburban Detroit and modern Jerusalem. In Jerusalem, she senses that people are watching her children and will care for them if trouble develops. She believes there are informal bonds between herself, her children, and people she does not know. In Detroit, she fears that no one really cares about her or her children. Social capital, the informal bonds of connectedness and trustfulness among people, seem to be missing. If her child is lost in Detroit, no one may care. Those who are concerned may not know how to reach her. In Detroit, car pools must be arranged, and day care is required. Lack of social capital makes us fearful of our neighbors and adds time and expense to our lives.

Social capital, features of social life that enable people to act together more effectively, is lacking in Detroit. People are less connected with one another and are less likely to trust others. Putman argues that social capital takes two forms—bonding and bridging. Bonding refers to ties that are inward looking and tend to reinforce identities and homogeneous groups. Church groups, ethnic fraternal organizations, and country clubs are organizations that reinforce connections that encourage bonding links among people. Another kind of social capital is referred to as bridging. These attachments are outward looking, tying people together across social cleavages and local attachments. Active membership in national professional organizations, national political parties, and participation in social or recreational organizations that are citywide or regional in scope are examples of bridging forms of social capital. Together, bridging and bonding attachments tie the individual to others both within or without his or her community. They enhance ties to others within the community and promote knowledge, understanding and tolerance in the larger world.

Critics of Putnam note that social capital can have negative consequences. Ku Klux Klan members and the bombers of the Alfred P. Murrah Federal Building in Oklahoma City are a part of both bonding and bridging organizations. Yet their existence is the antithesis of social tolerance. Some forms of social capital may weakly connect us to others, while other kinds provide stronger links. The concern expressed by Putnam relates to the positive consequences of social capital—mutual support, trust, and cooperation. The positive features of social capital encourage good citizenship and promote more effective public policies.

Evidence of the Decline in Social Capital

In what ways has social capital declined? Putnam collected numerous bits of evidence that lead him to conclude that the decline has been significant and in evidence throughout the society. Next, we will look at some of his evidence.

A most important source of evidence is the marked *decline in political participation.* Voting in presidential elections, for instance, declined from 62.8 percent of voting-age Americans in 1960 to 48.9 percent in 1996 (Putnam 2000: 36). This decrease occurred in spite of pronounced efforts to remove voting restrictions in the South and a large increase in the turnout of African Americans. Political knowledge and interest has also declined; participation in campaign activities has fallen precipitously since 1970. Putnam notes similar trends in local government activities. Attendance at public meetings declined from over 20 percent of the population in 1975 to nearly 10 percent in 1995 (2000: 43). All of this occurred, of course, during a time of increases in education, usually associated with voting and interest in public affairs.

Group membership also has fallen off considerably. This is particularly noted in PTA membership, which declined from over 45 percent of families with children under 18 in 1960 to less than 20 percent in 1996. Citizens today are less likely to serve as an officer for a local club or attend local meetings. While many Americans continue to join civic groups, most Americans no longer spend much time in community organizations. "We've stopped doing committee work," argues Putnam, "stopped serving as officers and stopped going to meetings. In short, Americans have been dropping out in droves. Not merely from political lives, but from organized community life more generally" (2000: 64).

Putnam finds similar evidence in other facets of life; *church membership, workplace organizations,* and *informal social connections.* He notes significant declines in union and professional membership, home entertaining, informal socializing, volunteering, and even card playing. Thus, Americans maintain fewer informal as well as formal connections among one another (2000: 81–105).

He argues that the cumulative effect of declines in social capital has influenced public attitudes. Today, fewer people would say that they feel others generally lead moral and honest lives (2000: 139). Public trust had risen significantly until 1960, when a long term decline in social trust began. The decline in trust is particularly large among younger adults.

Social Capital and the Inner Cities

Problems associated with declines in social capital are more severe in inner-city neighborhoods; they affect people's life chances and contribute to a less stable environment. Changes in the location and nature of jobs, and the movement of the middle class to suburban and outlying areas, leave these areas with few job opportunities and an absence of social clubs and churches, which served to integrate young people into the successful endeavors. All of this leads to a shortage of role models to assist those trying to enter the work force. Wilson found that young people there grow up with a weak connection to the working world. ". . . they grow up in an environment that lacks the idea of work as a central experience of adult life—they have little or no labor-force attachment" (Wilson 1997: 52). Consequently, they fail to develop the skills and habits needed to advance.

Without help from the community, being a good parent becomes much more difficult. "It is easier for parents to control their children," Wilson argues, "when there exists a strong institutional resource base, when links between community institutions such as churches, schools, political organizations, businesses and civic clubs are strong. The higher the density and stability of formal organizations, the less that illicit activities such as drug trafficking, crime, prostitution and gang formation can take root in the neighborhood. A weak institutional resource base is what distinguishes high jobless inner-city neighborhoods from stable middle-class and working-class areas" (1997: 64).

Political and social values and forms of community participation are severely affected by joblessness, according to an analysis of the residents in Detroit neighborhoods. Cohen and Dawson compared those living in areas with more than 30 percent of the population in poverty to other areas of the city. Those in high-poverty areas were less likely to be members of churches or social groups, less likely to feel that they could influence important decisions, and less often attended meetings about community problems or talked with family or friends about politics (1993). Social capital declines, then, are reflected in the extensive differences between inner-city neighborhoods and the rest of the city. The problems discussed in Chapter 3, of differences in wealth and opportunity within our cities, take on added importance. Residents of impoverished neighborhoods not only lack the means to make a living, they are separated from links to the world beyond the inner city and the support networks that could assist the less fortunate.

Social Capital and Public Policy: Is There a Connection?

ECONOMIC GROWTH AND SOCIAL CAPITAL

In 1940, Tupelo, Mississippi, was one of the poorest counties in the poorest state in the nation. It had no exceptional natural resources, and no great university or industrial concern to anchor its development, and no

(continued)

(continued)

major highways or population centers nearby. What was worse, in 1936 it had been ravaged by the fourth deadliest tornado in U.S. history, and the following year its only significant factory closed after a deeply divisive strike. A university-trained sociologist and native son, George McLean, returned home around this time to run the local newspaper. Through exceptional leadership, he united Tupelo's business and civic leaders around the idea that the town and surrounding Lee County would never economically develop until they had developed as a community. Concerned about the dim prospects of the county's cotton economy, McLean initially persuaded local business leaders and farmers to pool their money to buy a siring bull. That proved to be the start of a lucrative dairy industry that improved local incomes and made business more prosperous. To create a less hierarchical social order, the town's elite Chamber of Commerce was disbanded and a Community Development Foundation open to everyone started in its place. The foundation set to work improving local schools, starting community organizations, building a medical center, and establishing a vocational education center. At the same time, businesses were welcomed into town only if they paid high wages to all employees and shared this as a goal. Rural Development Councils were set up in outlying areas to encourage self-help collective action—from technical training to local cleanup campaigns—in a setting in which cooperative action for shared goals had been counter-cultural.

Over the next fifty years, under McLean and his successor's leadership, Tupelo has become a national model of community and economic development, garnering numerous awards and attracting a constant stream of visitors eager to copy the town's success in their own communities. Since 1983, Lee County has added one thousand industrial jobs a year, garnered hundreds of millions of dollars of new investment, produced arguably the best school system in Mississippi, constructed a world-class hospital, and kept unemployment well below the state (and sometimes the national) average. The community's success was based on its unwavering commitment to the idea that citizens would not benefit individually unless they pursued their goals collectively. Today, it is unthinkable that one could enjoy social prominence in Tupelo without getting involved in community leadership. Tupelo residents invest in social capital—networks of cooperation and trust—and reap tangible economic returns.

SOURCE: Robert D. Putnam, *Bowling Alone: The Collapse and Revival of American Communities* (New York: Simon & Schuster, Inc. 2000), 323–324.

As the story about Tupelo indicates, social capital is not lacking in all communities. Tupelo residents formed interpersonal and group connections at the very time when these kinds of connections were declining nationally. The ability of the community to unite behind a program of economic development that encouraged interconnections among the residents was, in Putnam's mind, the key to their success and it improved the well-being of all citizens. Social capital "allows citizens to resolve collective problems more easily and it . . . greases the wheels that allow communities to advance smoothly" (2000: 288). In other words, policies that encourage social capital formation may lead to positive results in various areas of public policy. Putnam goes on to analyze the

Citizens Making Their Views Known at a Public Meeting.

© Spencer Grant/PhotoEdit

influence of social capital on a wide range of policies, and he postulates that differences in social capital may affect public policy differently.

Putnam's analysis focuses on states, but the results should be applicable to differences among local communities. He constructs a social capital index for each state based on questionnaire responses, state level voting behavior, and organizational membership. Citizens in states that rank higher in social capital report greater frequency of membership in community groups, do more volunteer work, and serve more often as officers in community and social groups. They also spend more time socializing with friends and believe that people are more honest and can be trusted. These states also record higher voter participation and more non–profit organizations (2000: 291).

Putnam also compares the state's ranking on social capital with various indicators of policy performance. In most cases there is a strong relationship between the state's ranking on social capital and various indicators of policy. Figure 8.1 compares state rankings of educational performance with the index of social capital. It is apparent that states with higher social capital indices also produce better educational outcomes. He finds similar relationships for other areas of policy. A state's health statistics and mortality rate are related to social capital; crime rates are lower, and economic development greater when social capital is higher. Furthermore, tax avoidance is less common in states with a higher social capital index. Although one cannot infer causality from such connections (it is possible that other conditions in the state are the actual causes of the outcome), the links do support those who want to improve a community's social capital in the hopes that more social capital will help improve the quality of life. Indeed, cities today expend significant resources in the hopes of

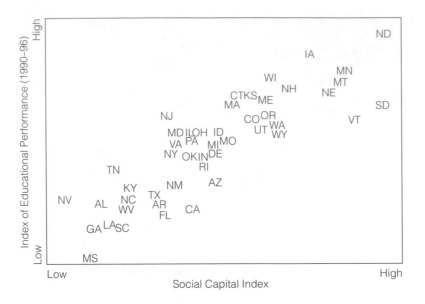

FIGURE 8.1 Schools Work Better in High-Social-Capital States.

Source: From Robert D. Putnam, *Bowling Alone: The Collapse and Revival of American Communities* (New York: Simon & Schuster, 2000), 300.

encouraging increased citizen involvement in government. It is their belief that improved community performance will result. We turn next to the several efforts that communities have undertaken to enhance the social capital of their residents.

APPROACHES TO EXPANDING COMMUNITY INVOLVEMENT

American cities have a long history of efforts to encourage community involvement. Activity often results from neighbors actively organizing to preserve their surroundings and to protect themselves from the negative effects of city policies. In other cases, government has created neighborhood political units and actively organized neighborhoods. Thus, the roots of current attempts to increase social capital are both anti-government and pro-government in origin. Before turning to specific strategies cities have used for inducing increased participation, we examine the ideas that support our traditional attempts to encourage social capital.

Public Order Is a Private Problem

Many argue that constructive community involvement would increase if citizens were allowed to manage their own public problems. Citizens fail to manage their common affairs because government handles the problem for them.

Police officers are called anonymously over the telephone when there is a disturbance, then the police arrive and manage the problem; the disputing parties need not confront one another. If the residents instead had no police to call, perhaps they would learn to deal with their neighbors and confront the problems personally. In the process, they would become more tolerant of differences and learn to deal directly with their problems with less expense.

Richard Sennett argues that people living in communities with less central government and more direct community control can create a freer, more tolerant urban environment. Individuals, when forced to deal with the common problems of the area, would confront their neighbors rather than rely on government officials. The result would be a community with greater cohesion and personal responsibility than occurs when control is centralized in citywide elected officials with significant power delegated to administrators.

> Let us imagine a community free to create its own pattern of life. Here also . . . would be found whites and blacks, who were blue-collar laborers, old people living in reduced circumstances, perhaps some immigrant clusters, perhaps a few small shopkeepers. . . . The outstanding characteristic of this area . . . would be the high level of tension and unease between the people living there. . . . And because metropolitan wide controls would be lessened, the threat of the assurance of police control would be gone, for the police would have the responsibility not of keeping peace in the community by repressing deviance but rather of dealing with organized crime or other similar problems. Precisely because the community was on its own, because people had to deal with each other in order to survive at all, some kind of uneasy truce between these hostile camps, these conflicting interests would be arranged by the people themselves. And the act of participating in some sort of truce would force people to look at each other, if only to find areas in which some bond, tenuous and unloving as it would be, could be forged. (Sennett 1970: 143–4)

Jane Jacobs was a journalist living in New York's Greenwich Village when she wrote her path-breaking book *The Death and Life of Great American Cities.* She reflected on the informal uses of power and influence in her neighborhood that she felt provided an example of how cities ought to be governed. Life in her neighborhood was influenced by informal interactions among the diverse residents. For example, keys were left with the corner grocer when people left their apartments because he is someone who knows the neighborhood and is trusted. She reports an incident where a man seems to be trying to get a young girl to go with him, and the girl appeared to be resisting. Shortly, the local bar owner, the delicatessen owner, and the local butcher were on the street giving the man menacing looks. "Nobody was going to allow a little girl to be dragged off even if nobody knew who she was"(1961: 39).

The strength of the neighborhood, to Jacobs, is the diversity and concentration of residents. People of various income levels and ethnicity and race are living nearby and they must interact regularly with one another. Most forms of individual commerce—groceries, entertainment, and dry cleaning—are carried out in the neighborhood. Consequently, everybody has a stake in the neighborhood's safety and vitality. It remains a successful neighborhood, she argues, because it contains diverse kinds of buildings with numerous kinds of owners and residents where life on the street can be easily watched, and it contains people who regularly go out of doors on diverse schedules.

Government's main task, Jacobs writes, is to assist in constructing this kind of neighborhood. Planning and zoning policies should encourage diversity and neighborhood organization. If the policies do so, the traditional functions of government often can be handled informally. "The first thing to understand is that the public peace—the sidewalk and street peace of cities is not kept primarily by the police, necessary as police are. It is kept primarily by an intricate, almost unconscious network of voluntary controls and standards among the people themselves and enforced by the people themselves" (1961: 33). To Jacobs, when public control lacks a community base, tyranny results. "In some city areas," she adds, "older public housing projects and streets with very high population turnover are often conspicuous examples—the keeping of public sidewalk law and order is left almost entirely to the police and special guards. Such places are jungles. No amount of police can enforce civilization where the normal casual enforcement has broken down" (1961: 32).

Like Sennett, Jacobs believes that individuals can learn to control most of the concerns of their territory if given the proper structure of government. She is most critical of governmental activities, particularly urban renewal and public housing, that destroy neighborhoods. Though she asks for government help in creating viable communities, she sees the foundation for good government as strong, independent neighborhoods. "City districts," she argues, "will be economically and socially congenial places for diversity to generate itself and reach its best potential if the districts possess good mixtures of primary uses, frequent streets, a close-grained mingling of different ages in their buildings, and a high concentration of people" (1961: 242).

Government-Induced Participation

A second school of thought argues that true participation, particularly in economically poorer communities, is possible only if government intervenes to ensure that the public will be represented and have their views seriously considered by policymakers. Thus, government agencies establish community decision-making bodies, provide resources for them, and give then responsibility for making important decisions. Provisions have been written into federal grants, for instance, requiring that community councils be established and that they participate in deciding how the grant should be spent. Some cities have established community councils that serve as advisory bodies for a wide range of city policies. The city often provides staff support for the councils and expects that input from the councils will have an important effect on city policy.

Several assumptions underlie this position. Power structures in urban communities are seen as a way to limit the influence of those with less resources. Unless higher levels of government intervene, therefore, meaningful participation will not occur. Further, historical discrimination and personal biases will silence minority members unless higher levels of government require community participation. It is also argued that poverty is, in part, related to powerlessness. Unless the poor have influence over the governance of their communities, they will not promote the values necessary to overcome the constraints of the lifestyle of poverty. Greenstone and Peterson, who studied the influence of community councils in the 1960s, claim this argument was the main rationale for the emphasis on participatory bodies in the urban legislation of that time. The poor, they maintain:

> . . . lacked such political resources as stable financing, social prestige, and easy access to decision makers. Generally they were known for low voter turnout where parties were weak and for the relative ease with which the vote could be 'controlled' by strong party organizations. Most important, the poor had few autonomous organizations which could articulate their collective demands and maximize their electoral influence, requisites for becoming more than a "potential group" in urban politics. In sum, poverty had a *political* as well as an economic dimension. Low-income citizens required not only improved services for individual clients; it was also necessary to mobilize community groups and to develop new political elites that could effectively articulate group interests. (Greenstone and Peterson 1973: 4)

These arguments supported changes in the federal grant and aid processes in the 1950s and 1960s to encourage and occasionally require representation of the poor in decisions concerning the spending of federal funds. The urban renewal program was the first piece of federal legislation requiring major citizen participation. The Housing Act of 1954 required citizen participation in the planning and execution of projects. Analysts, however, argue that the influence of citizens was generally pro-forma with little impact on policy (Cole 1974: 12). The Economic Opportunity Act of 1964, the so-called War on Poverty, placed significant emphasis on the formation of councils within areas receiving poverty funds and required broadly representative coordinating committees or poverty councils to determine policy and oversee the administration of funds within the district's territory (Greenstone and Peterson 1973: 2).

The establishment of participatory bodies in major cities led to significant criticism of both the theory and practice. Daniel Patrick Moynihan argued that Congress never intended to mandate actual representation of the poor, and blamed the structure of the program on well meaning but misguided social activists (1969). Others who looked at the practice of the councils themselves found many wanting in actual representation (Rose 1972). Powerful mayors like Richard Daley controlled the Chicago funds by appointing friends and cronies to the councils. In Los Angeles, where power was widely dispersed, the mayor and city council fought overt the structure of the program. Hence, few funds were actually distributed (Greenstone and Peterson 1973: 155–225). While many have argued since that the councils operated successfully in many cities (see Berry et al. 1993: 33), public opinion and the feelings of significant members of Congress became critical of participation efforts. The Model Cities legislation of 1966, for instance, watered down participatory requirements and channeled funds to the municipal government, not a participatory council. Participatory requirements remained a staple of federal legislation in many federal programs. The rationale for government-supported participation continues to influence attempts to expand citizens' influence on government policy.

METHODS OF EXPANDING PUBLIC PARTICIPATION

Let us look at the ways in which American cities attempt to encourage citizen participation in government. Current practice in American cities includes five distinctly different methods. They differ by the manner and extent to which government is involved and in their reliance on group or individual decisions. Government plays a major role in organizing and funding the effort in some cases and a less important role in others. In some programs we rely more on the response of individual citizens; in others we expect citizens to organize in groups. The approaches can be ranked according to the extent to which government is significantly involved. Table 8.1 lists the five kinds of participatory policies, ranked by the extent of government involvement. We will examine examples of each, with the aim of understanding how each approach assists in the creation of social capital.

Table 8.1 Participatory Methods and Government Involvement

LESS GOVERNMENT

- **Community Organized Councils.** Where community members, on their own initiative, organize members of the community and attempt to use their personal influence to affect city policy.

- **Community-Based Organizations.** Private, non-profit organizations within communities that perform a wide variety of services for community members and often receive government grants and support.

- **Internet Democracy.** The use of the Internet by governments to acquaint citizens with government programs and use the Internet to encourage public participation and access to government programs.

- **Government-Organized Councils.** Government establishes community-based councils, provides resources for them, and gives participants a role in public decisions.

- **Community-Based Policing.** Through the actions of police officer's, communities are organized and become a part of the governmental decision-making process. Citizens become co-producers of police services by helping control community disorder. Police assist the community by improving public services.

MORE GOVERNMENT

Community-Organized Councils

Baltimore experienced one of the century's largest blizzards in February of 1979. In Reservoir Hill, a largely Black, low income section of the city, looters began smashing the windows and looting supermarkets and liquor stores. The police were nowhere in sight; the snowfall prevented them from controlling mayhem on the streets. In the box "The Community Association in an Emergency," Matthew Crenson describes the response of the Reservoir Hill Community Association, an independent organization of residents funded by local contributions. The Association is a part of a network of similar groups operating in most neighborhoods of the city. Over 400 such organizations exist.

THE COMMUNITY ASSOCIATION IN AN EMERGENCY

Bernice Payne was standing on the front porch of her Whitelock Street home when Nancy Lawlor came by on the way to her job as director of a homeownership program at the Community Association offices. Mrs. Lawlor lived in Park Avenue, about a block further east in an area where young white families had begun to rehabilitate old townhouses. Mrs. Payne, a member of the Association's executive board, invited her inside for a cup of coffee. Not long afterward, two of the Payne children ran into the house with news of the first looting incident on Whitelock Street. Mrs. Payne ordered them to stay indoors and then began to telephone other women in the area, urging them to keep their children off the streets.

In the interval between calls, Stephanie Hall, president of the Reservoir Hill Community Association, telephoned to suggest that the group should open its Whitelock Street offices in order to respond to requests for emergency assistance from neighborhood residents. Mrs. Hull, a social worker, was one of the white home owners who had begun to renovate a house in Reservoir Hill. She had already spent the morning consulting by telephone with officers and board members of the

Community Association about measures that might be taken in response to the blizzard, and she had heard about the looting. Now, pulling a sled loaded with a supply of blankets and accompanied by her two children she set out from her home just as scores of would be looters were streaming southward through the streets to exploit a break-in at a supermarket.

When she arrived at the Payne home she was met by Nancy Lawlor. With Mrs. Payne's brother as an escort they walked toward Whitelock Steet, where they found Rudy Williams still doing sentry duty at the entrance of the Community Association's headquarters. Soon they were joined by Beatrice Payne and by Willie Mae Davis, a neighborhood leader of long standing who lived around the corner from Whitelock city on Brookfield Avenue. . . . A short time later, a team of volunteers had expanded to about fifteen members; during some periods over the next two days, it would include as many as thirty or forty people in a neighborhood where many families customarily buy no more than a day's groceries at a time. The distribution of food to snowbound residents was probably the volunteers' most pressing piece of

(continued)

(continued)

business. . . . To locate people who needed food or assistance, radio and television stations had already been asked to announce that neighborhood residents could contact the Offices of the Community Association for emergency help.

By afternoon, shipments of food were going out from the headquarters of the Community Association. Some were dragged or sledded to their destination by children. Others were transported as far as possible on a four-wheel-drive vehicle that had been pressed into service and then carried the remaining distance on foot. Several workers who were not engaged in the packing or distribution of food bundles were shoveling out the streets so that oil trucks could make deliveries and residents could get to their jobs. Others were helping a Whitelock Street merchant to clean up the wreckage in his store.

SOURCE: Matthew A. Crenson, *Neighborhood Politics* (Cambridge, MA: Harvard University Press, 1983): 5–7.

Crenson is describing community organizations commonly found in many cities. Neighborhood residents maintain these associations, and generally receive little or no funding from the city government. Fees from residents and small grants from local merchants and businesses supply minimal financial resources, but many rely exclusively on volunteers. Cities often work closely with neighborhood groups. They frequently compile rosters of such groups and provide assistance on a piecemeal basis. Thus, most of the effort is located in the neighborhood. Their strength varies significantly from one city to another and within sections of the same city. Some meet infrequently and do not actively involve citizens unless a significant problem emerges. Planning and zoning measures, for example, frequently activate near-dormant organizations because a threat to the lifestyle of the community is perceived.

Others operate with nearly the strength of the old ward system and a bit of a mafia Godfather. Crenson relates an incident where the community organization assumed a quasi-judicial role:

> . . . a young man was seen breaking into parking meters not far from the street where Mrs. Avara (the head of the neighborhood organization) lives. Some of the neighbors brought her a petition about the matter; it demanded that the culprit be arrested and prosecuted . . . They asked her to sign it and then present it to the appropriate authorities. Instead, Mrs. Avara decided to handle the case herself. Through her neighbors, she issued an unofficial summons for the accused. He was to present himself at her home for a talk. "I do it all the time" she says, "they talk to me . . . I tell them you don't fool with Mary. You know Miss Mary likes you, but don't you fool with me. Now I get the petition. I know you did it. Now either you stop or you're going to jail, And don't say Miss Mary's going to be behind me. I can take him to court. Those judges know me, When he comes over, I will not embarrass him in front of anybody. But he will not do that again, because the judges downtown know that if Mary Avara comes, that's it." (1983:156–7)

Some neighborhood associations are permanent and ongoing; others emerge or are activated when the interests of the community are threatened. Urban renewal and redevelopment projects that threaten to change the land use of neighborhoods and remove some residents from buildings frequently generate intense neighborhood reactions that take the form of pronounced organization activity. Henig looked intensively at six cases of neighborhoods threatened by urban renewal in Minneapolis and Chicago, evaluating the success of the communities in resisting the city's attempt to implement an urban renewal project. In each case, community members organized an attempt to preserve the neighborhood, but some areas were more successful in mobilizing community members and pressing their will on city officials.

The most successful neighborhoods mobilized residents quickly and received a responsive hearing from city officials, often succeeding in changing the city's plans. Generally, they were less susceptible to pressure from city officials. Other neighborhoods, however, responded slowly and failed to engage large numbers of people. These neighborhoods were less successful in getting their aims accomplished. Again, middle-class neighborhoods with a previous history of community organization were most successful. Those with previous experience in community activity and strong connections with city officials were able to alter or even cancel the proposal. Poor, fragmented neighborhoods had a much more difficult time being heard effectively in city hall, and urban renewal projects often pressed forward in spite of their opposition. Strong leaders did occasionally succeed in organizing residents in these communities and influencing city hall, but the leadership demands in these cases were most significant. Unless a strong and tireless leader emerged, these neighborhoods had little influence (Henig 1982: 216).

Evaluating neighborhood organizations is complicated by the many different forms these organizations take. Some are informal groups that meet rarely but are activated when community interests are threatened. Others are formal and rather permanent with a meeting place and a small staff. They seem to be most effective when neighborhood interests are threatened by land use decisions or urban renewal. Organizations in wealthier areas or those controlled by middle- and upper-class residents are usually more influential. In Seattle, for instance, a city with a strong tradition of neighborhood organization, Guest and Oropesa found that the effectiveness of community groups was directly related to the class structure of the community. Upper-class, homogeneous neighborhoods contained well-organized groups that seemed to effectively represent the needs of the residents. Lower-class communities were less effectively represented (1984). Perkins, Brown, and Taylor studied community organizations in Salt Lake City, Baltimore, and New York City. They concluded that participation was greater in communities with higher social and economic status and where residency was stable (1996). Likewise, Mesch and Schwirian found that home ownership and social and economics status were related to the effectiveness of neighborhood groups in Columbus, Ohio (1996). Crenson also found social and economic status related to the perceived effectiveness of community groups in Baltimore. High-status residents living in low-status communities were generally most able to influence the neighborhood organization and city policy. These associations were also most likely to suffer from internal conflicts. Since these associations are staffed by volunteers and their strength varies with the composition of the community and the skills of the participants, initiative is most likely to rest on those who are financially more able. As Crenson notes "Educational background, organizational skills, or simply confident beliefs that one's actions can make a difference for the neighborhood—any of these things may represent a political resource and the people who control these resources possess the wherewithal to exercise political influence. This means that privileged people who live in underprivileged neighborhoods are likely to have the capacity, not just the reasons for informal political action. . . . Political resources are more valuable in neighborhoods where almost no one has them than in neighborhoods where almost everybody does" (1983: 191).

Common today in many condominiums, cooperatives, and gated communities is the Residential Community Association (RCA). RCAs are mandatory organizations of property owners residing within a small area of the city. They are responsible for common problems of the residents and frequently manage public services. They also have the power to enforce standards on the property owners as specified in signed legal orders that are usually a part of the purchase agreement. Thus, they exhibit some of the characteristics of governments and in many cases can exercise more power than cities often possess. For example, RCAs enforce architectural and visual restrictions on property owners. They can cite owners for failing to cut their grass or paint their house properly. They can also assess members the cost of various repairs and services such as lawn upkeep.

In most ways, RCAs are closer to private corporations than governments. The members are property owners, not necessarily residents, and often the owners are absentee. Their tasks are largely business management, and profit making is the primary concern. Open meeting laws do not necessarily apply to their actions. At the same time, they do perform quasi-governmental functions and they usually have rather close relations with governments (United States Advisory Commission on Intergovernmental Relations 1989: 13–16).

RCAs have grown significantly in recent years. It is estimated that 12 to 15 percent of the country's population lives in units governed by them, a 26-fold increase since 1960. Are these organizations an asset to the quest for social capital? They exhibit many of the characteristics of governments; they include significant numbers of people, membership is mandatory, and they make decisions of basic importance to the owners. Critics, however, argue that the goals of RCAs, unlike neighborhood associations, are limited and inward looking— they avoid taking stands on local issues and limit their activity to zoning and permit issues with immediate impact on the development itself (Barton and Silverman 1994: 36). Some see RCAs as a tool for separating neighborhoods from the problems and concerns of the city (Davis 1990: 246). The corporate nature of the organizations and the membership of property owners with voting rights often based on the value of the property owned, would seem to question a comparison with a democratic government.

Community-Based Organizations

THE COMPREHENSIVE COMMUNITY REVITALIZATION PROGRAM, SOUTH BRONX

Since the 1960s, successive federal administrations have poured funds for education and social services into New York City's South Bronx through traditional program mechanisms without much payoff. The Comprehensive Community Revitalization Program (CCRP), launched in 1992 with support from the Surdra Foundation, used a quite different community-building approach in that area—one that is already yielding positive results. CCRP chose not to deliver comprehensive human services through traditional social work and educational institutions, but, through five existing Community Development Corporations (CDCs), the housing development activity over the years had become trusted by community residents. Community organizers were employed to develop broader resident involvement in both planning and implementation. Consultants were used in a manner that supported and reinforced resident decision making rather than replacing it.

Rather than beginning with a prolonged planning period, CCRP emphasized moving quickly to demonstrate results and make residents confident they could accomplish more. One early project that had substantial psychological impact entailed cleaning up the neighborhood—installing new lights and mobilizing 60 neighborhood youths to paint murals in a formerly crime-ridden pedestrian tunnel that had became a *cause celebre* in the community.

But CCRP activities have been comprehensive and typically broader in scope. The CDCs have already built new primary health facilities; developed and operated employment linkage and training initiatives; created a variety of childcare programs; developed partnerships with neighborhood schools to enhance education quality; initiated neighborhood safety and crime reduction measures; and undertaken several economic development projects (including a sizeable new shopping center and a micro-enterprise loan program).

One of the CCRP's most visible accomplishments has been its assistance in establishing the Mt. Hope Family practice; a partnership between one of its constituent CDCs—the Mount Hope Housing corporation and the Institute for Urban Family Health. While the neighborhood had one of the highest incidents of health problems in the country, healthcare services had always been fragmented and ineffectual. As a first step in addressing the issue, the Housing Company held intensive health education workshops in the community to build resident awareness of the importance of primary health care. The New Family Practice was opened in 1995 to provide continuity of care, special services and referrals, health education, and disease prevention. It employs a Spanish-speaking staff and makes special efforts to train and hire local residents for appropriate positions. The practice accommodated 8,000 visits in 1995, and has developed the capacity to handle 16,000 visits annually.

Noteworthy is CCRP's growing emphasis on preparing residents for and linking them to employment opportunities. In the past, CDCs have focused on job creation in small neighborhood businesses. CCRP's new Employment Service, in contrast, concentrates even more on job training to facilitate resident access to jobs outside of the community.

SOURCE: Kingley, C. Thomas, Joseph B. McNeely, and James O. Gibson, *Community Building Coming of Age* (The Urban Institute, 1998 //www.urbanorg/community).

The box "The Comprehensive Community Revitalization Program, South Bronx" describes the operation of a very successful Community-Based Organization (CBO). CBOs have some of the characteristics of neighborhood organizations: They create a forum for neighborhood residents' concerns, and frequently serve as a link between the citizen and the planning and administration of city services. Their functions, however, are much broader. They also directly administer services that are delegated to them by contracts with the city or non-profit agencies, or through their own initiative. They secure funds from governments, foundations, and the private sector and use them to support community programs. They may own property and manage banks and credit unions. Community members join the corporation and may collectively share in its profits. In a sense, they are a community non-profit business designed to improve the quality of life and expand individual opportunities. They do this by managing complex bargains between businesses, land owners, governments, and their own boards of directors. They own businesses and use the profits for community projects. One CDC director explained the kind of transaction common to many CBOs:

> I called it our Robin Hood type of arrangement where we actually get from the wealthy . . . in this case the for-profit Wendy's and give back to the poor. The land we acquired from the city . . . Wendy's of course leases from us. The difference between our annual payment to the city and Wendy's payment to us is a plus $6000. That $6000 goes into the low income trust fund that we then use to acquire additional land and or property to develop more low income housing. (Rubin 1995: 9)

CBOs also are actively involved in city affairs. When successful, they often become the primary distributor of many city services in their areas and in some sense a de-facto government. Ferman, for example, argues that the Pittsburgh Partnership for Neighborhood Development (PPND)—an umbrella organization of local CDCs, foundations, and the business community funded by Community Development Block Grant funds—is a major player in city politics. The PPND is engaged in the formation of community development strategies and secures coordination among CDCs for grant acquisition and coordination with city government. As a consequence, CDCs have become officially recognized as intermediaries between government and the neighborhoods. Over 80 percent of the city's capital budget is spent in neighborhoods coordinated by the CDCs (Ferman 1996: 99).

Because they can implement programs, CBOs can approach the problems of social capital formation from a broader perspective than do community councils. If jobs are needed to provide employment for youths, the CBO can acquire land and lend money to prospective businesses. They can establish job training and daycare facilities for residents to assist them in getting into the work force. Thus, they represent the residents' interests and improve community facilities. The goal is the development of deprived neighborhoods to permit them to build the characteristics of strong neighborhoods—employment opportunities, diverse housing, and community amenities. Here is the mission statement of one Chicago CBO:

> Bethel pursues progress on many levels at once, working to develop whole persons, whole families, whole communities. Good housing and well-paid jobs are central to building a healthy community, but so are health care, good libraries and schools and even such intangibles as food, parks, and a sense of local history. By addressing root causes in a comprehensive way, the wholistic approach creates a foundation on which to build stronger community. (Rubin 1995: 18)

CBOs are governed by a board of directors composed of community residents and others with a strong stake in the community (Imbroscio 1997: 107). The organizational model is closer to a corporation than a city government. The governing body sets general policy direction and empowers an executive director to manage the organization. The aim to is to bring about changes in the community and to improve the quality of life. The organization also must act to survive and grow. Managing a CBO requires a continuous search for funds from government, major foundations, and the private sector. Successful CBOs receive major grants from local foundations and are delegated significant governmental tasks. Federal funds, most particularly those from the Community Development Block Grant program, are often dedicated to CBOs.

It is difficult to gauge the strength of CDCs nationally. Their numbers have grown rapidly over the past 20 years. It is estimated that there were fewer than 200 CDCs in 1970 and over 2,000 today (Imbroscio 1997: 112; Ferman 1997: 141). Their influence varies from city to city. Ferman argues that CDCs have become institutionalized. They are part of the political and administrative system of Pittsburgh, and now are integrated into the city decision-making process. A similar, though less broad-based, incorporation also occurred in Los Angeles during the Bradley administration (Saltzstein, Ostrow, and Sonenshein 1986). Clavel, Pitt, and Yin see CDCs becoming more broadly involved in a diverse array of city policies and becoming a focus for community representation in the poorer parts of most cities. They argue that recent federal legislation—the Community reinvestment Act, the Empowerment Zone legislation, and the new welfare policies—place CDCs as intermediaries between local communities and the federal government (1997: 450–51). Thus, they expect their influence to expand, replacing relations between the federal government and local governments in many cases. In Chicago, however, CDCs are viewed as competitors to the political system, limiting their influence on policy and resource distribution (Ferman: 1997).

As a strategy for enhancing neighborhood social capital, CDCs work most effectively when they can become a part of the city's decision-making process and can coalesce successfully with key elements in the private and philanthropic sectors. There is a great deal of case study and anecdotal evidence that CDCs skillfully marshal resources, strengthen communities, and improve the quality of life (Gibson, Kingsley and McNeely 1997; Osborne and Gaebler 1992).

The context of the community and the cooperation of the many partners within the organization, however, frequently create tensions between community goals and the demands of those with resources. To be successful in the eyes of those who fund them may mean compromises with the perceived needs of the community. Thus, in successful CBOs there is always a tension between the ability to gain funds and programmatic responsibility and the community needs that might be sacrificed by operating so closely with the power elite. One CSC director revealed to Rubin:

> We are participating in some way in some measure in a fundamental change . . . that really calls into question the ways that decisions are made, the way control is exercised, the way resources are allocated . . . [if not] maybe we are just helping this lousy system work a little bit easier, to get by a little better. We often ask ourselves if we are not just the pimp for downtown. (1995: 5)

Internet and Urban Democracy

Open the Web site for Colorado Springs, Colorado and you are greeted with a stunning display of photographs of the city and its surroundings (Figure 8.2). Click on one of 14 buttons on the side of the pictures and much of the city is at your grasp. What is the crime rate in your neighborhood? A few clicks and you can find out. Want to know when your street will be resurfaced? Does the library contain a favorite book? How do citizens feel about the city? Who plays bass clarinet in the symphony? The Web site will tell you. The complete text analyzing a recent citizen survey, including colorful charts and graphs, is available. Are you interested in the city's strategic plan? A Powerpoint presentation can be viewed.

The site carries you beyond city hall. Which route should I take out of town? Live traffic cams give you instant pictures of traffic conditions at major intersections. Want to check the time of your flight out of town? No problem. Are you looking for a job or trying to locate a business in town? The Web site will help you.

And if you don't like what you see or you have a more specific problem, email anybody you like. All major department heads, the mayor, and the city council can be written to by clicking on their email accounts.

Some argue that the Internet has created a new form of political communications. By connecting people regularly in chat rooms, ideas among people develop and new knowledge grows. For governments, the consequence is an increasingly empowered citizenry. If these groups of citizens interact with government officials, a broader democracy will develop. City Web sites are a potentially crucial link in a system that will energize citizens. Brock Meeks, chief Washington correspondent for MSNBC, argues that:

> Using high-speed pipes now linking entire communities and subsidized through government regulation, entire networks will spring up dedicated to common use. At first, people will simply jack in to get to know each

FIGURE 8.2 Colorado Springs Web Site.

Courtesy of the Colorado Springs Municipal Government

other, amused by the novelty of it all. These will be clumsy, almost banal affairs, but crucial as people become familiar with the technologies and how to use them for online chatting or exploring the possibilities of full-motion videoconferencing links. . . . Once these families begin to form alliances, built around concern for their own kids it will spill over to the neighborhoods as well. Neighborhood watch programs will spring up in a more concerted fashion with more power and coordination simply hanging in ineffectual sign on doors and on street lamps. People will coordinate their own homes, via video and net links over specialized neighborhood channels. . . . City councils will be held more accountable as more citizens participate and voice their concerns (1997: 3–7).

Others, however, argue that Internet use strengthens but does not significantly transform political participation (Norris 1999: 73; Hill and Hughes 1998: 2–3). Thus, those people using political chat rooms are politically active initially and the use of the Internet only reinforces their political activity. The evidence from the use of the Internet in national political campaigns suggests that reinforcement is the most common pattern. Norris, for example, concludes "Net political activists were already among the most motivated, informed and interested in the electorate. In this sense, during recent campaigns the Net was essentially preaching to the converted" (1999: 89). High levels of Internet use are more common among right wing and Libertarian interest groups. (Hill and Hughes 1998: 71). One would expect a similar pattern in usage of city Web sites; most commonly they are used by those already active in city affairs.

Whether it effectively links citizens or not, the Internet has become an important tool for city officials. Much time, money, and effort is being invested in computerizing city offices developing sophisticated Web sites. Some argue it has revolutionized public business by increasing the responsiveness of the city to public problems, enhancing efficiency and more directly connecting the citizen to government. The goal in part is to more thoroughly connect the citizen to government. The question is whether we are better democrats as a consequence. Perhaps, if in fact Web sites regularly connect citizens with government, and involve them more directly and regularly with their elected and appointed officials. As the Denver case reveals, the development of a Web site is not without costs, both financial and political.

DENVER AND ITS WEB SITE: THE BEST THINGS IN LIFE ARE NEVER FREE

During his 1995 inauguration, Mayor Wellington Webb called for a brave new era in Denver government in which citizens would transact with the city through computer technology. "Too often when we need information from **city government,** we must come Downtown to some city building and wait in line for answers," he said in his inauguration speech. "That's not an acceptable level of customer service for either next year or the next century."

Denver, the nation's 26th-largest city, ranks fourth for Internet use. Although half of city residents don't have regular online access, 49 percent are studying, shopping, amusing themselves, emailing, trading stocks, and otherwise becoming entangled in the World Wide Web. City government first tapped the technology in 1993, when the Mayors' staff launched Denver's current site: http://infodenver.org. That site has grown; it now posts ordinances, council agendas, meeting minutes, city job openings, and lists of officials serving on various boards and commissions. But the site is difficult to navigate, especially for users unfamiliar with how city government is set up—unaware, for example, that animal control falls under the Department of Environmental Health.

So, for $45,000 in tax dollars, a private consultant studied the site and suggested Denver create a new Web presence that's easier to use and offers more information. Without seeking competitive bids from other computer experts, the city hired the consultant, former city techie Bob Schubring, to build the new site. Six months and $545,165 later, Schubring promises to offer property records, civil court dockets, and airport flight information updated daily. Bid documents, event calendars, volunteer databases, citizen suggestion boxes, and multilingual information about the Mayor's Office of Economic Development also will be available online. The site will enable users to register their bikes electronically and request that information such as council agendas and agency newsletters be emailed to them. It will offer forms for business licenses and disabled parking tags, for example, that users can download, print, fill out, and mail back to the city. It also will allow residents to type in their addresses and instantly see their homes on a map in relation to nearby parks and schools. And it will feature 360-degree pictures of Civic Center and views from the Capitol rotunda and Stapleton's control tower. Still, at least initially, the site won't feature many basic uses that city officials say it's technically capable of offering. It won't air the city's Channel 8 cable television programming, for example, nor allow the public to participate in hearings online. It also won't include credit card applications that would enable citizens to pay parking fines, renew license plates, or sign up for tee times at city golf courses. The site won't transmit live traffic

information, as do those in Seattle and Houston. And Denver's site won't feature electronic town meetings or online access to parcel maps, business license records, deeds, liens, birth and death certificates, or marriage and divorce documents, as does the site for Clark County, Nev. That government spent $75,000 on its Web presence, which offers nearly every service Denver's does, plus many more.

Denver officials say it could be months and possibly years before they add those uses, which will cost more than the initial $590,165 investment. They downplay the delay, saying new features will come when bureaucrats learn to take advantage of the technology, and when users demand better computer access to city services.

On content, experts have tepid reviews. Some say it doesn't do enough to grab users. Property records and court documents are useful, critics say, but most citizens would sooner log on for traffic updates, for example—information the site won't provide.

"Logging on to this, I see no information that I truly need. It's not a site I'd visit when I'm checking my e-mail," observed Gary Delius, project manager with Lexitech Inc. in Connecticut, a government Internet specialist which built Colorado Springs' Web presence. Added Paul Blodgett, Lexitech's product manager, "If the citizens are paying for it, it should be more useful, more compelling for them." Further, Internet users question whether the site is truly interactive, as Schubring promised, or simply an electronic bulletin board used to post information. Given its expensive technical capabilities, they say, it should offer more interactive uses. After all, they note, people typically don't visit city offices just for information, but rather for some kind of transaction—to renew their license plates or pay parking tickets, for example. Without such services online, they say, the site's motto, "Skip the trip," seems hollow. "Tell me, what

(continued)

(continued)

trip can you skip exactly?" Blodgett asked. Added Delius: "For $500,000, I think somebody in Denver ought to be raising some questions. Even projects we do for the federal government don't cost that much. And you know how they are. Maybe we should raise our prices."

Come Tuesday, the $590,165 doubtlessly will have given Denverites better Internet access to their city government. Mortgage companies and nosy neighbors will enjoy perusing property records online, and lawyers and news reporters will save time with electronic access to court dockets.

But, at least initially, the site hardly will revolutionize the way the city does business. Impatient drivers still will line up to pay traffic fines, and citizens still will have to struggle with 30-year-old microfilm machines in the bowels of city hall for images of most recorder's documents. In the mean time, Denverites will decide whether "that's an acceptable level of customer service," and, as the mayor had hoped, whether the city indeed has "the finest municipal Internet presence in the country."

SOURCE: From Susan Green "Critics Hit New Web Site; Find Denver's Net Presence Lacking," *The Denver Post,* February 19, 1999.

Unfortunately little is known about the effect of the Internet on the connection between citizens and government. Expanded use of the Internet is very new. Surveys indicate, for instance, that only 14 percent of Americans had ever gone online in 1995. This percentage increased to 42 percent in 1998, and is likely to be a majority today (Norris 1999: 75). While the percentage is lower among racial and ethnic minorities and the poor, many have argued that people in these categories are rapidly catching up. Cities are also pioneering in the placement of free computers in libraries, malls, and schools. Thus, it is possible to envision very widespread access to city Web sites in the near future. Today, however, governments still have a ways to go to reach universal citizen access (Mechling 1999: 181).

Availability, does not necessarily lead to city-citizen connections. To begin with, few cities have the Internet capacity evidenced in Colorado Springs, though more and more are expanding the coverage of their Web pages. When the Web site is available, we have little solid evidence of its use. Do citizens turn to city Web pages regularly? Do they use them to interact or only access information? If use is slight, will city officials find maintenance of the Web page worth the effort? There are few answers to these questions at this point in time.

Government-Organized Councils

Some cities commit much time and effort to encourage neighborhood participation in city policy. They establish advisory governing councils in all neighborhoods and locate city staff in a neighborhood office to aid council members in dealing with city problems. Certain city policies are expected to have the approval of the councils prior to implementation. Such councils rarely exercise direct control over government actions, but they are instrumental in influencing major policies. Though their control is modest, neighborhood councils can delay actions until appropriate compromises can be worked out.

Neighborhood councils differ from community-organized councils because they are financed and supported by city government. It may be common to combine the two in neighborhoods where an established council exists. There should, however, be a different outlook in a government-organized council. It is viewed as a part of government policy and meant to be a partner rather than critic. It also differs from a community-based organization because the organization provides no services directly.

Governments invest in neighborhood councils for numerous reasons. Government officials may be concerned about the general problems of declining social capital and hope that the councils will develop a firmer connection between the public and local government. They may also want more direct input on public policy from diverse sections of the city. City officials may hope that strong neighborhood associations will assist the city in implementing services. Organized neighborhoods may aid the police by reporting suspicious activities, and help the park system through volunteer aids. Neighborhood councils may also assist the city politically by preventing secession movements. As a forum for dissent, they permit city officials to respond to problems that, if left unattended, could lead to demonstrations or movements to separate from the city.

How successful are neighborhood councils? Several social scientists undertook a detailed and systematic analysis of neighborhood councils in five cities: Birmingham, Dayton, Portland, St. Paul, and San Antonio. These cities were selected because each had sponsored an elaborate neighborhood program. Councils were created in all parts of the city including from 2,000 to 5,000 people. In each case, the city provided staff support and regular communication with the councils, and in all cases the councils had significant advisory input in several areas of city policy. All were examples of serious and significant attempts to create participatory units. Additionally, the authors compared these cities with five other cities with similar characteristics but without neighborhood councils. In each city, a sample of residents were interviewed, while community leaders in all cities were interviewed in depth. The researchers also looked closely at important community decisions. The result is a large body of information about citizens, government policy-making, and the actions of the councils. By comparing cities with and without neighborhood councils, the analysts attempted to isolate the effect of neighborhood councils.

The authors pursued three central questions:

- Does the presence of neighborhood councils broaden the extent of political participation. In other words, do such councils increase social capital by encouraging more people to vote, become knowledgeable of community affairs, and become more active in their community?

- Do neighborhood councils encourage improvements in government responsiveness? Do government officials respond to the needs of neighborhoods more effectively when neighborhood councils are present?

- Do neighborhood councils empower people? Jefferson proposed that participation leads to values of tolerance and support for the political system. Thus, the researchers asked if people in cities with neighborhood councils felt better about other citizens as a consequence of participating with them. Are the residents in cities with participatory structures more tolerant of other people and do they express greater support for the political system?

FIVE CITIES, FIVE KINDS OF NEIGHBORHOOD BOARDS

Each city chose to organize its councils differently though all share common characteristics. Following is a · description of the councils in each city drawn from Berry, Portney, and Thomson, *The Rebirth of Urban Democracy.*

In Birmingham, the neighborhoods themselves are the key actors in the process. Since their officers are directly elected at the polls, they immediately gain a certain public legitimacy. And since each neighborhood makes its own decisions about an allocation of public funds . . . the neighborhood association has one clear mission right at the start. But the issue responsibilities run the gamut from housing and zoning to community education and jobs for youth. Twenty-one formal communities typically composed of three to five neighborhoods are the conduit to the citywide Citizens Advisory Board, a citizens forum on issues affecting the neighborhoods. While purely advisory, and not always able to get its way with city council, the board is seen as a means of focused dialogue between citizens and the city.

Dayton's Priority Boards, on the other hand, are almost agencies in themselves. They are seen by many citizens as quasi-governmental and by many administrators as a formal voice of the neighborhoods. In addition to their role in routing neighborhood concerns to the city and in carrying out the formal functions of an elected community board, the Priority Boards

perform a myriad of constituent service functions with individuals in their sector of the city. Their political culture is administrative: most board members see their role as making government agency-neighborhood groups directly. Each has a different representative base: Neighborhoods elect their own officers, while citizens elect Priority Board members by precinct and not, in most cases, through the neighborhood groups themselves.

Most of Portland's neighborhood groups, unlike many in Birmingham and Dayton, have a long history of independence from city hall. From the beginning of the Office of Neighborhood Associations, the individual neighborhoods fought any sign of structure or control by city hall. Only after several years did they accept district coalition offices, which play an intermediary role between the neighborhoods and city hall, even though the staff of these offices are hired by the neighborhoods themselves. Only after 14 years would neighborhoods accept written guidelines for their operations (on areas such as being open to all residents, reporting minority points of view, and fulfilling their responsibility for disbursements of city funds). The district coalitions, with boards made up entirely of neighborhood association representatives, are encouraged to work directly with the city council. Many additional participation opportunities, such as the citywide Budget Advisory

Committees, are open to individuals in the city without regard to neighborhood affiliation.

St. Paul's District Councils came out of a three-year process of negotiation between the city (especially the mayor, council, and planning department), existing citizen groups, and individual citizens. Each District Council has its own bylaws and election procedures, and many are separately incorporated and raise their own funds. More than in any of the other cities, these councils are the focus of neighborhood-city interaction. Their powers are substantially greater than the very limited sketch provided in the city ordinance describing their creation. If citizens want something done in their neighborhood, if developers have a project, or if agency leaders want to drum up support, they go first to the District Councils. With 17 neighborhood offices and an impressive array of community center buildings, the structural base of the system is more extensive than in any of the other cities.

Communities Organized for Public Service (COPS) in San Antonio survives not on city funds—in fact, it refuses to accept government money of any kind—but on its intricate network of parish organizations. Each of the 25 to 30 active parish groups finds its own way to support itself with varying degrees of assistance from the local church. Substantial annual dues— usually raised in the local church—make up the lion's share of the citywide organization's annual budget. The major constraint on the organization is that their active parish groups cover only about 30 percent of the city's population. The city has made some effort to encourage neighborhood groups in other parts of the city, and several neighborhood-based coalition organizations are active, but in large part COPS's sizable clout comes from a massive mobilization of citizens from its quarter of the city.

SOURCE: Berry, Jeffrey M., Kent E. Portney, and Ken Thomson. *The Rebirth of Urban Democracy* (Washington D.C.: The Brookings Institution, 1993), 57–9.

The Berry, Portney, and Thomson study gives us a mixed picture of the value of neighborhood councils. They found little difference between the two groups of cities in voter participation and citizen activity in general. Cities with neighborhood councils contained more highly active citizens. These were typically middle- and upper-class residents. Thus the presence of councils did not stimulate the lower class to participate more, and probably increased class differences in participation.

However, the presence of neighborhood councils did contribute to the responsiveness of the neighborhoods. The councils were particularly effective in reflecting community opinion on matters of local concern. They also had influence on the priorities of elected officials and agency heads. City officials in cities with neighborhood councils were more likely to listen to neighborhood problems and adjust spending and policy priorities. The councils also effectively dealt with business interests, and often were able to win important compromises from developers and industries when conflicts between their respective interests arose (Berry, Portney, and Thomson 1993: 133). The councils had less influence on citywide policy, and their impact on policy was often in reaction to the proposals of others rather than advancing their own agenda. Nonetheless, the neighborhood councils in these five cities are able to gain the support of the residents and have a significant influence on city policy.

The study's data lends support to the Jeffersonian ideal. Citizens who participated more were more likely to feel positive about their community and feel that the individual was listened to by public officials. Participators also exhibited higher trust in government and greater political knowledge. The authors conclude on a very positive note in this regard. "Community participation makes people feel better about their own political effectiveness and about the ability of the local government to respond to them. It contributes to the amount of political knowledge people possess. It does not necessarily make people more community oriented and less self interest oriented, but strong democratic activity appeals overwhelmingly to those with community-oriented motivations" (Berry, Portney and Thomson 1993: 279).

CAN NEIGHBORHOOD COUNCILS KEEP THE CITY TOGETHER?

Residents of the San Fernando Valley have often felt estranged from the City of Los Angeles. The "Valley," as it is usually called, was annexed to the city in 1917 as water from the Owens Valley was secured. An inland plain separated from the city center by mountains, it remained undeveloped and agricultural until the 1950s. The boom in the Los Angeles economy and the suburbanizing of the county in the 1950s led to rapid subdividing of the area. From 1950 to 1970, the Valley became the haven for the White middle class and developed a sense of identity separate from the central city.

Today, the Valley is much more racially and ethnically diverse but the feeling of estrangement and isolation from city hall remains. The fiscal problems of the city and the "Tax Revolt" that fueled Proposition 13 in 1978, increased the residents' resentment of city government. A petition requesting a study of secession of the Valley from Los Angeles was signed by over one-fourth of the Valley residents; over 132,000 signatures. Valley proponents then persuaded state, county, and city officials to pay for a $2.4 million study of the feasibility of secession. Following deliberation by the Local Area Formation Commission, a vote will take place, in the fall of 2002. The electorate of both areas must approve it. The new city would become one of the nation's largest. The Valley now contains 1.3 million people spread over 275 square miles.

City officials oppose the succession movement and hope that a new city charter, approved by the voters in June of 1999, will improve the responsiveness of the city to Valley residents. Two important changes in the charter may influence feelings in the San Fernando Valley. The new charter is best described as a subtle balance between centralized power in a stronger mayor's office and decentralization through area planning commissions and neighborhood councils. Land-use decisions are transferred to seven area planning commissions representing different parts of the city. Two of those are located in the Valley. Members of the commissions are appointed by the mayor with confirmation of the city council. The charter also tried to empower neighborhoods through neighborhood councils. The councils will be advisory, but might become important vehicles for community input. With the threat of secession hanging over the city's head, it is likely that serious attempts will be made to make the councils a significant part of the decision-making process. Will it be enough to forestall succession? Stay tuned.

Government-organized councils try to provide the tools for the re-creation of social capital. Effective councils intercede between the average citizens and a large, impersonal government. In the cities examined by Berry et al., they seem to be able to reduce some of the problems of impersonality by providing a connection between the citizens and government. They are less successful in generating increases in political participation. Whether they will be able to improve citizen responsiveness in a city as large and complex as Los Angeles remains to be seen.

Community-Based Policing

A "WALK ALONG" WITH THE LOCAL POLICE

Recently I spent an evening with my friend Ralph, a police officer in the city of Anaheim, California, a medium-sized city with a significant crime problem in some parts of the community. Ralph was part of a new program in the city referred to as "Community-Based Policing." His work was concentrated in the Jeffrey-Lynne area of the city, a lower-class neighborhood of garden apartments near Disneyland. The residents were largely poor Latinos employed in the service industries related to the Disneyland complex. Few had much formal education, and many could not speak English. They worked as maids, gardeners, cooks, and janitors serving the vast tourist crowd. Crime in the area was significant—gang activities and drugs were common and residents were fearful of the police. With a special grant from the state, the city designed a special program designed to upgrade city services and pay special attention to a wide range of needs in the area.

The Anaheim Police Department is a modern organization and highly professional; officers are paid well and many have college degrees. Generally, they operated as most good departments do, by placing officers in police cars and focusing their efforts on responding to calls and complaints. In Jeffrey-Lynne, they were implementing a different form of policing, experimenting with its

application in a neighborhood in need of much more than improved law enforcement. Park and recreation facilities and social services were non-existent; citizens had little knowledge of city services and weak attachments to the city. Schools were overcrowded and drop-out rates were very high. Following is the story of my opportunity to see this form of policing for myself and form some impressions.

The afternoon was spent walking the neighborhood; my officer friend Ralph, a code enforcement officer Jim, and myself. As we walked, children greeted us and both officers knew most of them by name. We stopped at a small park that was created by turning a street into a cul-de-sac and placing some playground equipment, a basketball hoop, and a few park benches around the area. Ralph explained that he proposed the park to the public works department and the parks department. The public works officials approved the changing of the street patterns and built the barricades. The parks and recreation department brought in the equipment. When we arrived, several children were shooting baskets, and young mothers were watching children on the swing set. "Before we came," Ralph explained, "people were afraid to stay in the street."

As we proceeded down another street, Ralph waved to a friend who

(continued)

(continued)

came by to talk. He was a former gang member who now runs a small social center in one of the vacant housing units, paid for by the city. Daycare facilities are provided, and he is on duty to deal with any problems that might develop. This position was also a new one that the police initiated and paid for with the grant.

The code enforcement officer was making careful notes of housing and building conditions. One of the strategies used here was upgrading the neighborhood's housing. Tenants were organized by Ralph and encouraged to report violations to the police and the landlords. Ralph, who knows a bit about real estate, had called meetings of the building owners and given instructions on how to upgrade their properties and improve the financing of their investments to get a higher return. He also promised to assist them in removing troublemakers from their buildings if they would cooperate with him. Ralph & Jim looked carefully at the lighting in the alley behind a structure where drug trades have been known to occur. Then, Ralph saw a large chicken on a window ledge and started to enter the building. "Let me go first," Jim suggested. He entered the building and returned a few minutes later. "It's OK," he said "It's a rooster." Anaheim building codes permit the harboring of roosters, but not hens.

We saw a car parked on the street with a young woman in the driver's seat. Ralph talked to her and she drove off. "What happened?" I asked. Ralph responded, "I didn't recognize the car. She doesn't belong here. She didn't have her driver's license, so I told her to leave." A truck selling vegetables was parked a few streets up. There are no grocery stores nearby so vegetable trucks are a major source of food here. Ralph talked to the merchant and looked over his produce very carefully. "Many of these merchants are good guys," he added, "but drugs are frequently sold by these guys or by people who loiter around the trucks. You have to check them carefully." We stopped at a small convenience store to buy soft drinks. Ralph talked to the owner at length to get information about potentially questionable activities that might be going on. "The neighborhood is pretty quiet now," he said to me. "It didn't used to be that way."

Unfortunately a few months after my visit to Jeffrey-Lynne, the grant ran out and Ralph was assigned to another task. The neighborhood reverted to its former state—the gangs returned and conditions deteriorated.

We usually view the police as specialists in crime control. They respond to criminal acts and try to find the perpetrators. They are trained to detect crime and find those who commit criminal acts. They are also part of a hierarchical organization where power flows downward and the patrolman on the bottom can exercise few discretionary acts. The community-based policing in Jeffrey-Lynne was something very different. In this case the police were part social worker, part urban planner, and part real estate specialist. They acted as a catalyst among city agencies, planning new programs and inducing non-police employees to help them. They also tried to get the community working with them, assisting them in controlling criminal behavior. The patrol officer, the bottom of the police organization, was the major decision maker and a central actor in the community. This is the new world of the modern police officer; community-based policing (CBP).

David H. Bayley, a renowned criminal justice specialist, lists four basic elements of CBP:

1. Consultation with community groups regarding security needs

2. Devolution of command so that those closest to the community can determine how best to respond

3. Mobilization of agencies, other than the police, to assist in addressing neighborhood needs

4. Remedy the conditions that generate crime and insecurity through focused problem solving (Gianakis and Davis 1998: 486; see also Skolnick and Bayley 1986: 210–20)

We see all of these elements in the preceding box. The officer is continually working with community groups and individuals to get them to help solve community problems. He is constantly making decisions; rarely does he need to check with his supervisor before acting. His work involves cooperation with other government agencies where he tries to persuade them to assist him in dealing with community problems. He looks for community problems which, if solved, might mitigate the causes of crime. A better street light here or there, a child that is being watched by a neighbor, a part time job for a family in need; all of these activities become matters of police work.

Community-based policing is an attempt to create social capital of a rather elaborate kind. If successful, community organizations whose members feel positively about government and the police are created in neighborhoods where values had been very negative. CBP aims to convert the very poor and those with very limited ties to the community into allegiant citizens who will aid the police in reducing crime. It deals with people with limited skills and little time to devote to community concerns. The task is difficult because CBP focuses on the most deprived communities, and the goal is to make very basic changes in community structure and in people's attitudes and values.

The role of government is also much larger. Community-based police officers do not simply aid groups who want to form organizations; they create the organizations and, in effect, run them. Thus, much is expected from the police officer. He or she must become a diverse community actor capable of understanding complex community problems, finding new and innovative solutions to these problems, teaching new skills, and sensitively bridging the need for law and order with the problems of a deprived community (Riechers and Roberg 1990: (111–12). One could argue that community-based policing is really a form of guided democracy. We expect the police officer to teach the residents how to organize themselves and also supply the skills needed to make these organizations effective.

How successful is community-based policing? Systematic assessment is difficult because the goal is long-range change in conditions that are difficult to measure. Community-based policing also means different things to different people (Giamakos and Davis III 1997: 496). The term is often applied to police departments that exhibit only some of the major characteristics. Many preliminary assessments are favorable (Kratcoski and Dukes 1995). Analysts report positive evaluations by community residents (Kratcoski, Dukes, and Gustavson 1995; DeLong 1995) and the concept has strong support among police professionals. Evaluations however focus on community attitudes toward the police, the views of police officers, and personal assessments. We really don't know if the elements of social capital are also accomplished. Do residents become more involved in their community? Do positive role models and more successful residents stay in the community as a consequence? Do new organizations establish a degree of permanence and become active in the wider community?

Some worry that CBP gives the police officer too much influence within the community. In our case, Officer Ralph decides who can park on the streets and who should live in private apartments. In the hands of the proper officer, such authority may be justified, but can we extend it to all officers? Perhaps we need to consider more civilian controls as a check on the potential power of the community-based police officer?

SUMMARY: THE SEARCH
FOR SOCIAL CAPITAL

Americans are losing their connections to one another and to their governments. The decline in social capital worries those concerned about the nature of American democracy. Furthermore, it may affect the life chances of those in our most deprived communities if those in the inner city are excluded from job connections and positive role models. Resolving the paradox of urban governance requires an informed citizenry that realizes the common needs of an urban area. With declines in social capital, resolving the paradox becomes more difficult.

We have surveyed several government and private programs aimed at strengthening communities and expanding the linkage between citizens, community organizations, and government. How successful are these programs, and who benefits most from them?

Citizen organizations have the potential to solve several of the most basic problems that stem from our paradox of urban government. If citizens can be attached meaningfully to government and become more directly involved in the delivery of urban services, allegiance to the political system will increase. With greater community consciousness, the unemployed can be connected to sources of employment and positive role models, thereby becoming more productive citizens. The delivery of public services will improve when citizens aid in the production of services; crime is reduced when neighbors cooperate with the police; and school performance improves when parents are a part of the education process. There will be greater support for the services needed to deal with the problems of increased urbanization and a closer connection will evolve between those who produce government services and those who receive them.

Contradictions lay beneath the search for greater social capital. *It is uncertain what the role of government should be.* Direct government programs aid in the production of social capital in many cases. Government-organized councils can improve the links between the citizen and government, although they seem to aid the middle class more than the poor. Community-based organizations assist in providing improved services to deprived communities, but it is unclear if this model can be broadly applied throughout an urban area. Community-based policing seems to improve the quality of life in deprived communities, but it may extend more power and influence to the police than is desirable. Moreover, all of these proposals seem to work better in some locations than in others. In Baltimore and San Antonio, for instance, private community-organized councils seem to operate quite effectively. In most cities, some parts of the city are better represented by one of these mechanisms, but general coverage is rare. Some community organizations serve as barriers to citywide cooperation, others encourage it. Unfortunately, we don't know what kinds of incentives would encourage positive neighborhood development and improvements in social capital.

We began the chapter with two basic problems. First, a general decline in social capital seems to affect all citizens, raising concerns about the nature of democracy. The connection between government and the lives of the citizens has become much weaker over the past 20 years. Second, our most deprived communities suffer from severed links between residents and employment opportunities and successful role models. Both problems are serious because, in each case, the citizen is lacking in essential connections to important groups and influences. For those in deprived communities, however, the main problem is associating with people connected to centers of employment. For the general population, the central focus is connecting the citizen to government. For the latter, community-based organizations and community-based policing can offer assistance. The concerns of the general population, however, are related more to community organizations, the Internet, and government-sponsored participation. Therefore, a successful plan requires the combination of several of the approaches, and important interests in the community may differ on the elements of a successful strategy.

REFERENCES

Barton, Stephen E., and Carol J. Silverman, eds. 1994. *Common Interest Communities: Private Governments and the Public Interest.* Berkeley, CA: Institute of Governmental Studies Press.

Berry, Jeffrey M., Kent E. Portney, and Ken Thomson. 1993. *The Rebirth of Urban Democracy.* Washington D.C.: Brookings Institution.

Chaskin, Robert J., and Ali Abunimah. 1999. "A View from the City: Local

Government Perspectives on Neighborhood Based Governance in Community-Building Initiatives." *Journal of Urban Affairs* 21: 57–78.

Clavel, Pierre, Jessica Pitt, and Jordan Yin. 1997. "The Community Option in Urban Policy." *Urban Affairs Review* 32, no. 4 (March): 458.

Cohen, Cathy, and Michael C. Dawson. 1993. "Neighborhood Poverty and African American Politics." *The*

American Political Science Review 87, no. 2 (June): 286–302.

Cole, Richard L. 1974. *Citizen Participation and the Urban Policy Process.* Toronto: D.C. Heath and Company.

Coleman, James S. 1988. "Social Capital in the Creation of Human Capital." *American Journal of Sociology* 94: 95–120.

Crenson, Matthew A. 1983. *Neighborhood Politics.* Cambridge, MA: Harvard University Press.

Davis, Mike. 1990. *City of Quartz: Excavating the Future in Los Angeles.* New York: Random House.

DeLong, Rhonda. 1995. "Police-Community Partnerships in Neighborhood Watch and the Neighborhood Liaison Officer Program, in Kalamazoo, Michigan." In *Issues in Community Policing,* edited by Peter C. Kratcoski and Duane Dukes. Cincinatti: Anderson Publishing Company.

Ferman, Barbara. 1996. *Challenging the Growth Machine: Neighborhood Politics in Chicago and Pittsburgh.* Lawrence, KA: University of Kansas Press.

Gianakis, Gerasimos A., and John Davis III. 1998. "Reinventing or Repackaging Public Services? The Case of Community-based Policing." *Public Administration Review* 58:6 (November) 485–498.

Gibson, James O., G. Thomas Kingsley, and Joseph B. McNeely. 1997. *Community Building Coming of Age.* The Urban Institute: http://www.urbanorg/community/combuild.htm.

Green, Susan. 1999. "Critics Hit New Webb Site: Some Find Denver's Net Presence Lacking." *Denver Post,* February 14.

Greenstone, J. David, and Paul E. Peterson. 1973. *Race and Authority in Urban Politics: Community Participation and the War on Poverty.* New York: Russell Sage Foundation.

Guest, Avery M., and R. S. Oropesa. 1984. "Problem Solving Strategies of Local Areas in the Metropolis." *American*

Sociological Review 49, no. 6 (December): 828–40.

Henig, Jeffrey R. 1982. *Neighborhood Mobilization: Redevelopment and Response.* New Brunswick, NJ: Rutgers University Press.

Hill, Kevin A., and John E. Hughes. 1998. *Cyberpolitics: Citizen Activism in the Age of the Internet.* Oxford: Roman and Littlefield Publishers Inc.

Imbroscio, David L. 1997. *Reconstructing City Politics: Alternative Economic Development and Urban Regimes.* Thousand Oaks, CA: Sage Publications.

Jacobs, Jane. 1961. *The Death and Life of Great American Cities.* New York: Random House.

Kratcoski, Peter C., and Duane Dukes, eds. 1995. "Perspectives on Community Policing." In *Issues in Community Policing.* Cincinatti: Anderson Publishing Company.

Kratcoski, Peter C., Duane Dukes, and Sandra Gustavson. 1995. "An Analysis of Community Policing in an Large Midwest City." In *Issues in Community Policing,* edited by Peter C. Kratcoski and Duane Dukes. Cincinatti: Anderson Publishing Company.

Marcuse, Peter. 1990. "New York City's Community Boards Neighborhood Policy and Its Results." In *Neighborhood Policy and Programmes: Past and Present,* edited by Naomi Carmon. New York: St. Martin's Press.

Mechling, Jerry. 1999. "Information Age Governance: Just the Start of Something Big?" In *Democracy.com? Governance in a Networked World,* edited by Elaine Ciulla Kamarck and Joseph S. Nye, Jr. Hollis, NH: Hollis Publishing Company.

Meeks, Brock. 1997. "Better Democracy Through Technology." *Communications of the ACM* 40, no. 2 (February): 75–82.

Mesch, Gustave S., and Kent P. Schwirian. 1996. "The Effectiveness of Neighborhood Collective Action." *Social Problems* 43, no. 4 (November): 467–82.

Moynihan, Daniel P. 1969. *Maximum Feasible Misunderstanding: Community Action in the War on Poverty.* New York: The Free Press.

Norris, Pippa. 1999. "Who Surfs? New Technology, Old Voters, and Virtual Democracy." In *Democracy.com? Governance in a Networked World,* edited by Elaine Ciulla Kamarck and Joseph S. Nye Jr. Hollis, NH: Hollis Publishing Company.

Osborne, David, and Ted Gaebler. 1992. *Reinventing Government: How the Entrepreneurial Spirit is Transforming the Public Sector.* Reading, MA: Addison-Wesley Publishing Company.

Perkins, Douglas D., Barbara B. Brown, and Ralph B. Taylor. 1996. "The Ecology of Empowerment: Predicting Participation in Community Organizations." *Journal of Social Issues* 52, no. 1 (Spring): 85–111.

Putnam, Robert D. 2000. *Bowling Alone: The Collapse and Revival of American Community.* New York: Simon and Schuster.

Putnam, Robert D. 1995. "Tuning In, Tuning Out: The Strange Disappearance of Social Capital in America." *P.S. Political Science and Politics* (December): 664–83.

Riechers, Lisa M., and Roy R. Roberg. 1990. "Community Policing: A

Critical Review of Underlying Assumptions." *Journal of Police Science and Administration* 17, no. 2: 105–14.

Rose, Stephen M. 1972. *The Betrayal of the Poor: The Transformation of Community Action.* Cambridge, MA: Schenkman Books.

Rubin, Herbert J. 1995. "Renewing Home in the Inner City: Conversations with Community Based Development Practitioners." *Administration and Society* 27, no. 1 (May): 27–60.

Saltzstein, Alan L., Raphe Sonenshein and Irving Ostrow. 1986. "Federal Grants and the City of Los Angeles: Implementing a More Centralized Local Political System," in Terry Nichols Clark ed. *Research in Urban Policy* 2:A 55–76.

Sennett, Richard. 1970. *The Uses of Disorder: Personal Identity and City Life.* New York: Alfred A. Knopf.

Skolnick, Jerome H., and David H. Bayley. 1986. *The New Blue Line: Police Innovation in Six American Cities.* New York: The Free Press.

United States Advisory Commission on Intergovernmental Relations. 1989. *Residential Community Associations: Private Government in the Intergovernmental System?* Washington DC: United States Government Printing Office.

Chapter Nine

The Governance of Metropolitan Regions

O n the eastern seaboard of the United States where the state of New
York wedges itself between New Jersey and Connecticut, explorers
of political affairs can observe one of the great unnatural wonders of the
world; that is a governmental arrangement perhaps more complicated than
mankind has yet contrived or allowed to happen. A vigorous metropolitan
area, the economic capital of the nation, governs itself by means of 1467
distinct political entities ... each having its own power to raise and spend
the public treasury, and each operating in a jurisdiction determined more
by chance than design.

Robert C. Wood, 1400 Governments: The Political Economy of the New York Metropolitan
Region *(Cambridge, MA: Harvard University Press, 1964): 1955.*

The central city government does not work in close cooperation with
those of suburbia; how could it? Suburban governments are themselves
uncoordinated, with no center of power and information. Yet the
cooperation of suburbia is frequently crucial to the programs in the
central city; traffic on a freeway system which ends abruptly in the main
street of a country town is apt to back up halfway to City Hall, and smoke
abatement will be less than complete until the suburban industrial park
complies. There is, however, no normative prescription in Jacksonian
philosophy for the forced integration of local government. Nor is there a
constitutional formula that frees the governmental structure from the
heavy hand of the referendum voter. Thus many important problems

generated in the metropolitan complex are insoluble within the existing governmental structure.

Scott Greer, Governing the Metropolis *(New York: John Wiley and Sons, 1962): 56.*

American law treats cities as subdivisions of the states and the states have organized them in a manner that has helped separate metropolitan residents into different, sometimes hostile groups. The design of cities' power to control land use provides an example of this phenomena. Most American metropolitan areas are now splintered into dozens and dozens of cities, and for decades state governments have authorized these cities to wield their zoning and redevelopment authority to foster their own prosperity even if it is won at the expense of their neighbors. This pursuit of prosperity has usually involved trying to attract the "better kind" of commercial life and the "better kind" of people while simultaneously, excluding the rest. Everywhere in the nation some cities are understood as having succeeded in this effort, while others have failed. Those that have succeeded have enticed millions of people to escape the problems associated with America's central cities by crossing the city/suburban boundary.

Gerald E. Frug, City Making: Building Communities Without Walls *(Princeton, NJ: Princeton University Press, 1999): 3.*

We began this book with the "paradox of urban governance"; the need for a common approach to the problems of American urban areas, yet the presence of numerous separate and independent governments in most urban areas. How can we manage to approach the common problems of all city dwellers if we insist on governing ourselves through numerous separate and distinct governments? The three statements that open this chapter focus on different aspects of the problem. Wood wonders how the concerns of a large economy with needs for sophisticated government services can properly function when so many governments are present. Greer worries about the effectiveness of broad-based public services like transportation and pollution control that span city boundaries when power is given to separate independent governments. How can separate and distinct cities possibly deal with these concerns that, by definition, are citywide in nature and can only be dealt with properly if all residents are governed by them? Frug sees our numerous cities dividing the population into rich and poor and exacerbating the differences between classes and races. Therefore, numerous cities contribute to the divisions in society and produce unequal levels of service divided by race and class. Here then, is the heart of the urban problem; has our Jeffersonian commitment to small government made it impossible to properly manage the problems of the American city?

This chapter examines the complex intergovernmental nature of urban areas and asks if cities would be served better by other governmental arrangements. Should we have fewer governments? Should regional governments be given some authority over the city governments and special districts? Some urban areas, in fact, contain few governments and others have created regional governments with some authority over certain policies. Do these cities provide us with models that could be used elsewhere? First, we look briefly at why and how this pattern of numerous governments developed. Changes in legal and public policy as well as social and economic changes led to distinctions between suburbs and central cities and the many governments of today.

Next, we examine the problems associated with the fragmented metropolis. Three kinds of concerns are frequently noted:

1. Fiscal disparities between cities often create differences in the cost to the citizen and in the quality of services in different parts of the urban area.

2. The presence of numerous governments may encourage inefficiency in the production of government services. When each city hires a city manager, a police chief, and its own employees, does the public end up paying too much for city services and getting a less cost effective and professional public service? Or does competition among governments encourage efficiency?

3. The performance of the economy and the social structure are affected by the number of governments. Some say that urban areas with fewer governments improve the quality of life for the residents; they promote greater social integration and improve the economic climate of the region. Others argue that without strong regional government activity, urban areas will be unable to make important choices that affect the quality of life. Residents, for instance, generally want single-family, detached housing and the ability to select their workplace and to travel there by automobile. When many people do so, however, travel becomes excessive, pollution increases, and open space is absorbed. Small, local governments do not have the authority or desire to make the kinds of decisions that these problems require. Others worry about the restrictions on personal freedom that a strong regional government might put into place.

The third section of this chapter looks at approaches that have been taken to improve the organization of urban areas. Drawing on different bodies of knowledge, two kinds of solutions have historically been proposed to deal with the problems of fragmentation. Because these proposals are radically different and have earned the support of prominent thinkers and practitioners, they continue to frame the debate about reform of our urban areas. The *metropolitan government* approach, drawing on organization theory and elements of the reform movement (see Chapter 4), argues that a single, large regional government would better service urban areas. This approach has been countered by those who see the urban area as composed of a competing series of governments rather than a single government. Proponents of the *public-choice approach* maintain that urban areas are better served by numerous competing governments, each providing a different set of government services with varying prices reflecting the value of the goods received. Central coordination, they argue, could be achieved informally through competition just as competing firms informally coordinate the economy.

Finally, we look at the practice of regional government. While almost all urban areas contain numerous cities, some have experimented with areawide or metropolitan governments; governing bodies that are regional in scope and have control over important public services. In other areas, regional special districts are given authority over particular services like air-quality control and water. In most of our cities, informal cooperation among city and county officials and advisory regional bodies deal with intergovernmental concerns. We will look at the success and failure of each of these approaches to regional problems.

THE RISE OF SUBURBIA
AND THE FRAGMENTED CITY

As was pointed out in Chapter 2, American cities developed with a strong dominant central city. In the early years of the twentieth century, while some wealthy residents moved to outlining areas and created suburban communities, most city residents were concentrated around the city core and were governed by a single city. As cities grew, city boundaries expanded to include outlying residents. The superior public services of the city encouraged outlying residents to join the central city. Cities used their public facilities to induce or often force suburban cities to consolidate with the central city, and they annexed large parcels of land. Early in the twentieth century, Los Angeles city officials correctly saw that improved public facilities could be used to expand the city. A thin strip of land was annexed from the original city center, 20 miles inland to the current location of the port. They used their control of the port to convince the existing cities of Wilmington and San Pedro to consolidate with the city in return for promised expenditures on port improvements and new highway links to the civic center. In one of the boldest public works ventures of all time, the city council and the voters authorized a $23 million bond issue to build a 200-mile aqueduct bringing water from the Owens Valley in Northeastern California to the city. Water was then used to encourage annexation and the consolidation of smaller cities (Saltzstein 2000: 9). These efforts expanded the city from its original 28-square miles in 1900 to 364-square miles in 1920, opening up the vast San Fernando Valley as a home for new residents.

Similarly, Milwaukee aggressively sought to annex open territory. Though the city was met with opposition from existing suburban communities, its efforts doubled the size of the city from 1900 to 1930 (Orum 1995: 81). In the 1890s, the present New York City was created from several autonomous boroughs. Several smaller cities joined the larger city to receive sewer connections, electricity, and lower water rates. Similar consolidation and annexation efforts successfully expanded cities as diverse as Cleveland, Chicago, Denver, Indianapolis, and Boston (Teaford 1979: 58). Teaford points out that the trend in most cities was for suburbanites to unite with the central city when it was in the interests of the residents to do so. "With superior capacity to produce public services, central cities were generally in a position to dominate the suburbs and induce residents in outlying areas to join the city. Suburban units could not yet compete as purveyors of water, sewerage disposal or fire and police protection; the central city provided superior services at lower costs" (1979: 63; see also Jackson 1985: 138–48).

By 1930, however, growth in most cities halted and a ring of suburbs surrounded the borders of the central city. City attempts to expand were met by new strength and aggressiveness on the part of suburban communities, and a shift in legal thinking favored suburban as opposed to city development. In city after city, suburbs developed the capacity to access increasingly sophisticated public services. Suburban communities combined to create water and sanitary districts to effectively counter the advantages of the central city. State legislatures permitted the establishment of metropolitan public service districts, covering city and suburb. Boston in 1895, Los Angeles in 1924, New Jersey in 1924, and Oakland in 1923 created metropolitan water districts (Teaford 1979: 80). Counties also became major service providers and competed successfully with cities as suppliers of urban services. Where strong counties emerged, residents had less need to annex to the central city. Los Angeles County expanded its influence over a major portion of the developable land by creating a market for urban services. New cities were able to contract with the county for virtually any city service. Consequently, annexation to the older cities of Long Beach and Los Angeles was less appealing. The result was the creation of 20 new suburbs and the virtual sealing of the borders of the City of Los Angeles (see Miller 1981).

Intellectual currents of the time also favored the suburbs. Muckraking journalists dramatized the ills of the central city and advocated the principles of the reform movement (see Chapter 3). Movement proponents favored suburban governments with high-status city council members and professionally trained managers over the machine-run central cities. Teaford points out that by 1940, "no longer was there as much rhetoric about services that only big cities could offer. Instead there was much talk of the advantages of life in the small community, a homogeneous home town where one's influence could be felt" (1979: 86).

An important shift in the court's role in city formation in the first third of the twentieth century encouraged small suburban jurisdiction at the expense of the central city. In the nineteenth century, states also facilitated the expansion of central cities. State legislatures redrew city boundaries to increase their territorial scope by allowing expansion of the city without the consent of the residents. State courts tended to support the dominant role of the central city on questions of consolidation and annexation (Briffault 1990: 17). Courts defined the city as a relatively built up, diverse, and economically self contained area and questioned the validity of the dispersed, thinly populated suburb. The Florida Supreme Court, for example, eloquently stated this position:

> The city of ancient Rome is the prototype for all municipalities of modern times. The desire to be in close touch with the glitter of social life and political activity presented problems of overcrowding. Bad

sanitary conditions, crowding of streets and public places . . . were all problems of the ancient municipia of the Empire of Rome.

These problems arose as population of the towns and cities increased. So it is apparent that before the legislative will may operate to establish a municipality, that is to say, to prescribe powers and duties for the governance of towns, villages or communities there must be in existence a town, village or community of people whose local public interests require in the orderly process of government, orderly administration under state authority. (Briffault 1990: 19)

By the middle of the twentieth century, state courts had changed their view of city formation significantly. Suburbs were now encouraged through loosened requirements for incorporation and the need for approval of the residents. The definition of city liberalized significantly to include limited purpose, small settlements that were wholly dependent on the central city for employment, and commerce. The Wisconsin court reflected this change in philosophy:

The villages of today are unlike the villages of 1848 . . . in many respects . . . . Many villages adjacent or near large cities are built up for the purpose of the convenience and comfort of the residents who are largely business men of a city who wish to get away from the noise and rush of the city to the quietude of country life. (Briffault 1990: 19)

Implicit in this interpretation is the right to exclude uses of land in the interests of the residents. As Chief Justice Burger stated, "Citizens should be free to shape their community so that it embodies their conception of the 'decent life.' This will sometimes mean deciding that certain forms of activity—factories, gas stations, sports stadia, bookstores and surely live nude shows—will not be allowed" (Frug 1999: 57). The Supreme Court and most state courts have allowed communities to shape their zoning policies in the interests of their own residents, even if this means requiring large lot sizes that effectively exclude all but the wealthy (Frug 1999: 77). Thus, legal changes and court decisions by the middle of the twentieth century permitted the formation of small cities and encouraged the differences in wealth and status between central city and suburb. The purpose of the suburb, to many, was keeping the undesirables out (Jackson 1985: 151).

As cities grew and changes in technology and government policy encouraged new growth outside of the traditional central city (see Chapter 2), new suburbs were created, legally separating the new residents from the old, and often the middle- and upper-middle-classes from the poor. African Americans migrating north in the 1950s were restricted from the suburban areas, thus becoming the new residents of the central city. In many urban areas, a ring of suburban communities surrounded the central city, effectively eliminating the central city's access to new resources. In these cities, the newer jobs and wealthier residents were located in the suburbs while poorer residents were concentrated in the inner city. Cities like Boston, San Francisco, Chicago, and New York absorbed the poorer immigrants within their city borders, while middle class and wealthy white residents moved to the suburbs.

GOVERNMENT FRAGMENTATION:
IS IT A PROBLEM?

By the middle of the twentieth century, most American urban areas contained an older central city and numerous smaller cities. To many, the proliferation of governments and the lack of central responsibility for the concerns of the entire urban area prevented the residents from dealing effectively with public problems. Several different arguments were raised by critics of the numerous governments in urban areas. Some believed that the pattern of governments and the failure to share resources between rich and poor communities lead to significant fiscal and public policy disparities between cities. Thus, residents in wealthier cities received better public services at less cost; while those in poorer communities paid similar fees and taxes but received decidedly poorer services. Some argued that policy performance improved when fewer governments were present; but others proposed that competition among governments improved efficiency. A third criticism looked at the influence of metropolitan organization on the social and economic performance of the region. Job growth, racial integration, and school performance were enhanced, some argued, when the central city boundaries included much of the newer areas that, in other cities, were located in suburbs.

Fiscal and Economic Differences: Cities and Suburbs

Suburbs attract higher-income residents and often adjust zoning policy to exclude lower-income residents. As the location of wealthier tax payers, suburbs can often attract commercial centers that enhance city income. Central cities, then, are left with a greater number of lower-income residents and less desirable industrial and commercial areas. The consequence of both of these conditions is greater income per capita in the suburbs and higher service needs in the central city. Thus, resources are more frequently found where there is less need for public services.

Over time, differences in wealth between cities and suburbs have increased, creating greater difficulties for central city policymakers. The percentage of jobs in the metropolitan area, for instance, increased by 23 percent in suburbs, but only by 12 percent in central cities from 1980 to 1986 (Downs 1994: 47). The proportion of residents classified as poor in the central city increased from 14 percent in 1970 to 19 percent in 1990, while remaining at 8 percent over that same time period in the suburbs (1994: 49). The median income of suburbs in 1990 was 38 percent higher than in central cities; 45 percent higher in urban areas greater than one million in population. In most states, revenue is not shared between city and suburbs; thus, funds for public services in central cities must be raised from a population with less average income. Additionally, most argue that the costs of providing many services is significantly greater in central cities than in suburbs. This is particularly true for police and fire services and education (Downs 1994: 48).

Aggregate differences, however, mask significant variations within central cities and suburbs. Some central cities are actually wealthier than their suburban neighbors. Many larger, western cities contain newer homes and shopping areas within their borders and retain the wealth that might otherwise migrate to outlying areas. Houston and Los Angeles are examples of urban areas where differences in wealth between city and suburb are not particularly pronounced. In all urban areas some suburbs become locations for poorer residents, declining industries, and less successful commercial areas. These "troubled suburbs" are often much less well-off fiscally and economically than their central city counterparts (Fernandez and Pincus 1982). Older urban areas are more likely to contain troubled suburbs though they are found in all urban areas and regions. Thus, whether a sharing of resources or a metropolitan area government would equalize resources and service outputs depends, in part, on the array of governments within an urban area. In many, but not all, cities, equalization would seem to lead to greater service equity.

In spite of the presence of some relatively well-off central cities, and the increase in the number of troubled cities, wealth differences between city and suburb have increased over time. In 1990, central city residents had a median income equivalent to 74 percent of that earned by suburban residents (Bahl 1994: 293). Central city expenses have increased as they have become home to a larger share of the area's social problems. Federal aid to central cities has decreased dramatically. Thus, most analysts argue that fiscal disparities between city and suburb remain significant (Bahl 1996; Bahl, Martinez-Vazquez, and Sjoquist 1992).

The Proliferation of Governments and the Efficiency of Public Services

So many little governments; surely the consequence is a great waste in public resources.

> Driving into Chicago from the west one enters the metropolitan area at the city of West Chicago, passing through the village of Winfield, through the bewildering array of Lombard, Villa Park, Elmhurst, Hillsdale, Westchester, Broadview, Maywood, Forest Park, Berwyn and Cicero before reaching at last the city of Chicago. . . . The result of this fragmentation is inefficiency, confusion of authority, and disparity in shouldering the burdens of the metropolis. Five municipal water authorities pump water to a region that could be served by one. Ten police departments engage in jurisdictional tangles that unified rule would eliminate. Twenty city councils enact ordinances for their particular segments, thus stymieing efforts at regional planning. (Teaford 1979: 1)

Yet others, as we will see, argue that numerous governments provide consumer choice and actually encourage efficiency by competing with one another for taxpayers. Smaller governments may also connect the citizen more directly to government decision making; thereby, more directly relating citizen wants with government policy. The concern is part of a general problem that was discussed even by the ancient Greek philosophers; what is the ideal size of government? Some services may benefit from larger scope, while others operate efficiently with smaller populations. The government that best connects the citizens to it may not be the size best designed to efficiently produce services.

Several major studies looked closely at the influence of the proliferation of governments on government spending. There seems to be little consensus in the literature (see Dowding, John, and Biggs 1994). Dowding et al., in an attempt to summarize these studies, conclude that there is evidence that the greater the number of jurisdictions, the lower their expenditure. However, the differences may be due to matters unrelated to competition among governments.

What Determines Regional Success?
The Influence of Open Space

Travel across the country and you will notice great differences in our urban areas. Some are booming with new industries with developers building elaborate new subdivisions; they have a reputation for being good places to live and work. Others look old and declining. Blocks of housing and commercial areas are boarded up, and major industries are leaving. Some are losing people while others grow. Poverty is concentrated and schools more segregated in some; others seem to be more socially and economically integrated. Some urban areas are pleasant places to live; places where the economy grows and new sources of wealth come, while others stagnate, and the better educated and more innovative people leave.

We used to think that problems in the larger economy caused some cities to prosper and others to fail. Sun Belt areas seemed to be the preferred location for new industries while the Frost Belt could no longer compete for new industries. Government policy, particularly defense spending and subsidies to the real estate industry, seemed to favor newer, warm-weather locations at the expense of the older regions of the country.

Yet some of the more successful urban areas now are located in the old Frost Belt. The resurgence of northern cities like Indianapolis and Columbus suggest that region and weather are not the only reasons why some cities prosper while others do not.

Government officials spend a great deal of time and resources trying to create a positive economic and social environment for their region. Subsidies are given to prospective new industries and commercial ventures, and developers gain inducements to locate in the region. Governments also try to aid those in need, hoping that such aid will improve the social environment and alleviate poverty. The goals of commercial and industrial development programs and aid to those in poverty are to improve the economic and social conditions of the community. However, these efforts are more successful in some communities than in others. Why is the performance of our urban areas so different?

Perhaps it is related to the structure of governments in the urban area? David Rusk (1995) thinks so. He collects much interesting comparative information on numerous urban areas hoping to discover why some areas prosper and others do not. His study is one of the few to look closely at the factors that may determine greater comparative success.

Rusk begins by dividing all urban areas into two categories. An *elastic urban area* is one where the central city has significant room to grow; much open area is contained within the city boundaries. Suburbs, in other words, do not ring the city's boundaries. Thus, as development occurs, it can be contained within the boundaries of the city. Albuquerque and Houston are examples of elastic cities. In both cities, much open land was contained in the central city that could be used as new sources of wealth as the urban area grew. Suburbs are present but represent a small percent of the total area.

An *inelastic urban area* is one with little room to grow. Suburbs surround the central city and limit it to a small, confined area. Boston, San Francisco, and St. Louis are inelastic cities. The central city is confined to the older, compact city center; new growth in the urban area must take place primarily in suburban communities.

Rusk searches for urban areas that appear to be similar in most respects but different in their degree of elasticity. Columbus and Cleveland, Ohio, are located in the same state and are of roughly similar size. Cleveland is a very inelastic city while Columbus is quite elastic. Likewise, he pairs Nashville, an elastic city, with inelastic Louisville, and elastic Indianapolis with inelastic Milwaukee. Rusk then examines whether the extent of elasticity tells us something about the general performance of urban areas. He compares the paired cities along several indicators of regional performance; Are elastic cities less segregated than inelastic cities? Do they contain less manufacturing growth? Have they lower bond ratings? His book contains numerous charts comparing the performance of paired cities. He also develops an index of elasticity for all urban areas and looks at the performance for all urban areas.

Table 9.1 is an example of the comparisons Rusk makes. Compared here is the growth in real income from 1969 to 1989. In each pairing, the elastic cities—Houston, Columbus, Indianapolis, Albuquerque, Madison, and Raleigh—are compared with their inelastic counterpart. Note that in all cases, the elastic urban area has increased its income to a greater extent than the inelastic urban area. With the exception of the Madison-Harrisburg comparison, the differences are rather large.

Rusk makes similar comparisons for indicators of population growth, racial segregation, poverty, and education levels. Following are his central findings. Those cities where the central city is defined as **elastic:**

- Experience greater population growth
- Are less racially segregated
- Have less segregated school systems
- Disperse poverty throughout the urban area
- Retain more manufacturing wealth
- Contain a more educated work force
- Earn higher bond ratings; thus, they can borrow money at a lower cost
- Create more new jobs
- Generate greater growth in real income
- Attract a more highly educated work force

Table 9.1 Elastic Areas Show Greater Gains in Real Income than Inelastic Areas

METRO AREA	PERCENTAGE GROWTH IN REAL PER CAPITA INCOME IN METRO AREAS, 1969–89
Houston, Texas	36%
Detroit, Mich.	26
Columbus, Ohio	34
Cleveland, Ohio	23
Nashville, Tenn.	49
Louisville, Ky.	30
Indianapolis, Ind.	32
Milwaukee, Wis.	25
Albuquerque, N. Mex.	41
Syracuse, N.Y.	29
Madison, Wis.	34
Harrisburg, Pa.	33
Raleigh, N.C.	62
Richmond, Va.	45

The first city in each pairing above is an elastic city; the second is an inelastic city. In other concerns, the urban areas are similar. The percentage growth in real per capita income from 1969 to 1989 is given on the right. Notice that the elastic cities experienced greater growth.

Why such dramatic differences in performance? Rusk provides few clues, but invites us to speculate. Why would elastic cities perform better both economically and socially? What is there about city boundaries and the presence of open land that would cause better performance? Job creation may be greater in elastic cities because a single large government can approach prospective new industries and can provide the resources needed to attract those industries. In inelastic areas, prospective industries are faced with numerous smaller jurisdictions, but none may have significant control over the key decisions that must be made, and each may have fewer resources at its disposal than would a large central city. Schools and housing may be more integrated in elastic areas because integration efforts can focus on a larger jurisdiction. School integration, for instance, is difficult to achieve in inelastic cities because integration orders are hard to enforce legally across city boundaries. Elastic cities will earn higher bond ratings because more of the wealth is contained in the central city, making the investment risk less. More educated workers are attracted to areas that are attracting new industries. All of these factors, then, may become related to one another. Firms want to locate in regions where their employees have diverse choices for housing and schools, where other new industries are locating, and where more educated workers are moving.

The boldness of Rusk's thesis has been subject to criticism. Some wonder about his use of comparison cities, for instance. One must assume that the paired cities are similar to one another in all other respects except elasticity. Some of the differences between elastic and inelastic cities are small, which leads some to wonder if other factors might explain the differences between cities. Though his methods can be described as less sophisticated than other quantitative analyses of city characteristics, the thesis has been the subject of significant comment and no one as yet has seriously challenged the findings.

Regional Government and the Interrelated
Problems of an Urban Society

Others argue that regional governments are needed to deal with the interrelated problems of an urban society. In their opinion, small, individual governments will concern themselves only with the immediate problems of residents and neglect the broader concerns of pollution, travel, open space, and the less desirable byproducts of a complex society.

Downs (1994) maintains that a strong regional government is needed to control what he sees as fundamental contradictions in the desires of individuals and the effect of these goals on the general health of the region. Most citizens, he maintains, want to own a detached single home, own an automobile, work at a low-density work place and live in an environment free from poverty. However, when those goals are pursued without regard for the effect on the region, several problems follow. Travel times become excessive, pollution increases, little affordable housing is built, much open space is absorbed by urban living, and undesirable byproducts of society—jails, halfway houses, and landfills—are not built. The region deteriorates as these problems multiply and ultimately it becomes a less viable area in which to live and work. All citizens will then suffer if the problems of urban life increase, industries leave, and residents with skills that are in demand find work elsewhere.

Dealing with the general problems of a region requires strong government efforts to build efficient public facilities for transportation, waste management, and criminal justice. Land use must be more carefully controlled to place people closer to their jobs and prevent the needless expansion of the city into open land. Governments must deal with the problems of the poor because all groups of people are needed to create an effectively functioning society. Only a regional government with significant authority can deal with these more general problems of the urban area. "Most Americans," Downs argues, "do not recognize their responsibility in causing the growth-related social problems they dislike. It will take strong, persistent leadership from those who do realize it to convince them" (1994: 16). Yet others worry about the restrictions on personal freedom and the economy that a strong metropolitan government assumes.

APPROACHES TO AN IMPROVED METROPOLITAN ORGANIZATION OF GOVERNMENTS

Government fragmentation is related to several basic problems within an urban society. Solutions to these concerns, however, are fraught with conflicts. Individual freedom may be related to the existence of numerous governments. The benefits of a market-driven economy are enhanced when governments operate efficiently and perhaps competitively. Citizens are often leery of large government solutions to problems. Thus, dealing with the difficulties of government fragmentation raises basic questions of political philosophy and values.

All approaches to metropolitan reforms are related to two general points of view. Some have advocated a large government model where smaller governments are consolidated into a metropolitan government. Others propose that urban governments be structured similar to the private economy with competing smaller governments. Twentieth century experience with both approaches has generally been negative. As we will see in the section "The Practice of Modern Regional Governance," contemporary approaches draw a bit on both perspectives. First, we will contrast these two approaches and discuss their application in current governments.

The Metropolitan Government Approach

The metropolitan government approach is premised on a straightforward argument. Residents in an urban area are a part of an interrelated social and economic network. The success of the area depends on common actions to deal with the interrelated problems of the area. Therefore, a single government for the entire region is the logical form of government.

The form that government should take drew its inspiration from the reform movement discussed in Chapter 4. Drawing on the writings of Woodrow Wilson, Fredrick Taylor, and Frank Goodnow, a common set of principles developed. Each major urban area should be governed by a single government, elected officials should be small in number and represent the region as a whole rather than in small districts, administration should be separated from politics and officials, and employees should be professionally appointed (Stephens and Wikstrom 2000: 32). Thus, the concern was both unified government for the region and a profoundly different way of making decisions and implementing them. When these ideas were proposed, most cities contained numerous independent governing bodies and central cities were run by partisan, often machine-dominated, leaders. This made the proposed change both organizational and political; a single government and a new form of politics—a bold proposition.

Support for metropolitan government rapidly became widespread among academics, reform-minded elected officials, and enlightened members of the business community. The National Municipal League, an organization of reform leaders, many of whom were prominent academics and elected officials, sponsored major studies of metropolitan areas and endorsed the goals of the metropolitan government movement. Political scientists in many of the major universities at the time contributed to these studies and endorsed their conclusion. Consequently, by the close of the 1930s, a consensus prevailed ". . . that the fundamental problem of the metropolis was the fragmentation of local government structure resulting in lack of a metropolitan-wide political perspective, conflicts between local governments and severe service problems. The only remedy for this condition involved the establishment of metropolitan government" (Stephens and Wikstrom 2000: 39).

Following from these ideas, most major cities formed Metropolitan Study Commissions. The commissions brought together the so-called enlightened members of the community; representatives of the major large industries, the press, and the universities. Money was donated to study the problems of the region and propose solutions. The reforms proposed were quite similar in nature; the elimination of smaller cities or the drastic curtailment of their powers and the imposition of a metropolitan-wide government with authority to make basic decisions for the region. Greer reports that by 1957 nearly one hundred metropolitan studies and surveys were undertaken. The results in most cases were quite similar. The proposal was endorsed by commission members and other prominent community leaders. A vote of the people was generally required. Significant funds were raised to run a campaign for its adoption, but most of these measures were soundly defeated (1962B: 81).

Analyses of these unsuccessful measures indicated that metropolitan government is a hard concept to sell to the public. By nature, proposals for significant metropolitan reform are complex; governments are dissolved and new structures put in place. The voter then is confronted with a wordy proposal that is difficult to read and understand. Surveys in these cities reveal that voter understanding and knowledge, in spite of significant media campaigns, was quite limited (Greer 1962A: 126). Existing elected officials, employee unions, and contractors who benefit from the present system are natural sources of opposition. Greer sums up the difficulty in promoting metropolitan change as ". . . fear of the unknown . . . caution . . . loyalty to and pride of place, the existing city, political suspicion of crusading outsiders who are not part of the team and whose campaign comes close to condemnation of the existing government. The normative structure of the existing political and governmental system easily translates the movement for change into a political contest with 'the enemy' " (1962B: 184–5).

The Practice of Metropolitan Government

Some proposals for governmental change were approved by metropolitan voters and legislators. Though none conform fully to the metropolitan ideal, several do approach the goals of metropolitan governance. We will look briefly at some of these and then summarize what we know about the metropolitan experience.

Miami The oldest and the most frequently discussed attempt at metropolitan government is the creation of Metropolitan Dade County in 1957. The campaign to produce the new government followed the general model described previously. With support of key business leaders, the Chamber of Commerce, the League of Women voters and the major newspapers, voters approved the new government in 1957. The Miami system of government at the time was one of extremely dispersed power. Thirty-nine separate officials were elected including five commissioners and 10 department heads. There was an absence of county-wide long-range planning and general fiscal and economic coordination (Stephens and Wikstrom 2000: 89). Residents of unincorporated areas of Dade County, an increasingly larger proportion of the county's population, were experiencing significant service delivery problems.

The system that voters approved in 1957 is best described as a compromise between metropolitan government and a system of independent cities. Cities remain but with significantly reduced powers. Cities retained control over local police patrol, zoning and planning enforcement, neighborhood parks and recreation, fire protection, and libraries in some cities. Counties retained control over tax collections, elections, regional parks, civil defense, public health, and agricultural services. The major change was the addition to the county of a rather wide array of functions. These included public transportation, environmental protection, solid waste disposal, libraries, regulatory services, air and sea ports, and mental health services. The county also assumed a major role in developmental planning and housing, and they passed a series of ordinances that applied to the entire county. These included a uniform traffic code, a uniform subdivision ordinance, and a criminal code. The county was designated as the producer of all local government services for the unincorporated areas, and most of the unincorported areas have remained in that state since 1957. The result was a political system with a dominant county responsible for many of the major governmental functions (see Sowers 1996: 194).

Metro Miami went through several years of court challenges, secession attempts, and political opposition. It has experienced varying degrees of public support over the years, though this is most likely a reflection on the severe environmental challenges the area has experienced. Most assessments of the metro Miami conclude that it has had a positive influence on the region and currently enjoys significant support (Nelson and Wikstrom 2000: 91–5; Sowers 1996: 200–1). Its accomplishments, however, fall short of the metropolitan ideal. Dade County contains roughly 60 percent of the metropolitan area population. Thus the county, at best, can coordinate only a portion of the affected population. Cities, too, retain some influence within the two-tiered system.

Indianapolis Indianapolis consolidated the city of Indianapolis, Marion County, and several independent cities, creating a new governmental structure commonly known as Unigov in 1970. Prior to the consolidation, the region was governed by over 50 separate governments with little central direction. When Republicans successfully elected Mayor Richard Lugar, a majority of the city and county officers, and took control of the state legislature and the governorship, the party was in a unique position in this highly partisan state to alter city government. Lugar worked to establish consensus on a reorganization plan within the city. Indiana law permitted reorganization to take place through an act of the legislature. Thus, in spite of some opposition from Democrats and African American groups, the reorganization was signed into law without a vote of the public.

In structure, Unigov resembles Metro Dade County. City and township governments are retained with reduced powers. County-wide functions were significantly expanded to include planning, zoning, land-use regulation, street maintenance, solid waste collection, and solid waste disposal. Public health and hospitals, mass transit, and the airport are provided by independent county agencies. Some services such as fire protection and public safety are shared by Unigov and the cities.

As a regional government, Unigov is credited with improvements in infrastructure and physical services. It has pioneered in public-private partnerships and general improvements in governmental efficiency (Bloomquist and Parks 1995: 85). Its electoral system has assisted the Republicans in retaining control of what had been a Democratically controlled city. Critics contend that the gains from the system have helped conservative interests through business investment and economic growth, but little has filtered down to the working class (Stephens and Wikstrom 2000: 86).

Jacksonville Jacksonville, Florida, was governed by a similarly dispersed political system with numerous city and county officials and independent boards and commissions. Public services were unable to accommodate the population growth of the 1950s. Hence, raw sewage was known to be directly deposited in the local river, and the schools had declined to the point where the senior high schools were disaccredited by the state. Local businessmen organized a metropolitan study commission that, following a series of public hearings, proposed the consolidation of Jacksonville and Duval Counties.

The voters overwhelmingly approved the city-county consolidation plan in 1967. It provided for a consolidated city and county government and several independent commissions. Four small towns retained their autonomy in the new system. It also provided for a two-tier tax structure. A *General Service District* levies taxes and provides services for all property owners. The *Urban Services District* levies additional taxes on residents residing in urban areas. Thus, in effect, a two-tiered system is present. The general services district provides police and fire protection, health and welfare, recreation, public works, housing, and urban development. Additionally, the urban services district adds street lighting, refuse collection and disposal, and street cleaning to a section of the urban area.

The consolidation is credited with helping promote an improved business climate in the region and with streamlining government operations and improving efficiency. It has also implemented several major public improvements, including a convention center. According to one observer, it has helped change the power structure from a southern conservative oligarchy to a modern conservative growth machine that promotes a regional perspective and an expansive role for government (Swanson 1996: 249).

Swanson points out, however, that the benefits of consolidation are not shared by the poor and African-American communities. The city remains quite segregated with significant wealth and standard of living differences between poor African Americans and the largely suburban White population (Swanson 1964: 249).

Assessing Metropolitan Government The three metropolitan areas examined are representatives of a larger group of urban areas with some form of metropolitan consolidation. Others include Baton Rouge; Nashville; Kansas City, Kansas; and several smaller cities (see Hamilton 1999: 96–7). Assessing the merits of consolidation efforts is difficult given the small number of examples, the differing goals each city pursued, and the significant differences in the regions themselves. Nonetheless, some tentative conclusions can be drawn.

In no case were the consolidation aims of the founders of the metropolitan government realized. All metropolitan governments are in effect two or, in the case of Miami-Dade, perhaps a three-tiered government. In all cities, concessions needed to be made to existing cities to secure support and passage. The multi-tiered systems assume that residents pay for the costs of urban services differently. The principle that suburban residents bear responsibility for the costs of an urban area is rarely realized in metropolitan governments.

Metropolitan governments seem to focus on physical improvements; public works, civic center improvements, and sports facilities. They also emphasize administrative efficiency, uniformity of standards, economic development, and public-private partnerships in service delivery. There is evidence of significant accomplishment in all of these areas in most consolidated counties. Rarely are efforts given to social services or community development. Critics frequently argue that the poor are not particularly well served by regional governments.

Reorganization is always a political process. Some interests gain and others lose when new governments are established and others eliminated or down graded. Critics have argued that it is no coincidence that elites in several southern cities became interested in metropolitan government when African Americans began to vote in significant numbers and became an increasingly larger proportion of the central city. In Indianapolis, it was noted that the Republican Party initiated Unigov and benefited from it politically. Proponents frequently cite improvements in the business climate as the major accomplishment of consolidation efforts. Thus, the winners in the consolidation game are more likely to be suburban and conservative interests at the expense of inner-city voters and the remnants of urban machines.

As a movement for general reform, metropolitan government experienced success in a small number of urban areas. In most cities, it was, at best, a very hard sell. Where it succeeded, the benefits, while often considerable, were limited to a small portion of the goals of the original reformers.

The Public Choice Approach

> If we give each governmental activity *to the smallest governmental unit* which can efficiently perform it, there will be a vast resurgence and revitalization of local government in America. A vast reservoir of ability and imagination can be found in the increasing leisure time of the population and both public functions and private citizens would benefit from the increased participation of citizens in political life. An eminent and powerful structure of local government is a basic ingredient of a society which seeks to give the individual the fullest possible freedom and responsibility. (Stigler, quoted in Ostrom 1984: 333)

Imagine a political system beginning with the citizen; his or her goals, needs, and wants. Yet we place that citizen within a metropolitan region where decisions must be made about the various kinds of services that are needed. Some of these services are local in nature: Do you want a nearby park? How frequently should refuse be collected? But others are broader in scope: Clean air and an efficient transportation system require that common decisions be made throughout the region. Yet the proponents of the public choice approach want to create governments as small as possible and focus on the goals and needs of the citizens.

Public choice advocates see the role of government similar to that of the economy. Capitalist economic systems work best when competing buyers and sellers are present. The value of the dollar to the citizen is highest when sellers compete for its use. Individuals get the most for their money when competing sellers provide alternative products at different prices. The rational consumer then compares costs and benefits and receives the best product. Sellers are forced to produce products that customers want at the most competitive price. They know if the price is too high or the quality is less than their competitors, their products will not be sold.

When we try to transfer the traits of the private economy to government, however, we find important differences between government services and those we purchase in the private sector. Many government services cannot be easily divided into units that are readily bought and sold. If I choose to buy police services for my home, for instance, my neighbor will benefit from the purchase since effective police services require that the area near my house be patrolled. If I choose to buy police services, my neighbor may see no point in buying them also since he will be protected by my services. We call such services *public goods*. They cannot be divided into purchasable units; they must be paid for and provided to all people within an affected area. Police services, air pollution control, transportation systems, economic development projects, and inspection services are examples of public goods. If all affected residents are not required to pay for these services, those that refuse to pay become what economists term *free riders*. They do not pay for the services, but they receive the benefits. Rational consumers would not pay for these services for long. Why should they if they would receive the service anyway? Thus, government must develop a way for all residents affected by public goods to share in the costs.

Other goods produced by governments create costs and benefits to some citizens only. When a landfill is located near one's home, for instance, the owner must deal with noise, odors, and probably decreased property values. If a factory in a neighboring community pollutes the air and you are down wind from it, you will experience costs but no benefits. Because the factory is located in a neighboring city, your city can do little about it. If a park is placed in a neighboring city next to your house, you benefit without paying the cost. Economists refer to these conditions as *externalities;* costs and benefits that occur from government actions that affect citizens, but due to the size of governments surrounding his or her property, the citizen has little control. To prevent externalities, the size of government must be large enough to include all effected citizens.

Designing a governing system that is similar to the economy but considers the nature of public goods and externalities complicates the system significantly. The goal is a system that provides maximum choice for the citizen but also accounts for public goods and externalities. Contradictions are clearly present; the system must be both large enough to account for public goods, but small enough to maximize citizen influence and choice. How can we build such a system?

We begin with an array of numerous small governments that supply basic services. Tiebout proposes that:

> The consumer-voter may be viewed as picking that community which best satisfies his preference pattern for public goods. At the central level the preferences of the consumer-voter are given, and the government tries to adjust to the pattern of those preferences, whereas at the local level various governments have their revenue and expenditures more or less fixed. Given these revenue and expenditure patterns, the consumer-voter moves to that community whose local government best satisfies his set of preferences. (Dowding, John, and Biggs 1994: 1)

Competing governments then provide different types of services for various prices. The citizen votes with his or her feet and selects the kind of services that satisfy his or her needs. Citizens must evaluate service offerings carefully and make the choice of location that best meets their needs.

However, when the affected area of the service is broader, a larger government must be created to prevent problems associated with public goods and externalities. Thus, governments for pollution control, transportation systems, and solid waste disposal must include most or all of the region within its boundaries. Districts for local policing must include a large enough area to include the source of crime for the citizens. In most areas the policing district would contain local shopping centers, the local high school, and a range of households. Small parks, refuse collection, and street maintenance could be tailored to the wishes of a neighborhood government since these services involve few external effects on those outside of the neighborhood. A representation of a public choice city is seen in Figure 9.1.

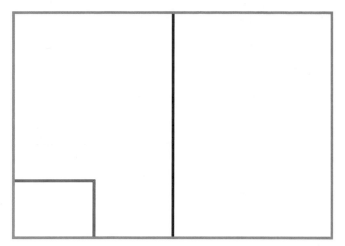

This is a very rough map of a public choice city. The smallest area in the left-hand corner is the neighborhood government, responsible for local collection services, local parks, perhaps daycare facilities, and any other service neighbors felt desirable and were willing to be assessed for. The larger square, roughly half of the map, is the government for services that contain significant externalities when handled by neighborhoods, but can be contained in the area above. Those services might include police and fire, traffic control, and regional parks. The largest area is the government for services that must be handled regionally to contain the affected residents. This government would be concerned with air and water pollution, major transportation networks, landfills, jails, and convention and spectator sports facilities. Each government would have its own separate governing body elected by the residents of the area.

FIGURE 9.1 A Map of a Public Choice City

One more concern needs to be raised. Many of our governments will be quite small. Large organizations, however, often produce services more efficiently or professionally. Large firms can take advantage of bulk purchases of raw materials and can hire specialists in a wide variety of areas. Small governments, then, may be disadvantaged because of their size. Proponents of the public choice approach propose that the small governments be permitted to contract with larger governments or the private sector for their services. Thus, a larger city might contract with a neighborhood government or the county for any of their service needs. The neighborhood government could compare the costs of contracting with different governments, the private sector, or doing the task themselves. By doing so they could take advantage of the facilities of a large organization but continue to tailor the service to the needs of local residents.

The consequence of the public choice approach is a governance system that is a series of governments designed to be as small and local as possible while at the same time large enough to include externalities and the affected area of public goods. Citizens would be members of several governments, depending on the appropriate area of the service. They would confront an array of choices and move to that area where the costs and benefits of government services met their needs.

Empirical Evidence for the Public Choice Approach

The public choice approach was both a description of an ideal political and administrative system and a challenge to the proponents of the metropolitan government approach. It raised many basic questions that academics and practitioners had taken for granted. Do smaller governments produce goods and services at lower cost? Do citizens prefer smaller governments? When deciding to move, was the choice and cost of government services an important concern? Are small governments designed to provide consumer choice?

Much of this literature is carefully summarized by Dowding, John, and Biggs (1994). Some of the major findings suggest both the promise and the difficulties of a public choice system.

- There is some evidence that smaller governments and competing governments produce goods at a lower cost. However, there is also evidence that small governments resist redistributive spending. Thus, lower cost may be served at the expense of services to the less privileged.

- There are mixed results on the satisfaction of citizens with public services in small as opposed to large governments.

- Studies indicate that taxing and service packages do affect citizen's residential choice, but opinions differ as to how important government services and taxes are in the choice of location.

- Governments today take advantage of contracting and privatization to improve service delivery and reduce costs. Therefore, the benefits of large governments are less pronounced.

Public Choice in Practice: Two Examples

The public choice approach describes an abstract, theoretical system of government. Yet it resembles the practices of government in many urban areas. We will focus on two examples: the St. Louis region, particularly St. Louis county, a large portion of the metropolitan area that is divided into many very small governments, and eastern Los Angeles county, an area of many small suburbs that was developed explicitly as an application of public choice theory. Together, these two jurisdictions dramatize the advantages and disadvantages of the public choice approach.

St. Louis   The St. Louis urban area is one of the nation's more fragmented urban regions. The city of St. Louis comprises the traditional heart of the urban area. However, it is a small portion of the region in area and has declined in population throughout the twentieth century. Once ranked within the top 10 cities in population, it is now comprised of fewer than 400,000 people and was ranked 34th in 1990. The city lost 27 percent of its population from 1970 to 1980 and another 12 percent from 1980 to 1990. The St. Louis region is among the nation's most highly segregated. The poor and racial minorities of the metropolitan area are concentrated in the city. In 1990, the African American percentage in the suburbs was 11.5 compared to 47.5 in the city. The difference in wealth between city and suburb is also among the highest in the country (Savitch and Vogel 1996: 10).

The county of St. Louis is one of 10 counties that make up the greater urban area, but it is by far the largest with over one million people. It is a largely suburban area adjacent to the city of St. Louis and legally separate from the city. The major forms of government in the county are 90 cities and a significant unincorporated area administered by the county. The cities range in population from 11 to 50,000 residents (Phares and Louishoome 1996: 81). The resource base to support services is unevenly distributed. Taxable property per capita ranges from $2,178 to $143,285. For all these reasons, the area provides a solid test of the costs and benefits of the public choice approach. Empirically one can examine whether distinct choices are offered to the public, whether efficient government results from the mixture of small and large units, and if cooperation and coordination on regional policies occurs.

The Advisory Commission on Intergovernmental Relations (ACIR), a federal agency created to evaluate metropolitan problems and make recommendations to Congress, closely studied St. Louis County in the late 1980s to see if in fact metropolitan problems were being satisfactorily handled within such a dispersed system. They looked closely at the operation of the governments and the nature of formal and informal cooperation among them.

The report's findings were generally positive. Fragmentation of governments did not seem to result in failure to capture economies of scale. Inter-organizational linkages among service producers were common as was contracting for services. They did find inequities in local finance—older citizens and minorities tended to reside in communities with relatively higher tax burdens. Fragmentation also seemed to have no effect on economic development. In fact, St. Louis County outperformed most comparable areas in its region.

Why was the region successful in spite of numerous governments? The commission attributes that outcome to the ability of volunteer associations of governments to handle regional problems, cooperative arrangements, and general rules of law that link the separate governments. State legislative rules allow the state representatives from the county to modify local government rules, enabling cooperative arrangements to be easily established. The county and various special districts also serve as integrating bodies.

Much of the success of the county is attributed to the work of individual entrepreneurs who gather groups of public officials together and through voluntary associations. Professional associations of public administrators and meetings of groups of mayors and city council members were the places where these entrepreneurs gathered and proposed common plans of action. Flexible agreements among the parties were often buttressed by changes in state laws.

The ACIR also found a particularly high level of coordination among police and fire departments, but less in street maintenance and schools. Generally, coordination among jurisdictions increased over time. They also found evidence of significant competition for service delivery, particularly within the smaller municipalities where some shopping around for different ways of producing services occurred.

Overall, the study concluded that indeed the system of very fragmented, small governments in a complex urban community was working.

> The experience of the St. Louis area in metropolitan organization has much to teach the rest of metropolitan America. Jurisdictional fragmentation can provide an institutional framework for a dynamic of metropolitan organization that continually offers new opportunities of coordination and productivity improvement. Jurisdictional fragmentation therefore need not lead to functional fragmentation. Effective metropolitan governance can emerge from local self determination and citizen choice, provided that the basic rules of governance lie within the local sphere of influence as well. (Advisory Commission on Intergovernmental Relations 1988: 169)

The positive view of St. Louis County governance is not shared by all residents. In 1987, a state sanctions board with the authority to propose changes in governmental structure subject to voter approval was appointed and developed a radical reorganization plan to consolidate many cities, equalize resources and services levels, and institute a form of regional planning. The proposal was controversial and ultimately was referred to the U.S. Supreme Court, which invalidated the board's action before a referendum on their proposal could take place. Thus, St. Louis County continues to operate with diverse and small independent governments. Others question the soundness of many of the smaller municipalities. Glassberg, for one, argues that many of the small municipalities are fiscally starved and barely able to deliver any municipal services (1991: 92).

Greater Los Angeles Radical changes in the economy and social structure altered American cities in the 1950s (see Chapter 2). Industry and housing moved to outlying areas of the cities as the truck, the automobile, and the airplane replaced railroads and waterways as the primary means of transportation. Mass-produced subdivisions gobbled up open land around the old central cities as government-supported home construction and freeways subsidized suburban development. The burgeoning defense industry encouraged the growth of Sun Belt cities. The decline of southern agriculture and the lure of the north encouraged thousands of poor African Americans to leave the rural south in search of a better future in the inner cities.

Nowhere were these changes more pronounced than in Los Angeles. The warm weather, the flat terrain, and the infrastructure that previous city officials had put in place proved to be an ideal site for post-war expansion. Consequently, the urban area grew at a much faster pace than other major urban areas. The city increased its population over 35 percent from 1947 to 1960. The county, on the other hand, nearly doubled in population, increasing from 2,747,962 in 1947 to 6,291,988 in 1961. It was the suburbs and the unincorporated portions of the county that experienced the bulk of the post-war growth. The city's proportion of the total county population actually dropped by over 10 percent from 1947 to 1961.

Mass produced new developments began within the confines of the city in the late 1940s and early 1950s. Westchester, North Hollywood, and Studio City, all located within the city boundaries, were among the first and largest of these developments that successfully merged factory-produced housing, new high tech industries, and commercial developments. As the economy expanded, developers sought large tracts of open land with access to centers of business and commerce. The San Fernando Valley, somewhat distant from the city center but within the city's boundaries, seemed the ideal location for new developments. The Valley grew significantly in the post-war years, from about 70,000 in 1944 to over 850,000 in 1950.

The city's ability to respond to the growth of the Valley was at best problematical. The Valley's sewers were so overloaded that many developers had to use cesspools, which often malfunctioned. Schools were placed on half-day shifts due to a shortage of classrooms. There were significant delays in adding curbs, storm drains, and sidewalks; common amenities in older parts of the city. Traffic jams and long commutes quickly became common as only two arteries connected the Valley to the central city (Nadeau 1950: 403). Developers frequently bore the brunt of criticism from dissatisfied new homeowners, though there was little they could do to improve the city's response. Thus, they looked for other locations where public improvements could be more easily obtained.

No location in the urban area was better suited for this kind of development than the open areas of the county south and east of the city boundaries. Located near the central city, the area was "freeway close" to downtown, the port, and the major airports; largely flat; and sparsely populated—developers hungered for the opportunity to locate new houses, commercial areas, and industries in southeastern Los Angeles County.

City and suburban officials, however, became concerned about how to finance services in the unincorporated areas. Los Angeles officials claimed that, in effect, city residents were paying for public improvements enjoyed only by the new residents of the unincorporated areas. Conflict over the subsidization of city services by the county surfaced in the state legislature in 1950 and 1951. The dispute threatened to limit further development of unincorporated Los Angeles County since developers were uncertain of the costs that would be assessed on the residents. The legislature could mandate that residents of unincorporated areas pay the full cost of all public improvements.

Incorporation was not necessarily a desirable alternative since the new cities would have to invest significantly in public services. Developers, however, feared annexation of the area by Los Angeles or Long Beach and were concerned that the larger cities would be added into taxes assessed in the new areas. Long Beach had already annexed a thin strip near the present city of Lakewood, considered a prime territory for new growth. Suburban annexation in the 1930s created a ring of cities surrounding Los Angeles, but some unincorporated areas remained adjacent to the city and they could be used as corridors to annex much of this area.

The solution for several developers and the county was the Lakewood Plan. Under the plan, the county would become the supplier of city services through contracts with newly incorporated cities. No longer could existing cities accuse the county of subsidizing development since the new suburban cities would pay for the contracted public services. The new cities, by buying services through contracts, avoided the capital investment most expanding cities face. They could simply purchase the needed improvements as demand warranted. This legislation appeased independent cities through state legislation aimed at controlling service subsidization. Legislation was passed forbidding counties from supplying services below the actual cost. Developers could now proceed knowing that they must pay only for the costs of new services as assessed by the county. The county remained as the major service provider for the new cities. The plan was a direct application of the public choice approach. New residents could select among many small cities with different kinds of services. Economies of scale were realized through the sale of services by the county or other cities. The Lakewood Plan became the poster child for public choice proponents. It is mentioned frequently, often approvingly, in the public choice literature (see Ostrom, Tiebout, and Warren 1961; Ostrom 1984).

The Lakewood Plan meant that residents could form a city in unincorporated areas without a reduction in service levels or an increased tax burden. Consequently, between 1954 and 1960, 26 new cities were created in Los Angeles County, and most of the southeast and eastern region was incorporated as cities. Twenty-five of these cities adopted the Lakewood Plan for most of their services. The county aided incorporation efforts by providing advice to city formation groups. The legislature sweetened the pot by passing the Bradley-Burns sales tax bill in 1956, that permitted cities to retain a portion of the sales tax raised within the city (Miller 1981: 21).

Consequently, in the eastern and southeastern sections of the county, development proceeded at a rapid pace. By 1960, nearly half a million people were living in the new cities of southeast Los Angeles County. Small enclave cities with specialized land uses became centers for particular kinds of wealth. The city of Industry, with less than 1,000 residents, became one of the region's prime industrial locations, for example. Today, 10 percent of Los Angeles County's industrial activity is located there. Other cities specialized in high-priced homes, heavy industry, and farming. Public administration specialists praised the Lakewood Plan for offering consumers a choice of services and lifestyles while at the same time benefiting the advantages of economies of scale in the production of services (Ostrom 1984). Cooperation among the new cities and the general oversight of the county may have gained some degree of regional influence on policy.

Behind the Lakewood Plan's success were hidden and arguably severe costs to the city of Los Angeles. Moving to the new cities were many White middle- and upper-class households seeking new homes. The prejudices of realtors, developers, and the public were reflected in the living patterns in the new cities. Miller reports that of the 32 cities created between 1950 and 1970, 28 contained less than 1 percent African-American populations. "Thus the Lakewood Plan cities were essentially White political movements," he adds (Miller 1981: 135).

The city of Los Angeles became increasingly poor and minority; the African-American percentage increased from 8.2 in 1950 to 27.9 percent in 1970, and the percent classified as poor increased from 10.7 to 13.3 in the same years.

The city of Los Angeles lost much ground economically from 1950 to 1970 while most of the Lakewood cities prospered. Manufacturing employment in the city decreased while it increased countywide. The city of Industry, alone, acquired an assessed value of over $13 billion by 1990, five percent of the total assessed value of the city of Los Angeles. Total per-capita revenue in Los Angeles decreased from $226.16 in 1950 to $181.50 in 1970, while the need for public expenditures increased.

By 1960, the county had expanded its influence in the urban area. The Lakewood Plan enhanced its influence over a major growth center. While the new cities had the right to produce their own services, very few did. The Lakewood cities became, in effect, clients to an expanded county bureaucracy. The city meanwhile was cut off from further expansion and lost significant wealth to the new suburbs.

Assessing Public Choice Governance Public choice theory raises important problems neglected by the proponents of metropolitan government. They proposed a political system that, in spite of appearing to be very abstract, was actually closer to the system of government in most urban areas. However, when we examine the reality of governance in cities that have chosen the public choice model, we confront several problems.

The public choice approach is closer to the reality of governance in most urban areas. We find no examples of a truly metropolitan government in the United States today. In most urban areas, many local governments of different sizes and populations are present and there are many single-purpose regional agencies. Through informal arrangements cities and special districts handle intergovernmental matters; often rather well. The public choice approach also recognizes the advantages of smaller governments. They increase the opportunity for citizen participation and, therefore, personalized government and more positive connections between the public and government. Thus, many of the concerns discussed in the last chapter are more fully realized within a public choice framework.

Proponents of public choice raise a valid critique of the efficiency advantages ascribed to metropolitan government. By tailoring services to the wishes of smaller groups of citizens, a series of small governments may be able to limit the production of public goods to those desired by the citizens. In contracting for services with public and private agencies, the advantages of big government are maintained without the disadvantage of large permanent bureaucracies.

Proponents correctly argue that regional problems can be managed without a strong regional government. Through cooperative arrangements, special districts, and governments mandated to include potential externalities, the aims of large metropolitan government proponents can be preserved without requiring a large metropolitan government. Indeed, most urban areas handle their regional problems through special districts, cooperative agreements, and informal coordination.

Problems of governance persist within the public choice framework. One such problem is that the model does not deal with the problems of fiscal disparities among cities. In Los Angeles, for example, there is evidence that many governments may increase fiscal disparities between city and suburb. The proliferation of small units of government encourages wealthy residents to live near one another and then act to limit racial and class diversity. They also can purchase a package of services at lower cost. The poor then remain clustered together without the means to pay for a good level of service without significant sacrifice.

Citizen desires and government policies are coordinated in the public choice framework through citizens voting with their feet—that is, moving to areas with a compatible package of public services at an acceptable cost. Therefore, a second problem is evidence that people make moving decisions based on their assessment of public services. Some argue it may be true for choosing schools (see Dowding et al. 1992) and for the elite (Teske, Schneider, Mintrom, and Best 1993), but there is little evidence that moving decisions are strongly determined by residents' assessment of public services. Applying the voting with your feet thesis to the poor is more problematic since the option to move into most suburban communities is usually not available to them.

Thirdly, discrimination seems to be ignored by the public choice approach. Proponents assume that those with means can move to the community of their choice. The study of Los Angeles cities and data on the residential location of African Americans in the suburbs questions the ability of all groups to move equally.

Lastly, the public choice framework assumes that services with major externalities and pure public goods will be arranged by a regional government. Proponents, however, rarely discuss how these services will be governed. One assumes that large regional governments will manage programs dealing with air and water pollution, environmental issues, transportation planning, and major leisure and recreation facilities. The necessity of regional government is contemplated by the public choice approach. However, the proponents offer little guidance concerning how such governments should be run.

THE PRACTICE OF MODERN REGIONAL GOVERNANCE

Sometimes we learn through our own mistakes and take to heart the analyses of our problems. Both of these approaches have their positive and weak points. Might there be a way of combining the positive features of each? Two urban areas have developed metropolitan approaches to governance that combine elements of the metropolitan government and public choice approaches. Like the metropolitan government approach, both areas created a new level of regional government with some important responsibilities. Yet local governments in these regions retain most of the responsibilities that proponents of the public choice perspective expect of cities. In this section, we examine the governing systems in Portland, Oregon, and the Twin Cities area of Minnesota.

PORTLAND

Portland's urban development prior to 1970 was similar to most large cities. The city is one of the oldest in the west, second only to San Francisco in population from 1883 until 1910. The population grew significantly following World War II as low density suburban development expanded the urban area and created a ring of suburbs in spite of attempts by the city to annex the areas. By 1956, the three central counties contained 176 separate governments. Planners were, for the most part, resigned to low density expansion. Abbot describes the planning process as:

> . . . several dozen suburban planners bent over their drafting tables and colored maps in the interest of rapid land development. Their active constituents were ambitious city councils, county commissioners, bankers and home builders; their mandate was to assist outward growth of the metropolitan area while holding down the most outrageous public costs. Suburban planners worried first about roads and sewers, second about zoning to protect new residential subdivisions, and only third about neighborhood amenities. (1983: 245)

By the end of the 1960s, the rapid growth of the suburbs was beginning to take its toll on the urban area as the city experienced heavy suburban traffic, an overburdened sewer system, and transit system failures. The central city remained the commercial and industrial heart of the region, but it was experiencing problems of blight. Central city commercial sales and trips to the central city declined markedly in the late 1950s.

The development of metropolitan governance in Portland followed from several independent actions that gradually came together as a strengthened Metropolitan Services District (MSD) in the late 1970s.

General concern for environmental management at the state level led to the passage of Senate Bill 100 in 1973, requiring cities and counties to prepare urban growth boundaries and allocations for low- and moderate-income housing. The tasks were initially assigned to a weakly structured council of governments.

- A Metropolitan Study Commission in the 1960s proposed two regional agencies in 1970; a metropolitan transportation agency, Tri-Met, and a Metropolitan Services District (MSD) to deal with problems of growth. Both were approved by the voters though the MSD lacked a tax base and initially had limited influence.
- Crises in the delivery of sewer services to the new subdivisions led to the creation of a Unified Sewer Agency, merging 23 sewer districts in 1970. The sewer agency was ultimately placed under the control of the MSD.
- Fiscal difficulties led to the transfer of the municipal zoo to the MSD in 1976.

The state legislature, following the results of another study commission, proposed a radically reorganized metropolitan services district. The new MSD was approved by the voters in 1978, creating the nation's only elected regional government. The new government was given responsibility for the zoo, solid waste disposal, the convention

(continued)

(continued)

center, and coordination of regional development over a three-county area. It also received a share of income and sales tax revenue in addition to revenue from landfill fees, the zoo, and the convention center.

The planning functions are the most far reaching powers of MSD. Senate Bill 100 and its extensions reflect concerns for the human as well as the natural environment. Local plans must encourage housing for all income groups, promote residential density, and take measures to assist the disadvantaged and the unemployed (Rusk 1999: 159). Thus, many of the basic concerns of traditional local governments are reviewed by the MSD. It can reject plans and has been able to get cities to accept housing targets and growth limits.

Over time, the MSD has increased its authority and influence. By most standards, the results of Portland's efforts are quite impressive. Urban sprawl has lessened significantly, park space has increased, an

efficient light rail system is in place, and 40 percent of the downtown workers use it. The central city remains very viable as downtown jobs have doubled and shopping areas are thriving (see Hamilton 1999: 328).

The MSD remains one government among many in the urban area. Transportation and the port are governed by separate districts and the cities and counties continue to be responsible for basic urban services. MSD's role is best described as an umbrella under which a variety of policy related functions are performed. It brings together regional interests and has the authority to approve or reject proposals under the guise of enforcing state laws (Stephens and Wikstrom 1996: 268). By independently electing the board members, this political team is independent of cities and counties. It is beholden to a strong state law, but can look after regional concerns with less pressure from individual constituents or governments.

TWIN CITIES

The Twin Cities (Minneapolis and St. Paul, Minnesota) region comprises a large dense urban complex of over two million people. Like most urban areas, its suburban areas expanded rapidly during the 1960s and ringed the central cities while the central city began to decline. Thus, the region faced problems similar to most cities in the 1970s; central city decay, urban sprawl, and significant fiscal disparities between the central cities. Job growth in the central cities also declined significantly and the minority population, while smaller than most urban areas became highly

concentrated in the older parts of the central cities. The region also contained a large number of separate governments—nearly 300 (Harrigan and Johnson 1978: 4). Minnesota is known for progressive, liberal politics and support for governmental measures to deal with social problems. Rivalry between the two cities, however, often limited civic cooperation. (One year, Minneapolis decided to convert to daylight saving time, while St. Paul remained on central time.)

Concern for coordination and expansion of urban services has a long

Downtown Minneapolis, with its modern office towers, is an example of successful suburban-central city cooperation.

© Steve Vidler/SuperStock

history in the region. In 1967, the state legislature created a Metropolitan Council responsible for setting policies on water quality, transit, housing, and land use. Gradually the influence of the council expanded to eventually become arguably the strongest regional government in the nation. In its initial year, the council successfully dealt with major health and sanitary problems through the creation of the Metropolitan Waste Control Commission, which constructed and ran treatment plants and trunk sewer lines. This successful endeavor proved to be a model for future concerns. The council set overall policy and established alternative organizations to handle day-to-day operations.

Over time, the legislature added numerous responsibilities. In 1969, the legislature put the Metropolitan Transit Commission under the direction of the Metropolitan Council. Later the council was given some control over airports and land-use planning. In response to state level initiatives the council created a housing authority with the ability to build moderate- and low-income housing in many of the smaller suburbs.

The council gradually assumed more authority over cities and special districts. Now, it appoints members of most metropolitan commissions, approves capital budgets, and establishes land-use guides for the cities. It acquired its own tax base and received funding through state and federal grants. Its first decade is described by Harrigan as one of unprecedented accomplishments (1996: 215). It oversees the dispersion of low- and moderate-income housing, creates a vast system of regional parks, controls growth and development into free-standing growth centers, and encourages supporting infrastructure improvements. The councils' most daring innovation, the Fiscal

(continued)

(continued)

Disparities Act, created a shared tax base created by new commercial real estate distributed to the commission and the cities.

The governance of the council permitted some degree of action independent of both the legislature and the cities. Commission members are appointees of the governor representing state senate districts rather than cities. Since senate districts generally overlapped several cities, or contained only portions of the central cities, distinct city representatives were unlikely to develop. Thus, while less independent than the elected members in Portland, they could exercise some independence from city influences. As appointees of the governor, they are a more direct link to state policy. Potentially the positions could become subjects of political conflict between the governor and legislators and the cities.

As difficulties within the region became more severe in the late 1980s and early 1990s, the council became a center of political conflict and in the process lost some of its hard-earned legitimacy. As differences developed between ambitious governors, legislators, and various public groups, the council was often bypassed on major land-use decisions. It had little influence on the decision to build a domed stadium (Klubuchar 1982), a world trade center, the nation's largest shopping center, and a new NBA basketball arena. Conflicts with the governor led to budgetary problems and a forced reduction of 20 percent of the council's planning staff. Harrigan attributes the problems to a general loss of consensus among key participants. Governors are elected on personality rather than party loyalty and program, business leaders tend to be absentee rather than home grown, and political parties no longer play a stabilizing role in city politics. Thus, metropolitan governing proceeds without highly visible political leaders pledged to cope with the problems of the urban area (see also Crosby and Bryson 1995).

In spite of these difficulties, crusading legislators and citizens proposed several changes in the council to increase revenue sharing among cities and to help suburbs expand low- and moderate-income housing and create an elected metropolitan council. The legislature did strengthen the Metropolitan Council in 1994, by placing all transit operations under its jurisdiction and giving it direct authority over waste control. The position of regional administrator, which is analogous to a city manager, was also created (Harrigan 1996: 226). The regional body now commands a budget of $294 million and has a staff of 3,800. It appears that the metropolitan council may be emerging from a time of political conflict and may again be capable of providing policy leadership.

Harrigan points to the need for regional leadership to permit the agency to resume its position. "In the last analysis," he argues "the key issue is still political. Alleviating regional disparities, containing sprawl, and positioning the region for global competition cannot be achieved by a bureaucratic agency" (1996: 227). It is possible that more significant leadership is emerging within the current council. Governor Ventura appointed a respected former state legislator, Ted Mondale, as chairman of the council. Mondale has written extensively on metropolitan concerns. He was the author of the Liveable Communities Act, which is considered a model for offering financial incentives to communities that build housing for the working poor. As Ventura's opponent in the last election, Mondale frequently raised urban and transportation issues. With a high profile leader committed to regional issues, the council may be able to assume the regional leadership position it formerly held.

New Approaches to Regionalism—a Better Way? Portland and the Twin Cities are not typical urban areas. Both are smaller complexes than our larger cities and wealthier than most. They share a liberal-progressive political ethos, and neither has had to contend with a large influx of immigrants or under-privileged ethnic or racial minorities. A form of metropolitan coordination and cooperation has improved governance in both areas, but problems similar to those in most cities remain. Nonetheless, important lessons can be gained by examining the common traits of these two cases.

Both areas retained the existing cities with most of the powers traditionally held by city governments. Neither tried to eliminate cities, nor were the prerogatives of cities significantly reduced. Both reforms learned from the criticisms raised by proponents of the public choice approach. Americans like small local governments, which, by and large, produce efficient and effective local services. Both areas also preserved a role for existing special districts that were assumed to be operating effectively. The reforms produced minimum disturbance of the status quo.

Both reforms followed directly from state laws that mandated rather precise policy changes. In Portland, an aggressive effort by Governor Tim McCall led to legislation mandating preservation of open spaces through urban concentration. In Minnesota, state laws mandated most of the controversial policy goals of the metropolitan district, and state legislators dominated the discussions. Metropolitan officials could defer to state officers and act as agents of the state when dealing with more controversial matters. They didn't need to be proponents as well as implementers.

In both cases, the metropolitan government gradually assumed more responsibility as problems developed with other agencies or there emerged a consensus to proceed. In both regions, the sewer system became the responsibility of the metropolitan agency when problems with the existing system surfaced. Portland's agency took over the zoo, relieving the city of what had become a problem. The metropolitan agency, then, is perceived as a problem solver rather than an aggressive power usurper, and its assumption of power has been gradual.

The governing body of both agencies is not beholden directly to existing governments. The Portland council is separately elected in districts unrelated to city council districts or city boundaries. The Twin Cities council is appointed by the governor to districts also unrelated to city boundaries or council districts. Representatives are not directly involved in city concerns and can exercise some degree of independence from city politics.

The Practice of Regional Governance:
How Most Regions Are Ruled

Regional governance in most urban areas takes place through special districts and authorities, through informal cooperation among elected and appointed officials, and within the confines of councils of governments—voluntary organizations with little formal authority but often with the power of reason and persuasion among government leaders.

Special districts of various kinds are typical conveyors of regional policies. Transportation districts responsible for transportation planning and implementation are common in most urban areas. They are organized on a countywide or regional basis. Elected officials are often members of appointed boards overseeing transportation services. The federal and state governments are major sources of funding for transportation; generally, they require comprehensive planning, citizen participation, and intergovernmental coordination. Transportation planning generally must be coordinated across counties and conform to standards of related policies such as air quality and housing needs. Transportation planners, therefore, coordinate their efforts with those involved in other policy areas.

Special districts for water and air quality are usually important regional factors. Air quality concerns have led to significant regional coordination because efforts to meet state and federal air standards in most regions require coordination of transportation and land-use plans. Since automobiles and trucks generate the majority of the pollutants in most urban areas, meeting air quality standards requires more efficient transportation systems and land-use plans that coordinate homes, employment, and commercial areas. Because of the interrelationships between most facets of life and air quality, the South Coast Air Quality Management Agency has become a de-facto regional government in greater Los Angeles. Its policies influence industrial and commercial locations, transportation plans, and the location of new subdivisions. The district's policies, though, meet with resistance from other governments who oppose the assumption of regional pre-eminence, and today its influence is diminished (Saltzstein 1996).

Other special districts and authorities act as regional agencies because of their control of significant resources. The Port of New York Authority, for instance, supports nearly 400,000 jobs in the region and maintains operating revenues of nearly $2 billion. Toll bridges, airports, the world trade center, and numerous smaller projects are a part of its empire. It is a significant player in the politics of the three-state region. In spite of its power and resources, however, observers argue that its influence on regional cooperation is limited. The Authority is governed by appointees of the governors of New York and New Jersey. It is financially independent of local governments and beholden to its bond holders. Thus, it operates more like a private corporation and has little incentive to reach out to other governments. As a consequence of pressure from the governors, it implements a regional development program that includes several economic development projects. These efforts, however, remain a small part of the Authority's activities (Berg and Kantor 1996).

Reliance on specialized regional districts and authorities has pronounced consequences for urban areas. Their mission is specialized and they are generally governed by appointees of state and local governments with particular expertise or interest in these policies. Council members are often competent overseers but generally they are policy advocates. Leaders concerned about air quality will seek seats on regional air quality districts, and transportation advocates will pursue the transportation districts. Thus, each district is governed by

Downtown Denver has become a center for
entertainment, tourism and commerce through extensive
public investment and redevelopment.

© G. E. Kidder Smith/Corbis

those who want to see the concerns of that agency expanded. While this may lead to competent oversight, it is less likely to encourage coordination across districts. Often, the single-minded purposes of special districts leads to conflicts among them for policy hegemony within the region. In Los Angeles, for instance, transportation and air quality concerns have frequently clashed; each argues that their agency should take the lead in transportation planning.

Another by-product of the reliance on special districts is a general increase in public expenditures. Foster studied special purpose government nationally with significant quantitative data on district spending patterns. She compared cities where common functions were handled by special districts with those where the same function was handled by a general purpose government. Her primary conclusion is that spending increases when the function is controlled by a special district. Thus, transportation and airport districts, for example, spend more when a special district operates them than when a city or county is the governing agency. A district with a single purpose and an independent funding source is likely to advocate the expansion of that function. When the same service is part of a more general government, it must compete with other service agencies for funds. The consequence of that competition is often less money for that service.

A final element in the regional decision-making process in all cities is the Council of Governments (COGs). COGs are mandated by federal legislation and expected to coordinate policy among all the governments in the region. They are governed by representatives of member cities, and generally have no formal powers. They usually develop studies of regional problems and act as a clearing house for several federal and state grants. Their power expands from time to time when certain federal programs mandate their review of certain programs. Currently, major transportation funds in urban areas from the Intermodal Surface Transportation Efficiency Act (ISTEA) and its successor, the Transportation Equity Act for the 21st Century (TEA-21), include COGs as a significant partner. The programs give urban areas significant freedom to spend the funds on various modes of transportation, and they rely on COGs to approve the final recommendation on the division of funds.

While COGs perform many useful functions and encourage regional cooperation, few argue that they have had a major influence on regional matters. Henig et al.'s conclusion on the operation of the COG in the Washington region probably speaks for many: "The member jurisdictions are not drawn to the COG by an overwhelming recognition that they are all rowing in rough waters in a single life boat. More significant, it seems to be their calculation that it is only through membership that they can share in certain federal grants and in the efficiencies gained through cooperative purchasing agreements and the like" (Henig, Brunori, and Ebert 1996: 126).

CONCLUSIONS: PRESERVING OUR RIGHTS
AND PROTECTING OUR REGIONS

The "paradox of urban governance"—the need for a common approach to the problems of our urban areas, yet the presence of numerous and separate independent governments—remains the most prominent feature of the governance of American cities. It is, in the words of Robert C. Wood, "one of the great unnatural wonders of the world." Wood peered at our cities from the vantage point of the early 1960s when the trends that now dominate our urban areas were in their infancy. Since his day, the size of urban areas has expanded, the central cities have declined in wealth, larger numbers of recent immigrants have replaced working-class Anglo's in the central cities, and more and more of the middle class has moved to the suburbs. What we used to call suburbs have, in many cases, become "edge cities"; separate urban complexes with little connection to the central city. Our economy has changed from heavy industry to knowledge-based processes, and we face significant international competition for our products.

Yet citizens remain committed to small government and, as we discussed in the last chapter, the connections between the citizen and government have become tenuous. Metropolitan reform today is not as simple a problem as it seemed in the 1960s. A strong case can be made for both smaller and larger local governments. Responsibility for the welfare of the urban area has become a more important concern while attachment to the central city has become less important for most citizens. The progress we see in Portland and the Twin Cities, however, indicates that some form of cooperative government can lead toward a governance system that might accomplish both.

REFERENCES

Abbott, Carl. 1983. *Portland: Planning, Politics, and Growth in a Twentieth Century City.* Lincoln, NE: University of Nebraska Press.

Advisory Commission on Intergovernmental Relations. 1988. *Metropolitan Organization: The St. Louis Case.* Washington, D.C.: United States Government Printing Office.

Bahl, Roy. 1994. "Metropolitan Fiscal Disparities." *Cityscape* 1, no. 1: 293–306.

Bahl, Ron, Jorge Martinez-Vazquez, and David Sjoquist. 1992. "Central City-Suburban Fiscal Disparities." *Public Finance Quarterly* 20, no. 4 (October): 420–32.

Berg, Bruce, and Paul Kantor. 1996. "New York: The Politics of Conflict and Avoidance." In *Regional Politics: America in a Post-City Age,* edited by H.V. Savitch and Ronald K. Vogel. Thousand Oaks, CA: Sage Publishers.

Bloomquist, William, and Roger B. Parks. 1995. "Unigov: Local Government in Indianapolis and Marion County, Indiana." In *The Government of World Cities: The Future of the Metro Model,* edited by L. J. Sharpe. New York: John Wiley and Sons.

Briffault, Richard. 1990. "Our Localism Part 1: The Structure of Local Government Law." *Columbia Law Review* 90 (January).

Crosby, Barbara C., and John N. Bryson. 1995. "The Twin Cities Metropolitan Council." In *The Government of World Cities: The Future of the Metro Model,* edited by L. J. Sharpe. New York: John Wiley and Sons.

Dowding, Keith, Peter John, and Stephen Biggs. 1994. "Tiebout: A Survey of the Empirical Literature." *Urban Studies* 31, no. 4–5 (May): 767–98.

Downs, Anthony. 1994. *New Visions for Metropolitan America.* Washington, D.C.: The Brookings Institution.

Foster, Kathryn A. 1997. *The Political Economy of Special-Purpose Government.* Washington, D.C.: Georgetown University Press.

Frug, Gerald E. 1999. *City Making: Building Communities Without Walls.* Princeton, NJ: Princeton University Press.

Glassberg, Andrew D. 1991. "St. Louis: Racial Transition and Economic Development." In *Big City Politics in Transition,* edited by H.V. Savitch and John Clayton Thomas. Newbury Park, CA: Sage Publications.

Greer, Scott. 1962A. *The Emerging City: Myth and Reality.* New York: The Free Press.

Greer, Scott. 1962B. *Governing the Metropolis.* New York: John Wiley and Sons Inc.

Hamilton, David K. 1999. *Governing Metropolitan Areas: Response to Growth and Change.* New York: Garland Publishers Inc.

Harrigan, John J. 1996. "Minneapolis-St. Paul: Structuring Metropolitan Government." In *Regional Politics: America in a Post-City Age,* edited by H.V. Savitch and Ronald K. Vogel. Thousand Oaks, CA: Sage Publishers.

Harrigan, John J., and William C. Johnson. 1978. *Governing the Twin Cities Region: The Metropolitan Council in Comparative Perspective.* Minneapolis: University of Minnesota Press.

Henig, Jeffrey, David Brunori and Mark Ebert. 1996. "Washington D.C.: Cautious and Constrained Cooperation." In *Regional Politics: America in a Post-City Age,* edited by H.V. Savitch and Ronald K. Vogel. Thousand Oaks, CA: Sage Publishers.

Hise, Greg. 1997. *Magnetic Los Angeles: Planning the Twentieth Century.* Baltimore: Johns Hopkins University Press.

Jackson, Kenneth T. 1985. *Crabgrass Frontier: The Suburbanization of the United States.* New York: Oxford University Press.

Klobuchar, Amy. 1982. *Uncovering the Dome.* Prospect Heights, IL: Waveland Press Inc.

Miller, Gary J. 1981. *Cities by Contract: The Politics of Municipal Incorporation.* Cambridge, MA: The MIT Press.

Nadeau, Remi. 1950. "Super Subdivider." In *Los Angeles: Biography of a City,* edited by John Caughey and Laree Caughey. Berkeley, CA: University of California Press, 1997.

Nelson, Arthur. 1996. "Portland: The Metropolitan Umbrella." In *Regional Politics: America in a Post-City Age,* edited by H.V. Savitch and Ronald K. Vogel. Thousand Oaks, CA: Sage Publishers.

Orum, Anthony N. 1995. *City-Building in America.* Boulder, CO: Westview Press.

Ostrom, Vincent, Charles M. Tiebout, and Robert Warren. 1961. "The Organization of Government in Metropolitan Areas: A Theoretical Inquiry." *American Political Science Review* 55, no. 4 (December): 831–42.

Phares, Donald, and Claude Louishomme. 1996. "St. Louis: A Politically Fragmented Area." In *Regional Politics: America in a Post-City Age,* edited by H.V. Savitch and Ronald K. Vogel. Thousand Oaks, CA: Sage Publishers.

Rusk, David. 1995. *Cities Without Suburbs.* Baltimore: Johns Hopkins University Press.

Rusk, David. 1999. *Inside Game Outside Game: Winning Strategies for Saving Urban America.* Washington, D.C.: Brookings Institution Press.

Saltzstein, Alan L. 2000. "Intergovernmental Relations in Greater Los Angeles: From Dominance to Governance."

Saltzstein, Alan L. 1996. "Los Angeles: Politics Without Governance." In *Regional Politics: America in a Post-City Age,* edited by H.V. Savitch and Ronald K. Vogel. Thousand Oaks, CA: Sage Publishers.

Savitch, H.V., and Ronald K. Vogel. 1996. "Introduction: Regional Patterns in a Post-City Age." In *Regional Politics: America in a Post-City Age,* edited by H.V. Savitch and Ronald K. Vogel. Thousand Oaks, CA: Sage Publishers.

Stephens, G. Ross, and Nelson Wikstrom. 2000. *Metropolitan Government and Governance.* New York: Oxford University Press.

Stowers, Genie. 1996. "Miami: Experiences in Regional Government." In *Regional Politics: America in a Post-City Age,* edited by H.V. Savitch and Ronald K. Vogel. Thousand Oaks, CA: Sage Publishers.

Swanson, Bert. 1996. "Jacksonville: Consolidation and Regional Governance." In *Regional Politics: America in a Post-City Age,* edited by H.V. Savitch and Ronald K. Vogel. Thousand Oaks, CA: Sage Publishers.

Teaford, Jon C. 1979. *City and Suburb: The Political Fragmentation of Metropolitan America, 1850–1970.* Baltimore: The Johns Hopkins University Press.

Teske, Paul, Mark Schneider, Michael Mintron, and Samuel Best. 1993. "Establishing the Micro Foundations of a Macro Theory: Information, Movers and the Competitive Local Market for Public Goods." *American Political Science Review* 87, no. 8 (September): 702–16.

Wood, Robert C. 1964. *1400 Governments.* Garden City, NJ: Doubleday Anchor Books.

Chapter Ten

Resolving the Paradox
of Urban Governance

The argument of this book can be stated simply: American cities can claim many accomplishments, but the governance of cities fails to achieve the promise of greatness. Residents of urban areas share a common destiny and a joint responsibility for the governance of the region. *The failure of cities to assume regional responsibility is a major constraint on the achievement of greatness.* Political leaders consider the problems of the poor, in both suburb and central city, the concerns of the particular jurisdictions they live in rather than the common concern of all residents. Hence, the locations of the poor receive inferior services and those with means who live in poorer communities move, usually to more distant parts of the region. Hence, while the cities may become richer, the concentration of poverty increases and the resources to deal with the consequences of poverty decline. As city residents move farther from their jobs, shopping areas, and entertainment centers, traffic congestion increases, and air and water quality decline. Ultimately the area becomes more expensive to live in and a less promising location for new businesses. Thus, the failure to promote common policies for the region may lead to regional decline.

All should share in the costs and take part in the decisions relating to the common concerns of residents of urban areas. Yet because we insist on dividing authority among numerous small and frequently invisible governments, the coordination among these governments is often limited. Political participation is also low and regional leaders have difficulty securing public legitimacy for their actions. Our cities are divided cities; few accept a common responsibility for their problems or their promise.

This concluding chapter summarizes the argument and discusses measures that would improve the governance of urban areas. We began with the "paradox of urban governance." Urban areas, by design and definition, require more government services and must devote resources to improve public facilities. Yet Americans cling to the ideals of small local governments and insist on creating numerous autonomous political jurisdictions within our urban areas. In earlier chapters, we examined how these conditions came about and we looked at what has been done in some urban areas to resolve the paradox. For most urban areas, however, the paradox is not fully resolved. Poverty exists among plenty, public services operate inefficiently, and cities encroach upon valuable agricultural land and prized natural resources. We close with a discussion of some far-ranging solutions that challenge the legal organization of urban areas and attack the relationship between citizens and the government in these fragmented regions. Some argue that city residents should be responsible for the governance of the region, not just the particular jurisdiction where they live. Legal challenges to our separate cities may ultimately be an effective way to reduce the problems of the urban area by forcing all citizens to bear the cost of public problems.

HOW DID THESE CONDITIONS COME ABOUT?

American cities developed with very concentrated populations. As discussed in Chapter 2, employment, living areas, and commerce converged in the city's downtowns in the first part of the twentieth century. Distinct, ethnically based neighborhoods and businesses developed in close proximity to one another. Business and commerce required face-to-face interaction, and residents needed to live close to centers of employment. A dense, vibrant downtown crowded with people and rich in diverse activities emerged.

Social and economic changes during the middle of the twentieth century encouraged the spreading out of the city. Innovations in transportation and production dictated that locations on the rim of the old city were more desirable. The central city was no longer the most viable area for commerce, industry, and housing. The Depression and World War II prevented many of these changes from affecting the city until the 1950s. When society opened up again, the change was rapid and haphazardly planned. Changes in the rural economy, particularly in the South, encouraged large numbers of African Americans to migrate to the cities at a time when the economy of the central city was declining. Discrimination prevented their movement to most suburban areas. Therefore,

© The New Yorker Collection 1998 Mort Greenberg from cartoonbank.com. All Rights Reserved.

the central cities declined while the population of poor, unskilled residents in the city center increased (Chapter 3).

Traditions of local self government and the legal concept of "home rule" required that city government handle most of the problems of urban life. In most cities, politics in the early years of the twentieth century was dominated by machines that dealt with the difficulties of urbanization, but they were often corrupt and undemocratic. In the middle years of the twentieth century, the reform movement attacked the machines and installed less corrupt and usually more efficient governments. The new reform governments, however, often detached the running of cities from large numbers of the public. Legal traditions and court rulings encouraged the incorporation of areas of small homogenous populations and separate communities. Thus, suburban residents frequently could exempt themselves from much of the governmental costs of managing an urban area. Cities were managed well, but at the expense of a close link to the public and a common sense of responsibility to all residents (see Chapters 4 and 5).

The influence of the federal government in cities has generally not been effective in dealing with the problems posed by the social and economic changes of mid-twentieth century America. Often it made the problems worse. Federal policies in housing and transportation initially encouraged suburban expansion and the exclusion of African Americans from new housing. Later, funds devoted to central city reconstruction often did more harm than good by destroying poor but viable neighborhoods and replacing them with segregated, concentrated public housing. In recent years, federal funding has declined significantly at the same time that local resources were also cut back. Urban managers today are faced with particularly daunting tasks; problems have increased, but funding has declined (see Chapter 6).

Urban leadership has, at times, been able to overcome the difficulties of managing the problems of cities. There is evidence of several effectively run cities managed by clever and intelligent mayors and city managers. The distribution of wealth, social status, and associational ties, however, requires that even the most liberal of mayors respond to the interests of the upper class. For these reasons, the influence of those less well off is generally limited in large cities (see Chapter 7). Sound urban leadership is, at best, a difficult task that is not necessarily the norm in today's cities.

The presence of serious violence in American cities reminds us of the costs of poverty, unemployment, weak links between the governors and the governed, and management failures (see Chapter 8). Though we seem to know more about the causes of violence and the means to prevent it, its periodic occurrence in cities suggests problems in governance.

HOW IS THE PARADOX RESOLVED?

The need for government power in the face of divided government and limited means to coordinate the many sources of power within an urban system form the *paradox of urban governance.* Despite the paradox, our cities survive, many prosper, and much significant governmental innovation occurs. The American economy is now the envy of the world, and most of the production and commerce occurs in our urban areas. Obviously, city officials find the means to govern well in spite of the difficulties of city life.

Public Officials Cross Governmental Barriers

Innovative city officials with a commitment to their regions are often able to bring about concerted actions to attack public problems. By working closely with other governments and the private sector, clever city leaders can often cut through the complexity of divided government and implement solutions to intergovernmental problems. The following case illustrates how astute city officials can do great things in spite of the problems mentioned previously.

The St. Paul example demonstrates how leadership and the cooperation of important members of the private sector and the federal government can overcome many of the impediments to concerted action. George Latimer found ways to coordinate finances and important people that brought about central authority in a normally divided and dispersed system. The example is not isolated. Osborne and Gaebler and other recent works trace the actions of effective

THE TRIUMPH OF ENTREPRENEURSHIP

Fifteen years ago St. Paul, Minnesota was a down-at-the heels, Frost Belt city that appeared to be dying. Its population had fallen below pre-Depression levels. Its central business district had lost 41 percent of its retail volume over the previous fifteen years. A citizens' committee had published a study projecting a continued drain of people and investment to the suburbs.

George Latimer, elected mayor in 1975, knew he would never have the tax dollars he needed to solve St. Paul's problems, so he set out to "leverage the resources of the city—combining them with the much more prestigious resources of the private sector."

Latimer started with the downtown, the most visible symbol of St. Paul's malaise. A huge two square block hole in the middle of town had stood empty for so long that residents had begun to call it a historic landmark. Latimer quickly found a private partner and nailed down one of the first Federal Urban Development Action Grants and together they built a passive solar hotel, two high-rise office towers, a glass-enclosed city park and a three level shopping mall.

The worst area was Lowertown, a 25 square mile warehouse district that made up the eastern third of the business district. Latimer and his deputy mayor, Dick Broeker, dreamed up the idea of a private development bank, capitalized with foundation money to catalyze investment in the area. In 1978, they asked the McKnight Foundation for $10 million to back the idea and they got it.

The Lowertown Development Corporation brought in developers, offered loans or loan guarantees and put together package deals with banks, insurance companies, and anyone else who would listen. Over the previous decade, investors had put only $22 million into Lowertown. In the Development Corporation's first decade, it triggered $350 million in new investments—leveraging its own money 30 or 40 to 1. Thirty-nine buildings were renovated or reconstructed. By 1988 Lowertown generated nearly six times the property taxes it had ten years before, and the Development Corporation was turning a profit.

Latimer and Broeker created a second corporation to develop the nation's first downtown hot water heating system; a third to develop affordable housing. They used voluntary organizations to operate recycling programs, to perform energy audits. And even to manage a park. They turned garbage collection and the city's Youth Services Bureau over to the private sector. They used millions of dollars worth of volunteers' time in the city's parks, recreation centers, libraries and health centers. And they created more partnerships with foundations than any city before or since.

By constantly catalyzing solutions outside the public sector, Latimer was able to increase his government's impact while trimming his staff by 12 percent, keeping budget and property tax growth below the rate of inflation and reducing the city's debt. Without massive layoffs—in fact while enriching the lives of public employees—he gave voters what they wanted: a government that did more but spent less.

SOURCE: From David Osborne and Ted Gaebler, *Reinventing Government: How the Entrepreneurial Spirit Is Transforming the Public Sector* (New York: Addison Wesley, 1992): 24–26.

politicians and administrators who have produced positive results for their cities (see also Moore 1995).

However, in the name of entrepreneurship, wrong decisions are also made. The example of Robert Moses (Chapter 7), reminds us that entrepreneurs can do harm as well as good, particularly if their actions are hidden from the public and they are able to gain excessive power. The bankruptcy in Orange County, California, demonstrates how entrepreneurs in one of the nation's wealthiest areas with good reputation for innovative government led government astray and produced catastrophic results. When the county faced losses of resources, its county treasurer stepped in with solutions and united cities, special districts, and school districts behind a large investment fund. Other officials were willing to follow his lead, ignoring signs of problems with his policies.

The World of Local Government Finance

A look at Orange County's problems requires some understanding of state and local government finance; where government's money comes from and how it is spent. Local governments receive their funds from a variety of sources. Historically, cities relied on the *property tax,* a tax on the value of real estate, for much of its income. The property tax is derived from an *assessed value* of each property, determined by a local official, called an assessor, who places a value on each piece of property, presumably based on its sales value and a *tax rate* determined by local governments. The assessed value multiplied by the tax rate determines the amount of taxes the owner must pay. Generally, as property increases in value, the owner pays proportionally more in taxes.

Local governments also generally receive money from *sales taxes* levied within the city boundaries and *licenses and fees* for services. Some state tax money is shared with cities. As discussed in Chapter 5, the federal government has been a major provider of funds to local governments, though these funds have declined significantly since 1978. In a small number of cities, a portion of the income tax is returned to the city. Many cities earn money through the operation of *municipal utilities;* power plants, water systems, etc.

Figure 10.1 lists the percentage of revenue the typical city receives currently. Charges are the largest contributor, totaling about 22 percent. The property tax and state revenue each contribute equals 16 percent. Income and sales taxes account for 5 and 10 percent, respectively. The federal government contribution is a scant 4 percent.

The property tax is viewed by many as a fair tax. Generally, as people's wealth increases, they acquire more expensive property. Renters as well as owners pay the tax indirectly since landlords determine rental rates taking all costs of the property into consideration.

However, the effect of the tax is keenly felt by those on fixed incomes when inflation occurs. Housing prices are very sensitive to rises in cost. Unless governments significantly lower the tax rate, homeowners will find their property tax bills increasing radically in times of inflation. In the late 1970s, increases in property taxes in California led to a grass roots rebellion that resulted in a

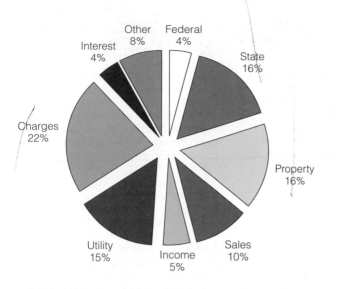

FIGURE 10.1 Revenue of Municipal Government, 1996–97

statewide initiative, Proposition 13, that radically lowered property taxes. The concern rapidly spread to other states where similar measures were passed. Sensitivity to the tax revolt has led state and local officials to decrease local government's dependence on the property tax. In 1962, for instance, property taxes totaled over 90 percent of all city revenues. Today, as noted previously, they represent 16 percent of the total.

Both taxes and the cost of government are affected by the economy. As the economy declines, property values often decrease since buyers have less income. If stores and factories shut down, value is taken off the tax rolls. As people buy less, sales taxes and fees for services decrease. Service demands, however, may increase. Crime increases when the economy declines; more people are eligible for social entitlements like welfare, public health, and food stamps; and numbers of the unemployed, the homeless, and those without health insurance expand. Since counties are the common providers of these services, hard times bring added strains to county officials.

Governments also borrow money. Short-term borrowing is common in local governments because tax money generally reaches them months after it has been collected. Thus, the government borrows until the money arrives and then pays the bank back. Longer-term loans are given for particular projects where the income will be received over a long period of time. Funds to build new highways are often provided from gas taxes paid over many years. To build the highway, money is borrowed and paid back gradually as the tax money is earned. Government borrowing policies have historically been very conservative. In Orange County, however, as their financial problems increased, an innovative county treasurer entered the world of more risky investments. The result was something no person could have imagined happening in one of the nation's wealthiest counties—bankruptcy.

THE ORANGE COUNTY BANKRUPTCY

Orange County declared bankruptcy in December of 1994, the largest municipal bankruptcy in United States history. The county is one of the nation's wealthiest areas and, with over 2.5 million people at the time, the nation's fifth most populous county. The pain of the bankruptcy, however, extended far beyond the county government since many cities and special districts, all the local school districts, and even individuals throughout the state had invested in their fund.

Today the county is solvent again. A series of austerity measures, much local debt, and a healthy economy has restored the county's finances. The pain, however, is felt by local taxpayers, employees who were let go, and public services that are only now recovering from the austerity that followed. The legacy of the bankruptcy for the long-range concerns of government is one of failed entrepreneurship. An aggressive and distinguished elected treasurer, Bob Citron, was permitted to risk the county's finances. Wildly leveraged investments ultimately collapsed as the bond market took a different turn than that anticipated by Mr. Citron.

Why Did It Happen?

Preventing the repetition of the Orange County bankruptcy requires an understanding of why it happened. Unfortunately, we have several theories but no definitive explanation for these events. Four explanations are commonly cited.

It Was Citron's Fault

Bob Citron is an unusual man; he appears to be at least two very different people. First, there is the quiet, soft-spoken grandfather over his head in the high financial circles he was placed in. Citron was appointed to the treasurer's position in 1970 when little discretion was given to the position. At the time, funds had to be held in safe liquid assets and there was a great deal of state supervision. Citron lacked a college degree and had little financial experience other than his years as a treasurer's assistant.

Financial concerns of the county treasurer changed, however, as local governments looked to investments as a source of income rather than liquidity. Citron was then asked to do things he really wasn't competent to do. Thus, perhaps he was easy prey for the "slick traders" of Wall Street.

At his trial, Citron complemented this impression by arguing that his mental facilities had declined in recent years. Senility had set in, impairing his judgment and leading him to accept advice without evaluation. It was also reported that he regularly relied on an astrologer for financial advice.

The other side of Bob is evident on the wall of his office, cluttered with awards and honors from the financial and public administration communities. The Orange County American Society for Public Administration Chapter awarded him its "Public Official of the Year" award six months prior to the bankruptcy. Supervisors and county administrators regularly praised him as a financial genius. A few months before the bankruptcy, one supervisor stated, "I don't understand how he does it, but the man is an absolute genius." Other governments and private individuals had so much confidence in Citron that they voluntarily invested their funds with the county. Judges often required settlements be placed in the fund to insure a good, safe return. Citron influenced the writing of state legislation that granted treasurers expanded authority to invest. Nationally, he was considered tops in his field. Senile, perhaps, but to paraphrase what Lincoln said of Grant, the supervisors wished all their employees were so senile.

It Was the Brokers Fault
When counties became more interested in the financial return of their holdings and state laws permitted more diverse investment opportunities, financial advisors and Wall Street firms became important players in local finance. A government as large as Orange County was a plum contract for a trading house; enough to make the careers of several individual traders. Orange County, through Bob Citron, was a regular customer of several brokerage firms and financial advisors.

Are these advisors responsible for bad advice when public funds are involved? County officials thought so and proceeded to sue several brokerage firms. Many of these suits led, collectively, to settlements that are among the largest received in the public sector. Over $700 million of the $1.6 billion dollars lost has been recovered through several court actions and mediated agreements. The success of these efforts suggests that the legal system finds fault in the advice given Mr. Citron.

*Governmental Structure
Is at Fault*
Authority in Orange County is divided between supervisors elected in large districts and several separately elected officials, including the county treasurer. The Chief Administrative Officer (CAO) was nominally responsible for budget preparation though, in fact, the supervisors and their staffs, and other elected department heads like the sheriff were strong players in the decisions. Consequently, few speak for the concerns of the county as a whole. "I am the CAO of my district," one supervisor stated when discussing why a strong CAO was not necessary.

Investment decisions were considered the prerogative of the treasurer in Citron's day, and influence

by the supervisors was resisted. To many, he guarded this authority carefully and often imperially. Current supervisor, Jim Silva, recalls his first conversation with Citron while he was running for office prior to the bankruptcy. "I asked him about the investment pool and he basically says he's doing a good job. He has a very good track record, and if I didn't believe him that I could read his press clippings. And he turned around and walked away from me." Supervisors claimed that, when they asked Citron for information about investment policies, he refused to give it, stating that he was allegiant only to the voters.

Thus, to many, the Orange County system was one of divided authority without central responsibility. Supervisors tended to focus on the concerns of their districts while centrally elected officials concentrated on their functional responsibilities only. Would a strong CAO whose job would include the treasury as well as expenditures place investment policy within a broader context? While the experience of governments and the writings of many of the stalwarts in the public administration field would say "yes," the voters and many key decision makers apparently disagreed when they soundly rejected the charter amendment.

*Environmental Demands,
Voter Mistrust, and Wishful
Thinking*
The last reason looks more broadly at social, economic, and political changes in the Orange County environment. Orange County has one of the highest per capita incomes of any county in the nation, but aggregate figures, while accurate, mask underlying problems of a large share of the population. The county's needy population expanded significantly from 1980 to 1990. Immigration from Latin America and Asia increased, leaving the county with the sixth largest Latino and fourth largest

(continued)

(continued)

Asian population in the country. By 1990, 27 percent of the population was foreign born and 26 percent had no health insurance.

Counties in California are responsible for most of the costs associated with poverty; welfare, public health, homelessness. Thus, these programs required higher budgets as the poverty population increased. The county is also the main provider of jails and the police force in unincorporated areas. Demands for jail space and more sheriffs increased as crime increased in the late 1980s and early 1990s.

Politically, the county remained conservative and its middle-class residents, facing some of the highest housing prices in the nation, were very sensitive to increases in taxes. Orange County voters had strongly supported the property tax cut of Proposition 13 in 1978 and subsequent tax-cutting measures.

State support of local governments had also declined during this time as a consequence of various initiatives that earmarked money to various concerns and a faltering economy that generated less state revenue. Several unincorporated areas of South Orange County incorporated as cities during the late 1980s, leaving the county with a smaller revenue base.

County board members faced an impossible problem. Demands for services had increased significantly and, in many cases, the county was required to serve the poor population at rates determined by other governments. Resources had declined and there was no reason to expect them to increase. Decision makers were limited in their search for new revenues and were opposed to increasing general taxes.

Bob Citron's pool of money and the magical returns he seemed to be able to produce became, perhaps, a solution to this awful conundrum. "Perhaps he really was a wizard," thought the Board of Supervisors. Each year the portion of the county's income derived from investments increased; it was estimated at 35 percent of the total county income in the year of the bankruptcy. Hindsight tells us that no government ever gets nearly that kind of income from investments, but to the board members, perhaps Bob could do it for just one more year.

Lessons for Urban Managers

We can absolve public administrators of any responsibility for the financial default of Orange County. Perhaps an apparently competent elected official lost his mind? Perhaps it was caused by a governmental structure that failed to provide central direction to the decision-making process? Or perhaps high demands for services and declining resources gave the decision makers no choice but to gamble on risky investments?

The setting of Orange County in the early 1990s made it difficult to warn the policymakers that bankruptcy might occur. Yet some did see the problem. John Moorloch, the present treasurer, campaigned for Citron's job in the spring of 1995 by raising concerns over the treasurer's investments, but few listened. Citron received the endorsement of most elected officials and won the election handily. Internally, some undoubtedly raised questions but few concerns were raised even when projected income from investments reached 35% of the budget.

This story is a classic case of short-range requirements overruling the need for long-range planning. Questions about Citron's investment policies could be raised only by those less dependent on immediate rewards or political benefits. It may be difficult for elected officials who worry about the public's immediate reaction to do so. Public administrators who are less governed by the reaction of the electorate, however, should be the ones to register concern for the general health of the organization.

Orange County needed whistle-blowers who were willing to inform elected officials and the public of the risk associated with Citron's decisions. To protect employees from recriminations, policies must encourage employees to come forth freely and superiors must be willing to listen to grievances.

A skepticism of authority on the part of all the parties is a final lesson of the Orange County bankruptcy. Errors were made here by those who had strong support from the public and political leaders. Major interest groups, the press, and leaders of other governments who invested in the county fund raised few concerns about treasury management. Everybody, therefore, should be alert to the potential for error even among those we trust.

Targeting Problem Areas

A second approach devotes resources selectively to areas of greatest need in an attempt to compensate for the advantages given to those of means. Federal aid is often targeted on the neighborhoods of greatest deprivation. Thus, we target low-income housing with special programs, and we aid deprived schools with free lunches and Head Start. Community-based organizations attract private and public funding for concentrated attacks on our poorest areas. Many of these programs have improved the life of the residents of poorer areas by increasing employment opportunities, providing job training, and aiding school children.

Several authors conclude that many inner-city areas have experienced major economic and social gains in recent years as a consequence of this strategy. Grogan and Proscio document significant improvement in the quality of life in the South Bronx, considered one of the worst slums as recently as 1970. "Today, new housing units have replaced massive public housing projects and community-based organizations and neighborhood groups have encouraged social cohesion among the residents and assisted the police in reducing crime. While poor, residents of the area are working and the schools have improved. Empty nesters have taken up residence in once-hopeless downtowns; merchants, police, and non-profit groups are restoring order and vitality to neighborhood markets. Communities are retaking control of derelict housing, parks, and even schools; capital is flowing into inner-city markets at unheard-of rates. Individually small and uneven, when these changes are seen together, they add up to something coherent and phenomenal" (2000: 241–2).

They attribute this improvement to four changes:

1. The strength and expansion of community-based organizations, which improves the life chances of a large number of residents.

2. A revolution in credit that has encouraged banks to invest in deprived areas. The Community Reinvestment Act requires banks to invest in poorer communities and has encouraged developers to invest in poorer areas. As a consequence of the Act, banks have expanded credit to the working poor.

3. Changes in policing tactics and community-based policing have made the neighborhoods safer.

4. The deregulation of public housing and schools through the privatization of public housing, welfare reform, and voucher programs has expanded opportunities. Together, these changes have made people less dependent on government and have provided the means for independence.

A study by the Department of Housing and Urban Development documents significant improvements in the central business district of 10 very diverse cities that have harnessed government aid and private sector incentives. Most striking of the cities examined is Newark, New Jersey, historically one of the nation's poorest and least successful cities. For several decades, they point out, Newark's job base had declined—private sector jobs dropped from 195,600 in 1969 to 110,800 in 1981. The population fell by nearly 19 percent from 1980 to 1997 (2001: 79).

Aggressive efforts by Mayor James Sharpe and innovative packaging of public and private sector resources have resulted in a significant economic and cultural revival. The construction of a major cultural arts facility and a minor league baseball stadium generated a new tourist and entertainment industry. New firms were attracted to the city center through the use of a Special Improvement District that cleared land and brought in infrastructure improvements including a fiber-optic network. A large community development effort helped provide safe, affordable housing and quality education and improved health care. Crime has declined markedly. Consequently, a number of high-tech firms have moved into Newark and the downtown is a becoming a center for culture and entertainment (2001: 77–82).

Critics, however, see these programs having limited effect on the broader problems of cities. Rusk points out that while community-based organizations do significantly improve the areas they operate in, often the area surrounding their territory declines. An analysis of 34 community development corporations serving neighborhoods found that all the surrounding areas had lost population and poverty rates had increased from 1970 to 1990. "In cities across the country, the thirty-four targeted areas served by the most successful Community Development Corporations, as a group still became poorer, fell further behind regional income levels, and lost real buying power" (1999: 49). The problem here is not the efforts of the corporations. Rusk sees much positive effort and efficient and creative management in the corporations. They fail to effect the social conditions of their surroundings because the source of the problems is beyond their borders. Without a regional approach to social problems and a serious redistribution of tax resources, deprived areas will continue to fall behind the more privileged neighborhoods of the urban area.

Regional Special Districts

A third approach relies on regional special districts and single-purpose governments to manage area-wide policies. The managing of major regional facilities is delegated to single-purpose districts. Regional districts can claim responsibility for many important achievements. The air in the Los Angeles basin today is much cleaner than it was 20 years ago. The aggressive work of the South

Coast Air Quality Management District, a regional agency covering a six-county region, is largely responsible for this success. The Port of New York Authority has improved the economy of the New York region and manages superior port and transportation facilities. By and large, urban sewer and water systems, often governed by special districts, create clean drinking water and safely dispose of wastes.

However, the single-minded goals of these agencies and their lack of visibility has often led to a waste of resources and a failure to consider the long-range effects of their actions. Thus, water is extended to new subdivisions without consideration of the effect of the new development on the use of land and the transportation congestion that may result. Single-purpose districts are rarely good vehicles to assess the joint impacts of separate decisions on the regional infrastructure. As we have seen, coordination of regional concerns through area-wide planning agencies is rarely effective (see Chapter 9).

BOLD APPROACHES TO THE PROBLEMS OF AMERICAN CITIES

Much good is often accomplished by the three approaches discussed in the last section. However, all provide only limited and often temporary solutions to the larger problems of urban areas—equalizing the costs and benefits of government policies; integrating classes and races; improving the life chances of the poor; and efficiently coordinating housing, industry, commerce, and open space. *Attacking these problems systematically requires strong regional governments with significant resources and the ability to make difficult, often unpopular, decisions.* The structure of government must provide access to public resources and incentives for leaders to pursue the general good of the region and act on it.

Regional governments can effectively deal with the common problems of urban areas. Proponents of regional councils find much to praise in the Portland, Oregon region and the Twin Cities area of Minnesota. Both areas devote significant public resources to common urban problems. Regional government in Portland makes primary land-use decisions and runs an effective transit system. Regional decisions mitigate the negative consequences of urban sprawl and protect the valuable environmental resources of the area. The Twin Cities region shares tax resources and promotes regional economic planning. In both cases, innovative local officials were responsible for developing the plans and convincing legislators and the public of the merits of the proposal.

In other areas, county and regional governments have taken important steps to deal with some of these concerns. Rusk concludes that Montgomery County, Maryland, has dispersed affordable housing throughout one of the nation's richest counties and Montgomery County, Ohio, which includes the city of Dayton, has taken control of major economic development efforts and promoted limited revenue sharing among cities. In both cases, the results are positive and generally supported by most residents (1999: 178–222).

Critics point out that these successes have occurred in middle-sized urban areas in states with democratic, progressive traditions. The cases are located in urban areas with small minority populations and generally less conflict among majority and minority groups. Can one expect our largest urban areas to voluntarily cede authority to metropolitan or even county-wide bodies? Without strong incentives from higher levels of government it is hard to imagine large complex urban areas with significant ethnic conflict and great differences in wealth and opportunity voluntarily ceding authority to regional or county governments.

The success of our smaller urban areas, and the extent of the problems faced by our larger cities, argues for intervention from the state and federal governments—intervention that would provide sufficient incentive for governments to cooperate in spite of the perceived differences between them. Two groups of authors propose more far-ranging solutions to the problems of urban areas through rules and laws imposed by higher level governments. Rusk and Downs argue that federal and state governments should require or strongly encourage metropolitan cooperation. Frug and Briffault propose judicial intervention to force cities to accept metropolitan responsibilities.

Creating Regional Governments
Through State and Federal Acts

How can state and federal governments encourage regional coordination and governance? State government establishes the rules of governance; following Dillon's Law, cities are the wards of the state. States can create or destroy cities and have the right to alter the powers of local governments. States can, in fact, create regional governments without a vote of the people if they so choose. As pointed out in Chapter 9, the regional government in Indianapolis was created solely by state action. "America is a *federal system*," states Rusk. "Within the bounds of our national constitution the states have sovereign powers. To varying degrees, local governments . . . are legal subdivision of state government. Typically state governments do more than merely set the ground rules for local initiative" (1995: 92).

Rusk would like to see states use their authority to encourage regional action. Several states have adopted growth management legislation that requires state-level influence in city planning and enumerates goals for affordable housing, urban revitalization, and preservation of open space. Portland's success is often attributed, in part, to strong state growth management provisions. He proposes that states expand the power of counties over cities where counties contain much of the territory within an urban area. He advocates state efforts to consolidate cities with counties and for counties to become regional governments where appropriate. He would also like to see states ease the process of annexation for central cities and limit the ability of unincorporated areas within urban regions to become cities.

Significant political support for state intervention is a prerequisite to state action. The examples of successful metropolitan reform discussed earlier spearheaded by state legislators who were often former city officials. In both Minnesota and Oregon, governors and state legislators campaigned for metropolitan reform and worked with other state officers to bring change about. State initiatives, thus, depend on the problems of urban areas becoming a focus of state policy. In both states, strong political movements were needed to overcome resistance from entrenched local officials.

The federal government's authority over cities is less direct but sometimes more powerful. Federal rules, funding, and tax incentives are arguably the single most important influences on the distribution of races and classes within our present-day cities. Historically, federal influence has also encouraged greater segregation, the decline of the central city, and the promotion of suburban sprawl.

Rusk asks us to turn the clock back. Instead of insuring mortgages in racially segregated communities, funding transportation programs that aided the movement of Whites only to these segregated suburbs, and tearing down the central cities through urban renewal, should not federal policy move us toward a racially integrated society with carefully planned cities? Many of the problems of today's cities would not be with us now had federal policy moved in this latter direction (1999: 327).

Why not act now to right the wrongs of the past? Rusk argues. The federal government remains a major funding source for housing, and through income tax and regulatory powers, it provides incentives that strongly influence the location of industry and residences. It also funds many major public works projects. Should we use the diverse program resources of the federal government to encourage improved organization and management of urban problems? Rusk proposes several actions the federal government should take to encourage regional cooperation.

- *Encourage formation of metropolitan governments through tax policy.* Rusk advocates reducing the allowable tax deduction on the federal income tax to 50 percent but providing a larger deduction for residents of urban areas with metropolitan governments.

- *Require that federal grant-in-aid programs for public works projects and various regulatory programs analyze the impact on urban sprawl and racial and class segregation.* If sprawl or segregated suburban development is encouraged by the project or policy, the federal contribution should decline.

- *Replace large federal housing projects with a voucher system for low- and middle-income residents.* He advocates destroying the large segregated public projects common in many large cities. Vouchers would permit the poor to live in suburban areas. The federal government could then encourage builders to create housing that, with the addition of the voucher, the poor could afford. It could also provide incentives to communities that increased the number of housing vouchers. Further, Rusk supports tax and financing incentives to encourage suburban residents to build or purchase housing in the central city.

Rusk argues for a concerted use of federal power to encourage a more racially and economically integrated city. Together, these measures would counter some of the problems caused by earlier federal programs and act to overcome the central problems of today's urban areas.

Downs challenges the argument that central cities have become obsolete and suburbs can therefore act without regard to the problems of the central city. In spite of the dispersion of economic resources and the decentralization of the economy, the welfare of suburban residents remains closely linked to that of the central city (1994: 52). The quality of life in the central city influences the location of businesses and the areas ability to attract future investment. Downs maintains that suburban responsibility for inner-city problems is both good business and the right thing to do. He provides evidence that urban regions with significant public service differences between rich and poor are also less prosperous generally.

Downs proposes that all residents must assume common responsibility for the problems of the inner city. Unless they do so, the viability of the entire region is threatened. The ultimate solution to the problems of urban America involves convincing the residents, especially non-poor suburban members, that "the interests they share with all parts of their metropolitan area are more important to their long-run welfare than the conflicting interests they more easily perceive" (1994: 204). Thus, regional governments with responsibility for dispersing the poor throughout the region, sharing resources between rich and poor area, and promoting regional land-use policies are required. Successful urban areas, he maintains, must promote strong regional policies through area-wide governance.

Downs places responsibility for reform at the state level. Because of the Constitutional dominance of the state over local governments, a state government can require that local governments exercise their power within a broader framework established by state legislation. He suggests that the framework contain these elements:

- The state legislature should develop planning goals applicable to all communities.

- Every local government must develop comprehensive land-use plans consistent with state goals, with a major role for citizen participation.

- A single government agency should be empowered to review all local land-use plans. The agency must have the power to withhold approval of local plans and be able to penalize non-conforming cities.

- The same agency should coordinate transportation, utility, and environmental protection plans (1994: 180–1).

Envisioned here is a strong coordinating regional agency, backed by clearly defined standards established by the legislature. The proposal would retain the existing structure of local government, but it significantly limits local government powers. It assumes that residents will become sufficiently concerned about regional problems and perceive the new structure as the best way of achieving regional goals. "The ultimate solution . . . involves convincing members of each metropolitan locality, especially the non-poor suburban members, that the interests they share with all parts of their metropolitan area are more important than the conflicting interests they more easily perceive" (1994: 204).

Encouraging Regional Actions Through the Courts

THE MOUNT LAUREL CASE

In April, 1974 Ethel Lawrence launched a lawsuit destined to dominate the suburban agenda of the country for the next two decades. The forty-one-year-old homemaker, a part time practical nurse, could not find a house she could afford in her home town of Mount Laurel, New Jersey. Heeding her minister's advice, she and her daughter, Thomascene, invoked the help of young legal service attorneys in their search for an affordable home. This simple action would become a flash-point in the nation-wide debate over exclusionary zoning and the destiny of American metropolitan areas. One immediate consequence was that the New Jersey Court undertook the boldest and most innovative judicial intervention ever to countermand exclusionary zoning; in the landmark Mount Laurel trilogy of cases, the court identified and enunciated a constitutional right for all people—rich or poor, black or white—to live in the suburbs. It went to extraordinary lengths to break down the legal fences raised against affordable housing in the suburbs. Mount Laurel also represented an attack against skewed distribution—by race, ethnicity and income—of metropolitan populations. It set the tone for all future legal encounters with discriminatory local land use regulatory barriers.

SOURCE: Charles M. Haar, *Suburbs under Siege: Race, Space, and Audacious Judges* (Princeton, NJ: Princeton University Press, 1996): 3.

The Mount Laurel case is particularly important because it challenges the right of cities to control the use of land if zoning decisions interfere with the citizens' right to housing. The citizens in question here are not residents of the city. Thus, the case provides a rationale for invalidating city policy in the interests of citizens living in the greater urban area. "The upshot is that towns may not refuse to confront the future by building moats around themselves and pulling up the drawbridge through enacting prohibitory land use controls" (Haar 1996: 193). Following the case, New Jersey cities had to develop a plan for low- and moderate-income housing and the state was able to sanction non-complying communities.

Progress in using the legal system to promote metropolitan cooperation, however, has been very slow. The Mount Laurel case itself involved three separate cases over a 20-year period. Seven states besides New Jersey have invalidated zoning ordinances as exclusionary, but most of those provide remedies that are less far reaching (Harvard Law Review 1995: 1129). A legal remedy to the problem of suburban exclusion is by no means an easy one.

Massive, racially segregated, public housing projects line the freeway
with the Chicago skyline in the background.

© Robert Maas/Corbis

The heart of the problem is a fundamental legal conflict between those favoring a metropolitan approach and a line of legal precedents that favors local
government power. The Supreme Court's position was articulated clearly in the
case of the Village of Belle Terre et al vs. Boraas et al in 1974. The small village
of Belle Terre's zoning ordinance restricted land use to one-family dwellings,
defining family as one or more persons related by blood, adoption, or marriage.
The owners of a house had leased it to six unrelated college students. The city
took the owners to court and demanded the eviction of the students. Justice
Douglas, speaking for the court, upheld the city argument that:

> The regimes of boarding houses, fraternity houses and the like present
> urban problems. . . . More people occupy a given space; more cars
> continuously pass by; more cars are parked; noise travels in crowds.

> A quiet place where yards are wide, people few and motor vehicles
> restricted are legitimate guidelines in a land use project addressed to
> family needs. . . . It is ample to lay out zones where family values, youth
> values, and the blessings of quiet seclusion and clean air make the area a
> sanctuary for people" (416 U.S. 73–191 1974: 5).

The argument of the court permits cities to legislate in the interests of their
own residents. The impact of the city's laws on citizens who live elsewhere does
not need to be considered. Thus a city can structure its zoning ordinance to
prohibit unmarried people, and by extension those of limited income, through
large lot sizes. Further, the court defines the city's interests as those of the residents and acknowledges the suburban ideal of quiet exclusive detachment from

the central city as a legitimate public goal. The Mt. Laurel case directly challenges the court's position. Until it becomes an issue before the Supreme Court, however, its impact will affect states that have ruled on similar cases.

Some legal scholars see in Mt. Laurel the hope for a future challenge not only over the right to exclusively zone but also more basically to rethink the legal definition of the city. By defining the city as a collection of homeowners, the interests of those who may work, shop, or travel through that city are denied the opportunity to live there. Yet city policies affect all who have contact with some aspect of the city, and city policies affect everyone who lives in the urban area. If Belle Terre can exclude the unmarried, single people will find their choice of housing restricted. If you work in a city, you may be affected by the laws of that city more than where you happen to be living. If you shop in a city that is different from the one you live in, the quality of government in the city you shop in is an important concern to you. As residents, therefore, we need to be citizens of all the communities that affect our lives; in most cases that also means the territory of the urban area. "By treating cities as autonomous individuals," writes Gerald Frug, "local government law fuels a desire to avoid, rather than engage with, those who live on the other side of the city line. Especially in prosperous suburbs the equation of city boundaries with the boundaries of private property encourages city residents to think of the city line as separating 'you' from 'them': crime, bad schools, and inadequate resources across the city line, far from generating pressure for inter-city negotiations, are dismissed as 'their problem'" (1999: 62).

Richard Briffault adds that city autonomy within an urban area advantages the wealthy. "Only communities with resources sufficient to meet their needs and content with the character of local development can use local zoning to its greatest effect. The power to exclude like the right to spend in public schools, is no boon to communities short on resources" (1990: 61). The right to zone, or to fund your own school, park system, or police department, is valuable only if your city has more income than most. The poor community cannot attract the rich through exclusionary zoning and hasn't the resources to improve its public services.

Scholars like Frug and Briffault, therefore, hope to provide the rationale to legally question the very existence of separate local governments within an interdependent metropolitan area. The goal is to challenge the ability of individual cities to exclude residents and maintain exclusive hold of the taxable resources of their citizens. They also hope to broaden the concerns of city residents to include those affected by city decisions who may not live within the city borders. Ultimately, the aim is to encourage all governments and their citizens to assume metropolitan responsibility.

★ ★ ★

American cities will always prosper. Our resources are great and continue to expand. Thus, we can survive the worst of our mistakes; Orange County can spend much more than it takes in, but recover and prosper. The wealth of the society permits the wasting of resources; therefore, dire consequences are unlikely if some resources are wasted. The tragedy of September 11, 2001, will remain a personal, but not a political, tragedy. New York City will survive and prosper thanks to the Rudolph Giulianis of the world whose leadership skills can overcome the centrifugal tendencies of our Madisonian system.

Our commitment to freedom allows us to tolerate differences in wealth and opportunity. Thus, the lives of the poor are accepted by the rich because we believe that hard work and perseverance will permit anyone to rise. We assume that industrious people with the right values can learn from adversity. We don't need to use government to assist them.

But shouldn't we expect more from our cities? Could they be more efficiently run, uniting business, commerce, and housing creatively and preserving natural resources? Could they provide equal opportunity permitting more to live in clean neighborhoods with less crime? Could we feel prideful of our city centers as places where all kinds of people meet freely to share in the benefits of city life?

REFERENCES

Briffault, Richard. 1990. "On Localism: Part II Localism and Legal Theory" 90: (January). *Columbia Law Review.*

Downs, Anthony. 1994. *New Visions for Metropolitan America.* Washington D.C.: The Brookings Institution Press.

Frug, Gerald E. 1999. *City Making: Building Communities Without Walls.* Princeton, NJ: Princeton University Press.

Grogan, Paul S, and Tony Proscio. 2000. *Comeback Cities: A Blueprint for Urban Neighborhood Revival.* Boulder, CO: Westview Press.

Haar, Charles M. 1996. *Suburbs Under Siege: Race, Space, and Audacious Judges.* Princeton, NJ: Princeton University Press.

Harvard Law Review. 1995. "State Sponsored Growth Management as a Remedy for Exclusionary Zoning" 108: 1127–44.

Moore, Mark H. 1995. *Creating Public Value: Strategic Management in Government.* Cambridge, MA: Harvard University Press.

Osborne, David, and Ted Gaebler. 1992. *Reinventing Government.* Reading, MA: Addison Wesley.

Rusk, David. 1999. *Inside Game/Outside Game: Winning Strategies for Urban America.* Washington D.C.: The Brookings Institution Press.

Rusk, David. 1995. *Cities Without Suburbs.* Washington D.C.: The Woodrow Wilson Center Press.

United States Department of Housing and Urban Development. 2001. *Strategies for Success: Reinventing Cities for the 21st Century.*

Village of Belle Terre et al v. Borass et al. 416 U.S. 73–191 (1974).

Index

Photo Credits

Cover, © Bryan Peterson/Getty Images; **p. 14,** AP/Wide World Photos; **p. 43,** © Bettman/Corbis; **p. 44,** © Corbis; **p. 51,** AP/Wide World Photos; **p. 81,** © Bettmann/Corbis; **p. 87 (left),** © Corbis; **p. 87 (right),** © Bettmann/Corbis; **p. 104,** © Robert Holmes/Corbis; **p. 105,** © Michael Cerone/Superstock; **p. 118,** © David Young-Wolf/PhotoEdit; **p. 120,** AP/Wide World Photos; **p. 153,** AP/Wide World Photos; **p. 157,** © Bettmann/Corbis; **p. 183,** AP/Wide World Photos; **p. 192,** © Bettmann/Corbis; **p. 197,** AP/Wide World Photos; **p. 206,** David and Peter Turnley/Corbis; **p. 212,** © Bettmann/Corbis; **p. 245,** © Spencer Grant/PhotoEdit; **p. 303,** © Steve Vidler/SuperStock; **p. 307,** G. E. Kidder Smith/Corbis; **p. 328,** © Robert Maas/Corbis.